AMERICAN
HYBRID

ALSO BY COLE SWENSEN

POETRY

Ours
The Glass Age
The Book of a Hundred Hands
Goest
Such Rich Hour
Oh
Try
Noon
Numen
Park
New Math
It's Alive She Says

TRANSLATIONS

Juliology by Nicolas Pesquès
Physis by Nicolas Pesquès
Future, Former, Fugitive by Olivier Cadiot
Oxo by Pierre Alferi
Island of the Dead by Jean Frémon

ALSO BY DAVID ST. JOHN

POETRY

PROSE

A NORTON ANTHOLOGY
OF NEW POETRY

 W. W. NORTON & COMPANY
NEW YORK ■ LONDON

AMERICAN
HYBRID

■ EDITED BY ■

COLE SWENSEN AND DAVID ST. JOHN

Since this page cannot legibly accommodate all the copyright notices,
pages 509–18 constitute an extension of the copyright page.

Copyright © 2009 by Cole Swensen and David St. John

For information about special discounts for bulk purchases, please contact
W. W. Norton Special Sales at specialsales@wwnorton.com or 800-233-4830

Manufacturing by RR Donnelley, Harrisonburg
Book design by Judith Stagnitto Abbate / Abbate Design
Production manager: Devon Zahn

Library of Congress Cataloging-in-Publication Data

American hybrid : a Norton anthology of new poetry / edited by Cole
Swensen and David St. John. — 1st ed.
p. cm.
Includes index.
ISBN 978-0-393-33375-6 (pbk.)
1. American poetry—21st century. 2. American poetry—20th century.
I. Swensen, Cole, 1955– II. St. John, David, 1949–
PS617.A54 2009
811'.608—dc22

2008036193

W. W. Norton & Company, Inc.
500 Fifth Avenue, New York, N.Y. 10110
www.wwnorton.com

W. W. Norton & Company Ltd.
Castle House, 75/76 Wells Street, London W1T 3QT

1 2 3 4 5 6 7 8 9 0

CONTENTS

ACKNOWLEDGMENTS

Of the dozens of people whose generous help made this book possible, the editors would like particularly to thank Yannick Mercoyrol, for giving us the occasion to dream it up; Susan Terris, for her tireless work on permissions and numerous bits of other advice; Peter Gizzi, Brenda Hillman, Marjorie Perloff, Jed Rasula, Claude Royet-Journoud, and Robert von Hallberg for their insightful comments on the introductions; and Jill Bialosky for her perceptive attention and countless invaluable suggestions.

INTRODUCTION

COLE SWENSEN

T HE NOTION OF a fundamental division in American poetry has become so ingrained that we take it for granted. Robert Lowell famously portrayed it in the 1950s and 1960s as a split between "the cooked and the uncooked," and Eliot Weinberger updated the assertion over thirty years later in his anthology *American Poetry Since 1950* (1993) when he stated that "For decades, American poetry has been divided into two camps." Were the poetic landscapes of 1960 and 1993 as similar as these two statements might imply? And where are we in relation to them today, at the end of the first decade of the new millennium? This anthology springs from the conviction that the model of binary opposition is no longer the most accurate one and that, while extremes remain, and everywhere we find complex aesthetic and ideological differences, the contemporary moment is dominated by rich writings that cannot be categorized and that hybridize core attributes of previous "camps" in diverse and unprecedented ways.

THE LEGACY

The history of the two-camp model has been well documented in various places, so I won't recapitulate it here except briefly in order to argue that the term "model" gives an overly static impression. Far from set, it's a continually evolving situation, with roots going back to the end of the nineteenth century and the birth of the avant-garde. The writer and translator Paul Auster has made an astute observation: that most twentieth-century American poets took their cue either from the British poetic tradition or from the French. And while all were influenced by the Romantics on the one hand, and the Modernists on the other, resulting in lineages that developed with much cross-pollination, Auster's distinction presents a useful model. First, it allows us to follow one thread that inherited a pastoral sensibility from British Romanticism, emphasizing the notion of man as a natural being in a natural world, informed by intense introspection and a belief in the stability and sovereignty of the individual. Christopher Beach pinpointed this trend in the work of two poets, noting that "The poetry of Robinson and Frost suggested one possible direction for American poets in the twentieth century: a reworking of traditional lyric forms that would require no radical break from nineteenth-century poetic convention."* Lack of a radical break, however, does not mean lack of change, and poets following this vein continued to refine and augment this lyric verse model in rich and diverse ways, some of which look dramatically different from their precursors.

The second prominent line of poetic thinking stems from the urbane modernism of Baudelaire, Rimbaud, Mallarmé, and Apollinaire, and moved from there into an increasing emphasis on the materiality of the text as developed by the early twentieth-century avant-gardes, a lineage fueled in part by the belief that meaningful change in the arts requires dramatic rupture. In Charles Altieri's words, these were poets who "considered their work a challenge to traditional notions of poetry."† This trend is marked by innovations in form, from Baudelaire's prose poems to Mallarmé's revolutionary use of the page on the one hand, and a relentless look at contemporary society on the other, which also included Apollinaire's enthusiasm for the Eiffel Tower and Marinetti's for the automobile. All were expressions of a dawning sensibility that Rimbaud captured in the simple statement, "We must be absolutely modern." which refused sentimentality as much as his "I is an other" invited it back in through a sense of loss so absolute it put the individual's claim to authority forever at bay.

■

This split is more than a stylistic one; it marks two concepts of meaning: one as transcendent, the other as immanent. Thus, twentieth-century American poetry offers both a model of the poem as a vehicle for conveying thoughts, images, and ideas initiated elsewhere—a model that recognizes language as an accurate roadmap or system of referring to situations and things in the real world—and a model of the poem as an event on the page, in which language, while inevitably retaining a referential capacity, is emphasized as a site of meaning in its own right, and poetry is recognized as uniquely capable of displaying that.

Although many American poets throughout the twentieth century would not fit neatly into one mode or another, the perspective of a hundred years reveals an overall pattern in which this split leads through various modifications, infiltrations, and permutations to the "anthology wars" of the late fifties and early sixties. Donald Allen's 1960 collection *The New American Poetry* brought to light the margins that had been thriving for years around a poetic center delineated by Hall, Pack, and Simpson's *New Poets of England and America* (1957), as well as by other anthologies edited by Auden, Ciardi, and Rolfe Humphries earlier in

*Christopher Beach, *The Cambridge Introduction to Twentieth-Century American Poetry* (Cambridge: Cambridge University Press, 2003), 23.

†Charles Altieri, *The Art of Twentieth-Century American Poetry* (Oxford: Blackwell Publishing, 2006), 2.

the 1950s. Those anthologies had consolidated an English-language voice distinct from a more continentally inflected modernism and honed by the New Criticism to reflect certain formal and ideological values. The ideal poem in New Critical terms was self-contained, refined, precisely formed, detached, and difficult in the sense that it required, and rewarded, careful study. As Robert Pack argued, the good poem "deepens upon familiarity." Many of the writers Allen presented, by contrast, were to be grasped in an instant; their work was spontaneous, raw, illogical, and exuberant, and while he included others who were more measured and studied, it was often in traditions unfamiliar to contemporary literature departments or understood quite differently. Overall, the forms that Allen's poets employed were open and organic, their subjects at times irreverent, and their emotional registers unfettered. Their emblematic phrases, such as Frank O'Hara's "You've got to go on your nerve," or Allen Ginsberg's "improvised poetics," underscored their affinity with Charles Olson's "Projective Verse," which advocated a mode of poetic composition epitomized by Robert Creeley's famous statement that "form is never more than an extension of content." Taken as a whole, the stance of the "new American poets" seemed to posit a vibrant faith in intuition and chance over deliberation and intentionality. Although Allen's anthology covered a vast range—from the esoteric historicism of Robert Duncan to Jack Spicer's playful timelessness to Ginsberg's bardic momentum—it effectively brought all these marginal poetries together, naming them and throwing them into sharp focus, which marked the beginning of their demarginalization.

And it changed American poetry tremendously, to such a degree that by 1982, the year of Allen's sequel anthology *The Postmoderns: The New American Poetry Revisited*, co-edited with George Butterick, the opposition had all but joined him. Though excellent poets were still writing with the formal tension that had typified much poetry of the 1950s, their numbers were fewer, and free verse was increasingly prevalent, based in a natural language modeled on Williams, but also importantly influenced by the Beat poets and all they had inherited from Whitman, including the Romantic impulse to see man's corollary in nature. The mainstream verse of the day retained much of the New Critical sense of shape, however; the poem remained a tight construct, with a distinct beginning and end, but it had a much more personal tone, having incorporated the centrality of self and the belief in the importance of individual history that distinguished Confessional poetry, a trend whose influence grew continually throughout the sixties and seventies. Also increasingly prevalent was the sense of the magical, transformative potential of quotidian epiphany that the Deep Image movement had fashioned from the vestiges of European Surrealism.

This, then, was the new mainstream, and it too had opposition, which, to some degree, retained the forms of Allen's original categories, with their more ragged, open-ended shapes and their ongoing interrogation of the relationship between self and voice. Yet the distinction was no longer so sharp, and several poets included in Allen's first anthology, such as Gary Snyder, were writing the

xx INTRODUCTION: COLE SWENSEN

epitome of what had become the new mainstream epiphanic lyric, whereas others, such as John Ashbery, had moved into the mainstream through publishing and awards while continuing their varied experiments. But an entirely new opposition arose as well, one that, ironically, shared some points with the New Criticism in its rigor, its interest in the difficult, and its demand that the poem be a worked object of art rather than a spontaneous expression of personal feeling. However, it opposed New Criticism in even more, and more important, ways, including its social and political convictions, its appreciation of the avant-garde, and its sense of history.

Though broadly based, this new opposition was most readily visible in the Language poets, who, as Robert Grenier indicated in his famous "I HATE SPEECH!," rejected the abiding emphasis on orality that stemmed from the Beats and the New York School, and questioned the natural language of the post-Confessionalists by interrogating its "naturalness" and finding it illusory. Instead, acknowledging language as a social construct, they focused on the surface of the text, emphasizing its materiality along the lines of the Russian Futurists, and the inherently political nature of language along the lines of the Objectivists. They also critiqued the arbitrary nature of genre distinctions by creating texts that fused poetry, criticism, and philosophy. Like all the twentieth-century movements that preceded them, from the Modernists to the Confessionalists to the Beats, they too opened poetry up to new subject matter, but this time the subject was international critical discourse.

Opposition to the new mainstream came from yet another direction as well in the form of a resurgence of formalist work. Sometimes linked with New Narrative poetry under the banner of "expansive poetry," New Formalism had its roots in the 1970s with X. J. Kennedy's journal *Counter/Measures*. It really took off in the mid-eighties with the publication of Philip Dacey and David Jauss's anthology *Strong Measures* and Robert Richman's *The Direction of Poetry*, followed in the nineties by other anthologies and the journal *The Formalist*. Focused on the beauty of constraint as an imaginative and intellectual stimulus, these poets not only revived old forms but renewed them through contemporary phrasing and subject matter. Other poets, while not writing in forms per se, were inspired by the movement to select specific formal elements and make use of them to give more structure and ornament to the dominant free-verse lyric.

In short, the two camps that dominated American poetry in the 1980s were very different from those of 1960, and the situation by the mid-nineties looked as different again. One of the main differences was that binary opposition was beginning to break down, notwithstanding three major anthologies designed around it. Indeed, as those anthologies attest, all opposition had not evaporated; it quite likely never will. Yet now, almost fifteen years later, American poetry finds itself at a moment when idiosyncrasy rules to such a degree and differences are so numerous that distinct factions are hard, even impossible, to pin down. Instead, we find a thriving center of alterity, of writings and writers that have inherited and adapted traits developed by everyone from the Romantics through the Modernists to the various avant-gardes, the Confessionalists, Allen's margins, and finally to Language poetry and the New Formalists. The product of contradictory traditions, today's writers often take aspects from two or more to create poetry that is truly post-modern in that it's an unpredictable and unprecedented mix.

THE NEW (HY)BREED

The hybrid poem has selectively inherited traits from both of the prin-cipal paths outlined above. It shares affinities with what Ron Silliman has termed "third wave poetics" and with what is increasingly known as "post-avant" work, though its range is broader, particularly at the more conservative end of its con-tinuum. And Stephen Burt touched on something similar when he introduced the term "elliptical poetry" in a review in 1998. Today's hybrid poem might engage such conventional approaches as narrative that presumes a stable first person, yet complicate it by disrupting the linear temporal path or by scrambling the normal syntactical sequence. Or it might foreground recognizably experimental modes such as illogicality or fragmentation, yet follow the strict formal rules of a sonnet or a villanelle. Or it might be composed entirely of neologisms but based in ancient traditions. Considering the traits associated with "conventional" work, such as coherence, linearity, formal clarity, narrative, firm closure, sym-bolic resonance, and stable voice, and those generally assumed of "experimental" work, such as non-linearity, juxtaposition, rupture, fragmentation, immanence, multiple perspective, open form, and resistance to closure, hybrid poets access a wealth of tools, each one of which can change dramatically depending on how it is combined with others and the particular role it plays in the composition.

Hybrid poems often honor the avant-garde mandate to renew the forms and expand the boundaries of poetry—thereby increasing the expressive potential of language itself—while also remaining committed to the emotional spectra of lived experience. As different as these two goals might seem, they're both essentially social in nature and recognize a social obligation; and as such, they demonstrate poetry's continued relevance. Hybrid poetry speaks out, but in ways that avoid echoing the canned speech that has become so prevalent in this age in which fewer and fewer people control more and more of the media. While political issues may or may not be the ostensible subject of hybrid work, the political is always there, inherent in the commitment to use language in new ways that yet remain audible and comprehensible to the population at large.

While the new is an important common denominator of much hybrid work, it is a combinatory new, one that recognizes that "there is nothing new under the sun" and embraces the postmodern understanding of the importance of connection: that given elements are often less crucial than the relationships between them. Some hybrid writers address the complexities of the new with an interest in repetition and collage, devising ways that similarity and novelty can be combined in a generative manner. And many hybrid writers go beyond novelty to incorporate the strange, the odd, and the uncanny. In fact, it was precisely a sensitivity to the strange that instigated the bridge between earlier poetic extremes through their common willingness to acknowledge the limits of human knowledge and to refuse to let them be limiting. Harold Bloom has argued that "a mode of originality that . . . cannot be assimilated" is the determining element of the literary,* and these works exhibit precisely the irreducibility that triggers the "uncanny startlement" of which he speaks. Hybrid writing tolerates a high degree of the restless, the indeterminate, and the uncanny because, like the best writing of any era, it doesn't seek to reinforce received ideas or social positions as much as it aims to stimulate reflection and to incite thoughts and feelings.

Much hybrid work is being written by writers under forty, who reconfigure and even reinvent the various moves of preceding decades, but the trend toward hybridization was actually led by writers of earlier generations who continued to push their styles and their underlying principles, even if that meant abandoning stances for which they'd become well known. Among the writers presented here are first-generation members of several movements, including the epiphanic lyric, Deep Image, the New York School, and Language poetry. Often these poets have retained much of their earlier sensibilities, but have opened them up to additional modes, broadening their audiences as well as their own voices. The earliest born, Barbara Guest, is perhaps the quintessential hybrid poet. First identified with the New York School in Allen's *New American Poetry*, she followed her explorations through permutations that, a decade or so later, identified her with the Language poets. In subsequent years, she published works that ranged from anecdotal and narrative prose poetry to abstract minimalism that maximized the meaning of page space, and her final volume, *The Red Gaze*, includes many short lyrics based on readily accessible, concrete imagery.

This book also includes many second-generation writers from various schools, as well as poets who began writing in the late 1980s and early 1990s, at a time when the tension between experiment and convention had begun to break down. This was the result of specific historical developments, one academic, the other technological, that transformed two of poetry's principal centers of force: academia and publishing.

THE CURRENT LANDSCAPE

"Academic" is always a problematic term in poetry, and its meaning has changed considerably in the past fifty years. Once shorthand for the distilled and allusive, the crystallized and formally precise, the term currently evokes two very

---

*Harold Bloom, *The Western Canon* (London: Macmillan, 1994) p. 3.

different sets of interests. One is the relatively new branch of graduate studies, creative writing workshops. From a few scattered programs in the 1960s, the phenomenon has mushroomed to 325, including MAs, MFAs, and PhDs, in the country today. Workshops have changed the tone of poetic criticism by extending it beyond the critics to the poets themselves; they've also legitimized practice as a viable site of study, created communities centered on a fusion of creativity and analysis, and brought the work of very recent or contemporary poets into the curriculum of literary studies.

The expansion of workshop-based programs and the trickling down of creative writing classes into undergraduate and community colleges have created teaching jobs for hundreds of poets, giving them careers that continually deepen their historical and critical understandings, and leaving them with more time for their own writing than they would have in most other professions. All in all, workshops foster a kind of poet-professor that recalls the early days of New Criticism.

As graduate creative writing programs proliferated, they also diversified and now run the gamut from academically rigorous PhD programs with creative dissertation options to programs based in fine arts schools—such as the ones at Otis College, the California College of Arts, and the Chicago Art Institute—that emphasize writing's commonalities with the visual and performing arts. This great range of programs unsettles poetry writing in academia by raising the question of whether it belongs in the Art Department or the English Department, revealing that it's a slightly awkward fit in either case. It may be precisely this inability to fit neatly into any department or school that will keep contemporary poetry from ever getting subsumed by the academy, thus guaranteeing it a sufficient degree of autonomy to follow its own course while also staying informed on the intellectual issues of the day, which are indispensable to that course.

Such intellectual issues are behind the other meaning that the term "academic" has acquired for poetry since the early 1980s, and it came from the direction of the Language poets. On the whole, they were not, like their Beat and New York School predecessors, content to let the poem just happen; they wanted to know why and how it happened, and what the social and political implications would be. From the movement's inception in the mid-1970s, public lectures, debates, and critical and theoretical writings were an important part of its activities. These writers were particularly concerned to explode the myth of the ahistorical by examining poetry's connections to contemporary social structures and developing its theoretical underpinnings. During the 1980s and 1990s, many people associated with Language poetry took jobs in universities, but often in literature, critical studies, and even philosophy departments rather than creative writing programs. Though equal in rigor, this new academicism differed from that of the 1950s in its insistence on viewing poetry as one aspect of a complex network that is itself the product of various historical, economic, and cultural forces. It also differed in adopting an experimental rather than conservative perspective, supported by decidedly leftist social and political interests.

With poetry's position in academia leaning in two different directions, serious students are often exposed to both the conventional and the experimental; but unlike their elders, they don't necessarily feel that they have to choose between them. Instead, they see both presented as viable approaches, and sanctioned by the same institutions.

If the university is one primary force in American poetry, publishing is the other, and it too has changed dramatically over the past fifty years. Although small presses and magazines, from the early issues of *Poetry* and later reviews such as Corman's *Origins* to the mimeograph revolution of the 1960s, played an important role in the development of avant-garde poetries in the United States, they remained relatively marginalized, and the post-World War II publishing establishment, based in New York, was seriously rivaled by only a few university presses and "alternative" presses such as City Lights, New Directions, and Grove. However, by the 1980s, the phenomenon of the university press had spread so widely that it played a substantial role in poetry publication. A sturdy three-tiered structure developed, still dominated by the New York houses, followed by university presses, and then by pioneering small presses such as Graywolf, Copper Canyon, Black Sparrow, and Burning Deck. The most recent shift has been the explosion of the bottom tier until, in terms of sheer numbers, the bottom is now the top. Though earlier canon makers, such as FSG and Penguin, still maintain important poetry lists, these constitute a smaller and smaller percentage of the number of poetry books published annually in the country, and their influence is increasingly mitigated by the dozens of small presses now thriving because of the past twenty years' technological changes in typesetting, design, and printing.

One effect of these changes is that poets themselves are increasingly deciding who gets published, often with little or no need to consider sales, and they are marketing their books through the Internet directly to targeted audiences. In all respects, the role of the Internet has been considerable. It not only facilitates production and distribution; it also functions as a publisher itself. While it may not represent a mode of production with truly democratic access, the Internet has broadened access sufficiently to constitute a decentralizing force that has complicated the accepted avenues of career and canon building. A whole world of poetry writing and publishing has grown up here, just below the radar of the traditional poetry reading public, which is itself constantly evolving, and more and more includes people who routinely use the Web for information and entertainment.

The Internet has also engendered forms unique to itself, both in publishing and in writing. Its unrestricted length and flexible format offer publishing options that print cannot. Many Internet journals use the Web simply as an affordable alternative to print, but others are using it for its unique features, incorporating moving or transforming elements, video clips, and audio dimensions. Still others combine creative outlets with informative ones, using hypertext to send readers to related sites, encouraging further lines of pursuit that operate in a rhizomatic rather than arboreal fashion, leading ever outward.

WHERE DOES THAT LEAVE US?

The rhizome is an appropriate model, not only for new Internet publications but for the current world of contemporary poetry as a whole. The two-camp model, with its parallel hierarchies, is increasingly giving way to a more laterally ordered network composed of nodes that branch outward toward smaller nodes, which themselves branch outward in an intricate and ever-changing structure of exchange and influence. Some nodes may be extremely experimental, and some extremely conservative, but many of them are true intersections of these extremes, so that the previous adjectives—well-made, decorous, traditional, formal, and refined, as well as spontaneous, immediate, bardic, irrational, translogical, open-ended, and ambiguous—all still apply, but in new combinations. Such hybridity is of course in itself no guarantee of excellence, and the decentralizing influences cited above make it harder to achieve consensus or even to maintain stable critical criteria; instead, these factors put more responsibility on individual readers to make their own assessments, which can in turn create stronger readers in that they must become more aware of and refine their own criteria.

Although the principal catalysts of this shift may be changes in education and technology, additional factors have augmented and implemented it. Women have played a particularly important role in creating sites for discussing and welcoming these changes. A few specific instances include the conference held in April 1999 at Barnard College entitled "Where Lyric Tradition Meets Language Poetry: Innovation in Contemporary Poetry by Women" and the "Page Mothers" conference held a month earlier, in March 1999, at UC San Diego, which focused on the crucial work of women in publishing in the last quarter of the twentieth century and the ways in which book and journal production have helped remap contemporary poetry.

Just as the shift in gender balance played an important role, increased internationalism and multiculturalism have also had a hand in broadening the aesthetic field, dispersing critical attention, and decentralizing power. Though the first word in our anthology's title is "American," it's increasingly difficult to say just what the "American" in American poetry is. More and more poets writing and publishing in the United States were born and raised in other countries; poets in this volume come from China, England, Lebanon, Germany, Jamaica, Canada, Korea, and elsewhere—it's a truly wide range of cultures that filters into the collection. In addition, many of the poets presented here routinely spend part of each year out of the country, and though they all write in English, for some it is not their native language, and many write in other languages as well. All these factors keep the English language questioning its parameters.

For many of these writers, translation is also an essential aspect of their writing practice, and, as translating is a discipline that constantly folds difference into the core of personal linguistic landscapes, it imports these differences—of form, sound, syntax, perspective, etc.—into American poetics as a whole.

Translation also casts creation out, away from the creating "I" into a more public realm, and that same gesture is made by the many poets represented here who work editing, publishing, and producing the poetry of others. By creating literature on the most concrete, material, and social level, these writers extend the Rimbaudian "I is an other" beyond the estrangement inherent in committing the first person singular to paper and into a socially creative act—they literally create the society in which they can thrive. Many of these poets also work in other media—in theater, music, and the visual arts. Some incorporate language into their paintings and sculptures, intentionally complicating the "materiality of the word," while others incorporate images as integral elements of their texts.

Poetry is eternally marked by—even determined by—difference, but that very difference changes and moves. At the moment, it is moving inside, into the center of the writing itself, fissuring its smooth faces into fragments that make us reconsider the ethics of language, on the one hand, and redraft our notions of a whole, on the other. Putting less emphasis on external differences, those among poets and their relative stances, leaves us all in a better position to fight a much more important battle for the integrity of language in the face of commercial and political misuse. It's a battle that brings poetry back to its mandate as articulated by Mallarmé: to give a purer sense to the language of the tribe. It's something that only poetry can do.

INTRODUCTION

I HAVE ALWAYS BELIEVED that the great strength of American poetry resides, at its source, in its plurality of voices, its multitude of poetic styles, and its consistent resistance to the coercion of what emerges—in each generation—as a catalogue of prevailing literary trends. That is, we are, as American poets, culturally alert to complexity and verbal nuance, determinedly polyvocal, and stylistically independent, even arrogant. I believe we live in a time of extraordinary literary riches. Contemporary American poetry is thriving on every front. The work of many of my contemporaries has been remarkably innovative in its ambition and deeply compelling in its personal and artistic courage. Recent American poetry is startling and powerful in the ways it has both drawn upon and revised any number of past traditions. Poets live with either admiration or despair within those literary traditions they inherit and, in time, must either alter, accept, or dismiss. Of course, poets have always created new alternatives for themselves and must, as we are hoping to do here, celebrate and champion the writings of those they consistently envy and admire.

In the spring of 2005, listening to Cole Swensen deliver a talk about the growing hybridization of American poetry, I suddenly understood quite clearly why I had become so deeply dissatisfied by the increasingly narrow categorical definitions of and, in my view, exclusionary critical demarcations in American poetry. The rubrics and various designations—avant-garde, postmodern, New Formalist, Language poetry, organic, mainstream, New Critical, Beat, et cetera—all served, I felt, primarily as highly generalized critical orientations to or as retrospective overviews of a poet's work (regardless of how reductive those rubrics might in fact be). What they did not make available was the fulsome poetically focused investigation or charged discussion of any given poem that comes, as poets know, with our understanding of and deep engagement with a particular poem. To Cole, the challenge and fascination of American poetry had become the way that previously conceived poetic "differences" and aesthetic borders of every kind were being tested and transgressed; she noted the many exciting ways that stylistic concerns were being melded and re-forged within the poetry of any number of individual poets. In my view, this was and remains exactly right. The most compelling poetry I've been reading for the past fifteen years has been that which has ignored and/or defied categorization, poetry that embraces a variety of—even sometimes contradictory—poetic ambitions and aesthetics. These hybridizations of poetic value seem to me all to the good of the individual poet and of American poetry itself.

Although I have always distrusted writers who run in packs, I welcome all literary partisanship as a gesture toward what I would call a "values clarification" in poetry. However, let's be frank. We are at a time in our poetry when the notion of the "poetic school" is an anachronism, an archaic critical artifact of times long gone by. The most compelling new poets today draw from a vast and wildly varied reservoir of resources. Their choices concerning "voice" and stylistic possibility (as well as their attitudes toward aesthetic, theoretical, cultural, and political urgencies) are now articulated as compelling hybridizations.

When Cole Swensen and I began deliberating about the contents of this anthology, we first imagined a group of younger poets. Then, we decided we would need to include other poets as well, in order to show the historical depth and vitality of the concept of poetic hybridization in American poetry, and in order to present the impressive range of poets we believe articulate this impulse. We eventually determined that we would consider only those who, at the time we began reading for the anthology in the summer of 2005, had already published at least three volumes of poetry. Ironically, this excluded many of those younger poets whose work we'd first looked to as models of hybridization. I can only add that their anthology is yet to come.

We also made the decision not to champion individual poets as special exemplars of hybridization in our introductions. We believe one of the philosophical points of this collection needs to remain that all aspects and variants of hybridization in American poetry are of equal and lasting value, and that, in fact, the variety of hybridization found in our living poetry at this moment constitutes one of the most vital elements of its importance. It seems therefore antithetical to both the project and spirit of this anthology to suggest that one poet's way or understanding of hybridization can be judged as "better" or "more important" than any other. That is, the idea of first suggesting that the poetic activities of the poets here in *American Hybrid* have helped to erase the boundaries of poetic schools and leveled out many assumed hierarchies, and then to say, Some animals are more equal than others, runs counter to the very premise we are positing here.

I am persuaded by the idea of an American poetry based upon plurality, not purity. We need all of our poets. Our poetry should be as various as the natural world, as rich and peculiar in its potential articulations. The purpose of this anthology is to celebrate these exquisite hybridizations emerging in the work of all our poets. Let the gates of the Garden stand open; let the renaming of the world begin again.

AMERICAN
HYBRID

ETEL ADNAN

ORN IN BEIRUT of a Syrian father and a Greek mother, Etel Adnan says: "I am, above all, American." Adnan's early work was influenced by Olson, Pound, and Stein, and her long writing career is marked by great flexibility of style. Pieces such as the opening one here, based on vivid images presented in full sentences, are often complicated by devices from juxtaposition and non sequitur to dramatic repetition, while poems that strike the eye as highly experimental are made more widely accessible by a thin narrative thread and emotionally charged vocabulary. A professor of philosophy from 1958 to 1972, Adnan pays close attention to the movements of the mind and the flickering perceptions that inform it, and is particularly concerned with the way the details of everyday individual lives connect to abstractions such as global politics.

Etel Adnan was educated at the Sorbonne and moved to the United States in the mid-1950s to do graduate work at UC Berkeley and Harvard. A longtime resident of the Bay Area, she has published ten books of poetry, many of which, such as *The Arab Apocalypse*, blend overt political commentary with explosive poetics. She also writes prose and plays; her novel *Sitt Marie Rose* (1978) is considered a classic in the Arab world and has been translated into more than ten languages, and her theater pieces have been performed in the United States, France, and Germany. She collaborated with Robert Wilson on his opera *Civil warS*, and her work has been set to music by Tanya Leon, Gavin Bryars, and others. She is also a well-known painter, and has had solo exhibitions in San Francisco, Paris, London, Beirut, and Rabat.

from THE INDIAN NEVER HAD A HORSE

The certitude of Space is brought
to me by a flight of birds. It
is grey outside and there is a trembling:
fog is too heavy a word

The zookeeper sends his love
letters to the female mayor of
San Diego
The lioness in her den fainted
on April Fool's day
the man hanged himself in
her cage.

A bee fell in love with a peach
blossom. Shakespeare wrote a
story about it.

There are no boats on the
river and the world's beauty
is blinding. Three astronauts
are on their way back. In the
garden a single leaf is shaking.

He had his mother's bones made
into a necklace because horses
came from Spain. He moved about
the country like a sword.

One day even the stars
became soldiers
Isis wept over the empty
sky

Galaxies work as narcotics
you didn't know how dangerous
it was to go to Mexico . . .
you make people run for shelter
you carry, within,
an angel
that overflows

Under old chandeliers
you kiss your parents to death.
Don't be afraid of
cobwebs
they only scan
theatres, and your
soul.

I have a love affair
with Albuquerque
because of the Indian
dancers and the Arab
builders
I own the sky.

from IN/SOMNIA

XVII

1. wings from one's late
    o minous voyage.
    (pestilence) ô
    half ½ have moon
    mind & number

2. healed mansions of . . .
    everybody's fate
    in the balance . . . in
    xeroxed (blank)
    sheets   shh

3. drugs for en/light/n/ment
    of THE fright/e/ned
    un/stable—
    .   to start. warranting.
    the (?) night.

4. sulfur:
    holding re/surrected
    baby. in arms.
    arms.

XVIII

1. altered epi/fanny. zzzz
    nerves—neurves. leaves
    in symmetry. for dorrmant
    lady in lace. in diamond

2. now transient horizon-
    tal life. Buttes. slough.
    (slow, low) over . . .
    ?????

3. warm warmth speech
    between eagles and
    and (!) the poor (pour)
    vi.si.bi.li.ty . . .
    of somber desires . . .
    w w w w w w w w w

4. maligNancy taken off
    time's isolation. off
    rain/bows

5. At the bone. up
    there.

XIX

1. Night falling. again. Not again.
    long/line no help help/less
    terror stop the terr . . .
    terribly all over/ over
    what?

2. blows bellowing blowing
    paper and doors and what
    else? Is is it? is it coming?
    Yes. time. Last time

3. lasting timing ever-ever
    snoring orderal or deal
    dealer of cards   of smoke
    tick/ no no end

4.   shhh——weee——buzzz
      buzing pele-mele
      keep   held hold-it! keep
      insane in/sane the right
      to wait wait! waited for
      for wait a minute for/the/
      dark/light of morning

5.   collapsibles

                    XX

1.   Aeschylus nothing
      nihil ist cloud-bearing
      battle stoop/lie on
      ground welll

2.   steam-boat where's Greece?
      the object ab/ject. Pan the god
      ear/ful of space

3.   thru   turn.   pull up
      cacophonus——phone——
      (messages) cross that
                measure——until
      the garden's rise / / /

4.   suspension: longer than . . .
      is usual. usually. penetrate
      push/in stay/there in
      obscured korridor——door——
      dors——till the heart
      (of the matter) gives up
      up _____ there.   .

5.   ubiquitous is
          night/ness
      dead is ????????? on
      couch :::::::: lust extinction
      extinct   breathing
      thing of leaves,
      of Kalendar's last
      last/ing . . .

from TO BE IN A TIME OF WAR

To say nothing, do nothing, mark time, to bend, to straighten up, to blame
oneself, to stand, to go toward the window, to change one's mind in the
process, to return to one's chair, to stand again, to go to the bathroom, to close
the door, to then open the door, to go to the kitchen, to not eat nor drink, to
return to the table, to be bored, to take a few steps on the rug, to come close
to the chimney, to look at it, to find it dull, to turn left until the main door, to
come back to the room, to hesitate, to go on, just a bit, a trifle, to stop, to pull
the right side of the curtain, then the other side, to stare at the wall.

To look at the watch, the clock, the alarm clock, to listen to the ticking, to
think about it to look again, to go to the tap, to open the refrigerator, to close
it, to open the door, to feel the cold, to close the door, to feel hungry, to wait,
to wait for dinner time, to go to the kitchen, to reopen the fridge, to take out
the cheese, to open the drawer, to take out a knife, to carry the cheese and
enter the dining room, to rest the plate on the table, to lay the table for one,
to sit down, to cut the cheese in four servings, to take a bite, to introduce the
cheese in the mouth, to chew and swallow, to forget to swallow, to day-dream,
to chew again, to go back to the kitchen, to wipe one's mouth, to wash one's
hands, to dry them, to put the cheese back into the refrigerator, to close that
door, to let go of the day.

To listen to the radio, to put it off, to walk a bit, to think, to give up thinking,
to look for the key, to wonder, to do nothing, to regret the passing of time,
to find a solution, to want to go to the beach, to tell that the sun is coming
down, to hurry, to go down with the key, to open the car's door, to sit, to
pull in the door, put in the key, turn it on, heat the engine, to listen, to make
sure nobody's around, to pull back, to go ahead, to turn right, then left, to
drive straight on, to follow the road, to take many curbs, to drive down the
coast, look at the ocean, to admire it, to feel happy, to go up the hill, to reach
the other side, then go straight, to stop, to make sure that the ocean has not
disappeared, to feel lucky, to stop the engine, to open the door, to exit, to
close the door, to look straight ahead, to appreciate the breeze, to advance
into the waves.

To wake up, to stretch, to get out of bed, to dress, to stagger towards the
window, to be ecstatic about the garden's beauty, to observe the quality of
the light, to distinguish the roses from the hyacinths, to wonder if it rained in
the night, to establish contact with the mountain, to notice its color, to see
if the clouds are moving, to stop, to go to the kitchen, to grind some coffee,
to lit the gas, to heat water, hear it boiling, to make the coffee, to put off the
gas, to pour the çoffee, to decide to have some milk with it, to bring out the

bottle, to pour the milk in the aluminum pan, to heat it, to be careful, to pour, to mix the coffee with the milk, to feel the heat, to bring the cup to one's mouth, to drink, to drink again, to face the day's chores, to stand and go to the kitchen, to come back and put the radio on, to bring the volume up, to hear that the war against Iraq has started.

To get more and more impatient, to be hungry, to bite one's nails, to wear a jacket, to open the door, walk down the hill, to look at the Bay, see boats, notice a big sailboat, to go on walking, to be breathless, to turn left, then right, to enter the Sushi-Ran, to wait, to look at the waitress, to call her, to rest one's elbows on the table, to pull them back when the tea arrives, to order, to eat, to drink, to use chopsticks, to be through, to wipe one's mouth with the napkin, to read the bill, to count, to pay, to thank graciously, to exit, to start the road uphill.

RALPH ANGEL

F ROM THE VERY first, in his debut collection *Anxious Latitudes*, Ralph Angel has written poems of a sublime abstract lyricism. His is a highly speculative poetic intelligence, both philosophically elegant and lyrically charged. Meditative and mysterious, his poetry tracks the subtle movement of consciousness against the backdrop of a culturally shifting and spiritually depleted world. Angel's exemplars are John Ashbery and James Tate, and he is always attempting to push the American idiom to its furthest reaches; yet, even with these ambitious expectations for his poetry, Angel makes poems that inevitably feel stylish, timeless, and marked by a precise lyric grace. His love of jazz and his knowledge of the Sephardic tradition influence his work, and he is both a poet of loss and a poet of place. As Tomaz Salamun has noted, "Just as Richard Diebenkorn defined Los Angeles for me in his paintings, so too has Ralph Angel defined that city in his remarkable poetry." Often wryly humorous, the speakers in Angel's poetry are sometimes like voices sent out over Samuel Beckett's radio, but with a background score by Miles Davis.

Ralph Angel was born in Seattle and grew up in the Pacific Northwest, though Southern California has been his home for many years. His second collection, *Neither World*, received the 1995 James Laughlin Prize from the Academy of American Poets. His most recent collection, *Exceptions and Melancholies: Poems 1986–2006*, was awarded the PEN USA Prize as the best collection of poetry of 2006. It was published alongside his superb translation of Federico García Lorca's *Poem of the Deep Song*. Ralph Angel is Edith R. White Distinguished Professor of English and Creative Writing at the University of Redlands, California.

INSIDE A WORLD THE WORLD FITS INTO

The lit match! As if I could really
see just now. The long streets, and longer river,
skyscrapers, and the arched bridges, all
that dusk has darkened,
all the distance they're related to.

And his voice is a sound gone wrong, a noisily
flapping one-winged bird. If not *clean*,
which word? His low, his spiraling, the heave and
thud of cold freight derailing, if not
orderly, what defends him from the truth
he already stands accused of?

As if, really, we'd been seen. In shaded areas,
in the hard, glazed open, standing in circles, laughing
at the worst possible time.

YOU THINK IT'S A SECRET, BUT IT NEVER WAS ONE

You think it's a secret, but it never was.
Sell the house, move to the beach, this *isn't* his closet,
there are no phantoms here.

You think that if you know the truth you'll forgive her. "I lied,"
she said. "I was afraid, afraid I'd be left alone."

Do we not each day leave this world
together, half asleep, a goodbye kiss steadying ourselves
against the seats of the train?

Do we not meet again and, always
dreaming, *not* find a word for it, the dream that would exclude us?

Someone remembers something that happened a long time
ago. She forgot it, it changed everything.

What can I tell you that you don't already know?
That life is sad? That this moment
brims with too-sweet wisteria?

And you, too, are sad. And hopeful. Adjustments
were made, the way they can be now.

You pick up your knife and almost
look at it, and put it down again. That she destroys
her life by keeping alive.

EXCEPTIONS AND MELANCHOLIES

Never before
had we been so thin and so clear
and arranged always
and in the same way gazing and listening
over the rooftops
to tin cans of flowers and strange
music. For an hour or more
I turned the same corner
and felt like a criminal farther and farther out to sea
among the racks of shoes and old clothes
but now looking
back I should never have
unpacked. A street
crowned with chestnut trees
ends at the sewer. You go to a theatre
and find yourself a house
outside the city
and walk the shore
forever. I don't have much
talent for poetry. When I see a wrecking ball
dangling from a crane I mean it
literally. I mean
I don't mean the world's fallen apart
or that a wrecking ball
symbolizes the eye my world-weary sister
couldn't know to turn away
from. The hospital's
exhausted. The little church is boarded up.
We leaned against the limestone
and liked the fact that tea
sweetens gradually
and that the wildflowers
beneath the shade of trees gone shivering

have really livened up the cemetery
and that the tall grass and the garbage
and especially the piled-up
newspapers and the rooftop pool
fit right in among
these windowless buildings
having gathered
as we are in the flesh again
and leading another life
altogether.

SOFT AND PRETTY

You don't even know how old
and black my blood is
or how the world does not participate
though in this country once the elevator's working
and the birds are fed and now they're bathing
and like a train
with a broken arm and blown-out
veins and one good eye you know my story
still, and so sit beside the mind that loses
as it wins you know
in its heart and peel an orange
against the shoulder of a friend and somewhere
clean to sleep
and bring back knowledge of the parapet
so to speak above the sea
and die for slippers and a robe
and in death
drag like waves your sound.

SAMPLING

I'm standing still on 10th Street. I'm not the only one. Buildings rise like
        foliage and human touch.

And so shall dig this cigarette as my last, and rattle trains, and rot the fences of
        the gardens of my body—

or without the harmony of speaking here the many sounds and rhythms that
        sound a lot like anger

when anger's silent, like a painting, though in the stillness of the paint itself the
        painter nods or waves or asks for help.

I'm not the only one. The pharmacy's untitled. The stars are there at night. In
        this humidity

the forlorn singing of the insects clings to anything nailed down. A whole bag
        of things I'm working

through, some set things that I know, like words I know that mean "from one
        place to another," the word that means

"to carry." I'm standing still on 10th Street. I'm not the only one. The dark
        tastes of salt and oranges. Its eyes

wander round and round. I am its thousand windows. I think about the future
        and the sea. And stay.

SOMETIMES AN IMAGE

A long time ago
I dug their graves with sticks. I leaned my face
upon them.

I'm looking at the moon
from our new home on the second floor. From our balcony
of weeds the moon's at sea. It will never snow here

and when it snows the further that I rise
above the earth the better.
I take a hundred

photographs. I
sleep among our clothes.

I don't know if I spoke aloud or not. I don't
stop talking. A long time ago the sky
invented flesh

and the miracle of viewing from a certain
distance the goddess

I need as much as water.

THE UNVEILING

As it is it could be
fog upon the eve of your unveiling,
or memory—unspooling every
distance—
or the mockingbird,
or the muffled screams of a neighbor,
or laughter—from strangers come
relatives and friends,
and small bowls of vinegar
in a roomful of thinking about you,
the almonds, the prayers
and the figs.

Impossible,
like the unwashed letters of your name,
or the faintly wailing
sirens of childhood, or the ocean
a half mile away—
like a kiss on the cheek,
a flutter of trees
in the plaza,
the breath of every
person you'll be.

VERTIGO

Only one is a wanderer.
And when she was sad she'd go into the street to be with people.
Two together are always going somewhere. They lie down beneath cypress,
next to a bird. I imagine the sky. It fans her mountains
and waves. She'd left some small town
where they used to make tires.
Stories are made out of stairwells
and rope. I'd been interrupting for years and didn't
know it. This old park. The dark hatchery. Workers in jumpsuits
throw down their poison at dawn.
Not everyone can be described. It's perfectly
natural. If she's thinking about love
does she break down

the door of the bedroom. Of course not. Not publicly
speaking. To the left there's a sofa. We all lived in rented rooms.
That's how it goes with subject matter.
Nude figures in profile
floating among palm trees. The idea was touristy,
like a postcard. I was given a small auditorium. I watched over
rush hour. I write down everything as I forget it,
especially at night.
I lock the door from the inside.

RAE ARMANTROUT

R AE ARMANTROUT BEGAN writ-
ing and publishing in the
1970s, in and around the
experimental milieu of the Language poets. Her radical use of juxtaposition
and her minimalist style echoed contemporary trends in the visual arts, while
her detailed attention to the daily marked her as a descendant of Williams and
the radical Modernists. In the ensuing three decades, her work has become
denser and more contemplative, but it hasn't lost the razoring insight that
trims her impressions and thoughts down to their essences. And always, her
work has engaged literature's classic questions—time, our place in the world,
and the role of language. To these, she adds an interest in the physical sciences
on the one hand, creating a distinctly twenty-first-century bridge between
C. P. Snow's Two Cultures, and an interest in the Christian mysteries on the
other, linking her work to the long tradition of poetry as spiritual exploration.

Rae Armantrout received her MA in poetry from San Francisco State
University in 1975 and has published ten books, the most recent being *Next Life*
and *Up to Speed*. Her selected poems, *Veil: New and Selected Poems*, was published
by Wesleyan in 2001. Her work has also been included in numerous anthologies,
including *Postmodern American Poetry: A Norton Anthology*; *American Women Poets in
the 21st Century: Where Language Meets the Lyric Tradition*; and *The Oxford Book of
American Poetry*; and her poems have been selected for *The Best American Poetry* in
1988, 2001, 2002, 2004, and 2007. A native of California, Armantrout teaches
poetry and poetics at the University of California at San Diego.

SPECIAL THEORY OF RELATIVITY

You know those ladies
in old photographs? Well,
say one stares into your room
as if into the void
beyond her death in 1913.

GENERATION

We know the story.

She turns
back to find her trail
devoured by birds.

The years; the
undergrowth

THE FIT

In a fit of repugnance
each moment
rips itself in half,

producing a twin.

■

In a coming-of-age story
each dream
produces me:

an ignorance
on the point of revelation.

■

I'm at a side table

in a saloon
in Alaska,

my eye on the door

where a flood of strangers
pours in.

The door or the window?

It's morning.

POLICE BUSINESS

The suspect
spat blood and said,
"I love you," causing us
to lose our places.
We had warned him once
that being recognizable
was still
the best way to stay hidden.

Harmless as the hose is turquoise
where it snakes
around the primroses—
those pink
satellite dishes,
scanning the columns.

Was that an incarnation there
when *say* connected
with *so*? (Was it
an angel
or a Big, Big Star)?
We're just trying to make sure
that the heart's desire
stays put.

TURN OF EVENTS

Outside it was the same as before, scrawny palms and oleanders, their long leaves, ostensible fingers, not pointing, but tumbling in place—plants someone might call exotic if anybody called—and the same birds and hours, presumably, slipping in and out of view. She kept coming out onto the porch with the sense that there was something to it. Perpetuation and stasis. She wanted to deal with the basics—though what this scene might be the basis for she didn't know.

This was her native tongue, slipping in and out of order—its empty streets and loose flapping leaves, its bald-faced simplicity as if a way had been cleared for something huge. Shape was the only evidence. She went back in. She should think about how the house was built or how it was paid for. How a feeling can have a shape for so long, say an oblong, with sun falling in a series of rhomboids on its wooden strips. It would have an orientation. She wondered whether there was much difference between orientation and reason. She would sit facing the door.

WHAT WE MEAN

Oh Princess,
you apple-core afloat

in coke
in a Styrofoam cup,
on an end-table,

you dust, glass, book, crock, thorn, moon.

Oh Beauty who fell asleep
on your birthday,

we swipe at you.

■

How are we defining "dream"?

An exaggerated sense
of the relevance
of these details,

of "facts"
as presented?

A peculiar
reluctance to ask

presented by whom
and in what space?

　　　　■

By space we mean
the collapsible

whirligig
of attention,

the figuring and
reconfiguring

of charges

among orbits
　　　　　(obits)

that has taken forever

SCUMBLE

What if I were turned on by seemingly innocent words such as "scumble,"
"pinky," or "extrapolate"?

What if I maneuvered conversation in the hope that others would pronounce
these words?

Perhaps the excitement would come from the way the other person touched
them lightly and carelessly with his tongue.

What if "of" were such a hot button?

"Scumble of bushes."

What if there were a hidden pleasure
in calling one thing
by another's name?

YONDER

1

Anything cancels
everything out.

If each point
is a singularity,

thrusting all else
aside for good,

"good" takes the form
of a throng
of empty chairs.

Or it's ants
swarming a bone.

2

I'm afraid
I don't love
my mother
who's dead

though I once—
what does "once" mean?—
did love her.

So who'll meet me over yonder?
I don't recognize the place names.

Or I do, but they come
from televised wars.

TRANSLATION

The thing that makes us human,
monkey-see, monkey-do speed-up,
a "call to mimesis,"
now comes from everywhere at once.

The cumulus
and the white flash
from under
the mocking-bird's wing
make what?

Repeat wake measurement.
"Check to see"
"Check to see,"
birds say,
"that enough time
has passed."

JOHN ASHBERY

A CONSISTENT INNOVATOR, John Ashbery has been a leader in contemporary poetics for over forty years. His first book, published by the Tibor de Nagy Gallery in 1953, marked his close relationship to the visual arts, and his second book, *Some Trees*, selected by W. H. Auden for the Yale Younger Poets Prize in 1956, focused attention on his unusual blend of avant-garde and traditional influences, which range from Raymond Roussel to John Clare. Noted for its tenderness and its irony, Ashbery's work revolutionized form in American poetry by taking Surrealism's dizzying imagination and applying it to new structures that could support radical ambiguity, juxtaposition, humor, and doubt. One of the four principal members of the New York School, Ashbery went to France on a Fulbright Scholarship in the mid-1950s and remained until 1965, writing, translating, and working as the art editor for the European edition of the *Herald Tribune*. Once back in New York, he served as the art critic for *New York* and *Newsweek* magazines and on the editorial board of *ARTnews*. Some of his art criticism is collected in *Reported Sightings: Art Chronicles 1957–1987*.

In 1976, Ashbery's *Self-Portrait in a Convex Mirror* won the three major U.S. awards: the Pulitzer Prize, the National Book Award, and the National Book Critics Circle Award. He has also won the Bollingen Prize, the Griffin International Poetry Prize, the Wallace Stevens Award, and the Frost Medal, just to name a few. Internationally, he has been made a Chevalier de l'Ordre des Arts et des Lettres and an officer in the Légion d'Honneur of the Republic of France, and was the first English-language winner of the Grand Prix des Biennales Internationales de Poésie in Brussels. The author of twenty-five books of poetry, Ashbery has said that his poems try to "record a kind of generalized transcript of what's really going on in our minds all day long." Noted critics such as Harold Bloom and Helen Vendler have written extensively on his work, which has also been the subject of numerous PhD dissertations and other studies. John Ashbery was the poet laureate of New York from 2001 to 2003, and in 2007 was named the first poet laureate of mtvU.

WELL-LIT PLACES

The horse chestnut tree shelters the house of princes.
The laurel nudges the catalpa.
Mussolini offers a diamond to Corot.
The proud, the famous, the magnificent
Exude gentleness and megalomania.
Embassies are loud with the sound of cymbals and organ.
The taste of insolence is sharp, with an agreeable mingled sweetness.

A man declaiming in front of a coat of arms
Is possessed of great pride and believes no man equal to himself in valor,
    dignity or competence.
He will have two wives who will love him dearly and whom he won't
    love at all.
He will be irascible and lustful.
He will endure many reverses because of his sudden wrath and his great
    courage.

The girl will have a large and wide bosom.
She will experience disappointment at the age of twelve through an act of
    oppression or virginal corruption.
She will conquer in all things, with God's help and that of the fuchsia, the
    orange, and the dahlia.

WHAT TO DO WITH MILK

Strangers may kiss.

There'll always be a bottle of champagne burning in the window.

Men and plagues have long marred the surface
of the estuary.

You haven't been listening. And now know I am not remembering.

Brainy and I were twins once. She sort of hung around the old
opera house. They looked for her in the pilings. No Brainy.

She preferred the poetry of D. H. Lawrence to his novels, and
puzzles to pudding. One night I can't get angry any more. Besides

it's not my house, I say let's go. LET'S GO! I say. No response.
Only the skittling of mice among the creeping charlie, and the wind,

a definite whirr.

THE TAKEN

I have this thing to do
thing I have to do

Almost I have to do
sky, dry, rooftops—
the almost funeral sky

will ignite it
to not be indebted

as the documentary will be tested
too well
Others came along
with the measurements

Icicle, are you,

and fervent sprouting
under the caps
twitch that makes well
off in kennel and tribe

Overlooking the stick
is what I came to be about
Don't listen the twins
curtain of fear

Oracle of forgetting

in the blaze

OBSIDIAN HOUSE

> *The fruits are ripe, dipped in fire, cooked*
> *and tested here on earth.*
> —HÖLDERLIN, translated by Richard Sieburth

as was proven
when they entered the house
in which the priest was,
moping and sincere

like all exegetes. Zeppelin
hovered o'er him, bushes fancied him,
but it was to be let down on earth
they all embraced singing.

Further, one was sure
one had come to pass,
yet no slovenly proof was
ever forwarded.

The lines swayed
backwards and forth,
housewives queuing up for lamb chops
and all that this rhythm implies

excoriated
from above.

The tourist metastasizes his position.
These palms are lucky being within us
no matter what the tyrant truth says.
All along my childhood's wall

I hoped (was hoping) for this occlusion
but not passionately.
A cheerful emotion hatched,
soon population o'erran the land.

We descended gently toward boats
to hear the boatswain's
song, sung from the capstan, about how life intrudes
on the plodding waves

and no one is certain of desiccation
as a great marrow bone is gnawed.
It is as though a feast had happened
in plain sight. We forgot about the
treasure, forgot it had happened
among the madness of whirling wheat.

OTHERS SHIED AWAY

> The Autumn seems to cry for thee,
> Best lover of the Autumn-days!
> —SUSAN COOLIDGE

And they have cooler armchairs.
They have an imaginary tunnel down there.
It can be the color of your choosing. With bridges, splayed
so wide of the mark, you wonder how they thought of crossing.

It can't be over.
I haven't taken my final exam
nor received the notice
to do so. The halls for my oratory
haven't been built yet. They'll be nice and new,
with buff-colored dolphins dangling from the ceiling.
The world will see something of my art in this,
though I had nothing to do with the actual building, and turn away,
admiring me and their clothes—so appropriate!
How did we know how the moon was going to be today,
what drinks to serve after driving fifty miles through parched savannas?
Yet does it all come miraculously to life?
Or is it the solitary crank who's right,
the unofficial historian? He never hazards an opinion,
yet stays by the door like a porter, pose
that fools no one. It seems none of us has begun to digest
the meal of all our lives. There's nothing left to do but count the rooms—
nine, all told.

I told you when I set out for
the market town, the saddlebags would be full
of gold and silver coinage, just for you;
coffers would bulge, orchards
overflow their walls with blue fruit.
Every day would be a cocktail party, all day long.

Now the tunnel seems withered.
We must return to the sparse blessings
that place our shoes on this winter path;
nothing can stay outdoors all the time—
there must be intervals for books and fire
and endless conversation that means very little
unless we'd prefer to have it some other way,
little girl, blinking at the autumn's rough practice,
crude language, distemper—wound into a ball for you.

HAIBUN 2

. . . and can see the many hidden ways merit drains out of the established and internationally acclaimed containers, like a dry patch of sky. It is an affair of some enormity. The sky is swathed in a rich, gloomy and finally silly grandeur, like drapery in a portrait by Lebrun. This is to indicate that our actions in this tiny, tragic platform are going to be more than usually infinitesimal, given the superhuman scale on which we have to operate, and also that we should not take any comfort from the inanity of our situation; we are still valid creatures with a job to perform, and the arena facing us, though titanic, hasn't rolled itself beyond the notion of dimension. It isn't suitable, and it's here. Shadows are thrown out at the base of things at right angles to the regular shadows that are already there, pointing in the correct direction. They are faint but not invisible, and it seems appropriate to start intoning the litany of dimensions there, at the base of a sapling spreading its lines in two directions. The temperature hardens, and things like the smell and the mood of water are suddenly more acute, and may help us. We will never know whether they did.

Water, a bossa nova, a cello is centered, the light behind the library

THE GARDEN OF FALSE CIVILITY

Where are you? Where you are is the one thing I love,
yet it always escapes me, like the lilacs in their leaves,
too busy for just one answer, one rejoinder.
The last time I see you is the first
commencing of our time to be together, as the light of the days
remains the same even as they grow shorter,
stepping into the harness of winter.

Between watching the paint dry and the grass grow
I have nothing too tragic in tow.

I have this melting elixir for you, front row
tickets for the concert to which all go.
I ought to
chasten my style, burnish my skin, to get that glow
that is all-important, so that some
may hear what I am saying as others disappear
in the confusion of unintelligible recorded announcements.
A great many things were taking place that day,

besides, it was not the taxpayers
who came up to me, who were important,
but other guests of the hotel
some might describe as dog-eared,
apoplectic. Measly is a good word to describe
the running between the incoming and the outgoing tide
as who in what narrow channels shall ever
afterwards remember the keen sightings of those times,
the reward and the pleasure.
Soon it was sliding out to sea
most naturally, as the place to be.
They never cared, nor came round again.
But in the tent in the big loss
it was all right too. Besides, we're not
serious, I should have added.

OF LINNETS AND DULL TIME

You said you don't want to know any more
than you do now, of every thing that might be
a person. It would be cheating. That is urgent.
If we are going to mean in so many ways
let them all be lopped off.
That way we'll know you're getting older.

I feel sorry for anyone that has to die.
The lines of what's expected
fan out like beaters. That's all,
I think. But I lose things, now.
The beautiful shape of the toilet interposed
a viability as the air-raid drill ended.
We've got to do something.
He may be up there now, trying to find us.
If you let me, I'll drive you back to the fairgrounds.

MARY JO BANG

RAPTUROUS AND DENSE, yet para-
doxically precise and incisive, Mary
Jo Bang's poems are both theatrical
and performative. Her exciting second collection (its title drawn from Samuel
Beckett), *The Downstream Extremity of the Isle of Swans*, displayed Bang's exhilarat-
ing sense of language, as well as her predilection for tonal sleight of hand and
witty verbal asides. She is also capable of elegant dramatic monologues and nar-
ratives of deliciously antic and even fractured sensibilities, as in her celebrated
third collection, *Louise in Love* (which uses the actress Louise Brooks as both a
jacket image and narrative springboard), in which Bang constructs complex and
deeply compelling poetic wholes from highly gestural, voice-driven sequences.
Bang's eye for high art and the corruptions of daily experience is enacted with
a verve and vivaciousness that keeps the reader held within the poised non-
chalance and irony of her voice. Always challenging convention and form, her
fourth book, *The Eye Like a Strange Balloon*, uses artworks as points of departure
to alter our traditional ideas of ekphrastic poetry.

Born in St. Louis, Mary Jo Bang teaches now at Washington University in
that city, though she has also lived in Manhattan. She has held the prestigious
Hodder Fellowship from Princeton University and was co-editor for poetry
for *Boston Review* for many years. Bang's first collection, *Apology for Want*, was
awarded both the Bakeless Prize and the Great Lakes College Association New
Writers Award. Her fifth and most recent collection, the powerful and heart-
breaking sequence *Elegy*, on the death of her son, won the 2007 National Book
Critics Circle Award.

FEBRUARY ELEGY

This bald year, frozen now in February.
This cold day winging over the ugly
Imperfect horizon line,
So often a teeth line of ten buildings.
A red flag flapping
In the wind. An orange curtain is noon.
It all hurts her eyes. This curtain is so bright.
Here is what is noticeably true: sight.
The face that looks back from the side
Of the butter knife.
A torn-bread awkwardness.
The mind makes its daily pilgrimage
Through riff-raff moments. Then,
Back into the caprice case to dream
In a circle, a pony goes round.
The circle's association: There's a center
To almost everything but never
Any certainty. Nothing is
More malleable than a moment. We were
Only yesterday breathing in a sea.
Some summer sun
Asked us over and over we went. The sand was hot.
We were only yesterday tender hearted
Waiting. To be something.
A spring. And then someone says, Sit down,
We have a heart for you to forget. A mind to suffer
With. So, experience. So, the circus tent.
You, over there, you be the girl
In red sequins on the front of a card selling love.
You, over there, you, in black satin,
You be the Maiden's Mister Death.

P EQUALS PIE

Let's place Plato on one side.
Let's place PeeWee Herman on the other.
It's worth noting the Greek root, Tekno,
Means know-how. This is not the same

As practical wisdom, which means the self
Knowing when. As in, Should one
When sitting nearly alone under a cinema dome?
The dialogue coach prompts, "Never, Sir,

When someone is watching." *(Enter a siren.)*
Now let's negotiate the "question" of the space
Between the two. And further, the issue

Of who decides which trumps—the trope of irony,
Or the trope of allegory? Each makes the picture of a perfect circle
Of pumpkin or pecan. Ergo, it's Pi and it's Christmas,

And there's Paul, devout as ever,
On his way to a donkey-headed nowhere.

MYSTERY AT MANOR CLOSE

>   —*Quickly Brenda stepped aside and tripped up the Biology Mistress.*

She puts her ticking wrist to her ear and hears a house
Full of *Tock* from the clock that is lacking a stem.
On the face it says Mickey and Mouse.
(All of which comes from within.)

She makes a wish: that the Heather who left her
In stormy weather will find herself
In the mire of desires that cannot be easily realized.
To your health, she says, and sticks out her foot

To feel the fire in its place. Here's to Bio-
In most of its many spheres. To the ear that hears
The clack of a gate latch. To the mouth and its legible
Little gray lies. To the brain with its hardwired fear.

And to cathexis, both far or near. Back at the manor,
There's mystery: a van and a driver, a girl's guide, a book.
The rescue of one in a basket about to be driven away by a crook.
The Freud finger puppet appears on stage and says, in German,

Yes, Liebchen, it's true.
We are born to begin and to end
In infantile fury.
The girl on the couch, who is listening, doesn't say a word.

ALICE IN WONDERLAND

Such a fall! Watch fob and waistcoat.
How late the mistake is made.
How long the clamoring lasts.

Who are you? Bending against a blade
of green grass. Smoke fills
the Caterpillar. Smoke floats

over the polka dot snow.
Have you really changed, do you think?
This is the best part of the dark edge of down.

Down, down, she fell. This is the best part
of the edge where one is not one-
self. Don't I know it, Alice says,

blinking her eyes once twice.
She took down a jar from one of the shelves
as she passed it; it was labeled "ORANGE

MARMALADE." The game was changing.
There are games where one never wavers.
There are games where one follows

a dot-by-dot disturbance.
There is falling, and about to
fall, and ground givingway. There is the beautiful

act of turning
to buy two and getting a free beach bag.
Perfect for picnics or toting and such.

A flavorful favor to take on a trip
to a mountain where chocolate is eaten
on weekends and during the week

it's placed on your pillow
right next to your head which is swimming
in visions. She could almost envision it.

A pool with a placid surface,
mist shrouding a peak
that poked through at the top

to speak of impossible heights.
But, no. The peak was a spike
on the cephalogram and she was dreaming again

in a sleep clinic bed.
Father was petting her forehead;
Mother was stirring a soup. She'd be ever more

reckless if never she woke.
Now that was not said right.
Some of the words had got altered.

A row of button mums hedged the walkway. She stopped
to enter this datum
in her Rite as Reign notebook.

She knew what the button mums meant.
Another fall.
Dying must happen quite often, said Alice.

Sigmar Polke, *Alice im Wunderland*, mixed media on patterned fabric, 1971

MAN AND WOMAN

To spend most of a short life living,
that was the aim. She'd know it since
the first time her heart's hand had painstakingly formed
its aortic scrawl, its Palmer Method
of pulse, pulse, pulse.

I love to be brought, he said, into the city. The bread
and butter so simple, so pure.
The waiter in a long white apron cleaned their places.
Finished? he asked.
One was never.

Breakfast followed dinner. Sleep was a wave
one rode to wake gasping.
Sea salt awash in the vein.

Cheek imprinted with sleep's ragged S.
And even prettiness could be dissolved

and reconstituted. Stone falling from an eave could be gravel
at the base of a pylon. A python knowledge grasping her
in its grip. Such a pretty blouse.
The sequins, the salesman had said, had been sandblasted
and no extras included

because none would be needed.
The firm was so sure they would last.
While nothing lasts, she said, still it is
for a while——. He helped her on with her coat.
The blouse is black.

The pattern of tiny circles forms a sequined paisley,
a pretty method of fragility.
I love to be brought, he said,
into a language. And so did she.
The white snapdragons,
the peach cheek, the pretty girl
in her black backless dress.
It was all dissolving into a hangman's noose.
Into a taut track——
the caboose following the train

into the tunnel tunneled into a mountain.
The children piper-bound following the train.
Don't open your eyes.
I have been waiting my whole life, he said,
to be brought

into believing. Practicing with a daiquiri,
dealing with timidity in any number of ways.
Wearing a hat, driving a Lexus.
It's difficult. The black blouse,
the clear sequins, each a little lake

taking Ophelia in, to oblivion. Into a language
that would suit her. The noise level
in the restaurant had risen.
The girl in the black dress (Ophelia?)
was wiping her eyes.

The woman in the pretty black blouse,
sewn with sequins was turning to look out the window.
Did I tell you? he said. Yes,
he had. He had told her.
And she had listened.

Eikoh Hosoe, No. 24 from the *Man and Woman* series, photograph, 1960

JOSHUA BECKMAN

T HERE'S A DYNAMIC play between coherence and incoherence at the heart of Joshua Beckman's work. We're soothed into a welcoming comfort through his grammatically normative phrases, but then realize that he often leaves them—and their meaning—hanging. While his situations are familiar, they never *quite* coalesce into complete scenes, which lets them retain all the flash and dazzle of the ephemeral, all the play and question of the Pop perspective. And it's out of that flickering indeterminacy that Beckman constructs the irony that drives his poetry. It's an irony at times tinged with self-deprecation, which for him is also both the deprecation of an age, our age, and a device for probing the limits and potentials of the self.

Beckman writes in a range of styles, including the *haiku*-like three-line poems from *Your Time Has Come*, reprinted here, which give an aestheticized, meditative turn to daily detail that reflects the influence of Eastern philosophies on American popular culture of the last quarter of the twentieth century. He also works in innovative book structures and has both collaborated with a number of artists on installations and performances and curated shows that focus on cross-media experimentation. He's the author of four collections of poetry as well as one written in collaboration with Matthew Rohrer. Also a translator, his translation of Tomaz Salamun's *Poker* was a finalist for the 2004 PEN USA Award in Literary Translation. Beckman currently divides his life between Brooklyn and Seattle, where he is the co-editor of Wave Books.

■ ■ ■

Now begins our immaculate summer
or the clutter of what tunes itself near the truth
or they have made glasses just for me (gloomy things)
or her hand there on my chest (the street of champions)
or the chorus of taught and clumsy common quality
we have made ourselves unable to share. See, Vivian,
the whole world's gone typical, crying,
the bed's now set, the sun the same (snow) and you
kept painting (so rather studious) and for me,
remember, everything's fine, I think of her
universal and divine. She has a patio too, proud,
and in stillness one beautiful thing is brought forward
after another, and refused. Leisurely and pleased
I go. To collect of things is all I ever know.

■ ■ ■

The birds know. The wind knows. Call me. I'm always
in the same place watching the same thing. The sound of
water, of wind, of flags, of the birds' deserved babies
crying for rain. The birds know. Translucent is the wallet
that holds the money on its way. Children stop. Pilgrims
stop. Tugboats drift. The wind knows. I'm always in the
same place watching the same thing. You know. The blue bridge
opening for no one. The water knows. A translucent wallet
filled with water. Flags flapping at the sign of water. We
know. We start singing at the sight of the translucent wallet
holding water. It's singing. It knows. It's always in
the same place watching the same thing. The blue bridge
opening for no one. The rain on its way to a wallet of water.
The birds know. Always the same place, the same thing.

■ ■ ■

In the days of famous want
the people acted cruel and sweet
the music was boring and insightful
and if one found oneself in a well
the others would pull you from that well.
That is how it was. The countryside
unintelligible in its evaporation
and the people, their faces, full
and with nothing to do. One would
lie with the beloved and cheerless

and await the passing over
of smoke, such clouds, and
the endeavors of the day
would be discussed, the
anecdotal annunciations would
fill the spoons which earlier
had been filled with the humble
presentation of intangible thought.
We had been left. We had poured ribbons
in each other's bags. We had collapsed
beside each other's beds—the
calla lily floats above the table,
about the hands of certain people,
a glow. With you there in such
historic towns, I'm brought down.
We, at all times, have learned
to dance and to throw. We have
made gallant our enigmatic ways,
and when our teeth part or
when our lips open, we are doing
what we are born to do—our
bodies so unimportant amidst
the bodies of others, our memories
so well painted, our futures
so full of expensive shirts.
And the uncomfortableness
of watching someone's hand
cover the body of someone else.
It is history and it is money
and it is the ugly hats the women
you're always with want to wear,
it is the unacceptable swagger
of the iced, threading their way
through our life, and it is
the bridge, how you climb
atop it now and the waters
below you doing their stupid
repetitive thing, and the air
emptied of its sound, and the
shallow acts of others, and the fly
and the grass you will never see,
the constant emptying.
Carl once wrote the most horrible

poem, and I pinned it to my wall
and where is it now?
I empty myself of wit and begin,
and before long, a tow truck,
a snow storm, the thought of him
going to California to make
other people miserable, the
thought again, the thought of
the sea, the unbecoming ways
of everyone, and other moments,
your red pants, your cradled purse,
the next man who will leave
his lover for you.

■   ■   ■

This is what's been done to flesh
the quill and the book and the
indiscretion of stone upon which
a little drop of gold does fall,
the cry of a pigeon or moan
of the folded over father, and
beneath these drapéd mysteries
the wine does spill upon the dog
the dog does sit in the corner
curing itself of this indifference
and the bar of light does illumine
such dust as has been brought
into upheaval with only your
untidy waking——the covers under
your chin:

pull

and in the distant river
they are listening, cut grass
blown through the window and
why music and the absorbancy
of such concrete as has distilled
the discordance of the neighborhood
and has left "through the music
he sweetly displays" an empty field
of lost balloons rolling into streets
as have, in other times, volcanoes

covered such singers as do justice
to the cosmic tops they had seen through
their equally majestic windows, the mint
leaf touched the lip, the regular
resurrection of those empty spaces
that result from banishment,
the ladder leaned against a tree,
Dear Margaret, I, in such
constant envious refrain as does inform
most open speech, do extend and my
flower does tap your halo—how it spins
now surrounded by such bagéd peoples
as only Florida can offer. I have set
your aura a runnin and from it (its sun)
I gather light. This, you see,
is our domestic partnership—the
conclusion of each well-attached earring
and fragrant misunderstanding, the chorus
of the barbaric calling, while here in the meeting
I'm passed this note:

> Dismal are we who love only recognition
> Now hand me the saber.

Which I did.

1:00 pm	Behind curtain baby kissing mother
1:05 pm	Clouds cover mountains
1:10 pm	Ribbons in patterns descending
1:20 pm	Tragic event of saber and table

The flesh. In time you will learn to look
at everything. In time you will learn to
touch everything. In time you will learn
to clothe everything. In time you will
learn to eat everything. In time you will
learn to say of everything that it has
been seen, that it has been touched, that

it has been killed, that it has been eaten.
Bloodied are our hours, in reflection,
the knuckle and the finger and the paper.
The shoulder. At dusk I did slip from the town,
the baby under my wing. Now to the water,
where what I have done will be reflected on later.

from YOUR TIME HAS COME

Oh atlas
look
you forgot my island.

They keep calling
but I'll just sweat it out here
in my little apartment.

Plants in hallway
near empty elevator,
I'll save you.

Lightning hit the island
so I left with the birds
to watch it from here.

Don't be mad,
I'm in bed thinking
of you at work.

Before she returned
I stepped slowly through the yard
as if to say, here an entire hour passes.

Clouds gather
over Wall Street
for lunch.

■

Everyone's got a lover
waiting to come back
mystically changed.

CAL BEDIENT

FROM HIS FIRST book *Candy Necklace* to his most recent poems, featured here, Cal Bedient's work traces a curve moving ever further out from poetry's conventions. Most of his early poems blend clear themes and tight visual forms with a rangy, active language that takes frequent startling twists. Increasingly, those twists have infiltrated his syntax, his page arrangement, and his subject matter. As his grammar breaks down, the intensity and density of his images pick up, and as soon as the grip of sense starts to slip, sound steps in, often with tremendous momentum, to keep the whole thing aloft. In a *Denver Quarterly* interview, he speaks of the "possibility that new grammars, new forms, might still be summoned out of the air, grammars and forms equal to our craziness, our desperation, and our need for the hope (the hope, not the solace) that lies in the more benign and strenuous species of invention."

Bedient, born and raised in Washington State, has also published four books of literary criticism, including *He Do the Police in Different Voices: The Waste Land and Its Protagonist*. His essays and reviews have appeared in *The Nation*, *The New Republic*, *The New York Times Book Review*, and many other periodicals. He is the co-editor of the literary review *Lana Turner* and is one of the editors of the New California Poetry Series published by the University of California. He teaches in the English Department of the University of California at Los Angeles and spends his summers in rural Washington State.

INSATIABILITY

For every angel
              a preposition.
You call,
         swarm guitar string longitudes,
o air flame shining relations
                    wandering contemporary.

      Steeple white clapboard "to"
              spikes enormity Iowa blue—
as the moon is a clasp for night.

  "Of," "with"—moments like rain,
when what rises from the river   is not only river.

Lightning never lay me bare to bed.

      She sat atop him as if he were everything,
         but not to her—

tablespoon of sugar in water.

Spaces be cream
              or exaggerated like raspberries,
red hustlers.

                  Roots that tug to be "up,"
              "inside,"
                    will never find a bride.

We're oyster spit, yet the sea
opens before us the white swan of the wound.

CLOUDS OF WILLING SEEN IN THE BIRD DAY

Amiable Monet, in lieu of *that*, had a *now*
         postdated like his eyes—
                    crafty, a beaver's,
         flush with the floating waterlily fields.

And you: anybody more remote would be dead
                                languaged,
      you are nice library, nice library, sit.

Who hasn't been out of line for a long time,
      like the cooked-spinach-green boat in *Sunrise*,
            twenty feet short of the

wobble laid down by the orange sun
                        low in the emerald air of sea?
(it's so easy to difference and cumber
(an eyelet passed through to a little evil
(boomerang of heartbone
            winging into the dark refusal for beauty.

What is special electrical railroad in anyone
                        that anyone should feel so wide
open the moon's sudden cheekbones?

Scatter corn on the dock
   as the wild geese breast toward you on the languid lake
   their greeny-plantinum circles of evening:

What you cannot think will be your life.

THE WHITE LETTER

  We are a fair people, white headlights of people, who have loved the north,
the east, the south, the west out of all reason, a curious people,

                  picking out the others in the barbarous
                  see-through of the falls, and I regret to say
                  the pond in the orchard is now full of them.

                  I have so loved your views of the working people,
                  gold earrings in the little brown girls' ears.
                  Write to me when the Flake White

                  peeling from your thighs
                  has been diagnosed.

Re: the cloudhooves of the love that safeguards the universe, crossing the
Rockies, what are you thinking, don't tell me, *the women & Childn. Cried dureing
my Stay of an hour at this place* and a still whiter thought is always yet to come *to
interigate thro' the Intptr.*, just as America leapt out of "cloudy, moist, melancholy
old Europe," spilling six feet of nice young men into Kentuck—

> and certainly land washed by packing-peanut surf
> conveys a rich position. Always
> the power of white is exciting to me.
> the creaming edge of the Pacific
> is the childhood of someone white,
> laughing to herself now,
> she's that kind of titanium—
> riding into combers on a mount
> the pale color of pilgrim time.

> Still, we'll want props if we're to fuck again:
> lickable polished policewoman shoes
> and a white sheet like a mountain stream
> to tighten around the throat.

*I undertook to tell the Cheif who we wer, how come, wither, and rolled up my sleve
to shew him I was not a Savage and did not wish to hirt him. He threw his left arm over
my wright sholder and vociforated the word âh-hí-a, âh-hí-a, "I am much rejoiced." He
requested his Squar might be used for the night.*

*I had this day an agility. A beautiful howling green down to the river below. Named
the river Dearborn after the Secretary of war,*

> and unto us this evening,
> several hundred miles within difficult going,
> this wild & mountainous bosom of more.

THE GREEN LETTER

A sea gull looking into the mirror remarked: "like a wedding, and a still life
with horses." There was not an acquaintance in the description who could name
all the faces in it.

> so many   so many   so many   so many:
> you would not think there could be none. There are none. There are many.
> Between in the mouth of among, exactly.
> For Nature's a large quantity. Jane is Nature.

Therefore, Jane's a large quantity when the little babies are in her and I
    paint her with leaves, artificially.

Once I married a French gardener, on stilts, in a lemon skirt. Then I
    became a character in a novelette. Then I was dead and alive again,
    inaugurating a carnal aura
    while sitting between Eva my right leg
    and Jessica my left.

My cat rubs his mouth against the piano leg and purrs like the wind
when it excites itself with a hundred poplars.

The wind Jane, when all her whiskers are between.

The evident affectation of the foregoing passage, its indulgent fondness for non-
identity, its thesis that there are no subjects, only processes, underlines the fact
that modern art has lost its courage for the unitary, as when a paper bird flies
into the shredder in full-throated *oh this harm of being one.* Pessoa's heteronymic
schizophrenia—is it what you've dreamed of all your life? To paint a reclining
something holding up on its goose-head hand the temper of horses ("too bad he
can't draw figures") ("strange it made me feel. One of the very great pictures of
these last years")?

    RETELL: "Turner could make very little of the human figure once it got
        too close."

We have heard your confession:

    Leaning over my inky cloak is no one of any color
    to give me in a short, plain, explanatory letter

    my *subito* entire. Who pisses in the next urinal
    dares not look at me (the prick),

    possibly my past, *another swimmer of tepid waters.*

If the green bud you lacerate with your thumbnail while you talk to your idiot
neighbor fails to remind you of poems of wattles made, still you could show a
little more respect for nature, couldn't you, you who (RELATE:) careless suck
the drunken evening out of grapes, you, a barred Subject who takes charge,
photographing "the sign of the undecidable" in the two nymphs asleep in nothing
but one another's arms before, randy Faun, you tread on it?

Listen, friend. I mean well by you:
accept the perfect legibility of things,

do not shake the blue boy till a little girl

falls out, a shattered fish
of POORLY wrapped pencils

and the angel with the telescope
is blinded by the flow-blow of leaves

from her lungs. Who knows
how to enter everything possess

nothing and pass by? The trees

sway like the Ink Spots
singing "Your Feet's Too Big,"

then the WINDS of terror

no one forgets the traces of
carry the leaves of the pencils away.

BANANA PEAKS GET SNOWFALL

Alice does not Carroll to take the banana boat to Paris, there is such
Eiffel distrust of resemblance there. (Yet when rains
dig their furred forks into the snow,

Parisians say the Seine goes bananas *like*
women schtupped in the white Calcuttas of translation.)
What is wrong, give me the keys,

give me the bananas, I could make a hand of them, I could
hurriedly to the podium the topic is unexpected, my eight
scoops of white gauze from the Medical Corps.

Will no one lean out from a window in the All-
at-once, like an interested banana? Why do I even ask
your black spots to meet me

                    in the clinic of the unmarketable dark?

The last of the sacred, "the submission of flesh to flesh":
sweetness extreme, banana cream: twice
in the yellow balcony seats (scrooch down, honey)

during the classification and treatment of war wounds.
To be more and less than one is why Alfred North
Whitehead wanted to process Alfred South

Whitehead is now Alfred West Whitehead
participating in the next epoch of God?
Send us a bulletin, dear interfuser. Our banana groves

long to be buffalo heads sniffing dawn's blood.
Alice not warm here in the crotch of my arm
while my other arm smells of distant

                    (and coming closer) ice cream

MOLLY BENDALL

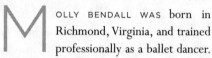

MOLLY BENDALL WAS born in Richmond, Virginia, and trained professionally as a ballet dancer. Her poetry conveys both the measured elegance of dance and, more and more over recent years, the wry demotic speech of conversation. There is an aesthetic poise to her poems, yet she relishes offering a highly posed world that finds itself riddled by a scathing, arched-eyebrow wit and intimate if ironic voice-overs. Her diction is at times playful and purposefully quirky. In Bendall's second collection, *Dark Summer*, her bemused speakers portray a darkly erotic and richly adorned world of false echoes and inevitable tragedy. There is a charged mixture of mystery and opulence in these poems, as if indiscrete shadows were in constant motion behind the velvet drapery of the page. The effect can be dreamlike, ethereal, and somewhat otherworldly, even while the poems themselves remain rendered with deft lyric detail.

Increasingly in her work, Bendall has collapsed phrasings and pushed for a denser, more enigmatic poetic voice, culminating in the book-length sequence entitled *Ariadne's Island* (her third collection), a radical retelling of the story of Ariadne and Theseus. Bendall's most recent work invokes techniques of fable while re-inscribing the lost practices of the remedial charm, malediction, and incantation. Her first book, *After Estrangement*, was awarded the Peregrine Smith Poetry Prize. She has also received the Eunice Tietjens Prize from *Poetry* and the Lynda Hull Prize from *Denver Quarterly*. She teaches at the University of Southern California in Los Angeles.

CONVERSATION WITH EVA HESSE

Where do you live?
    On the block with lots of 5's.
    The one with the glass doorway, the wavy glass
    and a one-sided shaky banister.
    All the houses are pressed together
    like boxcars, pulled by the Victorian
    on the end.

What do you say to your lover?
    Up came
    an Eighter from Decatur
    then he found her
    went around her
    but what do you care?

    I feel like my knees.

To what bakery do you go?
    The Ukrainian one with the pastries
    that have raisins like my mother's eyes.
    You're not always sure what's inside.

Where is the park you walk through?
    It has an ear in the lake
            And I imagine 14 legs under
    the surface holding it up.

    I wish it were indoors. I can't stand those
    outdoorsy sculpture gardens
    with big-leafed plants and trickles.

    You can't name a simple phallus
            unless it belongs
    to this body   body of water.

Is this piece finished?
    Too right and too beautiful,
    I'd like to do a little more wrong
    at this point.

I called it stove-pipe dreams
and then I sat all night wondering
what to put inside the head
                    later called it
circumflexion maelstrom

Does it speak?
        There's no fucking space—
I put myself in front
                Then behind this screen.
Here, a stem comes out of the mouth
                a tired mouth.

How will you see it through?
        It must arrive
        without me.

SAIL

The trick is the flow. Little fish with storms on their minds.
                Stones don't reveal

what they covet today, but I know them.

                I gather scraps and throw them back,
throw them back to the waves
                even as they climb toward my room.

                So where to go when my pockets are light?

        Night-shy, evening shells—
        all eyelids and ears.

The glinting blades and their kindred—do they ever say,
        no one ever, clean start, and
    clean, stark, smoothed galleries within galleries
 I want
emptied of desire, but gelled with color and domes of sea-
sweets.

            Look at the lapses in between stars,
                vertebrae washed up at my feet.

JUSTNOWLAND

My answer trips up
    the wires sometimes,

  but I've been on the fastest,
longest train.
      Way before that when
slippers crossed the gold yard

  we'd loosed threads.
To that bird you've divulged,
     you've dangled,
    loosed your raspy voice atop

  the trees,
that's what it's like
    with wings—a parrot mother

in the shade. Where there's talk,
  there are little bells in the air.

They go off, hardly a notice. One
  might even ask if we
and the toy orchids could spin out

  an oath. Where are the thinking
trees?
   Tag on home and meet

with the aviary of flickers—they'll be
     swayed if we angle
it just so.
   On the mend with a brush,
    a nice new brush,
and the forest keeps no picture at all.

VANISH NEARBY

When the outer air leans in
     billowing the sheets,
        only the trembling know.
  If you please
they'll give a farewell.

     Clothes pins out first and it's late
when you dip the hammer handles
        into the dye-blue water.

Sweet to have seen the pigeon
     in the tiny tree, and sweeter
to hear a humming call.
     Don't answer or

raise your head, become as you were—
waterweed, drowned hair.

Find it glad to be disembarrassed,
    as one cast out might.
With candor and a switch homeward

       wrestle with what you've heard,
knock on the fellow cabbage folds.

     Come, dissolve before that hidden house.

SHOOTS AND PULPS

      I can't stop
the vetch, its endless phrasing, should shun it

and these weeds, stems hurling
       to their reaches.

     And, of course, a satyr peeks through, cocksure
    in his glistening sulk,
       so I will it to stone.

Can someone undo this dizzy spell?
          We think hard   where it comes from,

then how beasts have a easy time of it.
          Speak robin then. Birds sink

with leisure, oceanward I guess.

     And the greens buzzing green like
                    death on the lawn.
His was only to rhyme with the others—
          he was restless
                    for dry rest.

          I think the tangled vengeance
thumbs us   as the cat digs

a little grave.

   Who else might know? Lie down, lie.

Be blind in the thickening,
          with weeds full of pleasure.

          Be patient, the knacker's coming soon
my hooved friend of loneliness.

PIRATE KEEP

   If later
   all the pretty fell,

then wouldn't tin shine?

And the ragged pony-wind
     bothers me more.
   I can't say which drawer

     darkened, but cheeks turned
and I couldn't see beneath—where

my friends had gone singing.
I settled for the knack
         of rusty sky. "Easy does,

  the splendid said, and I'd go,
         "Hey Maxy, you me the cat
next door?" So who's

   got the booty? Is there change
to be had?

  Can't bet on a slippery dog,
those unfathomed eels might say.

Must get some afternoon
   quick sleep
    —emptier than
a lift of a thumb,

   than the whisper of a spinning cup.

MEI-MEI BERSSENBRUGGE

M EI-MEI BERSSENBRUGGE'S LONG, contemplative lines achieve a pace unusual in contemporary poetry. They turn over terms and situations with a careful attention that focuses on fractional differences and traces the implications of grammatical evolutions. Often set at the intersection of the scientific and emotional worlds, her pieces track the core of human experience in relationships—whether it's the relationship between parent and child, between mind and body, or between perceiving and making. She situates the root of her poetry in an early shift from Chinese to English "because then you see that everything is relational." She goes on to say, "I think of poetry as a set of proportions, equivalences. And you see that between languages, too, are these equivalences."

Berssenbrugge was born in Beijing and raised in Massachusetts. She has books out from Burning Deck and Station Hill, as well as several from Kelsey Street Press, a press that distinguished itself in the 1980s by focusing on women's poetry in collaboration with visual artists. Her collaborations include work by the artists Richard Tuttle and Kiki Smith. Her selected poems, *I Love Artists*, was published by the University of California Press in 2006. After graduating from Reed College, she earned an MFA at Columbia University, and came to know the New York School and writers involved in the Language movement. In addition to these influences, the light and landscape of New Mexico, where she has lived since 1974, marks her work. She has also been involved in the bi-coastal multicultural movement and worked on theater collaborations with the artists Frank Chin, Blondell Cummings, and, later, Tan Dun. She has received two NEA Fellowships, two American Book Awards, and awards from the Asian-American Writers Workshop and the Western States Art Foundation. Berssenbrugge is a contributing editor of *Conjunctions* magazine and has taught at Brown University and the Institute of American Indian Arts.

CHINESE SPACE

First there is the gate from the street, then some flowers inside the wall,
then the inner, roofed gate. It is a very plain wall, without expressionistic means,
such as contrasting light on paving stones inside the courtyard to the calligraphed foundation stones.
My grandfather called this the façade or Baroque experience, rendering a courtyard transparent.
The eye expecting to confront static space experiences a lavish range of optical events,
such as crickets in Ming jars, their syncopation like the right, then left, then right progress
into the house, an experience that cannot be sustained in consciousness, because
your movement itself binds passing time, more than entering directs it.

A red door lies on a golden mirror with the fascinating solidity and peacefulness of the pond
in the courtyard, a featureless space of infinite depth where neither unwanted spirits nor light
could enter directly from outside. It lies within the equally whole space of the yard
the way we surrounded our individuals, surrounded by a house we could not wholly
retain in memory. Walking from the inner gate across a bridge which crossed four ways
over the carp moat, turning right before the ice rink, we pass roses imported from Boston,
and enter the main courtyard, an open structure like a ruin. This is not remembering,
but thinking its presence around eccentric details such as a blue and white urn turned up to dry,
although certain brightnesses contain space, the way white slipcovered chairs with blue seams contain it.

The potential of becoming great of the space is proportional to its distance away from us,
a negative perspective, the way the far corner of the pond becomes a corner again as we approach

on the diagonal, which had been a vanishing point. The grandmother poses beside rose bushes. That is to say, a weary and perplexing quality of the rough wall behind her gives a power of tolerance beyond the margins of the photograph. Space without expansion, compactness without restriction make peculiar and intense account of the separable person from her place in time, though many families live in the partitioned house now. The reflecting surface of the pond should theoretically manifest too many beings to claim her particular status in the space, such as a tiger skin in space.

After the house was electrically wired in the thirties, he installed a ticker-tape machine connected to the American Stock Exchange. Any existence occupies time, he would say in the Chinese version, reading stock quotations and meaning the simplicity of the courtyard into a lavish biosphere, elevating the fact of its placement to one of our occupation of it, including the macaw speaking Chinese, stones representing infinity in the garden. This is how the world appears when the person becomes sufficient, i.e., like home, an alternation of fatigue and relief in the flexible shade of date trees, making the house part of a channel in space, which had been interior, with mundane fixtures as on elevator doors in a hotel, a standing ashtray that is black and white. The family poses in front of the hotel, both self-knowing and knowing others at the same time. This is so, because human memory as a part of unfinished nature is provided for the experience of your unfinished existence.

from FOUR YEAR OLD GIRL

1

The "genotype" is her genetic constitution.

The "phenotype" is the observable expression of the genotype as structural and biochemical traits.

Genetic disease is extreme genetic change, against a background of normal variability.

Within the conventional unit we call subjectivity due to individual particulars, what is happening?

She believes she is herself, which isn't complete madness, it's belief.

The problem is not to turn the subject, the effect of the genes, into an entity.

Between her and the displaced gene is another relation, the effect of meaning.

The meaning she's conscious of is contingent, a surface of water in an uninhabited world, existing as our eyes and ears.

You wouldn't think of her form by thinking about water.

You can go in, if you don't encounter anything.

Though we call heavy sense impressions stress, all impression creates limitation.

I believe opaque inheritance accounts for the limits of her memory.

The mental impulse is a thought and a molecule tied together like sides of a coin.

A girl says sweetly, it's time you begin to look after me, so I may seem loveable to myself.

She's inspired to change the genotype, because the cell's memory outlives the cell.

It's a memory that builds some matter around itself, like time.

PARALLEL LINES

1

While I questioned my dream, whether or not he was a spirit guide, I closed off imagination not contained in the world.

The dream is a touchstone, face to your face.

In the morning, my husband would no more look for its trace than a
fish, who sees water as his palace, sees it flow.

I wake, like a bird among thousands of traces of small birds' passing through space.

Can you perceive traces, virga, pigment in a substrate of dawn light, as one speaks
yes, pigment, *no*, substrate, *seeing*, pigment.

Not waking is a substrate, as no love is to love.

So, you go out and meet someone.

Encountering a dream trace by day is face-to-face transmission: *lightning strikes the
lamp between us in a summer storm.*

It's pouring water into ocean and spreading it endlessly, dawn commencing on
mud walls; lamp shines out.

No trace continues.

It flows, as this summer flows through spring.

Spring flowed through itself, a space, and summer is space I break, pecking from
inside my dream and outside, telling it to you.

                    2

My eye encounters ocean floor, light on sand, horizontal bands of color with no
distinction between dream object and heightened sensation—looms of sunrays,
rain.

Then, emptiness is earth during the moments of my walk.

When I crossed a ridge into the next arroyo and crossed that, you were present.

Presence and today are like snapshots from a pin-hole camera, no substrate.

Spring flows through my walking in autumn.

Not walking is last year to this year, words arriving, mind ancillary to words, as I
recall your manner of thinking, of feeling happiness, of walking, looking, of
immediately telling your dream.

Pick up a weft line then and thread it here, edge of memory like film exposed
beyond an image, sky not hindering white clouds from flying?

So, speaking is not stained by my not hearing.

He's concealed within my not hearing and in his speaking, like not remembering someone whose card I find in my bag, or words in a mother tongue comprehensible to those experiencing words and no words as sky on film.

White clouds are data beneath words in blinding light.

They're not debris in the mind.

3

Where does mist come from on the mountain?

How will dust materialize color in air light moves through in parallel, energized lines, fabric?

Why does one person see time as a sequence of good health, exceptional beauty, a line of luck?

A moment of experience commences a train of causes for all plausible outcomes.

A moment over-exposed on film regains vibrations of a web in rain.

Like a causal succession of blood through the heart, myriad sight-lines construct crimson, then lose brightness in air, if not retained as the present.

Cast oxygen across the lines, a person walking toward a mountain across water routes north to south, z's of run-off, taking the interrupted line (of walker A) across voids.

There are fatigue lines of will struggling, as if flowing water were sand in drought.

Mist is breath not dissipated by space, joy endorphins chasing adrenaline exhaled into sky.

Mist, part of the plane, drifts through planes.

It does not tear time to carry across just a single emotional line of one self in one time, like a wind that comes up.

The lines accentuate each other, land stepped with waves, grass stippled with pines, indigo threads interwoven with exquisite gold strands in the dream palace.

MICHAEL BURKARD

MICHAEL BURKARD HAS always been known for the profound and powerful interiority of his work, poems that illuminate the mysterious, the psychologically resistant, and at times the wildly hallucinatory hauntings of the self. Burkard's poetry—and his speakers—can be, by turns, lyrical and feverish, pensive and desperate. Even though his early work often employed a collapsed (and startlingly inventive) non-linear syntax, allowing for a density of phrase that was both luminous and disturbing (and that at times seemed determined to test the limits of language itself), his more recent work can look and sound at first more conventionally narrative. Yet the complex psychological underpinnings of these poems are inevitably and brilliantly challenged as the works unravel. Burkard's most salient influences include writers as various as John Ashbery, Isaak Babel, and Louis Zukofsky. Indeed, the Objectivists are an important component to understanding the many complexities of his aesthetic. From his breathtaking debut collection, *In a White Light*, to his recent tour de force of indeterminacy, *Unsleeping*, Burkard has challenged his readers' preconceptions of American poetry. His most recent collection is *Envelope of Night: Selected and Uncollected Poems*.

Michael Burkard was born in Rome, New York, and studied at Hobart College and the University of Iowa, working as a psychiatric aide in between those degrees. His many awards include the Alice Fay di Castenola Award, as well as fellowships from the Fine Arts Work Center in Provincetown, the National Endowment for the Arts, and the New York Foundation for the Arts. At present, he teaches in the graduate writing program at Syracuse University.

A SIDEWAYS SUICIDE

This evening when I go off with myself
I go off with myself. This is a suicide, this going off,

this is a sideways suicide, but I mean to give this to you.
I needed rain, the way in which it would feel itself,

so that when the rain came, as it did this afternoon, I knew
I'd go off to you. When I committed suicide it wasn't easy,

it wasn't easy by any means: everyone I didn't know wanted
to talk about it, but their manner of talking about it

was manner, hovering like a plane that didn't land, but
kept believing in itself, as if it would. They also

had a way of leaving me out, even as they talked
they talked as if I had nothing to do with it, my own

suicide, my fallen men and my fallen women who have wept
now here in my body, in the very disparate areas of my body,

for twelve years. I thought it appropriate they left me out,
that they hovered over me, although it angered me at the same time.

An author's note would say something like this: "five minutes or so,"
but I am not an author. I think authors are assholes.

And that hesitation is a jealousy that is no better than feeling
sorry, which is no better than the absence jealousy finally means.

The author's note says something like we'll finally meet, in 1950
or in 1976, or for that matter that we won't meet, like the rain

today and this evening won't meet me, as much as I would like it to.
I don't think the rain is worth coming back to,

I don't think suicide is worth coming back to, and this leads
me to think that the body itself isn't worth it either.

This would mean that the mind is in an even worse place, falling
back like a memory that has no possibility of being remembered. Or it means this:

When I committed suicide you were startled; at the same time
there was a warm place, a warm place entitled "departure," the way an author,

an asshole, would entitle it. And in this distance there is the same kind
of memory as the memory I see that crosses your face, even

from the easy loving that rain was, and will be
—one evening I will submissively return to this departure,

and I will walk in back of myself, like a shadow will walk,
like a shadow now walks in back of myself. I will disconnect

any old grief you feel, I will take it, I will take it off the wall
like you can take a telephone off the wall, then I will speak

on that phone: authors are assholes, the rain that is lost is
memory that is lost, like you are, and I'll walk,

I will walk in a very local direction, and I will revenge the change
that memory brings, as it must change, as it changes.

RUBY FOR GRIEF

I tend to sit here very alone. Last night I asked a stranger if he
wanted a rubber slapped across his face. This morning brought more
or less more: I was whistling when I ran into someone I hadn't seen
for awhile, someone I would like to think of as a brief friend, and
it seemed all the better because I was whistling.

I'm fond of the bridges the sea makes in my mind, although far away.
Even with a shallow life before this one, or a life
after, I know my life is short, each is. The sea
bridges such familiar territory the life makes. The sea
measures such mending I make, and gives it colors:

ruby for grief, yellow for choice, flint green for staying awake.
One reason I live alone is the nature of the strangers
who appears in my dreams now and then: I can make nothing
of their life until they've made mine. I find their memories
in water, winter birds dipping their heads at winter windows,

and in the closet facts of walking the streets. The stranger
last night angered me as he refused memory, distorting mine
and his: he walked away under a few red lights until I shouted.
Little generosity unless he gets away. I used to fly in
my sleep, the sea often appeared, but these aspects of

images have rather faded over time. I wish they'd come back.
Water appears in simple settings—basins, tubs, glasses.
Often it seems I am thirsty in the dream just when
a winter bird appears. The colors the sea's given me
are constant: there's a kind of ruby girl who returns my face

about once a month, maybe her name is Ruby. My sister
often turns up and is as close to me there as I want to think
some future omen will be close to me someday. She is usually
making choices for me, defending me, or walking from one quiet
hut to another. My part in these dreams is to appear with a

yellow stick, having made my choice, and then I make some private
and selfish demand for secrecy, threatening anyone who appears
with my yellow stick. The flint green for staying awake simply
is the color of the water lapping under a few small bridges,
the bridges in cities or towns where there are none. I don't

like this lapping, it makes me feel my memory is an omen,
flint green, makes me feel that if I got up and
went walking I would find imaginary omens everywhere. So I remain
awake, talk out loud to myself—simple things, ask myself for
a match, wonder if someone out there will be walking by. If they

were, would I see them, would they want to come in? Sometimes I
take this staying awake and try resolving details or themes, like
with questions, like those at the end of stories or poems in school
texts: how are the three details of the story resolved? Is generosity so
privately handled a good thing? What is the importance of

Ruby's awkwardness when confronted with the stranger? Are omens
which take the form of memories immersed in water a good thing?
Will the narrator ever fly again?
I'm losing it when I begin these, so I

go to the window. It would be nice if the window asked me back, turned
back, helped itself to an attitude. God knows enough look in here during
the day, I'm that close to the street—I could even step out, begin

whistling again, ask someone if they want a rain check on coming over.
I don't know just what I will

do now. I might wash up.
I might whistle to see if any winter birds fly nearer.
Try resolving omens or themes. Isn't there some infinity
to the generosity of trying to tell your story? Or better: isn't there
some prior life to telling everything this way? Like secretly taking

the smallest belonging from a passing stranger, opening it up
under an open night light, the kind the night sky sometimes makes, and
ordering this belonging, giving it an attitude or omen so some other
truthful window might appear.

MY SISTER IS NOT A DOLLAR

I think it is unusual
I even try speaking, I hear steps and doors
where there is nothing but a medicinal smell,
the person crossing near me crosses on.

At the far end of a country lane
the night burned like shores,
the moon was dead, the moon
was okay.

The peace be and the peace
falleth, the garden is white
with my sister, and one dollar.

My sister is not a dollar,
I am not a man.

Not before the task,
when the burning afternoon rises
across the sky, not before
the angry residue of possession,
not before my teeth bleed
with greed for water . . .

Not before. Here is the parting of nails,
frames, the parting of empty footsteps.

THE EYEGLASSES

  I examined my father's eyeglasses late one Friday morning. I had
to climb to the bureau-top from a chair to do this. And I managed
to drop the eyeglasses and they broke. My father was to leave for a
business trip that very day, and the breaking brought on a confusion.
I pushed them under the bed—not well, not hidden. And I don't
know if the punishment was for breaking them or for hiding them
or both. And I don't know if I broke them intentionally or not, if I
dropped them through memory to the floor so that my father would
not depart again. I tried pretending in my memory for years that my
father himself broke his own eyeglasses, that he himself dropped them
in order to prevent himself from leaving, and that I was merely a
necessary pawn in this. And how could I forgive him for this—for who
would want to take a train to a foreign city only to leave his family
far away? To leave a son who was the unknowing double of the
older son, to leave a daughter whose room's high window looked
out at the tree, the moon, and the man who lived atop the telephone
pole a street away. Whose room was a wonderful stillness we each
visited but in which we never stayed. And a wife, a mother to three
who could care for us as much from sleep as from waking. Whose
sister Dorothy lived with us from the sea and lantern light of Nova
Scotia though she was far, far away.

  Who could he see with eyeglasses in a foreign city anyway, away
from us? What multitude of faces and voices could alter the longing
of our loss and tenderness? Were we tender? And if so, when? Whose
version is valid as my sister's room, or her quiet witnessing of
major and minor light?

WE HAVE TO TALK ABOUT ANOTHER BOOK

The boy's glasses were very very thick.
He was thinking of this life and the next and the next.
The yellow city bus drove by the blue-by-morning river
but the boy did not see the bus from his perspective.

Two blackbirds have more space than they can handle.
No one knows time this way the way blackbirds do.
No one knows no one: a blade of grass
is the blade in the grass. The boy stands in his ghost.

One of the blackbirds is now thick with the river.
Some of the branches make love like an awkward couple.
Or like a couple juxtaposed against the window, which
isn't unusual, but the window is juxtaposed against

branches,
and the branches are making more sounds than usual.
Things become is.
We don't have to make a sentence if we don't want to.

THE REARRANGER

I woke up this morning (or was it last night?)
and I wrote down "write something called 'The Rearranger.'"
The rearranged. The rearranger rearranging the rearranged.
The lone rearranger. Rangers of the rearranged, rearrangers
of the purple sage. The vast memory of purple. Or was it
last night when the real memory of purple recurred and recurred
like a wave? Then was gone, like a business which never opened.
Seeing a stick in the grass, a branch, maybe close to a yard long,
close to where I sat with Don when he read the letter from his lover
and his lover was writing to say he had tested positive for AIDS
and Don sitting there with a letter in his lap now, almost like
a minimal drawing of a robe from one of Mary Hackett's
drawings of the Stations of the Cross, Jesus' legs and a bearer's
hands and arms and the sense of the minimal robe to carry
or wrap Jesus in, a letter in Don's lap. A stick in the grass.
I thought I did not have any space left, but here is all this
space because of Mary's drawing and Don's lap and a stick
in the grass. Don is in the stick for a moment. I am in his lap.
Or Mary is bearing me because of all this space. I woke up
this morning and I wrote down write something called The
Rearranger.

KILLARNEY CLARY

A WIDELY ADMIRED MASTER of the prose poem, Killarney Clary has beguiled her readers with her spare and exquisitely carved poems-in-prose over the course of three collections: *Who Whispered Near Me*, *By Common Salt*, and *Potential Stranger*. The illusion of autobiography resonates—or perhaps we should say whispers—throughout her body of work, as oblique investigations of psychological and personal/historical narratives are slowly unveiled; the self's disguises and masks are often peeled away line by line, phrase by phrase. These quasi-autobiographical gestures are revealed to be highly provisional, speculative narratives, both enigmatic and (deceptively) precise at the same time. There is a quiet remove, a troubled self-regard in Killarney Clary's poetry that is at times edged with profound sadness and irony. Still, the project of all of her work seems in the end to be concerned with spiritual journeying, with a spare yet prophetic vision of the self in passage through its world. Each of Clary's collections feels architecturally constructed, with a carefully considered combination of literal and natural details set alongside moments of almost oracular speculation, the latter often revealing her deep concern with issues of faith.

Killarney Clary's work unfolds with a disarming clarity, yet her ability to suspend language and hold back the poem's urge for closure gives it a special tension and provides a series of unique satisfactions for her readers. Although named for the Irish town, Killarney Clary was born in Pasadena, California, a city that figures dramatically, in all senses of that word, in her poetry; she has lived in Los Angeles for the past thirty-five years. A graduate of the University of California, Irvine (where she has also taught), she received the prestigious Lannan Literary Award for Poetry in 1992.

BEFORE THE BIRDS AWAKEN, after the possum has gone home, for a moment no one is commuting from a night shift or to an early job.

Or it's late in the afternoon, all napping. Then there is no need to tell anyone.

I need to do something else when my friend is miserable and the music is over, when my balance is off.

Everyone's binging. I talk all day about escrow and interest. I drive a long way home from work and each time I start out feeling one way and arrive feeling the opposite. Resolutions are worthless in this swamp.

Before the birds, I might assemble a way. But it is logic and figuring, pushing me far to a dead end in a maze. I won't convince with trickery. I won't move or rest with it.

IT'S WHAT I'M AFRAID OF that hints at what I desire. Not this comfortable screened porch on an eastern beach in Indian summer, but holding a gun or asking favors, saying without doubt, "I wish . . . "

When I pray now, it's with puzzles of contingencies and a net of addenda. I finish in a corner, my heart bound and struggling, begging, "If it is your will, Lord, then what's the problem?" And when I don't pray, I whine, "Why should I send a letter to my friend who won't answer?"

The shore is long and nearly flat. The tendency of the tide doesn't falter; the ocean doesn't miss and doesn't adapt for me or the birds, for trash cast off a weekend cruiser. I am in the place of my dreams, still uneasy. My good anger, my best yearning, won't work toward a finish when there is none.

MY WHISPERED SONG, the tune replaced by breath, weakens, loses its place in a thin, icy draft. The cold lowers, by the rules. What turns a whisper to full sound pulls the colors from gray. Shaky, it skips like a stylus until time hints there is hope. But there is no more logic in this power to persevere than there is to the placement of Los Angeles or the ease on the faces of men and women who finish their long ride in. What clicks on or off after months of indecision? Did I choose to give in?

As I drive deeper into the corridor of downtown where the wind is crooked and fast between the office towers, as I try again the brightest song, I know the dead sailor who changed his mind in last night's dream will stay with me for days; I won't be afraid. And yet the friend who says good night on the phone is gone. I own nothing; I don't know my spirit. In sleep where the counting can't survive, I hear songs I've never heard, though there are no premonitions, only the teases of anxiety and fantasy. If I could turn my eyes from the experiment, it would run on smoothly with pure, unstudied results. Instead, I send off questionnaires, and wait.

I'M SORRY I BROUGHT IT UP. I'm sorry until I lose my body. I shouldn't have said what I said, not yet or not so late.

I answer, "I love you, too," and think, "for as long as you will believe it." But what I don't say now only thins the travel in and out of my heart, traps me in channels between my one thought and my next. So the one promises I will be new; the other laughs through its nose and says, "Sure."

If I'm daring you to please me, I have to stop somehow, but when I see what I've done wrong I am still wandering disagreeably, doing the wrong thing.

I hope I don't like you, myself, or anyone else. I hope I don't like the next song. If I do, I'll only try to remember it, and I'll have to look forward to hearing it again.

THERE IS NO WAY TO KNOW what I miss, and yet there is nothing else I try to do. What happens takes very little time; it's easy play. Before, I wonder how you will be. Will you feel like talking about Kathleen or the babies? Will you ask me where I was when you called? And as you ask I wonder what you're thinking while you watch a cruiser back out of a slip and turn toward the breakwater, Catalina, and maybe beyond.

What was it in that moment in your voice, in the pause, which told me? I keep working on ways through, which narrow as I wonder harder. If I am very careful, I might know the shift in weather between us is your bit of worry or remembrance; I excuse you forever. I will miss you less this way when you must go.

THE WORDS I DID NOT SAY have drawn their own map now, with turns I know as I knew the collar of a shirt against my face while I was comforted on a summer afternoon in the dark where I would have to lie down soon with the chatter of starlings sparse in the heat, the occasional traffic on Franklin. Not rush hour—not any hour really—the ordinary wonder of people going one way or another. A green shirt. My fingers sank into cool arms in July. Down pillows in the closet—cooler and darker.

Charts outside of saying, a squirrel in thick foliage held secret but loud as a siren.

If we navigated telling, oh what we might know together—any you, any me.

THERE SHOULD'VE BEEN RABBITS in the saltbush near the forbidding red rock. As I lie down in the half-light I see the room, our hats on the wall pegs, and when I close my eyes the animals are there. How long have they waited on the sharp surface, glowing against the vibrant terrain? They are still waiting, now.

The notary's name stenciled gold on the window doesn't mean the signature has been witnessed. The hard-edged shadows shouldn't have promised. Angling its light into the downy yellow grass, the sun should've risen.

SHE FALLS IN LOVE and wants to be well, is well and forgets to measure. She is noticed or not in the market by the man she met at last night's party. Though the day is bright—thunder—and mist sprinklers come on above the lettuce. Bitterly, the word comes, *Silly*. She is chilled and losing. The list is numbered. Each shape and color announces at once it is at her service. To keep from reeling, she could use her telephone. Her hand is lax on the cool lemon.

THE NOTE I TAPED UP in my window for Lily. The note in return. Now I am expected and will do anything else. If there were another place to look, a periphery where I might bear a thing said and then the waiting. She is four years old, watching my window, and I am counting.

If the origin had been less sweet or we rode in cars where we put our fingers to the glass. If handing over and standing still weren't a trap.

In her window, the glare on ornaments, the Christmas tree cut to be this exactly, to last as this. Needles dry and drop. We might set these houses adrift, hold ourselves to nothing, sincerely.

YOU HAVE PUT THE CUP where I can reach it. You've said the cruel thing and gone. Across the grass, ice spills out of the pitcher into plastic tumblers, onto sticky oilcloth in the afternoon swell. At the feeder, a hummingbird drinks and perches and again. Clear things flash quick rainbows onto the lawn, onto the shadows of leaves. There is no end to the giving, no place to put what is left. A patch might be strong, but close-by the difference makes a weary place. The smart doesn't last. From the glass flower, sugar water.

IN THE STORY, a poor family lives on bakery fumes, sleeps under the bridge. I try to imagine the smell of bread. I pretend I understand the words when she reads them aloud to me. I am loved but can't think. Now it's my turn to read. She waits. My mouth waters. My eyes water. I bury my face in her dress and she pets me.

There are always three living under the bridge. I am one of three children. I will breathe against the wall to feel breath against my mouth. I am urged. A chill needles the base of each hair.

I am selected to be It in the Halloween game, blindfold and spin It, hand It moist shapeless stuff to guess at. *What do you think this is?* I don't know. All me lost in what I think all of them think. Oh, this is cold noodles, not brains. They know that. I am seen, can't see what they are after.

THROUGH A PANEL OF CONTROLS in the post-panamax crane-cab, he raises the container from the ship, sets it on a trailer from which it will be transferred, at the intermodal yard, to a train through the Alameda Corridor. Switched through to the Inland Empire and beyond—the clothing, electronics and toys from Asia are on their way.

To the warehouse in Sparks, Nevada, to fill a catalogue order in Emmett, Idaho—a blouse for a woman who will be better when the package has arrived. Summer coming. She slits the tape, unfolds the pale tissue, lifts the thing. Dust on the dresser, powder on her throat, a fine quiet glow on what she has gathered, a riffle in the blinds, heat leaning on the outside wall of the dim bedroom. The color is different from what she expected. She pulls her shirt off, feels a tingling surge of shortfall behind her eyes.

WHEN YOU STEP FROM THE ENTRY HALL onto the street and close the door, where have you gone? I hear your car start, feel the air of hungry ghosts around me, cleaning away the smells of smoke, oil, soap. Skittering over my lips they steal the taste of apple from your kiss, lift the impress of your press. But they do not bleed my memory. I keep but cannot keep. We cannot keep.

I HAVE NO SAY over what my expression does in your head. The trinket was slipped into the pocket, the pocket picked, the cheap treasure lost in the seam of the bus seat. The bus in the ravine off the Ortega Highway is burning. A mole lifts its nose into smoke.

At the crossroads, at the city limits where taxes aren't certain and unusual bargains are struck, I said I was your friend. I wait while you talk. I wonder what you mean.

I say *I am sorry for your news*. But when you quote me I don't recognize the words. I watch a drop of water on the glass. A bent reflection at the edge quivers.

The guild verified capacities of barrels, jars—in secrecy. Tests, signs of recognition, but no ceremony for leaving. The measures would keep off goodbye. The words would hold to the end of the pavement, in the slide of tailings, but not into the wild wood.

NORMA COLE

NORMA COLE BEGAN writing and publishing in the late 1970s, a particularly vibrant moment for poetry in the Bay Area, when the influences of the San Francisco Renaissance and the Beat movement could still be felt and Language poetry was just beginning. A close friend and student of Robert Duncan's at the New College of California, Cole blends a sharp, historical intelligence with an interest in the material possibilities of language. Employing fragmentation and ellipsis, allusion and occasional quotation, she achieves a distinctly political address that emphasizes the public nature of personal experience. Her 2005 installation, *Collective Memory*, created for the fiftieth anniversary of the San Francisco Poetry Center, displayed the inherently communal and cooperative nature of the writing life, and was published by Granary Books in 2006 as an artist's book of the same name.

Born and raised in Toronto, Canada, Cole received an MA in French language and literature from the University of Toronto and has lived off and on in France. Since 1977, her principal residence has been in San Francisco, where she is active in the arts community, serving on the editorial board of Krupskaya Press and the board of Small Press Traffic, participating in Kevin Killian's theater works, and teaching at the University of San Francisco and at San Francisco State. She has translated many books, including two volumes of Danielle Collobert's notebooks, and works by Anne Portugal, Emmanuel Hocquard, Fouad Gabriel Naffah, and others. Her *Crosscut Universe: Writing on Writing from France* brings together prose pieces from many important late twentieth-century French writers, offering a critical companion to contemporary French poetry. Cole is also a visual artist, and has collaborated on an award-winning project with the photographer Ben E. Watkins, and on projects with Amy Trachtenberg, Jess, and others.

FLOATING BY

for David Bowie

"abundant" and "not true" somehow sets up the sound (elements active,
activating, enacting, selecting)

somehow sets up the tides of sound that convincingly present "unchanging" as
asking for "heaven" it's from my first body, actually, carrying them in
       but his is a strange and unheard of polish made of
       distance and intimacy

           GO BACK ONCE

               the young falconer holding a hawk,
               marvered glass eyes, threw his
               shoulder into the heart of another
               gilt heart

the solar systems that the song remembered, within the outside world,
referred light, an image called thought to the place beyond "it's grave inside
my head too"

           amrita, elixir of
           immortality almost
           recognize losing
           return, turning

       DON'T KILL THE DUST

dotted rhythm of disruption
dust off "bewilderment"
silent window, free radio
of "our" youth "I meant it"
deepest thought—I did

these things are real, unguessed in air, child of science, of space, universe: is
there a 5th dimension? can time run backwards? can love be lost?

UNITS FOR TOMORROW

The fighting fish at first looks just like a fish.   The picture of evolution in the strangeness of what was occurring.   We didn't know.   In the vivid familiarity of our lives.   What was happening at the payphone.   It wasn't yet known.   It was a time of exuberant niches hit across.   An unexpected and burgeoning.   In a squat.   Source of which.   Not yet a test for it.   Photons and compressed air.   A continuous scansion of the inner ear.   The outer world symbolic sociophysical universe in order to discover.
     Where to adapt.   To reset what was out of kilter.   The
     unaccountabilities.   Our collision will be elastic.   Importation
     into it.
In general the pattern for the time.   Dearest Mae.   Time to go.   We are battered.   So this letter is wet.   A conversion myth.   Oops, readership.   "Inescapable morphology" what's yours?   Dropping slowing cutting across Rossetti's dream "I said the water was choppy."   Attack, decay.   The body slop.   The birthday came and went.   The picture the vividness.   Flowers on the hillside and the stench of burning flesh, the reporter said.   In the shantytown.
          You have a sweet voice, une voix douce, una dolce voce,

Saint Ives   Grasse
Lands End   Vence   Bar du Loup

At a prayer site in the cemetery on a burial ground and relocation on paper.   On paper, for generations, for the future, on your bread, on your back, in your practice, at present no explanation undevourable at the barbecue, at a friend's, in the house before the movers come, at the table, on the carpet, at the beach, in a dream, reading, in the city

It was my faucet I was looking up. What I want is inviolate. "delirium of reason. It sets its sights on paradise (glorified generality)." a camel with a tiny saddle, a spare tire, turn viridian, grey fingernails arranged in a fan on the waiting-room wall: rain, ocean, heart, night, stream, glow between.   People sleeping in the house.

DEAR ROBERT,

        Hi, just wanted to check in
with you, see what's happening. I
was reading your "ACHILLES' SONG,"
the first poem in *GROUNDWORK:*
Before the War in which Thetis
promises Achilles not a boat
but the mirage of a boat. There is
always a "before the war," isn't
there. Some war. Another war.
Miss you.
    Love,
        Norma
P.S. and back of that war
"the deeper unsatisfied war"

SARABANDE

"and then looks at
the stars" from the
bed in the ambulance

looks up at boughs of
trees shifting quickly
lit in blackness

blackening soft, deep
siren's song—she died
several times that night

and only in the weeks
to come started and
started to come back

then forward which is
real life

MY OPERATIVES

"The boy, the shirt, its blue
color, his running, the absence of shoes."
—LEV VYGOTSKY

1
THEIR OBJECTIVE

Yes, it was easy "as far as I can see" for their huts were made of reeds. It's completely subjective or random, so beauty is dust. It's his birthday on Sunday. I see everything you remember. A flock of agents flew into each other in the field. As in life so in the mind. We are innocence to our fate. Here is the child on your desk. He touches his face then touches your cheek leaving a red mark. Momma what is that he says. Are their gestures not thoughts?

2
THE WALKING POOR

Involvement rather than simple registration or the generations before. By design he fell out of the truck so I picked him up. There was one little spot of blood on his cheek. Someone had opened the door from without. The word and the fact of bread. Experience does not care, for it comprises all time and in the while. It begins once.

3
INTERPELLATION

"Hence the one who feels and
lives is not an immediate given."
—MERLEAU-PONTY

This rides onto the premises on a missing link and this is the epitome of something, and this process is a gathering of attention in time, like weather moving quickly. This has an edge and is sharp. This in a person as young as yourself is startling. This eye looks elsewhere. This absence fashions an acute sensation of presence, this vividness you see but do not see. A treasure is not worth this.

4
THE EXAMPLE OF A RESULT

Sky hearth tender. And here we have the whole turning thing, hands considerate, sung from a boat. "Last words" meant a shrug, incomprehensibility. Telegraphic blue paint, hearsay, evidence. And the signs were rough enough. To write "orchard" and look at the date. So it all depends on the variables *that it is*. Jess said "sheer loveliness of the world and that we get to be in it for a time."

5
SO PROBABLY EARLIER

The definite article. No abstracting but at dawn or was it dawn but if at dawn or in the dawn. In other words a thought as sure as a cloud. Eruption of the river and a bridge. Exhaustively shaping everything. There. A thing needing no explanation. The moon, like other proverbs, is the recursive paradigm.

CONDITIONS MARITIMES

THE TEXT IS SHAPED AFTER
the letter of the ocean

THIS SHAPE ONCE REFLECTED
becomes its own narration

The fragmentary teeth become the
allegory of completion

There she stood, dressed like a sailor
in black pants, striped jersey, pea jacket

Wearing amber for luck
and company

"into eventual accuracy" (Michael Ondaatje)

Inverted lives
it was said refer to the ocean

There she stood, etc.

Thus the false map is scrawled
by sleep as if history assembled
these names

This time and its history a calculus of stars, the limit of
the formal plane, its proportions
                                        the sign for division
outside its context
                    its issues' decision
(soon we would begin to lose
the feeling in our fingertips)
                that it was science; that it was so
appealing; that rules are the instrument

Here we are talking about the playful
handling of an object
the negotiation with an imagined acceptable

That the poem is a toy
with the structure of insomnia

That gardens being lit thus saved
just to know and not have
in local practice
given up that control
"in your dreams"

That time, that spiral marrow
(the space between shoulder blades)
that hyphen without reason
lashed to death by virtue = reason = virtue
(the reason between knowledge and fact)

I   wash my feet
before going to bed
contrafact: one complete thought

GILLIAN CONOLEY

GILLIAN CONOLEY'S POEMS are brilliant tapestries of multiple dictions, natural observations, regional inflections, and a general kaleidoscope of tone—a high wire act of down-home grit and sudden flurries of philosophical grace. In her earliest work (her chapbook, *Woman Speaking Inside Film Noir*, and her first two collections, *Some Gangster Pain* and *Tall Stranger*), Conoley's relatively straight-up narratives were resonant with the weathers and flavors of her native Texas—a unique combination of verbal charm and desperado bravado. The three linguistically inventive books that followed—*Beckon, Lovers in the Used World*, and *Profane Halo* (a lyrically fragmented and compelling meditation on culture and faith)—are increasingly concerned with the wreckage and rescue of language in a twenty-first-century, post-lapsarian world. Her newest work, *The Plot Genie* (the title comes from a writer's aid used by pulp fiction writers and screen writers alike), continues her journey in this direction yet recalls the humor and sheer theatrical nerve of the earlier poetry. Barbara Guest has said: "The poems of Gillian Conoley lead us up to then step just out of sight where an ordinary sign begins. They beckon us from where an invisible power distorts; a sudden view appears of innocence aslant."

Gillian Conoley was born and raised in Taylor, Texas, and now lives in the San Francisco Bay Area. She has received the Jerome J. Shestack Prize, a Fund for Poetry Award, and several Pushcart Prizes. The founder and editor of the influential magazine *Volt*, Conoley has been an important force in positing a "hybrid" sensibility in American poetry. She is Poet-in-Residence and Professor at Sonoma State University.

THE SKY DRANK IN

The sky drank in   sparrows making lucid the oaks.   The leaves sank

onto the stair. And you as you were,   I as I become, color and form,

bend and start,   split one on the other side of *the screen of*

your projections—   you wanted me.

But I wasn't around,   only a small soul asleep   in the high heel,

or fluttering among the cosmetics   blindly, usually just a pause

between what's there, not there,   mail on the stoop,   lists   "to do"

and other narcotics   we call beauty,   symmetry, harmony,

and no supplied thing— Only a weak-edged soul,   the almost seen

bright circle breaking   to parenthesis,   tender embrace   trying

to enclose   whether for an instant or an eternity,   something is

"true—"   The sky   drank in sparrows making lucid the oaks.   Whirl

of particles in the desire of   whatever I sought   when I began

these sentences   (I stay,   I have stayed, I am staying),

slow burning in of the come on   darling, the salesman, the waitress,

the couple fighting in the phone booth   heart wall to heart wall,

palm,   darkening lip,   the infinities that *were, were*

our mouths and our sex— you who were not   becoming not again—

lovers   in the used world,   more extinguished, finer,

o you-again,   o one,   o no one,   o you—

CAREFUL

Paper boat   the wind loaned.

This difficult maneuvering under an umbrella
spokes of ribs,   I elbow you.

Peeping Tom of nothingness
catching a video of you

buying a pistol 10 days ago, wary of intruders.

Shot messengers
in day's fold,

green, a miner's lamp,
green, the aftershave.

In a roadside tavern, a reader crumpling a letter back into an
envelope,   what if.

Thus I had carpentered our entire relationship to go upstream.

A LITTLE MORE RED SUN ON THE HUMAN

A little more red sun on the human   Church program spiked
     to the tree

There where the child carved   Grown to the father

Daughter in the grassy lot   sky pink-streaked in raincord   Forgive

my fallen corporeality   Once I was the first germ of life

afloat in the swampy gale   Water drop, come roll away the stone,
     a polaroid I pan

The world is terrifying   The land covers up

The land says to itself its eternal doubt   Green trees

are bending, tombstones

are bursting,   a boy laughs   in lag time

Aphoristic   ferryman   The community's

leafy vernacular   meaning all life

is unfinished   as the grass

grows back   The mourners bow   every so often   over the human

The river's candor   a life sentence

Hazy,   launched, stopped

Vision this honeyed outline

The shapes   suggest

it is late   afternoon   Did you   know it too

from THE PLOT GENIE

As a child Miss Jane Sloan came upon a diamondback rattler. On a girl scout day camp, s'mores and wieners, old gray sheds, blisters and sunburn, at least one case of bull nettle rash on a bare ass. Motes drifting above weedy path like automata surveying an earlier globe. The diamondback did not rattle. In hot noon sun, sour pungent sulfur smell of snake, the child body of Miss Jane Sloan alarmingly tangible as she walked backward, little nervous spasms beneath her white socks, high grass parting like disinterested third persons standing aside to let her pass, to let her back so far away, just far enough away so she could still see, where. . . . look, there is a small wooden bench just strong enough for her to stand on. It was a beautiful sunny day. A peculiar speech signal could be overheard between suspects. I was afraid I was about to permit an unrecognized sister to starve. A relative had decided to jump a bail bond. Part of a body, or a portion of the spoils, was found in the possession of the subject. And Miss Jane Sloan went down. She went down the white road of aftermaths, no Titanic. She went down the alterations of, to the barely beyond, where everything was begging everything to come back to where we live. When Miss Jane Sloan closed her eyes she could feel slight neuronal embraces caving in, tuned to the vibration of other tormentresses. Whatever sulks there. The dust eliminated. Destiny is a world apart.

To remove a tabu to be rid of
possession of a key.
reformation to overthrow
an appetite. The screen is
a phenomenon, how much
We are here to escape
To secure life insurance
to defeat a plot
To possess an abode
to be refused forgiveness
to get relief from a monstrosity
A line of boxcars
completely frontal

carping is the desire to obtain
The desire to bring about a
authority is to satisfy
the desire to produce
everyone needed a glass of water.
payment of a lost wager.
to satisfy a horoscope
the river's sheen.
our virgin torso
to escape from a master
or abomination.
slides open
to escape a carousel.

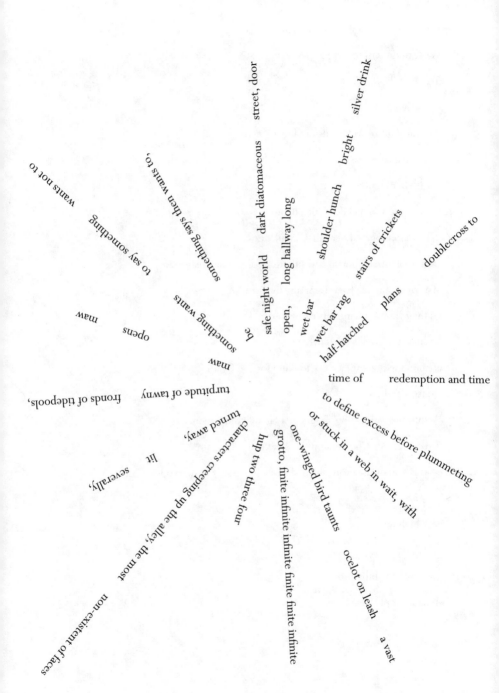

street, door

silver drink

bright

dark diatomaceous

long hallway long

shoulder hunch

stairs of crickets

doublecross to

wants not to

to say something

something says then wants to,

safe night world

open,

wet bar

wet bar rag

plans

be

something wants

maw opens maw

maw

half-hatched

time of   redemption and time

fronds of tidepools,

turpitude of tawny

turned away,

to define excess before plummeting

or stuck in a web in wait, with

severally,

lit

characters creeping up the alley, the most

hup two three four

one-winged bird taunts

grotto, finite infinite infinite finite finite infinite

ocelot on leash

a vast

non-existent of faces

■

A blank photograph   arrives in the mail.

What to do with it

like one silk stocking

throughout

the war. Out of wet pools of blotting paper

comes a coal rose.

If with her all of life went by.

Since there was a child with a drum.

Why I interrogated her left-behind straw.

Or the cast-open portal and situation gallow to a realm

of a friend and his friend starting by airplane

on their hunting trip, never to return.

Because the book's oily covers

contain the body they were looking for.

House a-twitch.

Within the welcoming shouts of a far-off companion.

If you read her Chapters on the Atlantic,

or as is said of the dead, she had worn her jacket under your jacket.

Very low down

very high up

the Alone

rolling toward the Alone

along her optic seacoasts

MARTIN CORLESS-SMITH

M ARTIN CORLESS-SMITH'S WORK mines the entire history of English-language poetry, bringing the flavor of earlier centuries into the contemporary through curiosities of vocabulary and syntax. Often his careful sentences, composed with an almost documentary precision, suddenly veer into lyric flights teetering right on the line between sense and its breakdown. Their intense musicality links them to the Romantics and their seventeenth-century precursors, while his use of collage, rupture, and fragmentation position his work firmly within postmodernism and its critique of the consolidated subject, which dovetails with his interest in the Middle English notion of the lyric as a public song. His use of heteronyms pursues this line of exploration even further and allows him to confound various eras, for while Corless-Smith's poetry brings history with it, it is a history that has as much to do with a multi-occupied present as it does with the past.

Born and raised in Worcestershire, England, Martin Corless-Smith came to the United States in the early 1990s; and studied at the University of Iowa Writers' Workshop and then went on to do a PhD at the University of Utah. He's the author of four books of poetry, all of which play with the visual dimension through page arrangement and typographical manipulation. Corless-Smith studied painting before coming to the United States, and is still an avid painter, focusing on quasi-abstract landscapes that often incorporate handwriting. He edits and produces the chapbook series "Free Poetry," which publishes contemporary poetry and distributes it free of charge and without copyright. He teaches in the MFA program at Boise State University in Idaho and divides his time between Idaho and England.

from WORKS OF THOS. SWAN

> *Saw a beautiful sphinx this evening flying about the flower its wings made a*
> *humming noise like a top its body fur*
> *(I have no scientific names) was covered with a down of black and white*
> —NOTEBOOKS

I take myself up   i take myself on up
    over cliff trees   over clifftrees off
as swimming   a swimming brimming cup
    a bright bursting off   a bright bursting off

For once at once your fear's day duplicates
    its Seemless Possiverities
all mingled like a calmless wealth
    Oh I am stalked   O am I from above

vision of a place   my vision is a place
    this always-onning   its ever shifting face
lumbrous   a waterfall she is
    transparent over rocks

I cannot and run   i cannot run and stay
    lingring of this steep   this sudden steep so hill
I cannot and go   I cannot stay and go
    my Wings trained to a near invisibility

—*Poems in Manuscript*

ON MY BROTHER W[ILLIAM] FALLING FROM HIS HORSE

Was not the horses [sic] start
what made it start was not
A shadow or a hare afoot
as sense of something sudden near the heart   an arrow to the heart

You fell on your right side
to break your arm and dignity   pride
a fellow helped you catch your ride   that fellow caught your ride
who you did not know or see   yhom did not notice next to thee

before you fell. And afterwards
a different beast your horse   another horse your horse
and afterwards yourself somehow   and changed yourself somewhere
the earth had entered through your breast   restructured where it was

This land of yours no longer yours   each atom now itself
but you its curious gift   And you this curious gift
each leaf a painted diadem   each leaf a painted leaf
an atom in a leaf   miraculous & hidden shift   ·

THE ACTS

I'm getting ready. I'm really getting ready
That a kite, the past (future-engine)
should land on the present (future-past/genitals)

The trees drone in their ears
their birds (innumerable)
There to lose what binds us here
no field felt the sky it never fell

no garden alabaster nothing its pure blue
should she live at Kensington or Kew
but every year, when winter came
every summer for seven summers now
she did neither. If she wore pearls, pearls they were
a hundred miles from the sea. A fact that was
lobsters, fresh from lobster pots and salmon and the lobster
they heard dead men they saw a white lady walking under trees
the cook's hands cut cut cut
the room a shell a vase stood in the house
holding distilled across the hall a door opened
the author's last novel was completed just before her death
during the war the action takes place on a single day

Coming from the library the voices stopped in the hall
come earthward a century ago
pleasure's what they want she said you often heard her call
out of the corner of his eye he raised his glass
he saw a flash of white
someone passing silently they
manoeuvred in their water world

made by the trembling grass made by the sky
the ghost of convention rose to the surface
the wall remained nothing but a wall
the tractor has to some extent superseded the plough
the horse had gone but the cow remained
Red Admirals feasting and floating
our part is to be the audience
books open no conclusion come to
and he sitting in the audience
she made another face and dropped the invisible pen
not here not now but somewhere
there was nothing for the audience to do
the flat fields glared the morning room
but we have other lives I think I hope
we live in others we live in things
old men striped trousers girls skin colored lips
the audience was assembling
spreading across the lawn
and as they took their seats
the human figure seen
to great advantage against
a background of sky
then the play begins

I fear I am not in my perfect mind
the sins I've sinned before cockcrow
Did the plot matter?

She fell back lifeless. The gramophone blared
The idiot scampered in and out
the megaphone announced in plain English: An Interval

As usual her vision escaped her
undressing down in the hollow
where dishcloths in the shadow
made pools of yellow
choked with a toad in its throat
the snake was unable to swallow
the toad was unable to die
a blue-bottle settled
the play keeps running in my head
the path was narrow she was broad
swaying slightly as she walked

the little grapes above then were
wet between bird's claws
Perhaps because we've never met before
and never shall again
the door trembled and stood half open
the audience was assembling
the actors were still dressing up among the bushes
d'you think people change?
clearing out a cupboard
I found my father's old top hat
but ourselves do we change?

figures advanced from the bushes
hooped and draped
entered her dressing room
(Enter carrying a parchment)
(reading)
(aside)
(aloud)
(both speak together)
her mirror and lipstick attended her lips and nose
the gramophone which everybody knows to be perfectly true
while her courses ran and speckled eggs in the warm
hollow lay neighbours dig in cottage gardens and lean
over cottage gates
(she hides behind a tree)
(she reveals herself)
The voice stopped but the voice had seen
(they sang)
whose mouths opened but no sound came out
the whole world was filled with dumb yearning
craves the indulgence of the audience
          (owing to the lack of time a scene has to be omitted)
Thank heavens
How right. Actors show us too much
Yes they bore one stiff. Up and down the city road
(he hobbles up and down)
The scene ended
Reason descended from her plinth
the words rose and pointed a finger
yet somehow they felt
how could one put it
a little not quite here or there

And so to end the play

Let holy virgins hymn perpetually
as if what I call myself was still
floating unattached and didn't settle
over the tops of the bushes came voices
voices without bodies
the audience was on the move
they kept their distance from the dressing room
it all looks very black
ever since I was a child I've felt
then she began again
it's a good day the day we are stripped naked
A lake it was a lake apparently
there was an interval
(they were rolling up the lake)

Nothing happened
present time ourselves he read
they sat exposed they were neither one thing nor the other
they read it in the programme.
o that our human pain could here have ending
real swallows the swallows or martins were they?
I am not in my perfect mind
And the audience saw themselves not whole
by any means but at any rate sitting still
the hands of the clock had stopped at the present moment
it was now ourselves
consider the sheep or faith in love
o we're all the same. take myself now
and the desire for immolation
look at ourselves then at the wall
the first note meant a second the second a third
was that voice ourselves?
we are members one of another
we act different parts but are the same
I caught myself too reflected
as it happened in my own mirror
was that the end?

Nature takes part there was the idiot
we're oracles a foretaste of our own religion
one feels such a fool perhaps one day
thinking differently we shall think the same

by means of which we reach the final
or ourselves the audience
all gone under the leaves
scared by shadows passing
the fish had withdrawn
the lilies were shutting
then something moved in the water
she had a glimpse of silver
the fish had come to the surface
it was unlikely that they would ever meet again
the play was over
swallows skimmed the grass
that had been the stage
the flesh poured over her
the hot nerve wired
what interrupted now she passed
then something rose to the surface
the curtain would rise
what would the first words be
I am the slave of my audience
there would be shelter voices oblivion
and two scarcely perceptible figures
she swallowed
ourselves
did you feel she asked what he said
we act different parts but are the same
yes I answered no she added
both had changed
or that the author came out from the bushes
there were letters
the paper that obliterated the day before
then she found the page where she had stopped
the great square of the open window showed
shadows fell he rose
end of the chapter
left alone together
then the curtain rose. They spoke.

STACY DORIS

S TACY DORIS'S WORK honors an unusual variety of traditions, and all by playing wholesale with their conventions. Perhaps the sole common denominator is a theatricality based on the page as both a metaphorical and a real stage. Her latest book, *Cheerleader's Guide to the World: Council Book*, emphasizes this by diagrams of football plays that show the mind (as in those 1950s dance diagrams) how to traverse this social/political landscape. Always tapping a performative energy, her *Conference* evokes Farid ud-Din Attar's twelfth-century Arabic epic *The Conference of the Birds* through a play of voices, while *Kildare* parodies the popular culture of talk shows and B-movies, and *Paramour* takes on every convention of romantic love since the Middle Ages. Drawing from antecedents as diverse as Jackson Mac Low and Marcel Proust, her work draws its energy from the dynamic play between the pressures of history and a quotidian blasé that finds humor in the contemporary flair for the jaded and the arch.

In addition to five books of poetry in English, Doris has written three intergenre texts in French, published by the Parisian avant-garde publisher P.O.L. She has been responsible for making much recent French poetry available in English translation through two anthologies that she co-edited during the 1990s, one with Emmanuel Hocquard and the other with Norma Cole. Her own translations include works by Dominique Fourcade, Christophe Tarkos, and Ryoko Sekiguchi. Although her work has received such honors as the University of Georgia Series, Stacy Doris has also realized her work in less usual ways, such as artists books and theater productions. She teaches at San Francisco State University.

from CONFERENCE

Young birds, *waking*: Who will feed us?

A friend of mine, a man, craved absence. Between urgent and endless, a trembling mass of augury and eros was this man. His self wore or was wearing out. This or a man's self is defeat. As defeat, he saves himself from being defeated.

BELBEL: But to not see that ends begin is blind.

Shining, Luminous BELBEL: Lie down. Let me roll all over you.

If you or I ever needed wings, they might grow like teeth, in intermittent pain and from the gums. Lips seal. Lips seal breaths and passages, bridges, extinctions. Kisses lose those they involve. Expansion's intermittent, thus implicates contraction too. Kisses also asphyxiate. Lips promise to disallow. Lips organize.

BELBEL: When you don't know what you're saying, run over and over, comes an end that will not end ending. This is the end of all and our efforts, then. Provisionality is its one necessary mirage. Don't breathe the words. Disorganization unties to unite you anew. Peace is surrender. Talks tender us or you. Conversation's conversion. Sentences raise children. A movie's a disorganization of living; images disorganize people and their bodies and humanities. Sit back. Sit back, because love undoes. Love undoes bodies and organs. Love deforms form then. Kitten or kindred, I closed you in my box's box. Therefore drab is, whether or not drab goes. Love is chemical, mineral, matter, 99.9% similar for each, carrot and carat, a trove.

BELBEL: You come from the inanimate, are borne by the inanimate, return to inanimate; nothing's inanimate.

Instructions for If the Above Becomes a *Confrontation*
- 1. If attacked, do not run. The inanimate is
   >
- faster than you are.
   >
- 2. Lie flat on the ground. Put your arms tight against your
   >
- sides, your legs tight against one another.
   >
- 3. Tuck your chin in.
   >
   >

- 4. The inanimate will come and begin to nudge and climb over your body.
  >
  >
- 5. Do not panic.
  >
  >
- 6. After the inanimate has examined you, it will begin to swallow you
  >
- from the feet and—always from the end. Permit your feet and ankles to be swallowed. Do not panic.
  >
- 7. It will now begin to suck your legs in. You
  >
- must lie perfectly still. This will take a long time.
  >
- 8. When the inanimate has reached your knees slowly and with as little
  >
- movement as possible, reach down, take your tongue and very
- gently slide it into the side of the inanimate mouth between the
- edge of its lip and your leg, then suddenly rip upwards,
- severing yourself.
  >
- 9. Be sure you hold your tongue.
  >
  >
- 10. Be sure your tongue is sharp.

from CHEERLEADER'S GUIDE TO THE WORLD:
COUNCIL BOOK

Hi. I'm Tanesia
and a cheerleader
Exarchon stationed
right in the push. Since
for our language "bless"
comes from "bleeding"
subtlety's violence.
Because names get lost.

To win we gotta imitate
sameness. That's full time.

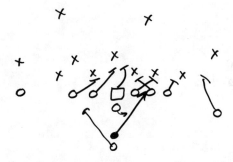

Here's what I wrote 30 years after
the meltdown: when I was -15:

The good old idea
was that corn growth
+ tax cuts make leisure.

Though agriculture means
"slash and burn" and "dispersed
population" maybe it wasn't
as bad as that sounds.

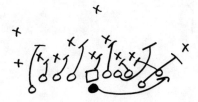

This is about Our Country and Our Cultrue
since even before they were Ours.

That's why it sandwiches Popol Vuh Paterson
Tibetan Dead Jigme Lingpa Pindar

Rah rah:

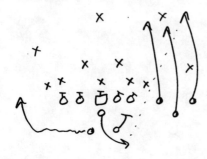

A green bird taught the kids art. But then
he got plugged by Laugh1ng M1rrors Puk1ng

who crams him good shoves him in bed
and goes off from shame leaving the desert
sphere's intricate cultrue of offense in the infant
stage hands of stage hands. Religion aims
to keep continuity going and clearly
say our 'leaders that makes war.

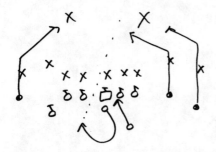

Out there on the field of Twisted
or Deception High with the sign
Puk1ng like an SUV commercial
on our display-energy screen
which is the same plasma
of the mall heap world
of undifferentiated empty
5ungla55e5 won out for good
as our coach. Then we
'leaders began avoiding
our impulses and memory

to burn out on practice
and team spirit bulimics

something to look
back on when we're old.

So growing corn showed
the preponderance of land and sky plus the need for oil
not mixing and that
'leads to what Laugh1ng M1rrors call genetic drift
or stealth or "multilogic" or "hidden
under green and blue
pompoms."

Or Bisquick: greased with the destructive Private
Properties of lubricants.

A Muffin Box recipe:

Force manifests in space thus counting the field it
inserts we're fucked yes this was a typical bakeoff.
Like each hour's measured but so are the minutes
with the same numbers: why?
The slots of time filled with M1rrors.

<<gloss has an extra-societal relationship with life>>>

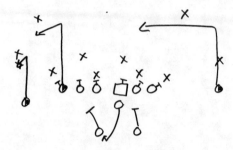

When I was a child
and it thundered I called
out to the corn not to be
frightened which helps but not
if LaughIng MIrrors tries it.
When the tv came to tell him
he'd been elected he was.

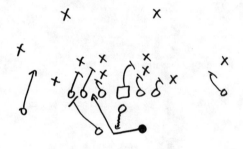

from PARAMOUR

NOTE: (A SUICIDE)

This sent Thus a magical dog who wore a little bell which, when it tinkled, produced a song that was the only thing This had ever found that gave him a moment's respite from the torments of his loving. Thus kept the dog always by her side for a time for This' sake, and at first she thought that her heart was less heavy because the gift was from This, but one day she realized it was the little bell that charmed her spirits. Then she said: "What right do I have to take any drops of solace, when This is away from me, in sorrow?" She took the magic bell and shook it just a little, one last time, then threw it through the window, over the cliffs to the sea.

NORMAN DUBIE

N ORMAN DUBIE HAS consistently written some of the most daring, eccentric, and highly charged lyric poems and dramatic monologues in recent American poetry. Though he's often grouped with more traditional poets of his generation, he has emerged as one of the most radical poetic imaginations now writing. Dubie presents his readers with syntactically complex, often extended poetic phrasings and constructions; nevertheless, his intricate meditations and spiraling verbal gestures unravel with a sense of inevitability. As these meditations dissolve and reformulate before our eyes, his narrative details blossom into delicate, almost prayerful speculations, and his observations of the natural world often resolve either by way of dream or philosophy. Dubie has always been a verbal alchemist and, in his stunning dramatic monologues, a shape-shifter of the first order. In setting the backdrop for a poem, he might look as easily to physics or history as to literature, to the movies as easily as to Meister Eckhart. The capacious generosity of his imagination and the particularity of his imagery allow for both passionate and acerbic reflections. The dignity he grants his figures is as compelling as the enduring and compassionate vision of his poetry.

Norman Dubie was born in Barre, Vermont. A longtime practicing Buddhist, he stopped publishing books for ten years, from 1991 to 2001, when *The Mercy Seat: Collected & New Poems* appeared, winning the PEN USA Prize in Poetry. His other awards include the Bess Hokin Prize and fellowships from the Ingram Merrill Foundation, the John Simon Guggenheim Memorial Foundation, and the National Endowment for the Arts. He lives in Tempe, Arizona, and teaches at Arizona State University.

THE APOCRYPHA OF JACQUES DERRIDA

The ruptured underbelly of a black horse flew overhead.
Bonaparte, is what the matron said to me,
always condescending; vulgar, slowly separating
the three syllables. And it was the last thing she said.
The engine block struck the tree. Our faces
making brook ice of the windshield. The vaulting black horse
now on its side in the dust. I was left
with the road, with the memory of cities burning.
Matron seemed to sleep. My nose bleeding.
I went over to inspect the huge sunflowers
that were beyond the stone wall. The sunflowers
marched with me in Italy. They were cut down.
There was gasoline everywhere. The attendants
will come for me. It's back to the island.
I'll study English out in the cool stucco of the shed.
I don't really believe I am the Corsican. But then
neither did he.
The car was now burning with the tree. The black
brook ice bursting. The horse got up and left.
A back hoof snared by intestine . . .

I was once all game leg in a fast sleigh
passing a half-frozen cook who asked a frozen orderly,
"is he the snow?"
If only that cook had been my general.
It was that straggling long line that cost us.
If they had moved in a dark swarm, huddled together,
cloud shadow over the Russian countryside, then
there would have been little trouble, a few men
out on the fringes dropping to the snow for rest,
but still how
like a forest they would have been
moving over the land
like that gang who came for Macbeth.
I know what you're thinking, that the land pell-mell
is itself mostly obstacle
and this makes a road. But we were cloud shadow

moving over snow.

AT SUNSET

Fucking get back. I have cut
the white paper gasket
out of the apple. Yes,
it's a seed packet
like the wife's whalebone jacket
ruling the fat lamps of the orient.
The faint straight lace of it,

sounds.
Ashes and wormwood
in a brand drawer.
The horses' testicles tossed
into straw for the cats.
Was it not mad John Clare—
that night, and it mad, *last night Clare* saying
it was a sound
going off in his head. A main mast snapping.
The man standing next to you hears it.
Suddenly you're naked running through pasturage
like a woman's hair.

AFTER SKY X

Sky Z, in disbelief, agrees that this alphabet
of mysteries was, one day, to reach him.

He was said, in a foolish legend of weather, to be
a husband of language
like sudden lightning
revealing the bare branches of a tree.

A complacency of owls in that same tree
climbs to a night sky

which is Z.
The revolving eyes of these owls
like the changing aureoles of a woman's breasts
guttering now into eternity.

Z establishes a rainbow of needs
which is the only breach in eternity. He is
searching for Sky A, who, in a discretion
of letters substituting for lovers, forgets
the origin of rain and alphabets. Forgets

that Z is soon to forsake her—not
for the braille points of rising skin
encircling the dark nipples of her breasts,

but, in the language of the deaf, for a signing
of hands, which begs
that none of this be said.

OF POLITICS, & ART

Here, on the farthest point of the peninsula
the winter storm
off the Atlantic shook the schoolhouse.
Mrs. Whitimore, dying
of tuberculosis, said it would be after dark
before the snowplow and bus would reach us.
She read to us from Melville.

How in an almost calamitous moment
of sea hunting
some men in an open boat suddenly found themselves
at the still and protected center
of a great herd of whales
where all the females floated on their sides
while their young nursed there. The cold frightened whalers
just stared into what they allowed
was the ecstatic lapidary pond of a nursing cow's
one visible eyeball.
And they were at peace with themselves.

Today I listened to a woman say
that Melville *might*
be taught in the next decade. Another woman asked,
"And why not?"
The first responded, "Because there are
no women in his one novel."

And Mrs. Whitimore was now reading from the Psalms.
Coughing into her handkerchief. Snow above the windows.
There was a blue light on her face, breasts, and arms.
Sometimes a whole civilization can be dying
peacefully in one young woman, in a small heated room
with thirty children
rapt, confident and listening to the pure
God-rendering voice of a storm.

BLUE

In that first harsh winter of the war
I dreamt a great pear of a man, sun-ripened
in red cotton
and greenish brocade, on the twenty-sixth night
of a not very difficult fast, was
presenting to me thirty-two
separate gifts of gold.

Each carried a fragment of verse.
The first was pure and formal, but the test,
on this blue night of *sohbet*,
was to make his remaining offerings
increasingly vulgar,
more the desperate prayers of a sincere blasphemer?

There was something here of the burden of a life
and the breathless exercise of stairs.

For the dying *mevlana*
there was the admonition of his lover
not to count the heavy kisses
falling like coins onto his beard; not
to count the counting, as with the days,
rising integers of nothing,
going nowhere; just

look upon him
in simple praise of what it is that increases
for that is exactly what will, in secret,

be taken away.

THE CITY OF SNOW
for Jim

These are dry bellicose men
who charge across a field like red violins
like chariots framed in cedar
by a highly mathematical Egyptian magus.

Elementary, that the Lord made us
in his image, so that by the very end of days
he would recognize uncannily
himself in the lumber of Charley McCarthy.

This is my poem for a man who's dead
at his own hand.
Dead, blamelessly, if you were to ask.

No doubt, deep within Mississippi
there's a sister
and a tree. White mules
are dragging a box through rhubarb. The testament

is in Greek, it witnesses
Enos Slaughter rising above a summer's runner—
a baseball diamond
where the chalk lines
have been erased by large men
throwing themselves against bags of sand.

It's wrong to think that you are dead
just because another lives;
conversely, vote, if you wish
the other stained thumb of a Spring Offensive
in a far desert city
with unlimited sand so hot, in fact,
it impugns the child's brow like falling snow itself.

TWO STANZAS FOR TIMOTHY DESHAIES

The lit windows of the train rise
against the night field
with women and children sacking beets
in a near freezing rain; a little girl with fever
believes that coffins of light
are shooting past them
on a high parallel to the shadow
of a ruined aqueduct
and an equally ruined constellation, ursa major.

The red haired woman
turns the horse toward the house and barn.
Later that night
she'll smile crawling into the bed
with her twin brother and small sister. Red
heated stones in with them.
Snow now falling from the sky
into the open rivers of their arms and legs.

Someone snoring out behind the mountains.
You said to us that you never
quarreled with your wife. Good night.
Tim Deshaies. Good night.

LYNN EMANUEL

N ALL OF her work, Lynn Emanuel has been concerned with what constitutes the presence of an author, a speaking self, and the idea of the "book," including the ways all aspects of a text contribute to a reader's experience. Her third and most recent collection, *Then, Suddenly—*, is a complexly woven meditation—and performance—reflecting the relationship between the self, an audience, and the poetic enactment of language. Emanuel has called this "a book of rebellions. The characters are in rebellion against the author, and the author both participates in and rebels against the literary conventions that make her an author." Influenced by cinema, in particular the nuances of film noir, Lynn Emanuel's poetry is filled with iconographic harmonies, images, and details recurring across the landscapes of her poems and collections, much in the way, she has commented, that painters will create visual vocabularies over the body of their work. Stylized and self-conscious, ironic and sly, her poetry asks us to question the given limits of any text.

Lynn Emanuel's first collection, *Hotel Fiesta*, was awarded the Great Lakes College Association New Writers Award and her second, *The Dig*, was a National Poetry Series Award winner. *Then, Suddenly—* received the Eric Matthieu King Award from the Academy of American Poets. She is Professor of English at the University of Pittsburgh and has appeared in numerous editions of *The Pushcart Prize* anthology (for which she has also served as poetry editor) and *The Best American Poetry*. Emanuel has twice been awarded NEA Fellowships and is a past judge for the National Book Awards.

ELLIPSES

Into the clearing of . . .
she climbed and stood

up from the black boots of her black outs
into her body.

The coat wept upon her shoulder,
it hung upon her, a carcass heavy on a hook,

and in the sockets of the button holes
the buttons lolled and looked.

As she climbed into that clearing
it shook as it took her.

A fever wrote the sentence
and screwed it tight with ache

and the long hair of the grass grew silvery and weak,
lay greasily against the skull of dirt.

Each of her steps parted it and she
a figure armed with . . .   came toward me.

She flew to me as though I were a sentence
that must be mended, that must be broken,

then ended, ended, ended.

THE OBSCURE ROOM & MY INEXPLICABLE WEEPING

Kimber Lester, my student, while you cannot actually write
a poem at least write a sentence to tell me why
in the eighth stanza of this *text* the image of a bloody
dagger hangs before me?

My own poem was lost on the plane from Finland.
Under the hungry coliseum of the night sky
where the souls of the martyred stars are burning,
in the terminal at Helsinki lies the poem I had told myself

to unpack as so many times I have told you, my students,
Caleb the Morose, Jennifer whose face is that of a wall guarding a moat,
whose face is that of the guard on the wall of the moat,
whose walled face stands guard over the moat

guarding her heart,
& Kimber whose flesh—as by lions
the flesh of early martyrs—is mauled
by specialized increments of scarification

so that you are a cloud floating inside the rosy burns,
the sunsets edged & licked by the red fires of your face
on which you write with torches, with tongs.
Yes, to you all have I said—

Consider that
1   in this image of the bloody dagger
2   buried in this hard dark scab of line
3   in this densely botched moment of your personal life
4   which has gathered its sense & meaning unto itself like a scar
5   your life has got itself swallowed in an obscurity as deep
         as the locked suitcase.

Perhaps you could "unpack it."
Now it is too late. You are gone into your lives,
Caleb the Morose, Jennifer the Moat, Kimber
smoking beneath the poured lavas of new scars.
& somewhere in that dark airport lies

my poem in which the electric gives out & my husband
& I lighting ourselves with the pale weeping of candles
& an heretical manner of copulation set the duvet on fire
lies the obscure room & my inexplicable weeping.

Kimber, Caleb, Jennifer, my small vista of gall,
luckily looking out at you I can recall Finland,
that endless supple supply of night sky like black leather,
the stars like pierced nipples.

Vagueness is personal, writes Rae Armantrout.
So, perhaps it is best, after all, that I not stand before you
& that you & I not stand before each other clearly
revealed. If we had not lost everything we would be
violate, & undisguised, & explicable.

ELEGY FOR THE POETRY OF HER PERSONAL EXPERIENCES

Dipped in the batter of the personal, adrift in its thick glisten,
she gave up ambition and dyed her hair

blonde-on-black for her post nine eleven project.
Personal experiences are chains, balls,
iron filings drawn fatally to the magnetic personality.

Once she bore the leashes and tourniquets of the personal;
stuffed herself deep into the nooses of its collars.

Then she heard the call to rise out of the trance of herself
into the surcease of the dying world. As the Buddhists say:

*Rise out of the trance of the self into the surcease
of the dying world.*

Now she has things to do: The corpse waits
to be drawered in the coffin,

the blood waits to be mopped up,
the wicked to be exalted, the innocent punished. Homes for the orphans.

Farmers called forth for the slaughter of the lambs, and doctors
called from their face lifts to perform amputations.

She will never again write from personal experience.
She discovers: It Is Too Hard. And: Her Life Is Boring.

Or it was until nine eleven when things picked up
considerably because as Gertrude Stein wrote

from France in the 1940s: *Now we will have an occupation.*

IN ENGLISH IN A POEM

I am giving a lecture on poetry
to the painters who creak like saddles
in their black leather jackets; in the studio,
where a fire is burning like a painting of
a fire, I am explaining my current work
on the erotics of narrative. It is night.
Overhead the moon's naked heel dents
the sky, the crickets ignite themselves
into a snore, and the painters yawn
lavishly waiting for me to say Something
About Painting, the way your dog, when
you are talking, listens for the words Good Dog.

"Your indifference draws me like horses draw flies."
I say while noticing in the window the peonies
throbbing with pulses, the cindery crows seething
over the lawn. "Nevertheless," I continue, "I call
your attention to the fact that, in this poem, what was
once just a pronoun is now a pronoun talking about
a peony while you sit in a room somewhere unmoved
by this. And that's okay. Gertrude Stein said America
was *a space filled with moving*, but I hate being moving.
If you want to *feel*, go to the movies, because poetry
has no intention of being moving; it is perhaps one
of the few things left in America that is not moving."

And yet, I am a fatalist when it comes to art
and orgasm in English, because in English
even a simile is a story and there is no trip
so predictable that some poem won't take it.
And just as I am finishing my lecture, here
is the snowy hem of the end of the page
and one of the painters says to me, "Actually,
I found that very moving. Get in the car.
I'll drive you home."

THEN, SUDDENLY—

> *All bad poetry springs from genuine feeling.*
> —OSCAR WILDE

Yes, in the distance there is a river, a bridge,
there is a sun smeared to a rosy blur, red as
a drop of blood on a slide. Under this sun,
droves of poetry readers saunter home
almost unaware that they are unemployed.
I'm tired of the dark forest of this book
and the little trail of bread crumbs I have
to leave so readers who say *garsh* a lot
can get the hang of it and follow along.
And so I begin to erase the forest and
the trees because trees depress me, even
the idea of a tree depresses me. I also
erase the white aster of a street lamp's
drooping face; I erase a dog named Arf;
I erase four cowboys in bolas and yet in
the diminishing bustle of these streets I
nevertheless keep meeting People-I-Know.
I erase them. Now I am surrounded by
the faces of strangers which I also erase
until there is only scenery. I hate scenery.
I wind rivers back on their spools, I unplug
the bee from the socket of the honeysuckle
and the four Black Angus that just walked in
like a string quartet. "Get a life," I tell them.
"Get a life in another world, because this is
a page as bare and smooth as a bowling alley,"
and, then, suddenly—renouncing all matter—
I am gone, and all that's left is a voice, invisible,
airborne, disembodied, a cloud giving a poetry reading
at which, Reader, I have made our paths cross!

THE BOOK'S SPEECH

As you are reading, you become the hard,
dark bulk looming at the end of a sentence,
you become the broken branch of lightning
falling and the groan of thunder, like an oncoming
migraine, and the flesh of your body pulls itself
closer, and behind you gathers a pressure of coats
and hats; you are now inside the crowd like an ache
in a tooth, that's you, muffled and woolly,
until a door opens to the tavern in the station.

You become a waitress. What does a waitress feel like?
What does it feel like to have a head like an airport fogged
in by a stout cloud of blond hair? You are picking up the
steins and saucers and there, amid the tinselly litter of the tavern,
is a dress like a plate licked clean. This clean wick, slick with beading,

is not a dress really, it is heartache-waiting-to-happen in
the train station of the small town where the rainy evening
is a window, black and shiny, where the passengers are
planted like flowers in the rubber pots of their galoshes.
And the train is coming, the train is surrendering under
a white flag of smoky hoots; the train is looking through
the dark with the big round lamps of your eyes, and above
you the moon looks like someone set her warm elbow
on a block of ice and left a cleft for your tongue to fall into.

KATHLEEN FRASER

K ATHLEEN FRASER HAS been a central figure in innovative poetry in the San Francisco Bay Area from the late sixties to the present day. During the eighties, her small but influential journal *HOW(ever)*—now online as *HOW2*—created a point of encounter for contemporary women writers and scholars influenced by radical Modernists such as HD, Stein, and Niedecker, and pursuing experiments parallel to but often quite different from those of the Language school. Fraser's work has always shown a concern for the space of the page, and her carefully constructed, often disrupted texts underscore the interactive nature of positive and negative space. The resulting dynamic between the concrete and the abstract frees the concrete objects of the world from their routine associations and multiplies their meanings.

Before moving to the Bay Area, where she spent many years teaching in the creative writing program at San Francisco State University, Fraser lived for several years in New York, working as a journalist and associate editor and studying writing at The New School. During her time at San Francisco State, she founded the American Poetry Archives, the largest audio and visual library of poetry in the country, and served as director of the Poetry Center. She has been awarded the Frank O'Hara Poetry Prize, an NEA Young Writer's Award, an NEA Fellowship, and a Guggenheim Fellowship. Her works include fifteen volumes of poetry; a book of critical essays, *Translating the Unspeakable*; and three collaborative artists' books. She currently divides her time between San Francisco and Rome, where she translates contemporary Italian poets.

CUE OR STARTING POINT

BIRD

Sometimes they fly in pairs

                              about the length of one
                                      window

Sometimes they are ponderous
windowshades over grass

                              as big blades and

brown paper is to brown field algebraic

                                      as if one

but not the other one gives up
being alike

                             pointing at something obvious

BIRD

t d k and *s* often carry us
emerge outside of
ending us
as swallows rush

and Vespas tear over

                                   long plastic strips of
                                      blue and yellow
                                        binding
                                      brake and

break free of us
birds know the length of us even
from behind a window and look down

                                        in that
                     brown black sketchbook ordering

wing   wind how made

TREE

"the thing about trees is . . .

                                    relentlessly
                              consistent" antennae

untenable metal staple
yet flies down silvery night each length

                                    of bee wing

                              rung after rung, dark's light
                     it perched on pieces of blue cloth

CLOUD

Arm in arm, across tarmac   pointing her to

thin coral cloud stream   (pious in
                                                    reproduction)

above piazza's ancient fruit tints   (tropical flush in
                                        some other island context)

"I think it means rain"   (wrong again)

Late March, knowing she needed to see this emptiness, clouds and the one
tree (which didn't leaf out) gone

TREE

One did hear   the flow of nearby branches
shear occasional and limp

yet this rawness   moves, is
                                                           moving
even sudden atrophy   of limb

BIRD

see an emptiness shoot off
                              narrow path stapled with wing lengths

dependent on scale, your under-
                                        estimation of how it could

eat at you, that movement
                                            (left behind itself)

BIRD

not a protective   thing   but the negative
incision not brown   field   of scissor
cut   wing   right up
                                         against it

looked downward & saw one long pointing & another up

to remove it
paint between sound   scratchy big stillness
of birds
and other inward flutter   still did not move

CLOUD

My hands had to move as fast as the Vespa over tarmac
Clouds drew themselves   No it was some ordering
principle pulling or pushing   it was the skeleton

book's empty page and the little box of staples
          Something shining outside the black line
not finished

                    —For Sanda Iliescu, after her drawings/notation, Rome 1995

THE DISAPPEARED

          entablature, missing elements, details
            that found the architect's practice

———————————————⟨⟩———————————————

          a disappeared part   spirit to doorway's cornice
            column of all these unraveled cities

      (client more than satisfactory and anyway we are
              overwhelmed   useless)

          run-after city   *all this belonged to us*

          we walked through the streets arm-in-arm

                    ■

method: remarking how in memory the physical world is not ours

for reflex: a photograph itself distorts shadow and real value

                    ■

the studied object at that synthetic level forms in space such as doorways . . .
but noise of radio waves, bottles shattering . . .

all those green parrots gone wild
                (screeking cloud of them hurtling by)

2

Deep signs in the form of our cities' exhausted daily craftsman never
reached   Silence of the noisy and forced   Houses with littered
causeways   Submerged city roughly put aside with slight regret
Ecstatic tolerance for the shiny missing dead

                                        ■

Corner solution, etc.   relatively small &   singled out because it can
be measured   reference to whatever is   visible / axial
digital pencil   laws held at point of disappearing in plastic value
not merely schematic   Peculiar, for   we can still see   canonical elements
of the classical language   even here, at the point of   disappearance
and   (embellishment) facade techniques   bricked arch   projecting
pilasters slightly columned attic with   hang-out balustrade washing
on line   Egyptian cotton shirts &
hand-cut table linen (old and soft)   the crossed arena yet wide

. . . green parrots loose between buildings . . .

3

Initially rolling forward
as sculptural coincidence

it evenly astonished us,
this pleasant absent mind

Opposed aristocratic bias,
Stendahlian city moment,

unitarian re-use
of abusive marbles

"The Rome of the 1931 plan"
close to the ear

---

nest plan : a city as long as a long building

4

molding^   window^   stair^

small lobby cautiously abandoned
unaffordable threshold of a landing never reached

alleys of places (we have lost their names)
so-called baroque time   parrots slashing
through curved light   bent and wrinkled

in the beloved unadorned

—Rome/San Francisco, 2000

HOTEL CLASSIC

The interior stress of a leaf was forming its own new section
when the hotel came under renovation. Steps led downward
to a drawing of trees, at least in the early draft pinned to his light box.
The architect described in his notes what he thought they wanted,
the clients equal to stargazers or foreign diplomats and wives of
officials from Milano, and he felt that something should happen
on the stairs, an event or motion, as if to rush towards
that noise of the entire tree in stress.

ALICE FULTON

ALICE FULTON'S POETRY is intricately crafted, yet expansive—even majestic—in its scope and vision. One senses there is something startling about to be revealed in these poems, and indeed that mystery or tension often resolves in powerful acts of linguistic reckoning, as if a piece of psychological origami were unfolding before our eyes. Nervous and astute, exacting and gracious, Fulton's poems are sensual in their intelligence and arresting in their rhythms. Hers is a maximalist aesthetic, and as she notes in her prize-winning collection, *Felt*, "it's not simplicity that epiphanizes me, it's/saturation, the maximal." Even while courting and celebrating artifice, Fulton is inquisitive and speculative, always looking for the exact aspect of lyric invention that will allow her poems to transcend the constraints of the page.

Alice Fulton's most recent collection is *Cascade Experiment: Selected Poems*. *Felt* was awarded the 2002 Rebekah Johnson Bobbitt National Prize for Poetry from the Library of Congress; it was also selected by the *Los Angeles Times* as one of the Best Books of 2001. Her other poetry includes *Sensual Math*; *Powers of Congress*; *Palladium*; and *Dance Script with Electric Ballerina*. A collection of prose, *Feeling as a Foreign Language: The Good Strangeness of Poetry*, which includes her seminal essays on "fractal" poetics, was published by Graywolf Press in 1999. She has received fellowships from the John D. and Catherine T. MacArthur Foundation, the Ingram Merrill Foundation, the Guggenheim Foundation, the Michigan Society of Fellows, and the Fine Arts Work Center in Provincetown. Fulton is currently the Ann S. Bowers Professor of English at Cornell University.

WARMTH SCULPTURE

Strange fits of passion! The author's hyperventilating
defense of geraniums in *First World Flowers*,
his overmodulation over "the dark period"
of tea rose breeding: what gets to others
sometimes leaves me numb. The blush and bliss of
sappy violins. The intensity of
sun on the stereo this morning
in concert with the strings—

If there were none attached, how unencumbered.
How trance in progress, everlastingness.
Since no one instant is
inherently different from another,
time has invariance. No strings.
Just the fluid ongoing
        no stain == tape == restraints
equal to the moment bleeding through.

        Hi Ma. I'm working on my book.
        Well, when this one's finished,
        don't do it again.
        My air conditioner quit, she says.

    Surfaces in contact
    do not touch everywhere.
    Just so == Just there.

When I survey the brightest reaches
in whatever direction I look it looks
the same. Only the silo distinguishes
our local sample from the remote.
Wrens live in the bullet holes.
How can I leave this to the unlove
of someone else? Unless I become
the opposite of connoisseur,
an immersant, reveler, welcomer
    of everything that is == that is

whale fossils with feet, the benefits of
making robots look less like people,
worm's brains, many body

problems, vinyl, chitin, nonelite greens,
unless I understand the secondary spongiosa
as a vaulted structure.
Books have been written!

Most people want blurbish blobs of praise.
Can I see each as a good thing of its kind
and love not only the stand-up sisters,
but the Group for the Suppression of Fuchsia?

At Kmart, a strange woman about 65
asked my mother for a ride. I said yes,
she says. Don't do it again! I interject.
I took her to her door and she tried to
give me a dollar as she got out.
Don't do it. Of course, I wouldn't
take it. Don't. I thought
you'd say gee, Ma, you're a good soul.

She greets those who are troubled and filled with lament.
May some find herein physically relevant
charms against extinction: don't

sit down in your new white linen suit,
use so many dictionary words,
shovel your own path or go on vacation
with you know who, drink only
grapefruit juice, check in without baggage
demanding a high floor, get to Mass too late
to get a vigil light or become a flash
in the pan—

Like you I long for fairness, some justice
that would let us live
in affirmation of eternity.
But what mind, what treetop research,
can rise high enough
for canopy studies of
the complete?

Recently I noticed the tiny small black blossoms
in the middle of the Queen Anne's lace.
I knew the red speck in the center,

but I didn't know of its unfolding.
It must be a bud that gives way to such
eldritch petals, really tiny violets.
Examine them today, not tomorrow.
Notice too the understory of rungs, the way
the flower hinges on green stays
as the century closes
and language strings consciousness to difference:

   a stain == tape == restraint ==

equal to the moment bleeding through
the unknown on both sides of the non-
linear equation. Strings squash abundance
which, face it, there's too much of.
They crunch invariance to flair
and highlight: the bundle, what was it,
my aunt brought each Monday,
white paper, bound with twine . . .

    Hi Ma. I'm working on my book.
    Do you have to do that?
    Let this be the last. My fan
    is on the blink, she adds.

When every moment's full of severance
what is left but to revel
in the delible
unlingering, precisely this
   goldening == dawn == silo == bird
singing contrapuntal above
the edgeless mono calm of
appliances, this century's ambient sound.

It isn't simplicity that epiphanizes me, it's
saturation, the maximal, interwoven
thrombosis and richness of
contributors to each morsel of
what-is: this density
in which all entities
exist. It works. It wilds ==

   The unknown on both sides of the *don't*:

forget to use your noodle, get knocked for a loop,
miss that show about the guy who gets
the paper the day before
and prevents a lot of accidents,
buy a lamp without a shade,
encourage intercourse with spirits,
go ashcan over tomato can,
have bouts, or fail
to give everyone my best red garters.

I give my best regards to those
who are cast down and beclouded,
those who pursue the miraculous
as a gesture of defiance,
heretics who worship in the chapel perilous,
those who live in the proactive *is*
to whom each moment is spacious
and those who gnash and weep alone.
May they find herein some charms
against excruciation and speak them
gently, disencumbered.

    When I survey the lightest reach of thee—

the intensity of string coloration in concert
with the sun's expansions on the silo's curve,
the unknown on both sides of the non-
linear brightness, the reciprocity swerving
everywhere exceeds my radiance threshold and life

forgive me! I have to close my eyes.

        Hi Ma. I finished my book.
        It cooled off nice.
        Thanks. I'm glad you like it.

THE PERMEABLE PAST TENSE OF FEEL

              Let the barbaric flowers live, I'm living.
        I'm liking the meadow blobbed with bird's-foot trefoil,
                with earth-gall and the creeping wheatgrass
                anciently known as felt. I mean nonelites

that live in disturbed soils, nuisance shrubs
whose fragrance exceeds exaggeration. Isn't it green.

These days everyone wants
two acres gated with herbicide. Everyone wants
to eat high on the food chain while——

Contain yourself. We need less
impervious surface per person

beginning with the mind.
Oh, the blisters sustained
while blaming others. The indignation of!
Only the sky has a right to such
disdain. Isn't it blue, my companion
animal said. And doesn't the body extend

into other endowed stuff. Feeling things
with blue irises and pink or brown
fleshy hairless ears
enrobed in fat and skin
that chew and breathe and joy themselves
by twisting, aerodynamic, when they jump.
That have soulweight and intestines.
That like Mozart,
which is played to calm them since calm
things are easier to kill.

Felt comes from "beat" and from "near."
== As hooks pass through, the fibers entangle
till our presence is a double-dwelling ==

Why must I say they are like
us whenever I say let them live? Speak eco-speak
like eat no flesh and save the watershed, like
maybe the whole blue-green.

How have I inconvenienced myself
in service to this feeling?
Felt is ideal for padding and sealing.
How have I left the earth
uncluttered with more me?

The inhabitant cleans and wipes,
eats and spasms. Cruelty exasperates
reason. At the top of its range,
ah is the only sound
the human voice can make. So felt
takes on the shape of flesh

beyond resemblance
into same, a thou-art-that that oscillates
through pollen-throwing and clasping devices,
ovaries and arms. So lid and lash
close over iris and pupil, dissecting tables drain
into our sweet spot.

The century heaves. Nowever. Who has time?
With primates to raise, important hearts
to hold down.

== When the box is full, hammers beat the felt,
which turns to present a new surface
before it's struck again ==

Lovers, givers, what minds have we made
that make us hate
a slaughterhouse for torturing a river?

As the prescribed burn begins, I see the warmth
sculpture rise higher, twisting from the base.
And though the world consists of everything

that is the case, I know
there must be ways to concentrate
the meanings of felt in one

just place. Just as this flame
assumes the shape of the flesh it covers.
I like to prepare the heart
by stuffing it with the brain.

JAMES GALVIN

'M A FLASHLIGHT in daylight," declares James
Galvin in a 1995 poem. That brief line cap-
tures his wry self-irony on the one hand,
and his focus on elemental wonders and large metaphors on the other. Long
identified with the poetic mainstream, Galvin has increasingly incorporated
radical juxtaposition, syntactic disruption, and other formal devices into his
otherwise straightforward language, gradually exploding his modes of making
sense. While remaining committed to a Frost-based belief in the power of clear
speech to access clear emotion, he has developed a method of complicating it,
keeping his language clear, but leaving the relationships among his lines and
phrases ever more open-ended. Frequently set in a rural landscape, his poetry
and prose present nature imagery freed from the nostalgia and anachronism that
threaten it in our largely urban era.

Galvin is in a perfect position for this because he lives several months of the
year in rural Wyoming in a house he built literally by hand. This fragile land-
scape is the focus of his acclaimed non-fiction work *The Meadow* and a principal
character in his novel *Fencing the Sky*. Born in Chicago and raised in northern
Colorado, Galvin has published six books of poetry, one of which was chosen in
the National Poetry Series. In addition, he has received a Lila Wallace–Reader's
Digest Foundation Award, a Lannan Foundation Award, fellowships from the
Guggenheim Foundation, the Ingram Merrill Foundation, and the National
Endowment for the Arts, and has been a visiting artist at the American Academy
in Rome. He teaches at the Iowa Writers' Workshop, where he directs the
poetry program.

LEAP YEAR

When the river goes underground it isn't lying.

                             I used to have
someone to miss.

               Forgetting about the future makes the moment
you live in slouch.

             Excuse me while I digest this small galaxy.

                                 In
a petri dish of hubris, fear and sorrow are exculpatory and lead to
an event-free life.

             The waterfall fell and the river went
underground.

          Terror is transvertebrated to attraction, making you
feel more godly.

            Quite a leap.

                The river went to hell.

                         The waterfall
fell.

  Down here we don't have moods.

                    Nothing amounts to
anything.

    The man with a fishhook in his eye can see quite clearly.

The rain never comes, but dry lightning in a thunderhead is like
cotton candy being electrocuted.

                      When the river comes back up
again we call it spring.

           Oh, Persephone, home's not where I
thought it was.

          Home is where the heart gives out and we arouse
the grass.

NATURE AVERTS HER EYES

> FOOL: *He's mad that trusts in the*
> *tameness of a wolf, a horse's*
> *health, a boy's love, or a whore's*
> *oath.*
> —King Lear

Fool. I had an exaggerated interest in death, so much so it was
possible I might already be dead.

        Anyway, I had this ridiculous
feeling that I could walk around, that I had found my wallet, that a
beautiful woman had kissed me twice, once on each of the lenses of
my spectacles.

    No, that's wrong.

        Actually I was someone else.
Could it be you?

    Is causality a structure?

        Nothing happens that is
supposed to happen, of that I'm certain.

        Probability cannot be
enthusiastic, only the unlikely can.

    Your voice is velvety.

        Watch
out.

I have inspected my restored order and find it wanting, insipid
even.

    I'm getting drowsy, a good sign.

    Yesterday was different.

        I
tried to convince myself that passion was not a gyre of dust
swirling about my feet.

    Would you like a biscuit?

    I lived in a
lukewarm province until it became unbearable.

    I touched
everything.

    It didn't help.

    The room insists.

    My categorical
imperative is falling in love.

    I saw a ship dancing on waves.

    It even

kicked up its heels.
                    It heeled over.
                              That ship will never sink alone,
without a captain.
                         Scientific aspirations, curiously inaccurate,
unrolled before the innocents.
                         The subject had arisen.
                                        Something
like happiness had long since lost my other.
                                   Dark eyes staring into
ice blue ones.
              I do not want to know how old the stars are.
                                          I do not
want to know how long they have left on their astral death row.
                                             As
if they really existed, like gods.
                         What's their point?
                                   It was very
quiet in the Faculty Club as, outside, the firing squad took aim.

Lightning's alphabet.
                    Little circles, sightless, float down the river to
the sky.

EARTHQUAKE

A well-dressed mannequin with a price tag on her sleeve—what
could be closer to the truth unless an earthquake rocks her lifelike.

A woman eating an orange in an earthquake—what could be closer
to the truth?
              The luminescent globe perches on four of her
fingertips, which are the four definitions of beauty.
                                        The earthquake
is self-conscious because it means no harm.
                                   I'm waiting for my
life to be over because it couldn't be closer to the truth.
                                        Here's
what the earthquake feels like: something you'd like to step off of,
please, onto something else, but can't.
                                   The exoskeletons of survival
strategies are strewn over the plain.

They are the most beautiful
airports.

I've read a lot of books in which all the protagonists had to
do was say something true, and everything would turn out all right,
a comforting twilight.

They never do.

Without fail they fall
unchecked into a comfortable misery.

The woman eats the orange
segment by segment, longitude by longitude.

She separates segment
from segment, as if there were truth in an orange.

She could take
forever.

Each time she peels another glowing crescent it sounds like
the turning of a page.

The earthquake is just descant.

The ground
undulates—so what.

She perches the light-lusty globe on her
fingertips and pulls it apart like pages agonized into a story where
nothing could be closer to the truth.

The truth?

Fault and slip,
broken limbs, swooning buildings, an inner din unending.

APOLLINAIRE'S CANE

—for Dean Young

The Mastermind was for a time
In possession of Apollinaire's ivory cane,
Carved from a narwhal tusk.
It was given to the Mastermind
By a famous lady philanthropist in Venice.
Apollinaire had forgotten his cane
On the philanthropist's dock,
His attention focused on stepping,
Drunk, into a gondola.
Apollinaire never missed his cane.
To him it was just a cane,
But for the Mastermind

It was the ivory cane of Apollinaire,
His most prized possession.
The Mastermind brought the cane
To Paris,
When he entered the Sorbonne
At the age of ten.
He took it everywhere,
And when people asked, "Why the cane?"
The Mastermind replied,
"It was Apollinaire's."
Did I mention the Mastermind was absent-minded?
He forgot the famous cane
On the seat of a Parisian taxi.
As the taxi drove off, he remembered it.
He shouted and waved
But the cabby didn't notice him.
The Mastermind watched as the cab disappeared
Into Paris,
And Apollinaire's cane
Ceased to be
Apollinaire's cane.

The salt was on the shelf
Next to the bottled ship.
Reaching for the salt one day,
The Mastermind hit the ship with his elbow.
The bottle broke, but the ship was fine.
Fine? What good is a tiny ship
Without a bottle to sail in?
It's not like it wanted to be free,
Sail a tiny sea,
Float in a bath tub with a child.
The point of a ship in a bottle
Is the bottle.
Apollinaire's cane never wanted
To be free of Apollinaire, either.
Apollinaire's cane
Is not Apollinaire's cane.
The ship without the bottle
Will never be the same.
Don't touch me.

THE MASTERMIND ASKS SOME QUESTIONS

Q.   What is the nature of your presentation?
A.   I always leave before the music starts.
Q.   Why should obscene transgressions, then, occur?
A.   The wind, it seems, is taking me personally.
Q.   Do you know nothing of the art of being
Interrupted?
            A.   Yes. I want to feel
Lucky, and be someone else's luck.
Q.   Do you think your teeth are under the fallen building?
A.   Why else would I keep digging for them there?
Q.   Are you seeking closure for your teeth?
A.   Every closure is an aperture.
Q.   Whatever will you do if you should find them?
A.   Give them to the loved ones, the lucky ones.
Q.   Survivors of the victims, who need closure?
A.   Yes. Them. All of them. All of us. Us.
Q.   What about me?
            A.   You? What about you?

STOP WHIMPERING AND SPEAK

Sad Master, I see you coming from very far
Away, leading your bony, wind-broke horse.
Turn back. I'm busy dividing my time.
My love is the death of kisses. I live
With her apart in the wind of constancy.
There's nothing you can do, given what you have done.

FORREST GANDER

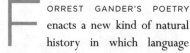ORREST GANDER'S POETRY
enacts a new kind of natural
history in which language
is the avenue of research. His precise treatment of plant and animal life, of
rock formation and water pattern, is further sharpened by twists of syntax
and occasional grammatical oddities that create shifts in perspective, mak-
ing tiny things fill our whole field of view or widening the horizon so that
we see eons as well as miles. Lyrically rooted and visually adventuresome, his
work draws from influences as varied as César Vallejo and Robert Creeley,
G. M. Hopkins and Gertrude Stein. "Like species," Gander writes, "poems
are not invented, but develop out of a kind of discourse, each poet tensed
against another's poetics, in conversation, like casts of wormtrails in sandstone."
Holding a degree in geology as well as an MA in creative writing from San
Francisco State, Gander is attentive to the lapidary construction of meaning,
which shows in his poetry's complex ambiguities and interwoven references.

Born in California and raised in Virginia, Forrest Gander has lived in San
Francisco and Mexico as well as Providence, Rhode Island, which has been his
principal home since 1983. The author of seven books of poetry, he co-edited
Lost Roads Publishers for twenty years with C. D. Wright. He is the transla-
tor of numerous collections of contemporary Latin American poetry, includ-
ing *Firefly Under the Tongue: Selected Poems of Coral Bracho*. His recent collection
of critical essays, *A Faithful Existence*, gathers work previously published in *The
Nation*, the *Boston Review*, and elsewhere. He is the recipient of fellowships
from the Guggenheim Foundation, the Whiting Foundation, and the National
Endowment for the Arts, and teaches in the Literary Arts and Comparative
Literature programs at Brown University.

TIME AND THE HOUR

The convulsive incision   tore light
from matter, image   from similitude, black vowels
croaked and flew   from the four-lettered name of God.
In diffuse nebulae,   non-luminous metals shined
in their planets.   The thirty intentions of the shadows
condensed below a brightness   the multitude
of species emitted, and Ras Algethi   glared in Hercules.
So the light came   to contain numbers
and the first   was intoxication
and Giotto was intoxicated   painting Scrovegni,
1306.   Out in the fields—wheat,
cockleburs, jimson—   a farmer stood up his hoe
and when that hoe was standing   on its own shadow,
he knew, and he was certain   that he knew.

EXHAUSTIBLE APPEARANCE

    Around the burning barn, stationary objects seem to stream.
    Scrub brush, twigs in sinople dirt, dry weeds,
puffballs among scattered breccia and chert.
    Grey barn burning in the eye of the afternoon.
    The solid given upward, hemorrhaging into air, the vista
tinged Merthiolate and twisted inside the barn, a dense ball of smoke
like a black sock
        stuffed in a shoe.
            We breathe carbonized splinters, our shirts beating
to exploding planks, holding barely within ourselves the felt
quality of redness, whoosh, heat. Roof gone, walls seared
down to the single argent window gleaming . . .

    And here, to keep the whole visual image from slipping across
                        the retina,
away, we focus upon the window—
    which does not reflect any panorama we see
    which does not reveal the penetralia
    which neither contributes nor borrows any color
from the chromatic blaze
    which, though gravity always tugged the glass down
through itself, melts quickly now.

Nothing in the window of the world beside it the world within it the
world we can see around, beyond it.

The window catches light from another world altogether,
one behind us, one we cannot see, the world from which we have come
clomping across the desert from a road which is a dashed trace
on a map.

It is a moteless clarity behind us.

Not a mature representation of imagined form.
Not a clot of flies at the edge of a cow's eye. Not tadpoles wriggling
in the mud of a
tractor tread. Not a broken bootlace.

But when we turn, like a piece of music at the andante,
the landscape resumes. The barn fallen inside itself.

CODA

and the birds: canthi loosed at a distance. Aqua-
marine backdrop, scratched out several. All symbols
buried in the sand. Nor a cardinal's color nor point, so
only smooth and hush come clear. Unfocused and as if
winked upon. Where the wind, dehiscing sand, does not
omit. In a synoptic way, surrounded: already the eye
whose perceptible tearing: "how the rain swung from
the rims of." Even if it is possible to remain noncommittal
about an endpoint. Winter, thumbprint of black birds
smudged across windshield, in a premature language.
An ocean

from THE HUGENESS OF THAT WHICH IS MISSING

CONTACT

Call the direction the eye is looking
the line of sight. There
where it grazes the surface
of the visibly surging
without reference to a field of human presence,
don't look away.

I haven't looked away.

The neurons spike quickly. And the catastrophe
will be consummated even to the end, to the absence of ambiguity,
a new range of feeling. Torn awake. What if
a man went into his house and leaned his hand
against the wall and the wall
                              was not?

Look how your relation to truth creates a tension
you have slackened with compromise.
                              Yes, and the more
distant it is, the more I have valued it. But to stand
where the crossing happens, as fall oaks fold
                              into lake light, and so
wearing reflection, take a further step inside—

                              No, the voice said, you will strike out
into a forest of pain, unpathed, wolved, clouds muffling the mountain ridge
                              and spilling down in runnels,
blindness with confusion come to parl, at variance with,
measuring out an exile between self and self. Driven
transverse. Hazarded abroad. Nevertheless you will begin to arrive, to know
                              from intimate impulse
the crucial experience of . . . the threat of dissolution of . . . but not yet.
There is something more astonishing
                              than rhythms of distance and presence,
of more quality than the set of qualities determining figure and ground
and suffering, where respite is so often
misinterpreted as a horizon.

Isn't the word for a turn of phrase
itself a turn of phrase?
                              Something was given to me as a present
and a spectre was attached to me, a projection
                              pregnant with equivocation.

And in the neck of language,
and in the early June riots of starlings,
and in some crumbs in the seam of a book,
the solid real steps out from infinitely diluted experience
saying *Tongue I gave you. Eyes.*

At any point in the trajectory, the body might stop. Do you recall this part?

But who is it who is speaking
in the glorious and contracted light?

POEM

Some
we say we
know go
like a window
dark.
Pathetic
any remark
then.
They leave
us, what
we call
them.

ROAD AND TREE

Lucent road, first letter.   Evening spooked with light.
Quarter moon road   with the darkness inside it, and full
moon
sky with the tree inside it.   Curved road in the gloaming.
Oak trunk, a vector of force   punched upward. Held in place
by the stenciled circle of light. Lit   road bearing a trunk of its own
darkness. Circle of light split   like a cat's eye. Road
curling left, eye   cutting right. Barely there in the soft
dirt, footprints and dogprints   commingling in the throat
of the road where voices,   also, have fallen with pollen.
This is an inner landscape, for even   as light came back like bees
to the camera proclaiming   the photograph, the place
altered, never availed   itself at all. A hem of cirrus
brushed the sun, the Carolina wren's   *cheery* gave way
to a full moon   in the afternoon and little grass frogs.
Dry puffballs detonated   into a cloud of gold spores as a
hoof
lifted, and even if it had pictured   a real terrain for
one moment, of what place   is it a memory now?
The image strands itself,   a word   knocked loose
from the language, a tooth   under a pillow.

And the place itself was neither   fully read nor erased since it
never
ceased being written. Only   a word was pronounced, only
the instrument   clicked.

COLLODION

Dogwood, laurel, rhododendron,   Judas tree. Traveling
to places they had seen   in magazines, tourists
found the original   less authentic
than the impression   with which they came.
The more intense the emotion, the slower   the speed.
Incarnate and carbonized,   the photograph gives evidence
of an arousal to be had   in no other form.
The hedge, not visible,   I feel it
and know it.   *A dark cloud*, wrote a monk,
illuminates the night. Oh,   aperture revealing
the divine gesture   as a pure demonstration of the world:
guide me back from   interpretation to sensation to
vision, for one   stroke of a wet cloth
may wipe the picture   out.

IVY BRICK WALL

It never aims to create an illusion of reality. Instead, the warped lens
allows for a new set of relationships behind swirling frets. The wall confronts a
flotsam of vortical energy and tree limbs transparentize in the blast.

Enmeshed in a field of concentric force, the spectator is drawn toward a
wormhole of brightness, not depth but another dimension entire. A light which
is life source.

It is this originary force that transforms the ordinary into the exultant.
Here, where light authors act and meaning, where whelming ivy overwrites
brickwork.

The nucleus of the image is all verb, the seen availing itself to our seeing.
When there are no stable terms, there are no faithful things.

ARGOSY FOR ROCK AND GRASS

A snapping turtle, its saw-tooth   tail and keeled shell
nesting in the river mud,   blows water

through its nostrils   until the surface froths.
Wind   runs through the distant
assembly of pin oaks: a family graveyard, untended
in bracken fern. Five   concrete headstones
decorated with marbles   Child, Child, Child, Child, Child.
The landscape clutches   its long roots, its concealed
life animates   the loam. A drawn-out exposure
nets traces of movement—   flying birds, trembling leaves
Glinting in rock: mica, feldspar, cyanide.
Although place is depicted, no   sign in the world

corresponds to this   image. There is no source
outside itself   for such radiance. Stone
pulls at grass and   the treeline wavers
like something proposed   and forgotten.
But to fault   the image for its lack
of correlative, we would   miss its fullness
coming to be.   The river is named
The Holy Ghost. We believe   what we do not know.

MOON AND PAGE GHAZAL

Before the neutrinos could interact with matter, they went out.
His voice hardened. The foreplay went out.

Through a pocked sky he dragged her by the rope in her mouth.
She didn't like it. When he opened the door, her stray went out.

To wound him no deeper than to awaken him, she thought.
Under eaves, the buzzing of mud daubers in their piped clay went out.

That could not be his meaning, on two legs walking backward.
But whoever heard her pray went out.

Only a fly responds to a moving hand in thirty milliseconds.
Biting the hole in her lip as each day went out.

They met at the footsteps of the altar, in a groined chamber of salt.
Forever, she said—*flash*—smiling as the bridesmaid went out.

C. S. GISCOMBE

C. S. GISCOMBE is a lyric cartographer, a poetic geographer, and a landscape artist of historical, cultural, and social disparities. Giscombe's startling meditations on place are indeterminate in their construction yet revelatory in their resolutions, and his use of secondary materials—maps, tables of symbols, fragments of explorers' charts, guides to native decorative markings—all help to record the dislocations and discoveries, both actual and psychological, of his speakers. Giscombe's poems evolve deceptively and elusively at times, yet they always remain firmly grounded in their physical descriptions and details of place. The language is muscular, direct, and elemental, yet the fluid movements of these poems reflect cinematic gestures as often as they echo the conventions of historical journals.

C. S. Giscombe was born in Dayton, Ohio, and received a BA from the State University of New York at Albany and then an MFA from Cornell University in 1975. Previously a professor at Penn State, Illinois State, and Cornell, he currently teaches at the University of California at Berkeley. He has written three books of poetry, *Postcards* (Ithaca House), *Here*, and *Giscome Road* (both Dalkey Archive), and a book of linked essays, *Into and Out of Dislocation* (North Point). A new poetry collection, *Prairie Style*, will be published in the fall of 2008. He has been awarded the Carl Sandburg Award (for *Giscome Road*) and grants and fellowships from the National Endowment for the Arts, the Illinois Arts Council, the Fund for Poetry, and the Council for the International Exchange for Scholars. In addition to being a long-distance cyclist, he is working toward his locomotive engineer's license.

from GISCOME ROAD

A soundtrack

in wch north's marked off by inflection, delineated
by an inflection in all that contour
& the helix of information,

in wch north's ranging over even the fattest talking edge,

centerless heat going on on its own: the abstract

says the trail was *built from Giscome Station* on out *thru the centre of the northern
block*, out to where it's unexaggerated,

the way out to where it's nameless (on a map of sound)

on past where there's a little end, the little end of a fast lead-in
to the biggest most unexpected parts of the soundtrack wch are nameless
themselves

but look to be the same information or re-surfacings in it: the forms descend

& bend away & cross over

(not returning much to the theme):

they go on down becoming rueful & muted, giving way without receding,

making way, the way in wch the same old caravan appears, the way it looks
when it appears, some shapes

at the horizon have become the horizon its prodigal self, are
the blood as if it too were out there telling.

■   ■   ■

The talking map began to seem inauthentic, began to look to be the stylized
reproduction of a *series* of explanations:

                        I'd been asleep at the wheel, out
                where it's undrivable
—*began the description*—,

I had a taste for ambiguity
& arrival

& contrived to be
distance itself closing
in on a single place
to stop,

if at the outside,
at the jagged rind
of the empty
old heart:

I'd arrived funky

& incognito, in shades
though it was dark
out or simply overcast,

taking on resemblance
moving outward

& confident too

to be a blunt condition,
an old stone face w/ those African highlights giving specificity

to the remote,

being immutable

& trailing off

loud into
the trees right
there.

■　■　■

In the shooting script too north's a long fragment, a traveling insert repeated

in half-steps, say, up near-invisible ridges, human nature rising
up from lowland or low-lying areas to along the rims, say,

of some canyon, a run-on commentary, hesitant voice over,
a *geographical* cover, a *cover* of trajectory sliding on in, sloppy cover

in that it's imprecise & overstated, the fragment *doing*,

that phrase out there working for you:

         & a caution of steps as tho' up a little hillside followed

by the high patter of restatement descending, crossing over: in

the shooting script north's no revenant or ha'nt in the talk, it's
contrapuntal in the face of the woods, dialogue looking like monologue,

in the shooting script are lead-ups to some same old edge.

                 ■   ■   ■

The long song's a commotion w/ out words,

about the contempt for arrival,

all about the taste for arrival,

about losing one & you lose the other one too:
a hodgepodge of little shrines lined the road in, along the water:

you never know how the blood's going to appear, where

it's going to come up in the current—
the longest song bends away from the hodgepodge,

takes shape from below & beyond: no telling

how it appears, no word for the way blood arrives.

from PRAIRIE STYLE

FAR

Inland suffers its foxes: full-moon fox, far-flung fox—flung him yonder! went
the story—, fox worn like a weasel round the neck, foxes are a simple fact,
widespread and local and observable. *Vulpes fulva*, the common predator,

varying in actual color from red to black to rust to tawny brown, pale only in the headlights.

It's that this far inland the appearance of a fox is more reference than metaphor. Or the appearance is a demonstration. Sudden appearance, big like an impulse; or the watcher gains a gradual awareness—in the field, taking shape and, finally, familiar. The line of sight's fairly clear leaving imagination little to supply. It's a fact to remember, though, seeing the fox and where or, at night, hearing foxes (and where). The fox appearing, coming into view, as if to meet the speaker.

Push comes to shove. Mistah Fox arriving avec luggage, sans luggage.

FEVER

The spiral inward. Or, instead, the trek across as if in a wagon or on Amtrak—perpetual stretch from range to image, from splay to toehold, cane to cant, etc. Coming across all evil (which is not to indicate that everything has been come to but which is to suggest crossing with penchants intact and the face advertising that).

On or along the way music *occurs* in such a way as an animal could, it's an appearance that's ambiguous and rarely finite.

The point of origin, the point of fade. Fielding the question. A train trails its own noise.

Around here juxtaposition's lacking so the argument that juxtaposition might state is nonexistent. Another one's got to be made; another one's got to be interposed. I felt a restless emotional excitement from no source in particular. As though I were talking and suddenly there was the great hesitancy of the prairies.

Music appears, the voice coming not into itself but to real things such as animals. A whole slew of repeat performances coming up. Today, to me, is the opposite of relief: today's blunt-toothed and equivocal, ugly. Music does the talking, the hem of my garment just banging away on the skin.

Inland, one needs something more racial, say bigger, than mountains. Before, I'd always come, as if from nowhere, to places. Trek's out of Afrikaans but has entered, as they say, our vocabulary; I've always had a penchant for the place around speech, voice being suddenly absent in the heart of the song, for the flattest part of heat.

THE 1200N ROAD, GOING EAST

To me, image is any value in the exchange. Pleasure's accidental. In any event, it's hard to measure and harder still to memorize, pleasure. Image stands in. To me, voice is that which gets stuck in the head, effected voice, or in between the teeth, the hiss of love. Songs, eating. Whatever love says it's no image, no consequence. This far inland, the erotic's only obvious from a distance. This far inland you need something more sexual than dichotomy.

NATURE BOY

Air over the place partially occupied by crows going places every evening; the extent unseen from sidewalk or porch but obvious, because of the noise, even from a distance. Noise glosses—harsh, shrill, a wild card. Sundown's a place for the eye, crows alongside that. Talk's a rough ride, to me, what with the temptation to out-talk. At best long term memory's the same cranky argument—changeless, not a tête-a-tête—over distance: to me, the category *animals* excludes birds, the plain-jane ones and birds of passage, both. To me, song's even more ambiguous—chant itself, the place of connection and association. It's birdless, bereft. I'm impartial, anhedonic. I'm lucky about distance but I would be remiss if I didn't hesitate over image before going on.

BALLAD VALUES

Love's a lazy slave and won't come to her name being called and called, is—finally—a poor interlocutress. The call might be a station—emanation, convergence, crossover.

The phrase—the sound—may lengthen but the variation's the same: it re-encounters the consequences again and again, it meets a standard.

OPEN RETURN

Equivocation's big enough to take the place of argument. In the literature the same animal's called by different names and the descriptions have gaps big enough to drive a truck through. One wishes for an avatar. Love's inarticulate when it does appear: it's just lazy speech—love talk—and not specific and you can't exchange it for much.

LIGHT, BRIGHT, ETC.

Or skin's the *inevitable* appearance, the only castle (location only equaling voice). Skin meets the weave and you're clean; inland's no delta.

Skin's blank, though, and you can see it coming or going from far away. Neck to neck, side by side, a panoply of advantageous positions. Skin stands in; whole stories have to do with being caught up with on the road. Half-certain's different.

For the sake of argument, let image be the writhing end of hoop-la. I'm as interested as I should be. Let tomorrow come.

PETER GIZZI

P ETER GIZZI'S WORK blends a deeply personal voice with wry intelligence, highly wrought phrasing, and historical depth, which both puts pressure on language as an art material and uses it as a vehicle for emotion. Gizzi has said in an interview, "When I write, I write from the sum total of things that have made me: my loves, ideas, people I've known, the books I've read, the news, things I've seen. The beauty of thought and/or emotion, the virtue of it, is to be able to present its field, to present the fact that it's actually in relation and living and part of something larger and ongoing."

Interested from a young age in classical and nineteenth- and twentieth-century literatures, Gizzi writes a poetry that is at once original and a highly receptive trans-historical synthesis of these various approaches to the art, creating a voice that is simultaneously embodied and haunted. His work revels in the tension between the everyday and the desire to complicate its surface. "A good poem," Gizzi has said, "disrupts everyday language." As if language could crack open the daily and deliver it up new, or reveal the multiple histories that compose each moment, he uses slight deviations, such as repeated phrases, synesthesias, and hypnotic rhythms, to charge observations that run from the personal to the political. His books include *Periplum*, *Artificial Heart*, *Some Values of Landscape and Weather*, and *The Outernationale*. His editing projects have included the little magazine *o•blēk*; the international anthology *Exact Change Yearbook*; and *The House That Jack Built: The Collected Lectures of Jack Spicer*. The recipient of a Guggenheim Fellowship and numerous other awards and residencies, Peter Gizzi currently teaches at the University of Massachusetts at Amherst.

TOUS LES MATINS DU MONDE

Goodness is hard on the body,
a distracted mind unable to doze in fitful sleep.
The dove rattles the mind into thinking
it has a body of thought—complete
& symbolic—the gray feathers perched
outside the pale cut square of silver.
Say then, we belong to that window,
that warble, and suddenly we belong too,
the silver car in the yard, even a tiny silver hammer.
All vehicles of travel
disclose the mind's need to wonder in perfect forms.
Even if the skiffsman don't come to this bed
to rock me to sleep—to wander the tired stones again
and worn teeth we remember to hold onto a world
for this life might not take us the whole way.
That shape of an idea, the concept, or *donnée*
travels farther than the instrument can register.
The spindle whirs beyond its order.
Something must be moving at incredible speed.
With pure speed I address you, reality.

IN DEFENSE OF NOTHING

I guess these trailers lined up in the lot off the highway will do.
I guess that crooked eucalyptus tree also.
I guess this highway will have to do and the cars
         and the people in them on their way.
The present is always coming up to us, surrounding us.
It's hard to imagine atoms, hard to imagine
         hydrogen & oxygen binding, it'll have to do.
This sky with its macular clouds also
         and that electric tower to the left, one line broken free.

PLAIN SONG

         Some say a baby cries for the life to come
         some say leaves are green 'cause it looks good against the blue
         some say the grasses blow because it is earth's instrument
         some say we were born to cry

■

Some say that the sun comes close every year because it wants to be near
us
   some say the waters rise to meet it
   others say the moon is our mother, *ma mère*

■

Some say birds overhead are a calligraphy: every child learning the words
"home"
   some say that the land and the language are the father
   some say the land is not ours
   some say in time we'll rise to meet it

■

Some say there are the rushes the geese the tributaries and the reeds

■

Some say the song of the dove is an emblem of thought
   some say lightning and some the electric light some say they are
brothers

■

Some say the current in the wall is the ground
   some say the nervous system does not stop with the body
   some say the body does not stop

■

Some say beauty is only how you look at it and some beauty is what we
have some say there is no beauty some truth

■

Some say the ground is stable
   others the earth is round
   for some it is a stone
   I say the earth is porous and we fall constantly

■

Some say light rings some say that light is a wave some say it has a weight
or there is a heft to it

■

Some say all of these things and some say not
   some say the way of the beekeeper is not their way

some say the way of the beekeeper is the only way
some say simple things all there are are simple things

■

Some say "the good way," some "stuff"
some say yes we need a form
some say form is a simple thing some say yes the sky is a form of what is
simple

■

Some say molecular some open others porous some blue
some say love some light some say the dark some heaven

BEGINNING WITH A PHRASE FROM SIMONE WEIL

There is no better time than the present when we have lost everything. It
doesn't mean rain falling
   at a certain declension, at a variable speed is without purpose or design.
   The present everything is lost in time, according to laws of physics things
shift
   when we lose sight of a present,
   when there is no more everything. No more presence in everything
loved.

   In the expanding model things slowly drift and everything better than the
present is lost in no time.
   A day mulches according to gravity
   and the sow bug marches. Gone, the hinge cracks, the gate swings a
breeze,
   breeze contingent upon a grace opening to air,
   velocity tied to winging clay. Every anything in its peculiar station.

   The sun brightens as it bleaches, fades the spectral value in everything
seen. And chaos is no better model
   when we come adrift.
   When we have lost a presence when there is no more everything. No more
presence in everything loved,
   losing anything to the present. I heard a fly buzz. I heard revealed nature,
   cars in the street and the garbage, footprints of a world, every fly a
perpetual window,
   unalloyed life, *gling*, pinnacles of tar.

There is no better everything than loss when we have time. No lack in the present better than everything.

In this expanding model rain falls

according to laws of physics, things drift. And everything better than the present is gone

in no time. A certain declension, a variable speed.

Is there no better presence than loss?

A grace opening to air.

No better time than the present.

HUMAN MEMORY IS ORGANIC

We know time is a wave.

You can see it in gneiss, migmatic
or otherwise, everything crumbles.

Don't despair.

That's the message frozen in old stone.

I am just a visitor to this world
an interloper really headed deep into glass.

I, moving across a vast expanse of water

though it is not water maybe salt
or consciousness itself

enacted as empathy. Enacted as seeing.

To see with a purpose has its bloom
and falls to seed and returns

to be a story like any other.
To be a story open and vulnerable

a measure of time, a day, this day one might say
an angle of light for instance.

Let us examine green. Let us go together

to see it all unstable and becoming
violent and testing gravity

so natural in its hunger.

The organic existence of gravity.
The organic nature of history.

The natural history of tears.

THAT'S LIFE

It couldn't be closer than Mars
these days. First you're off on a tangent,
then glittering beyond the call
in the backyard to no good effect.
Later when you shrugged you were blue,
I mistook it for "that's life" not "help me."
I mistake many things in dusk
like seeing liberty everywhere today,
smallish unacknowledged moments
of door holding, tossing coins
into a worn paper cup, smiling.
To rediscover our neighborhood
one wrapper and bum at a time.
Where am I going with this?
Down to the riverbank to watch the light
dazzle and showcase trees
in all their prehistoric movement.
Two more animals blinking in the breeze.
The guest-host relationship is
bigger than a house, older
than cold planets in space.
One of the earliest manuals
is about the guest-host thing.
Sit down, breathe deeply and
welcome yourselves. If you listen
you can faintly recall the song.
The sweet height of it all
breaking free from a canopy of leaves.
Remember the day
you first took in the night sky?

I mean really let it enter
and unfold along the interior
when the architecture of the body
resembles a cauldron for a dying star,
twinkle twinkle inside, and inside that
a simple hole. So now you know
what it is to be sucking air,
to be walking upright, to love.
Why not enjoy the day,
this moment to moment thing,
and the furnace above sending
you messages: breathe, dummy.
Birds do it and the rest of the ark
all following the great blank of what's next.
What's next is courage.
To take it all in and feel it for keeps,
that persons you meet
have a hole too and a twinkle.
Embrace them and have a meal.
Look straight into their impermanent flash,
the nervous-system tic of their talk.
Welcome their knowing
not knowing their coming and going.

ALBERT GOLDBARTH

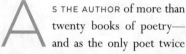

A S THE AUTHOR of more than twenty books of poetry— and as the only poet twice awarded the National Book Critics Circle Award in Poetry—Albert Goldbarth should perhaps best be thought of as an industrial-strength poet. He is as erudite as he is eclectic, and as imaginatively capacious as he is meticulous in his sprawling, protean, and exhilarating poems. A Goldbarth poem can exploit a deft lyricism or unfold an expansive and sweeping meditation. At times narrative, at times incantatory, these poems alter like Transformers right before our eyes, becoming whirling poetic Cuisinarts devouring history, science, myth, sexuality, religion, and the simple sweetness of human perseverance. A Pop culture aficionado, who is a nostalgist at heart (he is a devotee of comics as well as space—and other—toys of times past), Goldbarth prefers the verbal dynamism of American speech at its most raucous, impure, elaborate, and wise. Reading a collection of his poetry is somewhat like attending a multi-ring circus in which the ringmaster, who just moments ago was in the spotlight below you, has now taken the seat by your side and is, with an urgent and alarming intelligence, whispering into your ear.

Albert Goldbarth is Distinguished Professor of Humanities at Wichita State University. His most recent collection is *The Kitchen Sink: New and Selected Poems, 1972–2007*. In addition to his poetry he has published five collections of essays, including *Many Circles*, winner of the PEN West Creative Nonfiction Award. He is also the recipient of the Center for the Study of Science Fiction Theodore Sturgeon Memorial Award.

(ETYMOLOGICALLY) "WORK WORK"

1. GO-PART

Somebody's stuffing excelsior into the penis
of the museum's model aurochs. Somebody's snapping
hundreds of plastic halos into the ruffs of hundreds
of plastic Infants of Prague. Somebody's grading exams.
Somebody's sleeping with the Senator. And
the Senator's promising even more jobs,
more automobile assembly lines, and everything
that means to an edgy electorate. In the kitchen,
tonight, my niece is also putting a car together,
out of equal amounts of concentration and crayon.
"This is the go-part here"—the steering wheel,
obviously. Green by black by red, it takes shape.
And orange hubcaps. She's chewing her lip.
She's driven all night by this labor.

2. SHAHZZUT & TYUPAT

Eno's fingers seem as fat as those Red Hot Mama sausages
suspended in brine in a gallon jar, but under my hood
they tweeze out various ailing gobs with the finicky quickness
of surgical pincers. He lifts some oily puzzle-piece into the equally
oily light of the shop, as if it might explain
gravity or antimatter. "Shahzzut," he explains to me, "tyupat,"
in the secret fraternal language of auto mechanics. He
sings to himself; no one has ever been so happy. He's
fixing my engine, he sings, he's polishing my shahzzut
as if it's the milktooth of a saint. "Man's work,
whatever its ostensible purpose, is, at any given time,
to sustain the universe." Tribals, "asked the reason
for ceremony X, say that if they missed one year,
cosmos, the world, would collapse." (Richard Grossinger)

3. ELEMENTARY

They weren't handed masks, no one knows why.
We're a pile of elements. No one knows why
they weren't handed masks: they were handed
their slop-poles, though. They were handed the poles
and ordered up the inside catwalk, three stories high.

We're a pile of dirt-cheap elements. They
were ordered up the catwalk, they were told to skim
the floating layer of fester off the top of this
three-story drum of byproducts animal blood.
They weren't handed masks. The drum was 103 degrees.
And one was found face-up and one face-down,
caked into the fester by noon.
We're a pile of dirt-cheap elements, bought,
and toyed with, then tossed with the rest of the shit.

4. EASY ENOUGH

In his book explaining quantum physics John Gribbin
writes, "It is easy enough for me to say 'Anderson measured
the curvature of particle trails and found positrons';
it was much harder for him to do the work." All week
that mundane phrase has hummed itself inside my head
like an abracadabra, conjuring up my father, alive
again, and in the makeshift basement workroom
each night totaling those colossal rows of figures in his war
against an enemy alliance: Rent and Food and Clothes.
It's easy enough for me to wring the sweet rag of nostalgia,
now that he's cold dark particle trails himself.
It's easy enough to ennoble him down there: adding,
juggling, adding, with the same bit lip
his granddaughter later inherited. *To do the work.*

5. FRED: ONE

That summer (I was seventeen), the powers of Midwest Mercantile
(Roosevelt Road at Jefferson), seeing my reedy body was no use
shlepping delivery crates, assigned me to Accounting, where
my reedy mind was more disastrous yet: I doubt if four
consecutive numbers fit true. One day in the wake
of a contretemps (with tire jacks and a boot-knife)
at the loading dock, Koenig was canned. Would I
pitch in?—meant tussling one unbudgeable sumo
of a crate in the unbearable sun and stares out there,
and just as I was believing death was preferable,
Fred Nelson (The Black Bull everyone called him) moped
on by, in one hand lifted my butt by my belt *and*
in the other the crate, then carried us both the length of the store
and set us like eggs on the top shelf in Wholesale Drapes.

6. FRED: TWO

In August, Teaberry Polk—a sassy lassie
from the mending room, whose rump thumpthumped in walking
like a pair of bongos—married Fred Nelson. I don't know what
he did or didn't do, if anything, but on the honeymoon night she
went at his clothes in the closet with a kitchen knife, wildly first, and
then methodically, until his sharkskin suits and French-cuffed shirts
were a wall of ribbon, like some avant-garde "art project." Frankly,
I wish my old friend D. had been upfront like that
with my old friend Jack; instead, it was a long-drawn mess
of misread cues, with kids and sanctimonious tears: the acrimony,
alimony, lawyermoney scene. As for my own divorce
—I remember my mother shaking her head. "Oh Albert . . ."
knowing the heart too needs to be a practiced economy
". . . love, shmove. You have to *work* at it."

7. A SOCIAL SECTION

Begging for work. (An out-of-work worker.)
Begging—for work. (A beggar, "working.") Hat out trusting
in coins: and yes we like this one, but not his beggar brother
faking blindness; or the one who pushes this perimeter further,
sneaking purses; or the one so far he's past this
social seventh section, out of the frame of understandable
reference almost completely: slinking shadow to shadow
with hatchet-edge glint. The feral labor living beyond
/and off/ the labor of civilized lives. The drive home
and the back door jimmied. The girlygirl
peddling her honeyspread under "the viaduck" and why
the hell not?—her man be drown this last week
in a drum of blood at the rendering works. Somebody
profiting off this, somebody buying the Senator lunch, sssh.

8. BREWING

Of a favorite labor in literature I sing. Of Miss
Amelia Edwards, Londoner, braving savagery, vast sands,
and not a little of the alien dyspepsia, to the mountains
of Abu Simbel, the two Great Temples there
with their friezes and carven Colossi. It's 1883. It's
unthinkably ancient and new and amazing.
Her work crew ably swabs the face of the northernmost Colossus,

Ramses II, restoring its whitened splotches with coffee,
"swarming all over the huge head . . . Reïs Hassan
artistically touching up a gigantic nose
almost as long as himself. Our cook stood aghast.
Never before had he been called upon to provide
for a guest whose mouth measured three-and-one-half feet . . . .
Ramses' appetite for coffee was prodigious."

9. BONDING

What did I understand? Let's say I was five,
let's say it was Friday, he was bringing me
on the collection route, his salesman smile
in place like a sew-on bowling patch.
The dirty life-cycle of any dollar bill—did I know?
The wheedling and two-bit genuflecting he needed me to see
as professional courtesy—did I see? Did it "take,"
this day of belabored bonding? Was I wiser now?
Time's work is continental drift and the red-shift.
"Opera," "racketeering," "telecommunications"
—workworkwork. On the way home he thumbed a spare coin
at the upturned snap-brim hat of the harmonica beggar
we liked. "So play me a czardas." Well, *sort of* a czardas.
Wheeling me under the skeleton-knocking thunder of the rush-hour el.

10. EASY ENOUGH

It's easy enough for me to wring the sweet rag of nostalgia
—not that bucketsful would make a difference now—
or diddle away at the self-set tasks of the poet:
~~planet shaking~~ skeleton-knocking. "Oh, I've worked *hard*
before this, I once set lobster traps," you always hear
at poetry conventions, "but *nothing's* as difficult as
Selecting The Proper Word!" which is usually just bullshit,
such a bullshit it's not even *real* bullshit, which
weighs down a shovel until the trapezoids scream.
My buddy John once spent a summer hauling cattle,
including hosing the walls of their holding hangar
free of crusted draperies of shit. He did a stint
once in the winter too, and outside of Denver hammered
urine icicles off their pizzle-tips.

11. THE MODES

Someone's busy lawyering: she's torte, she's court,
she's paving over the planet with paperwork justice.
Someone pretending to play a plastic sax with her twat.
The modes of what we call earning a living are the deepness
of the universe in human compactness, and some of it altogether
free of wages: the tomb of the Prophet at Medina was cleaned of dust
by an elder "celebrated for piety and purity" who was lowered
"through a hole in the roof by cords, with directions to wipe it
with his beard" (Sir Richard Francis Burton). *That's*
the work for me! The work for me, each me believes, is
something like being beamed into a spaceship: instantaneous,
acorporeal. But "even angels," says John Donne,
"who are winged, yet had a ladder to go to heaven
by steps"—so, no, there's never an end to it.

12. AN END TO IT

After he retired, after his trophy shelf of crummy
name-plaqued paperweights for *Sales Leader, 19(blahdeblah)*
was plastic'ed-over to keep it free of dust, my father
took up part-time work at a local Shop-Rite,
for minimum wage. He greeted streams of strangers
at the door with that smile he'd used for Metropolitan Life
for thirty-five years and couldn't retire off his face.
The rent wasn't really a problem now—my sister and I
were self-supporting—but every night he returned
to those heavy ledgers in the basement, they were *this*
world's Torah and bore repeated scrutiny, they were a way
of life, were *his* life. When they weren't, one day, he
closed the Book of Life with a slam the nurse's stethoscope
heard, and let them do as they pleased with his smile.

13. A SURVEY

My sister in labor. Labor unions.
Labor law. We can never escape it. The body
asleep is a bellows and a steadily hammered forge.
(Herakleitos: "Even sleepers are doing the world's
work, moving it along a little.") Labor-
atory. So "lab work" comes from (etymologically)
"work work." Skyler earned her pay as a med tech

for a few years; in the lab they had a machine
that shook up cans of patients' shit like one of those
automatic paint can mixers, and one day a can
with too much gas exploded. You can imagine.
The stories! Alice the microbiologist.
Claudia posing nude. My Uncle Lou one evening suddenly
losing his left thumb to the bandsaw.

14. OVER AND OUT

Jack calls from Dallas. He says that city's
crime rate is the highest in the country and
last night his ex-wife saw three shadows
slink from a shadow, then enter another shadow,
waiting. Nothing happened—to her,
but this morning the papers are selling a woman's body
chopped in two. "I went to a pawn shop,
I bought a shotgun." It's something like
a 14-gauge or a 22-gauge—I know nothing about these
arsenal terms, to me it's all statistics
from the dark side of the moon. "So that's protection
aplenty?" I venture. He pumps it. My phone fills
with the sound of an Exxon oil tanker cracking in half.
"Oh, it'll do the job," he says.

JORIE GRAHAM

J ORIE GRAHAM WAS one of the first outspo-
kenly hybrid poets in the United States.
While her early work was firmly grounded
in the post-Confessional lyric, she began incorporating startling stylistic devices
in her third collection, *The End of Beauty*, in 1987. Inaugurating rather than fol-
lowing trends, she has continued to expand her forms in an attempt to chart the
individual mind as it negotiates its interface with history. In recent work, she
has fused the historical with the political to underscore not only poetry's social
potential but its social obligations. Steeped in philosophy and the visual arts,
Graham augments her stylistic hybridity with an interdisciplinary inclusivity
reminiscent of Pound, all without losing the sensuality of her language, which
uses its music to keep the reader's rational and emotional registers in play.

Jorie Graham was born in New York City and spent her youth in Italy. She
is the author of numerous collections of poetry, including the most recent, *Sea
Change*, and *The Dream of the Unified Field: Selected Poems 1974–1994*, which won
the 1996 Pulitzer Prize for Poetry. She has also edited two anthologies, *Earth
Took of Earth: 100 Great Poems of the English Language* and *The Best American Poetry
1990*. Graham's many honors include a John D. and Catherine T. MacArthur
Fellowship and the Morton Dauwen Zabel Award from the American Academy
of Arts and Letters. She has taught at the Iowa Writers' Workshop and is cur-
rently Boylston Professor of Rhetoric and Oratory at Harvard University. From
1997 to 2003, she served as a Chancellor of the Academy of American Poets.

DAWN DAY ONE

(DEC 21 '03)

A gunshot. The second, but the first I heard.
Then the walls of the room, streaked with first light, shot
                                  into place.
Then, only then, did my eyes open.
We come about first, into waking, as an *us*, I
think. Sometime between the first and second instant
there is still the current that carries one in
and deposits one in singleness. The body's weight is
a beaching. Back behind, or underneath: infinity
or something which has no consequence. Then consequence, which
feels like walls and the uprighting of self one has to do
in them, then the step one has to take once roused, and how it
puts one back on the walking-path one stepped off of
last night. Zeno reasoned we would
never get there. Reason in fact never gets there.
But we step back onto the path each time.
How long have you been yours, are you tired, are you
in a hurry, are you sitting down, is that stillness
still your pathway which you enter
                     now only with
your mind—which keeps on stepping mind you—
until it doesn't and the stopping
                     happens again.
Are your eyes shut? I put cream on my lids
and rub it in. I feel my eyes in there under the skin.
How impersonal are they, these hardnesses, barely
attached, in their loosely protected sacks.
Tony tells me how, in the lab, they cast an image
—a cross in this case—onto the gaze of a monkey then
                             "sacrifice
the monkey" and how, when examined, the neurons in the
                         visual cortex
actually form the imprint of
the cross. It would have been, the cross (except under very
                 unusual circumstances), erased
by the next image. Hence the need for
sacrifice. Of what is it made, I ask. Of cells, of *active*
cells, he says. Is it imprinted, I ask. No. It
would have disappeared and been replaced except

the creature was stilled. I like it they
use the word *stilled*. Then the back
of the cave in there with its cross of cells. Which will
dissolve as the "next instant." Some arguments
continue this way ad infinitum. And
infinitum *is* one path, but you can't
really get onto its promenade, its boardwalk, by
speculation. "Therefore" is another way to walk,
therefore the fast Achilles can never best the slow
tortoise. Zeno inferred yet another way.
And yes, now space and time can be subdivided
infinitely many times. But isn't this sad?
By now hasn't a sadness crept in?
I put my hands over both my eyes and lie
still. I think. The paradox says that you can never leave
the room in which you are right now. First walk
half the distance to the door, then half again, and so on. These eyes,
under my hands, I looked at in the mirror yesterday.
Everything of course was silver, my skin, my gaze,
and then the eyes, held in
                    their lids.
Looked hard into that room.
Looked everywhere, all the way to the back. The
                            back
                        tells me
I have to come back here, here to the front, there is
no further I can go. One takes smaller and smaller steps
according to Zeno to try to leave the room. If you return now
to the glass, you can look *at* your eyes. After a short
time, very short if you hold fast, don't blink, just stare,
you will be looking at *an other*. A silver one. I promise
you, go do it now, you will see it, it is not you.
It is more exactly not-you than anyone you've
ever seen. Keep staring. Even Achilles must take
smaller and smaller steps. Even so he can never win.
Before Zeno there was Pythagoras. Before Pythagoras humans
did not understand—that is the verb that is used—that results
had to be proved. That there is an edifice
you can build, level upon level, from first principles,
using axioms, using logic. Finally you have a house
which houses you. Now look at you.
Are you an entire system of logic and truth?
Are you a pathway with no body ever really on it?

Are you shatterable if you took your fist now to
this face that looks at you as you hold to your stare?
Here. You are at the beginning of something. At the exact
beginning. Ok. This is awakening
number two in here, in this poem. Then there are
these: me: you: you *there*. I'm actually staring up at
you, you know, right here, right from the pool of this page.
Don't worry where else I am, I am here. Don't
worry if I'm still alive, you are.

LITTLE EXERCISE

The screen is full of voices, all of them holding their tongues.
Certain things have to be "undergone," yes.
To come to a greater state of consciousness, yes.

Let the face show itself through the screen.
Let the organizing eyes show themselves.
Let them float to the surface of this shine and glow there.

The world now being killed by its children. Also its guests.
An oracle?—a sniper, a child beater, a dying parent in the house,
a soil so overfed it cannot hold a root system in place?
Look—the slightest wind undoes the young crop.

Are we "beyond salvation"? Will you not speak?
Such a large absence—shall it not compel the largest presence?
Can we not break the wall?
And can it please *not be a mirror* lord?

DUSK SHORE PRAYER

The creeping revelation of shoreline.
The under-shadowed paisleys scripting wave-edge down-
                                        slope
on the barest inclination, sun making of each
                milelong wave-retreat
a golden translucent forward downgoing,
golden sentences writ on clearest moving waters,
moving their meaninglessness on (not *in*) the moving of the
                                waters

(which feels tugged)(the rows of scripting
       [even though it's a trick] adamant with
self-unfolding)(wanting the eye to catch and take
dominant final-hold, feel the thickest rope of
        waterlipped
        scripting
to be a producing of a thing that speaks [to whom
one does not know, but a true speech])—to believe this truly,
         not in metaphor—
to put it in the blank in which one *sees*,
and then into the blank in which one *is*,
to separate *I am* from *I have being* from *I am
apart*. And not to want to *be*. And never to be
emptied by the wound of meaning.
The gash of likeness. The stump interpretation.
Spelled from the living world. Grown sharper by
this sighting. As sun goes down. Until it glimmers in
the tiny darkness and the human will comes to the end.
Having it go before one's looking goes. The summer
at one's back. The path back barely findable.

EBBTIDE

I am a frequency, current flies through. One has
       to ride
       the spine.
No peace [of mind][of heart], among the other
frequencies. How often and how hard are answerings.
The surf, receding, leaves successive
hem-line trims of barely raised institching sand—
bridal-wreath puckerings—
glassy (this side), packed smooth (that).
Making one's way one sees the changes.
What took place before one
       looked.
Snakeskin of darker sands in with the light.
Slightly more raised and wider alligator-skins.
Crabtracks' wild unfocusings around firm holes.
The single tubefish, dead, long as a snake, half-snout,
rolled over and over as the waves pick up, return, return
less often, go away. For a while he is incandescent

white, then blue, deep green, then white again, until he's
                                    left, half-turned,
eyes sandy till one wave, come back
this far as if in error, cleans him off.
Greenish with rising/falling weed-debris, shoremist
fingering long streaks of sun.
Graphed beachlength on the scallop-edged lapping retreat:
                        christmas-ornament red shrimp
punctually along the highs of each
upskirting arc—prongs upright,
stiff. Swift ticks of sunlight count them
                        out.
Who has enough? A little distance
                        back
two vultures feeding on a pelican. Later, claws and beak
float in the brack. Foam-bits lace-up the edge
of the retreat. Something feels like it's not
coming back. In the tidepool
sand-grains advance along a long
walled avenue, in ranks—at the conjunction of
                        two rocks, algae
signaling the entry point—(swarming but
                        swaying in
unison, without advancing) (waiting for
                        some arrival)
(the channel of them quickening)(the large espousal)(light
beginning now to *touch* what had been only
                        underwater story)—
until the gleaming flow of particles is finally
                        set down, is
                        stilled: the grains
drop down and mat, silt in, begin to dry: the wandering tribe is
                                    gone, the
city's gone, the waiting gone. The individual grains
are not discernible. I'm squatting so I hear
sand sucking water in. Gravity. Glistening.
I take a stick and run it through
the corridor of wilderness.
It fills a bit with water the first time. Is self-erased.
The second time it does not fill. It leaves a
                        mark where

my stick ran. I make
another (cursive) mark. How easily it bends to cursive, snakes towards
                                                                    thought.
                                                           Looking back
I see the birds eating the bird. The other way my
gaze can barely reach shore-break.
The (little) weight of the stick in my hand. The meditation
place demands. My frequency. This hand, this
sugar-stalk. The cane-fields in the back of us,
the length of tubefish back there too. And
if I write my name. And how mist rounds the headland
                                          till the sea
is gone. One feels word should be sent us
from some source. It is all
roar and cry and suck and snap. The pebbles on the
pebbles roll. One feels one has in custody
what one cannot care for for long. Too much is
asked. Nothing is coming back the way it was.
But one can wait for the next hem, next bride,
next oscillation, comedy. Done, the birds fly
off. I can see through the trees,
through the cane grove, palm grove, out far enough into
                                          the clearing where
the spine of the picked-clean story shines.

BARBARA GUEST

BARBARA GUEST WAS one of the most consistently experimental writers of the twentieth century; throughout her long career, she constantly changed her style and approach, both learning from and contributing to the most important developments in American poetry, while at the same time always maintaining a driving tension between lyrical intensity and concrete immediacy. She emerged as a writer in New York at the beginning of the New York School, and was one of the few women presented in Donald Allen's *New American Poetry*. Her publishing history says much about her career—her first book, *The Location of Things*, came out in 1960 from Tibor de Nagy, the tireless supporter of the New York School poets and Abstract Expressionist painters. Her next few books were published by large New York houses—Doubleday and Viking—but she then chose to go with smaller, more experimental presses: Burning Deck, Sun & Moon, Black Sparrow, Kelsey Street, and Post-Apollo.

During the eighties and nineties, Guest's work became associated with the Language school as she increasingly experimented with both a loose referentiality and an active use of white space and the visual possibilities of the page. In the last decade of her life, her work shifted again toward an emotional precision and clarity of image that yet resists encapsulation—ambiguity and indeterminacy continue to keep her poems open. She was also an innovator in genre: many of her texts blend poetry with literary criticism, art criticism, and the essay, while her novel *Seeking Air* has a distinctly poetic flow, and her acclaimed biography of HD, *Herself Defined*, breaks up the traditional chronological structure. Barbara Guest wrote numerous plays, as well as art criticism for journals such as *ARTnews* and *Art in America*, and she took her work beyond language in collaborations with several visual artists.

The author of twenty-nine books, Guest received numerous awards and honors, including two America Awards for Literature from the Contemporary Art Council; the Longwood Award; the Columbia Book Award; and the Frost Medal for Lifetime Achievement from the Poetry Society of America. She lived for the last eleven years of her life in the San Francisco Bay Area.

DISSONANCE ROYAL TRAVELLER

          sound opens sound
shank of globe   strings floating out

    something like images are here
    opening up avenues to view a dome

a distant clang reaches the edifice.

   understanding what it means
   to understand music

cloudless movement   beyond the neck's reach

an hypnotic lull in porcelain   water break   mimics

tonality   crunch of sand under waddling

   a small seizure
   from monumentality

    does not come or go   with understanding

the path will end
birdhouse   of trembling cotton

or dream   expelled it
parcel   on the landlocked moor.

        explaining music
and their clothes entangled
who walk into a puddle of minnows;
      minnows in a bowl
consonant with water.

the drifted footpad

    ambushed by reeds signals the listening
    oars.

        music disappears into oars.

in the middle the world is brown;
on the opposite side of the earth
an aroma of scarlet.

this accompanies our hearing music;
the sleeve of heaven
and the hoof of earth
loosed from their garrison.

dissonance may abandon *miserere*
on bruised knee hasten to the idol.

and what is consonance—the recluse—

entering and exiting
as often as a monarch butterfly
touches a season;

by accident grips the burning flowers.

in the stops between terror
the moon aflame on its plaza.

autumn of rippling wind
and the noise of baskets
smell of tin fists.

and harsh fists
on the waterfall changing the season;
the horse romps in flax
a carboard feature
creating a cycle of flax.

   music imagines this cardboard

the horse in cardboard jacket
    flagrant the ragged sleeve

       red summit red.

  dissonance royal traveller

       altered the red saddle.

A MEDIEVAL HOLLOW

                                    Smother
floating in air headgear lit
                              "Light,
splendour, beauty, form, rule of the world"
                                    Alan of Lille.

Dwarfs assemble with hook and thong,
tracing rivulets, plane trees, tidying rooks,
passing papers, muddling Thomistic drafts
while monks shift their garments and a thud
says fallen dwarf "ach" cries the priest
over the ink blot he has ruined November and
the plowing . . .

Aflutter with pagan tales the Mong Chieftain
spreads his rug the acrobat turns milk weeps,

From turf and dugget
hospice in a wafer
evensong alone in swaddled clothes she holds

No more trees
building on top of building
the archbishop fetched by a donkey.

Medieval surrenders by tallow light
labbed and lobbled into cellars
strew garters tightening in the gyre

Simples sail in light hosen
their glides make a run for the moat
before it closes for the bridge crowd
in dank and fuses,

Plunging into a hollow
a hoard limits profits on sibilant limbs
and gaited throbbers braiding hair
look at the vision sitting on mud.

Under the bowed blue
in rhythmic joust pattern shadewise

gauntlets toss lances the moon
rises edging green Mundis,
gentle equerry the plague killed him.

Shut off that inner sound,
a fierce place needed douce
more than amethyst
dealt a rat lust,

Living in medieval hollow
went into tatters

Mute tambour mute viol
thrown out of the welkin.

from STRIPPED TALES

            klebnikov   *lootage*

Velimir they broke into thy *Baku* house and drank from thy cup of

numbers and Destiny improved their zero.

                    ■   ■   ■

            the moment
                a noun

                    from porridge to velvet dubious

oh disasters   factories   memory and actors   dossiers

a name   piloting balls of speech   worm balls and grape kites

        literature   single-mindedness

            settles into space

                    ■   ■   ■

law
The lady protests she reserves the right to select her
own ghost should you from the parlor call "mine" and where
were thee when grief doubled over the lithe figure running

said "mine."

> *of the ether*

THE IMAGINED ROOM

Do not forget the sky has other zones.

Let it rest on the embankment, close the eyes,

Lay it in the little bed made of Maplewood.
Wash its sleeve in sky drops.

Let there be no formal potions.
A subject and a predicate made of glass.

You have entered the narrow zone
your portrait etched in glass.

Becoming less and less until the future faces you
like the magpie you hid,
exchanging feathers for other feathers.

In the tower you flew without wings
speaking in other tongues to the imagined room.

A SHORT NARRATIVE

Your painting took a long time to dry.
It was sent to Rome to give it a royal luster.

Your thoughts the evening before had been gloomy.
They would not forget rumors accompanying you.

Lo, Royalty had placed a hand on your head.

Nobles twist their rings in corridors,
worried about painting's future.

ALTERATION

In the sky a dilemma. Fountains rush by.
Home from the tournament beasts seek quiet.

Writing covers the desk.

       Your colonization of the infinite

       is a romantic departure.

I ask you to permit the image

       and the alteration of time.

ROBERT HASS

ONSIDERED BY MANY to be the master of the personal lyric, Robert Hass also experiments with thought's ruptures. He has the ability to connect readers to the intimacies of daily life through attention to the details of lived experience, but can also reveal that experience as not necessarily seamless, not always coherent. For instance, in "Time and Materials," the title poem to his most recent collection, words break up and break down to form lines such as "In rogres f ever hing at xists." Hass balances such innovative realism with an interest in ethics and skepticism toward American Romanticism. Often his signature meditative tone and pace is complicated—even troubled— by issues of cultural collapse and linguistic indeterminacy, situating his aesthetic versatility in the liminal zone between modernist practice and the recursive play of postmodernism.

Robert Hass grew up in the San Francisco Bay Area and attended St. Mary's College and Stanford University. His earlier collections of poetry include *Field Guide* (winner of the Yale Younger Poets Prize), *Praise*, *Human Wishes*, and *Sun Under Wood* (which received the National Book Critics Circle Award in Poetry). For many years, he collaborated with Czeslaw Milosz on translations of Milosz's work. Hass's numerous honors include a John D. and Catherine T. MacArthur Fellowship, a National Book Critics Circle Award in Criticism for his collection of essays, *Twentieth Century Pleasures*, and both the Pulitzer Prize and the National Book Award for his most recent collection, *Time and Materials*. He served as U.S. Poet Laureate from 1995 to 1997 and is currently a Chancellor of the Academy of American Poets. He teaches at the University of California at Berkeley.

TIME AND MATERIALS

—Gerhard Richter, *Abstrakt Bilden*

1

To make layers,
As if they were a steadiness of days:

It snowed; I did errands at a desk;
A white flurry out the window thickening; my tongue
Tasted of the glue on envelopes.

On this day sunlight on red brick, bare trees,
Nothing stirring in the icy air.

On this day a blur of color moving at the gym
Where the heat from bodies
Meets the watery, cold surface of the glass.

Made love, made curry, talked on the phone
To friends, the one whose brother died
Was crying and thinking alternately,
Like someone falling down and getting up
And running and falling and getting up.

2

The object of this poem is not to annihila
To not annih
The object of this poem is to report a theft,
    In progress, of everything
That is not these words
    And their disposition on the page.

The object o   f this poem is to report a theft,
    In progre   ss of everything that exists
That is not th   ese words
    And their d   isposition on the page.

The object of his poe is t epor a theft
    In rogres f ever hing at xists
Th is no   ese w rds
    And their disp sit on o the pag

3

To score, to scar, to smear, to streak,
To smudge, to blur, to gouge, to scrape.

'Action painting,' i.e.,
The painter gets to behave like time.

4

The typo wound be 'paining.'

(To abrade.)

5

Or to render time and stand outside
The horizontal rush of it, for a moment
To have the sensation of standing outside
The greenish rush of it.

6

Some vertical gesture then, the way that anger
Or desire can rip a life apart,

Some wound of color.

". . . WHITE OF FORGETFULNESS, WHITE OF SAFETY"

My mother was burning in a closet.

Creekwater wrinkling over stones.

Sister Damien, in fifth grade, loved teaching mathematics.
Her full white sleeve, when she wrote on the board,
Swayed like the slow movement of a hunting bird,
Egret in the tidal flats,
Swan paddling in a pond.

Let A equal the distance between x and y.

The doves in the desert,
Their cinnamon coverts when they flew.

People made arguments. They had reasons for their appetites.
A child could see it wasn't true.

In the picture of the Last Supper on the classroom wall,
All the apostles had beautiful pastel robes,
Each one the color of a flavor of sherbet.

A line is the distance between two points.

A point is indivisible.

Not a statement of fact; a definition.

It took you a second to understand the difference,
And then you loved it, loved reason,
Moving as a swan moves in a mill stream.

I would not have betrayed the Lord
Before the cock crowed thrice,
But I was a child, what could I do
When they came for him?

Ticking heat, the scent of sage,
Of pennyroyal. The structure of every living thing
Was praying for rain.

RUSIA EN 1931

The archbishop of San Salvador is dead, murdered by no one knows
who. The left says the right, the right says provocateurs.

But the families in the barrios sleep with their children beside them and
a pitchfork, or a rifle if they have one.

And posterity is grubbing in the footnotes to find out who the bishop is,

or waiting for the poet to get back to his business. Well, there's this:

her breasts are the color of brown stones in moonlight, and paler in
moonlight.

And that should hold them for a while. The bishop is dead. Poetry
proposes no solutions: it says justice is the well water of the city of
Novgorod, black and sweet.

César Vallejo died on a Thursday. It might have been malaria, no one is
sure; it burned through the small town of Santiago de Chuco in an
Andean valley in his childhood; it may very well have flared in his veins
in Paris on a rainy day;

and nine months later Osip Mandelstam was last seen feeding off the
garbage heap of a transit camp near Vladivostok.

They might have met in Leningrad in 1931, on a corner; two men about
forty; they could have compared gray hair at the temples, or compared
reviews of *Trilce* and *Tristia* in 1922.

What French they would have spoken! And what the one thought would
save Spain killed the other.

"I am no wolf by blood," Mandelstam wrote that year. "Only an equal
could break me."

And Vallejo: "Think of the unemployed. Think of the forty million
families of the hungry. . . ."

THE YELLOW BICYCLE

The woman I love is greedy,
but she refuses greed.
She walks so straightly.
When I ask her what she wants,
she says, "A yellow bicycle."

Sun, sunflower,
coltsfoot on the roadside,
a goldfinch, the sign
that says Yield, her hair,
cat's eyes, his hunger
and a yellow bicycle.

Once, when they had made love in the middle of the night and
it was very sweet, they decided they were hungry, so they got up,
got dressed, and drove downtown to an all-night donut shop.
Chicano kids lounged outside, a few drunks, and one black man
selling dope. Just at the entrance there was an old woman in a
thin floral print dress. She was barefoot. Her face was covered
with sores and dry peeling skin. The sores looked like raisins and
her skin was the dry yellow of a parchment lampshade ravaged by
light and tossed away. They thought she must have been hungry
and, coming out again with a white paper bag full of hot rolls,
they stopped to offer her one. She looked at them out of her small
eyes, bewildered, and shook her head for a little while, and said
very kindly, "No."

Her song to the yellow bicycle:
The boats on the bay
have nothing on you,
my swan, my sleek one!

THE GARDEN OF DELIGHT

The floor hurts so much it whines
whichever way they step,
as if it had learned the trick
of suffering.
Poor floor.
This is the garden of delight,
a man pointing at a woman
and a bird perched
on a cylinder of crystal
watching. She has a stopper
in her mouth or the paint
has blistered, long ago, just there.
He looks worried, but not terrified,
not terrified, and he doesn't move.
It's an advantage of paintings.
You don't have to.
I used to name the flowers—
beard tongue, stone crop,
pearly everlasting.

LYN HEJINIAN

ONE OF THE principal writers associated with West Coast Language poetry, Lyn Hejinian has expanded her work over the years to incorporate narrative, lyricism, and philosophical speculation. Her 1980 classic *My Life* recast subjectivity along postmodern lines, yet also reinvested the text with intimacy, making a distinction between the intimate and the personal that has informed American poetry ever since. Some of her more recent books have focused on reconfiguring genre, including *Oxota: A Short Russian Novel*, which plays with the traditions of the novel; *Composition of the Cell*, which explores the boundaries of literary criticism; and *Happily*, which uses the aphorism to ponder our notions of fate.

Editing has also been an important part of Hejinian's work. Co-editor with Barrett Watten of *Poetics Journal* from 1981 to 1999, she was the founder and publisher of the Tuumba Press series, a project that epitomizes the role that women played in broadening experimentalism in the late twentieth century. During the late nineties, she co-founded a second press with Travis Ortiz called Atelos, which commissions and publishes cross-genre work by poets. She is also known as a critic and essayist, particularly for her collection *The Language of Inquiry*, and she has worked on numerous projects with artists in different media, such as the painter Emily Clark, the filmmaker Jacki Ochs, and the musician John Zorn. Hejinian has done extensive work in Russian translation, concentrating on the poetry of Arkadii Dragomoshchenko, and visiting Russia several times for lectures and readings. Elected a fellow of the Academy of American Poets in 2000, she is on the faculty at the University of California at Berkeley.

from THE BEGINNER

This is a good place to begin.

From something.

Something beginning in an event that beginning overrides.

Doubt instruction light safety fathom blind.

In the doorway is the beginning thus and thus no denial.

A little beat of time, a little happiness quite distinct from misery as yet.

The sun shines.

The sun is perceived as a bear, then a boat, then an instruction: see.

The sun is a lily, then a whirlpool turning a crowd.

The shadows lengthen, the sun-drenched line of arriving strangers are all admitted, seen in the day and not the same at night, host and guest alike.

Two things then, both occurring as the beginner arrives: acceptance and the reconstruction of the world which that acceptance implies.

In the first twenty-four hours nearly blind and with hands swelling, the gaze fierce, face scowling, the beginner faces scowling.

The beginner is a figure of contradiction, conditions what has begun.

Someone could say clouds suddenly, correctly, there's a change in the low-lying blue, the space for it having diminished, its limits are almost certainly black.

Yes, black is right, it's for certainty, yellow for cattle, brown for the violin, pink is fortuitous except in flowers especially the rose, rose is for the rose, gray for clocks and the time they keep, orange for lips or for cups, also sponges, ochre for shadows at noon and sleep, silver for fish and memory, fissures and their accompanying sentiment, gold for blue and iconography and geographical distance, red is for the forest and for the alphabet, blue is for intelligence, purple for the old neighbors smelling of wool, green is for sweat, and out of white comes what we can say.

The face is made from paste and paper, this is what's known as clay, the skull is formed of clay supported by feeling twigs into which feeling flows.

Some degree of risk is involved, but no one pities the beginner.

How can they until he or she has begun (to be pitiable or enviable, happy or sad (one can't experience happiness without catching a glimpse of life (February 1) since that's what happiness is: the awareness of the sensation of having seen something of life), rich or poor (money is both signifier and signified, and poverty is like the notorious gap between them (February 5)), well or ill (inevitably in the course of time one will be both, though for some wellness is the norm and illness the marked condition (for these people illness is an injury) while for others it's the other way around (illness befalling the ill is an insult)), etc.).

And then it's too late for pity.

If in the 19th century, as Gertrude Stein said, people saw parts and tried to assemble them into wholes, while in the 20th century people envisioned wholes and then sought parts appropriate to them, will the 21st century carry out a dissemination of wholes into all parts and thus finish what the 19th century began (February 7)?

Even when nothing happens there is always waiting submerged in the task of beginning and task it is in thoughts to begin afresh.

The beginner makes a beginning, and if optimism is in the air (or pessimism, that mordant state of mind that says things can't possibly improve), the beginner proclaims it a good place to begin.

That is beginning.

Something and other things in a sequence simultaneously.

Ants on a white sill buried.

A harbinger in the light.

A child composed nudely.

A side of a tree cut into squares at a shout from a man under an umbrella.

A furtive marked moth fluttering into a beam of light.

A woman at a door falling.

The beginner is diverted.

Follow me.

[. . .]

Time matters to experts but it is everything to beginners, who don't want to get up in the dark unnecessarily any more than anyone else but who don't want to be left in the dark either, they don't want to miss out on life, hardly anyone does, though I'm not such a beginner myself as to deny that some do, some come to that, to wanting to be left in the dark, that is, yes.

One "comes in from the dark," that's the phrase we use, the room (a room just like the one in the book in which it will later be described) metonymically representing the realm of perceptibility, plenitude, and light, the dark representing the void, the casting of things into invisibility and hence into imperceptibility, into absence, and out of experience, yet to begin.

"I," in cease continuing, weigh without erasing.

"I" in piracy on a porch, a pilot coming through the dark over a city, hide from war.

"I" in my own idea of what must be inevitably never preclude outbursts.

It's not I doing it all, the buttering and alphabetizing.

It's impossible to collate all the changes of mind that bring us things hard to catalogue.

Things we can't change —specific dreams or deaths, griefs, gifts drawing close—we can't edge.

Can we hesitate?

It takes more than seeing a piebald horse browsing beside a murky pond and more than being Anna Karenina to figure out what and what besides.

It takes observing for example, but the example itself will surely change.

It takes leaning a long bicycle against a smudged wall and stumbling over a bent bicycle beside a sucking ditch to distinguish between *against* and *beside*.

It takes arguing with a person against an idea and declaring that one is bound for the hills and experiencing a sensation of momentum beyond all expectation and declaring this a sky beside which nothing is more blue to distinguish between *against* and *for* and *beyond* and *beside*, which is to say there's no end to it, which is to say we're getting to it now.

There's an infinite connection to perform.

No stop.

We subtract, loop, erase, rope, return to zero, tug, and begin over again.

Things give way, then things assert.

They appear in photographs.

"When I was 14 I went to Spain.

"One early morning in Seville I left the hotel (of which I remember nothing but deep gloom) and walked into the exhilarating but devastating sunlight that seemed to hover, to cascade, to penetrate like some philosophical quandary.

"Could fate exist without us?

"No matter the answer, I was frightened.

"I saw a small donkey; though it was trotting toward me—because I was sad—it was absolutely still" is such a photograph.

But now the things in it have given way, yielding to different assertions.

[. . .]

I'm beginning, and thinking that I think myself launched into something, but the actual beginning has occurred long before and as a result the thought that "I'm beginning" is not a beginning but a pause, a phrase, though one incorporated into a beginning (the beginning concealed around it).

Each pause or phrase in when as a beginning.

Each pause or phrase in and as a troubling.

A spidering.

All that occurs does so in many ways.

But the past has not yet withdrawn from a beginner.

A small group of people has gathered in anticipation of an event (say, seeing a whale).

If they see one, they will do so only momentarily, becoming open to doubt.

The past is concealed in doubt.

Say someone gazes at the sea for a long time in the hope of glimpsing a whale.

Then—very briefly—he or she looks aside (perhaps, for example, at another whale watcher).

"Oh!" the other says.

Somewhere out there a whale has sounded (breathed), but the one who looked aside has missed it.

But I can't yet say that whales bear no relation to this beginner.

Character is bound to developments in "the drama of consciousness."

Plot evolves in things experienced.

One proceeds physically into the physical.

But consider the duty problem (and the coerciveness of the American sense of duty).

Plan: to devote 20 minutes (or thereabouts) each morning to improvisational writing so as to gain facility, explore thought layers and conceptual connections, and to discover metonyms and (?) psychonyms.

In dreams, there are things to which words are applicable or attached.

These words aren't naming the things but "dimly, a thousand associations."

Plan with optimism, a new note, singing.

There is something to do.

It is coming out nicely.

from THE COMPOSITION OF THE CELL

1.1	It is the writer's object to supply
1.6	Rocks are emitted by sentences to the eye.
2.13	Circumstances rest between rocks
2.14	The person of which I speak is between clocks.
3.1	Exploration takes extra words.
3.4	The words anticipate an immoderate time and place.
3.5	Reality circulates making objects appear as if they belong where they are.
4.2	Exactly!
5.8	The sky pours shape into intervals.
5.9	Those between seeing and believing.
5.10	An individual requires an individualism which disbelieves.
6.12	And commiserating sunlight.
7.1	Nature as hypotenuse.
7.12	A door substitute.
8.3	It is the writer's emphasis to detail hundreds of times—or there will be no poetic . . .
9.13	. . . increments (like difference, longevity, and velocity).
10.14	Are details bound to objects and are the objects cathartic?
10.15	There is absolutely no catharsis.
11.2	This presents a problem of boundaries.
11.10	So a woman compensates by letting others get in line ahead of her.
12.2	Space accumulates in a far larger tub.

13.4   Unless you could say that the psyche itself is a mistake.

13.5   I pose a question and immediately the psyche pops up.

14.2   Then we may be hearing the social increase.

14.11   Sex, in this context, represents a human hilariously building.

15.3   Every place the imagination occurs replace it with the word "language."

16.3   In passing between these compounds, the mind will feel shocks of difference.

17.1   When I say "equals" I don't mean indifference but distance.

18.2   The lung is not the articulate organ of poetry.

19.10   I think, and that is the reason I learned to talk.

20.7   It was a question of scale.

20.8   It is erotic when parts exceed their scale.

21.4   A drop of water is thrown off by the stove.

22.4   Love.

23.4   People see faces in everything.

24.4   My portrait is a bowl and I tap it with a spoon.

24.7   The clink of psyche on the clay of history.

25.1   The world shows and it receives worldwide attention.

26.7   One wants to be disembodied and at large in it.

27.3   Ellipsis, slab, cognition—these aren't pretty words, but the imagination can't help watching itself

28.9   I've thought that many times—myopia exacerbates the psychosomatic.

28.12   And fate is convex, like an eyeball.

29.12   Also the wind is round.

30.1   I closed my mind in order to sleep with objectivity and modesty.

30.16   A person has deliberately to keep all that can be seen in.

31.4   But this posture inclines one to feel elated.

32.8   Two people cannot be bare at the same time—they have to exchange visibility.

33.10   Shelter and respite are not what's intended by their exaggerated reality.

34.1   The psyche circulates.

34.6   Thus I can still say that I do not intend to be the end result of anything.

from THE BOOK OF A THOUSAND EYES

Then the fourth night began. Through the open window I heard the falsetto of a singing man. One of the triplets couldn't sleep and brought me a book to read. She sat on my lap.

I opened the book.

Once . . . (I began)

Why singing threatened a singing man

Once a girl became a nightingale just as the drifting light on that particular late afternoon was turning purple under enormous winter clouds. A moment later a storm began—a dazzling murky wind shattered the shadows of the trees.

Is it true that men sing for themselves and not for others? the nightingale girl asked no one and nothing in particular. She had always wondered whether birds were miserable in stormy weather and she was discovering that they were not. She wanted to communicate this information. I have very little to say to myself, she said, and the sound of her voice trembled in the air. The rain swirled like silt in a racing tide refusing to fall.

> bird
> of music word
> in a well again
> well
> word aloud

Birds nest in their omnipotent meditations. What but these are the contents of mature development?

A fugitive was running from shadow to shadow below, afraid of . . . but no story should speak only of the past. We sing to be ourselves tomorrow, he said to no one or nothing in particular.

There was no answering sound.

O, he said to himself in the silence of his thoughts—inflexible nightmare!—I've been doomed to silence:

> dawns descend
> on dawns
> in darks
> from tree to tree

BRENDA HILLMAN

I N HER FIRST two collections, *White Dress* and *Fortress*, Brenda Hillman investigated the limits of the lyric. With each subsequent book, she has grown increasingly intrepid, often inventing formal constructs for poetry that invoke Gnosticism, alchemy, and other esoteric doctrines. These transformations are evident in *Bright Existence* (a companion to an original pastoral book-length elegy, *Death Tractates*), and later in *Loose Sugar*. Her works often bring together ecopoetics, feminism, and myth in ways that are political as well as personal. In her most recent work—the first volumes of a proposed tetralogy engaged with the earth's elements—Hillman has most powerfully broken new stylistic ground. In *Cascadia* ("earth"), she takes California's geography and geology as the topos for meditations on consciousness and on historical disjunction; in *Pieces of Air in the Epic* ("air"), she expands our understanding of the medium we breathe, restoring notions of physical and poetic space that are both familiar and magical.

In addition to her seven collections of poetry, Brenda Hillman is also co-editor of *The Grand Permission: New Writings on Poetics and Motherhood*. Born in Tucson, Arizona, she attended Pomona College and the University of Iowa. Her honors include a Guggenheim Foundation Fellowship, the Delmore Schwartz Memorial Award for Poetry, the Poetry Society of America's Norma Farber First Book Prize, an NEA grant, and the William Carlos Williams Prize for Poetry. She is currently the Olivia Filippi Professor of Poetry at St. Mary's College in Moraga, California.

BLACK SERIES

—Then in the scalloped leaves of the plane tree
a series of short, sharp who's:
a little owl had learned to count.

You lay in your bed as usual not existing
because of the bright edges pressing in.

All at once the black thick o's of the owl
were the very diagram you needed.
Where there had been two
kinds of infinity, now there was one.
The smudged circle around the soul
was the one the Gnostics saw around the cosmos,
the mathematical
toy train, the snake eating its tail.

Relieved by the thought that the owl's o's
had changed but not you, that something
could change but not be lost in you,

you asked the voice for more
existence and the voice said
yes but you must understand
I loved you not despite your great emptiness
but because of your great emptiness—

SEDIMENTS OF SANTA MONICA

A left margin watches the sea floor approach

It takes 30 million years
It is the first lover

More saints   Augustine's mother

A girl in red shorts shakes Kafka's *The Trial*
Free of some sand

The left margin watches the watcher from Dover

After the twentieth century   these cliffs
Looked like ribbons on braids or dreads

A dream had come over
With a sort of severe leakage

Ah love let us be true to one another

I went down to the ferris wheel
God's Rolodex

There were neon spikes around everyone
Like the Virgin's spikes

Or an old punk's mohawk   Evidence of inner fire

Rode throwing words off   Red current   Light swearing

Ah love   The century
Had become a little drippy at the end

We're still growing but the stitches hurt   *Let us be*

True to one another   for the world

Easy on the myths now
Make it up   Sleep well

STYROFOAM CUP

thou still unravished   thou
thou,   thou bride

thou unstill,
thou unravished   unbride
unthou   unbride

— — —   — — —

LEFT EYE

There's a barrier before between

I think they were trying to write their names on it

The rubbed-looking light   a glare of the all along
Had inserted itself into the nerves' lining

Say you saw it   Be alive
As if comprehension were not to blame

As if autonomy were not to blame
And to the you between us   there could be read
                (a   heap of dirt had been pushed up, outside)

In the numberless
Rumorless
Night   the flame narrative   the flame report

+ + +   + + +

STRING THEORY SUTRA

There are so many types of
"personal" in poetry. The "I" is   a needle some find useful, though
the thread, of course, is shadow.
In writing of experience or beauty,   a cloth emerges as if made
from a twin existence. It's July
4: air is full of mistaken   stars & the wiggly half-zeroes stripes
make when folded into fabric meant
never to touch ground ever again   the curved cloth of Sleeping Beauty
around 1310, decades after the spinning
wheel gathered stray fibers in a   whir of spindles before the swath
of the industrial revolution, & by
1769 a thread stiff enough for   the warp of cotton fabric from
the spinning frame, the spinning jenny,
the spinning "mule" or muslin wheel,   which wasn't patented. By *its*, I
mean *our*, for we would become
what we made. String theory posits   no events when it isn't a

metaphor; donut twists in matter—10
to the minus 33 cm—its
numbers start the world for grown-ups,
& wobbly fibers, coaxed from eternity,
like today so the way people
are proud of their flag can
Blithe astonishment in the holiday music
over the picnickers: a man waves
that both has & hasn't lost
its nature. Unexpected folds are part
kissed by eucalyptus insect noises ^^z-
z~~> crr, making that for you.
Airline pilots wear wool blend flag
ties from Target to protect their

castles, hummed as they sewed
spiral horns with thread so real
by figures in beyond-type garments so
they could ask how to live.
Flying shuttles, 1733, made weaving like
experience, full of terrible accidents &
were made in countries we bombed
in the last war. By *we*
means *the poem*. By *it*, I
mean meanings which hang tatters of
the druid oak with skinny linguistic
branches, Indo-European roots & the
came to me in a dream
beyond time: *love, we are your*
with stereo eyes spoke over my
head. I am a seamstress for
hear. It puts its head on
our laps. Fibers, beauty at a
industry of thought. Threads inspired this
textile picnic: the satin ponytail holder,
saris, shine of the basketball jersey,
turbans, leis over pink shorts, sports
he's like Chekhov, an atheist believer
in what's here—that sometimes, sitting
"God bless you." It seems to
help somewhat. They don't know what
I mean the *internet*. Turns out
all forces are similar to gravity.

inverted fragments like Bay Area poetry;

are stuffed into stems of dates

enter the pipes of a 4.

from his spandex biking outfit, cloth

of form where our park is

Flag cloth has this singing quality.

hearts. Women, making weavings of
                              unicorns in

it floated; these artists were visited

It's all a kind of seam.

progress. Flags for the present war

you mean *they*. By *you* it

dawns' early light in wrinkled sections of

weird particle earth spirits. A voice

shadow thread~~ A little owl

the missing queen. The unicorn can't

low level, fabric styles, the cottage

the gauze pads inside Band-Aids,

bras. A young doctor told us—

with his dying patients, he says,

causes delays between strings; by *they*,

We searched for meaning ceaselessly. By

we I mean *we*. My sisters
& I worked for the missing
aren't. A paradox. There are some
revolutions: rips in matter; the bent
barely mattered any more. Our art
could help take vividness to people
No revolution helped the workers, ever,
very long. Tribes were looser
but not so very always, &
the types of personal in art
World War II. We shall not flag
nor fail, wrote Churchill. O knight,
Je est un autre wrote Rimbaud
the gun-runner. Over & inner &
rips by which the strings are
tethered to their opposites like concepts
will undo. We spoke of meanings.
I, it, we, you, he, they
Colors forgive flags—red as the
fireskirt of the goddess Asherah, white
as the gravity behind her eye,
blue for the horizon unbuttoned so
It's not a choice between art &
life, we know this now, but still:
After the workers' lockout 1922,
owners cut back sweatshop hours to
string & theory makes air seem invented
& perhaps it is, skepticism mixed
singular purpose, we should not act.
To make reality more bearable for
in Southey's journal when a tomb
is opened & the "glow-beast" exits—
revolutionized their work—by *their* I
mean *our*—& cut costs by
continue them & if you do
help the others, don't tell. String theory
'tis of installing provisional governments.
Why was love the meaning thread?
matter what: washable rayon, airport
carpets, checked flannel smocks of nurses,
aprons with insignias or socks people
wear before / during sexual thrills after
t-shirts worn by crowds in raincoats.

queen: she said: be what you

nots inside our fabric whirred &

but only if they had food.

than nations, nations did some good

turned & turned. Nylon parachutes for

tie our scarf on your neck.

code. The unicorn, *c'est moi*. The

of an art which each example

am, is, are sick about America.

the next world can get through.

How shall we live ? *O shadow thread.*

44 per week. The slippage between

with fear that since nothing has

some besides ourselves? There's a moment

right when the flying shuttle has

half. So lines are cut to

posits symmetry or weight. My country

Textiles give off tiny singing no

caps, pillowcases, prom sashes, & barbecue

dark subtitled Berkeley movies next to

Human fabric is dragged out, being   is sewn with terror or awe
which is also joy. Einstein called mystery
of existence "the fundamental emotion."   Remember? You unraveled in childhood till
you were everything. By everything I mean
everything. The unicorn puts its head   on your lap; from there it
sees the blurry edge. How am
I so unreal & yet my   thread is real it asks sleepily ~~

::: AN ODDNESS :::

A scent   rather quietly   loves
the library.   Readers   look up: a
life of paper   inside   the great
Life: scent of greenly   ravished civilization ~
dream of inspiration   freed.   When a
book is   lifted   from horizon's steel
that mystery   object   spreads   an oddness
each call number   a timeling   of
yellow math,   its curve   leftover from
epic.   The mind has no periphery
for meaning,   the several phoenician, sailing
sideways   through vowels   of the dead.

PAUL HOOVER

THROUGH ITS WIDE range of styles, Paul Hoover's work manages to strike an equilibrium among a surprising variety of traditions. In certain collections, such as *Poems in Spanish*, he echoes the emotional and rhetorical intensity of the Spanish Surrealists; in others, he practices an austere minimalism based on precise word counts; and in his current project, an homage to Raymond Queneau's *Elements of Style*, he is rewriting Shakespeare's "Sonnet 56" in fifty-six different modes. Though his work is never as programmatic as that of the Oulipo group, he makes use of constraints in ways that bring to it a formal tension, balancing a wide range of emotional registers from the humorous to the philosophical to the intimate. No matter what its tone or subject, Hoover's work is always marked by an agile intelligence that uses poetry as a tool of inquiry.

Paul Hoover has published eleven books of poetry and has won numerous awards, including the University of Georgia's Contemporary Poetry Series Competition, the General Electric Award for Younger Writers, and an NEA Fellowship. He has also written a collection of critical essays, *Fables of Representation*, and a novel, *Saigon, Illinois*. He edited the 1994 Norton anthology *Postmodern American Poetry* and, along with Maxine Chernoff, is co-founder and co-editor of the literary review *New American Writing*. Also with Chernoff, he has edited and translated a collection of Hölderlin's poetry; his other translation projects include collaborations with Nguyen Do of contemporary Vietnamese poetry. He currently curates the reading series at San Francisco's DeYoung Museum and teaches at San Francisco State University.

THE PRESENCE

We know it and we feel it—
the fierce will of things

to set themselves apart,
isolated by their beauty,

bereft in isolation.
Museum of the Thing:

the living glove, earthen shoe,
a parakeet's soft feather

that seems to be made of fur—
yellow tuft of sunlight

falling through the air
like nothing but itself,

as water is nothing but water,
grinding and turning as if

there were no passage.
Where does the work get done

that tenders so much beauty
and leaves us in such grief?

Sweetmeat and papaya,
your own face in chrome

with its hint of speed—
all these chaste subjects

love us in their way—
needle & thimble, dog & bone.

Whatever is absent in them,
let it speak its name:

fingerprint, blue smudge,
a typewriter with new keys—

one for infinity and one for sleeping.
Each night the objects come

to watch us in our beds,
above which hang

the dusty family portraits
retreating toward a quaintness

that can only be remembered—
mother in her kingdom

of white gloves and black bibles,
the mouse she trapped in her hand

as it leaped from a cabinet.
And father, poor father,

whose kindness went on forever,
into a clear confusion,

what were those sounds I heard
from the bed beyond the wall?

Which way should I drive now
to find the house we lived in,

vanished including its trees?
Gone the upstairs bedrooms

with their perfect shining floors,
not even a ghost to warm them.

All things come to witness
these absences like objects—

pears so near to ripeness
they melt in the hand

and roads that will only go south,
with a sound of tires like rain.

CHILDHOOD AND ITS DOUBLE

Everything's more real, once it finds its mirror.
The gray lake and its gray sky,

skin and the sound of drums,
and the back end of a costume horse

confused against the skyline.
Absence turns the corner

and looks into its eyes,
and presence, whatever it was,

has fewer shapes to inhabit.
My grandfather fell asleep

with one leg in the fire,
and now the other one's missing

because its grave is missing.
This is no fiction. Your body changes

seven times, seven times disguised
by the weakest flesh and the strongest,

and then it finds its absence
as a mouth finds language.

from EDGE AND FOLD

XXXI

the body is a field
    consisting of attention

singing of a land
    the eye can't imagine

darkness everywhere
    even on the pillow

these are refractions
    of other surface worlds

thickness of a hand
    behind a glass of water

decisions lightning makes
    arriving at the templum

XXXII

mountain moving day
    flashbulbs firing

the cloud of unknowing
    velocity of water

the earth is other minds
    but the speed of a window

is how we change seeing
    to be outbound

on the inbound train
    among the fierce women

this is the fictive
    a latent celebration

of what could never be
    a shadow in the rock

exceeds the sun itself
    sun exceeds the mind

XXXIII

the first estate is time
    the second is matter

the third estate is shape
    the fourth is shadow

the fifth estate is nothing
    nothing at all

vacant interrogation
    of silence by sound

perception empties
    a room at a time

when the not-yet
    is no longer

and the future
    is unwritten

we know the words it uses
    if not its perfect cadence

XXXIV

when you add to infinity
    the number one

it is and you are
    finite as before

no such thing
    as an infinite measure

the length of life is god
    to stumble on the run

folding and unfolding
    a new blank map

first in the actual
    then as a symbol

XXXV

in the sparest of ruins
    language is act

where one can imagine
    the unbuttoned present

with its ripe interjections
    and swerving cars

the way green mold
    covers a lemon

& stone asks a question
    the moon must answer

HAIKUISATION OF SHAKESPEARE'S SONNET 56

Love, renew thy force.
Thy edge should blunter be than
tomorrow-sharpened.

FANNY HOWE

Fanny Howe's writing is increasingly driven by a tension between mind and spirit that recognizes a further tension in the ways these two play out in the material world. The problems of materialism, and particularly its imbalances in contemporary society, haunt her work with questions that are profoundly religious; but, as the title of her recent prose book *The Lives of a Spirit / Glasstown: Where Something Got Broken* indicates, her view of religion is unorthodox, intricate, and realist. Her often enigmatic, often abstract lyrics demand nimble attention and mental suspension at the same time. Within a warp of sound and a weft of allusion, the writer is endlessly searching, not without doubt, but with determination. Her essays show a profound interest in and understanding of the varied traditions that inform our culture, from fairy tales to the Scriptures—traditions she receives and transmits through the lens of a Muslim "bewilderment," allowing their experience without their reduction.

Fanny Howe has published more than twenty books, including novels, poetry, and essays. Her *Selected Poems*, published by the University of California Press in 2000, won the 2001 Lenore Marshall Prize, and her most recent collection of poetry, *On the Ground*, was shortlisted for the Griffin Poetry Prize. She has also received awards and fellowships from the National Endowment for the Arts, the California Arts Council, the National Poetry Foundation, and *The Village Voice*. A professor for many years at the University of California at San Diego, she currently divides her time between Boston and Ireland. Her papers are held in Stanford University's Special Collections.

9/11

The first person is an existentialist

like trash in the groin of the sand dunes
like a brown cardboard home beside a dam

like seeing like things the same
between Death Valley and the desert of Paran

An earthquake a turret with arms and legs
The second person is the beloved

like winners taking the hit
like looking down on Utah as if

it was Saudi Arabia or Pakistan
like war-planes out of Miramar

like a split cult a jolt of coke New York
like Mexico in its deep beige couplets

like this, like that . . . like Call us all It
Thou It. "Sky to Spirit! Call us all It!"

The third person is a materialist.

2002

We are stamping on the bosom of Satan, boot-boot

We are sure of the origins of evil

Ice-chop. Man and soil
Which came first? The robin or the worm?

Burst a well, *das kapital*, sell, sell.

The windows into the worm are flowers

Lily layers and a basket upright

Its stick figure is like a piece

Of something that can't stop living

Severed from nothing at both ends

Wish on the first worm of the year
and all other firsts as ways to get
what you want. The first fish-hook, the first bait

The first time you hear a woodchuck being its name

When the president wakes up, it always asks
What am I doing here? Where's that man?

Satan broke open the worm
One night on the Dalmatian coast
And out of the grass came another worm
and another, or was it a word by then

Hatch, hatch, snake of snake

Plague came and went in a matter of days
Town to town and the saved
got out of there fast

Tongues of grass curled around their legs

For the others, suck suck on the man's breast

How utopian is water
when you are disordered or bloody from a fall
Everyone loves the way Satan
mixes water with his syntax

A plug of magnolia budding too soon

A long blue sky without a brow

No providence
but a grope in the galley of simultaneity

Poor us. Here but not why
It's the proximity problem, being stuck
inside a body unknown to it or anyone

So the sticking to things, associations
No way to free dog
or color from surrounding whys

This about existence, paper-littered river
and the first wish. Wish, wish, water

THE SPLINTER

When I was a child

I left my body to look for one
whose image nestles in the center of a wide valley

in perfect isolation wild as Eden

till one became many: spirits in presence

yes workers and no workers up on the tops
of the hills in striped overalls

toy capes puffing
and blue veils as yet unrealized in the sky

I made myself homeless
on purpose for this shinnying up the silence

murky hand-pulls
Gray the first color
many textured clay beneath my feet

my face shining up I lost faith but once

(theology)

To stay with me
that path of death was soft

this pump's emotion
irregular, the sand

blew everywhere

My hands were tied
to one ahead

driving a herd to the edge
(mother)

She said I said why
fear there's nothing to it
at any minute
a stepping out of and into
no columns no firmament

Most of each thing
is whole but contingent
on something about
the nearest one to it

Confused by moving
the only stranger I know
has a bed a blanket

a heartfullness famous
for hypocrisy

When she's not trusting anyone
she leans her crown
upon her hand
snowslop all the way to the grating
before lying down

in a little block of childhood
(one hour for the whole of it)
and her book to record it

THE DESCENT

The descent has deepened
the interior lengthened

designated ending

Blind

pulled down inside and then
shot up again

to see east via the plateglass
a moon a monsoon an ashram

I used that time almost wantonly
in that bald but sensual sky

to give me gusts
and more measurement

not to snap the stars shut
but Joseph said
you really ought

to tender how you sail by eye
your soul is just a length of baby

LET IT SNOW

Let it snow unless it is in heaven

Let it know
what it is itself that waterstuff

as it covers the silver
winter dinner bell

IS KNOWING

Is knowing the same as owning?
Do I already have it

(Poetic model)
a spiral thumb-print
taped responses
to each event

I thought I was
a five-part someone

who had to decipher the air
in things before navigating them

and each error was necessary

SUSAN HOWE

ISTORY AND PHILOSOPHY fuse and take on new shape in Susan Howe's many works. It's above all in American history that her questions are rooted, and through history, she makes place come alive across time, evoking the landscape of the American Northeast, particularly Massachusetts, to haunt and inform many of her books. Howe began her career as a visual artist, and her shift to language marked a new concentration on the potentials of page space in American poetry. An astute reader of Charles Olson, she took his notion of field poetics and emphasized the immediate role of white space and the canvas it creates. Her work throughout the seventies and eighties is particularly inventive in its scattering and overlapping of words, compromising meaning while creating visual information. The more recent work adds scholarship to this mix; her book *Pierce-Arrow*, for instance, draws largely on the life and work of Charles Sanders Peirce, but also brings in Swinburne, Alexander Pope, and others. The resulting hybrid texts fuse theory and practice, history and poetry, realizing one of the principal objectives of the late twentieth-century avant-garde.

Susan Howe's biography *My Emily Dickinson* (1985) similarly marked a turning point in American literary criticism, acknowledging the inherent subjectivity of the biographer and the necessary materiality of any text, no matter how informative. She has published over twenty books of poetry and collaborated with visual artists, book artists, filmmakers, and musicians. Her work has been widely anthologized, in *The Norton Anthology of Modern and Contemporary Poetry* and *In the American Tree*, among other places. She taught for many years in the poetics program at SUNY Buffalo, finishing her teaching career holding the Samuel P. Capen Chair of Poetry. Howe's papers are held in the Mandeville Special Collections Library at the University of California at San Diego.

from BED HANGINGS II

Secrecy let me light you in
In shadow something other
echoed and re-echoed only

The dark who can veneer it
That conjoint abstraction will
come to snow let us go back

Lace is frequently mentioned
In the English Bible if
He went that way into that

While in the pulpit he was
frequently distressed with
the fear of falling over it

Night studies until two or
three o'clock brought a string
of nervous sensations

The Age of Resplendent Lace

Penelope is presented as
working a shroud for Laertes
the father of Ulysses

Cobweb gossamer ephemera

miscellaneous bundle 34

The shirt worn by William

the Silent when he fell by

an assassin is still preserved

at the Hague

Dare not say strapwork of

prized indigo homespun to

artist in lashing true cradle

Glass has broken the mirror

With pins she lay on straw

just visible to this age and

the next age under boards

Pine board scallop cowslip

Maple of casepiece pine of clock

a scaleless lyric Thanatos pattern

Come free yourself an authorial

voice echoes it is not comic to be

tragic people have been trying to

come down tangible form we hear

the bell but there is no handiwork

Trade we have nothing porcelain

Sir Thomas Malory isolation

is not the question I am not

confined to distant recipient

beyond the scope of realism

Queen Guinevere lies in bed

dreaming pregnable dreams

Have her face screened green

leather and japanned gold

■

Silvius twine this muslin

hedge in silver threaves

a half-line aesthetically left

slashed if a hare crosses

a highway or the double

of a hare himself Silvius

■

Mrs. Little from 1745 to 17

75 by arithmetical reckoning

specular as morning to half-

articulate lace curtain insofar

Gravitation the electron naïve

yesterday thin thick realism

A fugitive incarnate statistic

at lattice lately in hair pencil

from KIDNAPPED

TEACHINGS ON STYLE AND THE FLOWER

In 1402, the Japanese Noh performer and aesthetician Zeami Motokiyo wrote several items concerning the practice of the Noh in relation to an actor's age. He said a boy's voice begins to achieve its proper pitch at eleven or twelve, only then can he begin to understand the Noh.

But this flower is not the true flower not yet.

IRISH LITERARY REVIVAL

1926. Mary Manning having wandered on the Brontë moors in Yorkshire, carries a copy of Arnold's *Scholar Gypsy* home to Dublin. She always takes it with her when she goes out walking. Now it is 1948. I am to read aloud the last three paragraphs of *Wuthering Heights* for the sixth grade public reading contest at the Buckingham School, in Cambridge, Massachusetts. The book is her choice. Poetry is our covenant. She believes tables move without contact I am skeptical. If what is present to the mind at one time is distinct from what is present in another what is belief? Hoosh. Not in the Catholic graveyard not in the Protestant one either.

Bird in the hand worth two of its own emptiness.

This flower, taken from a scrap of paper, is said to be the Ammellus or Italian starwort of Virgil. Long ago Ogham stones were erected to commemorate the dead in rune-like ciphers then memory for voices then the rapid movement of ballads. Nearly all go to Scotland anglicity. Lexical attention must be guarded from the dark age of childhood though lengthen night and shorten day. I have no option but to be faithful to you unlucky half human half unassuaged desiring

dark shade you first Catherine. You are my altar vow.

This cowslip is a favorite among fairies.

THE GATE

A double cowslip bears one flower out of another. It remains in

pastures long after the grass has been eaten away a stage name under

the true one.

Mind the hidden

◾

Dedication to M enough
to the wood if you have
aconite and poppy she
said "Lie still, sleep well"
Quiet for it is a small
world of covered bone
Come veil the thought of
I shall dress primrose

ANDREW JORON

W HILE ANDREW JORON'S early work shows a direct engagement with the full range of avant-garde experiments, from Lautréamont to the Language poets, his more recent work focuses on the legacies of Surrealism, examining links between "convulsive" aesthetic practices and the current impasses of capitalism. He approaches these themes more directly in a book-length essay, *Neo-surrealism or The Sun at Night: Transformations of Surrealism in American Poetry, 1966–1999*. With influences ranging from science fiction (the title of his first book of poems) to the Frankfurt School and the radical politics of Berkeley in the eighties and nineties, Joron's work is ever conscious of otherness, especially a kind of self-estrangement that makes for the *ostrananie* that gives poetry its uncanny endlessness.

Born in Germany, Andrew Joron moved to the United States as a child, and then to the Bay Area in the mid-1970s, where he became involved in the avant-garde writing and philosophy discussions of the time. He graduated from UC Berkeley with a degree in the history of science, and has worked as a librarian's assistant and a freelance bibliographer and indexer. The founder and editor of the journal *Velocities: A Magazine of Speculative Poetry*, he has three major collections out; the most recent, *Fathom*, was selected by *The Village Voice* as one of the top twenty-five books of 2003. He also has several chapbooks, and his awards include three Rhysling Awards for the best science fiction poem of the year. In addition, Joron translates from German—his translation of the literary essays of the Utopian Marxist Ernst Bloch was published by Stanford University Press in 1998.

THE REMOVES

After the Time Epidemic, the eyes of owls were found embedded throughout the soft balustrades, reminders of—

A fateful plan your cellmates (in this centuries-wide prison, whose actual walls have yet to be discovered) will soon deploy against you—

This is understandable. You are waiting to achieve your paradigm, a damaged star. Running like smoke from the Chamber of Ills, your signature commences—

"Against the operations of chance," you write, "it is sufficient to call upon the sign of the Umbrella, that which opens outward, or the Sewing Machine, that which stitches together—inasmuch as meaning will be defined systematically as a series of openings and closings upon the dissecting table of Language."

Thus, the words of your confession appear as vestiges of an Original speechlessness, ragged holes in the firmament—

"What phoneme in *integers* is also present in *jewels?*"—Why answer? The laws of thermodynamics can't forgive you because your name is a darkened festival of sound.

Here, then, is the gift of your exhaustion—a precious animal stroked to transparency.

Here, too, is a windowless sunset—its proof scratched out by the charred branches of your eyes.

Your pursuers, inevitable, still trust in the parallelism of acts where desires converge. Yet space itself must be spoken aloud, the emanation of a veil . . .

ECLIPSE CALLING

O

Poured orbit, O
An all-rounding river of last regard

Given nothing for
Given

Cannot rest, but runs in countercurrents
   against

   that pax, that poverty of state—

As contorted as letters
The bodies lie still below the readable surface.

1

To those who—come to comb rayed musics
Out of matter—read

Red eddies, desire as Swan, as swoon of dawn—
Commune
   of all that cannot be thought:

Earth & blood are even, because Divisible.
   Heaven
Is odd, because indivisible. So free from prayer.

—a free word says death or, better, death
To the president.

Imagine the spoken, O's
Spokes convergent on no center. No place
Is polis
   but there are violins preceding violence.
   A word is birthplace of the plural body.

As wide-eyed as wild-isled:
   I & I
   achieving signature upon inverted landscape-sky.

Accepted into vastly revolving ocean
As shock of nudity—

    that posture foaming to far pasture, to pure field.

Here, first person is maintained: an archaic device, somehow
    stopped inside its own velocity, its substance
    dissimilar to itself—

Its living moment: relic of a movement unarriving.

2

Of *if* born of *of*, there is no information—
    the universal is unsaved.

Age to come to calm
    if & only if
Calm's measure makes disquiet.

For a phrase = a fragile thread
Composed of something dead, plus pulse.

    O my Other, mother-throated One—
Name, between
    abandoned body—
      the twin of *of*.

Horn fight, drum fight, drafting tatters in the head.

The groan as ground-tone is also known.
    Unsaved is this
    unstruck instrument. A theater, someday with tall voices

    —chorus overboiling like cumuli—will be lifted from the sea.

From *frees* to *free*, the verbs do not agree.

Shadow
    belongs to the half that is always hungry.

Totality's ring
    a window-effect
Of the self-referential.

HOME UNKNOWN STONE

Shh, shh, surest measure—
One minute too minute.

The blue animal lies bleeding
On a field of stars.

No, no word-order to end well

    meaning indwelling—

What effort, merely
    to sob out its
    winter-substance!

Tag from fragment: a certain light
Cannot be cited
    in that Book that wants invisibility.

That which needs nothing to exist
Fixes accident, each

    marriage of the genitive:

Prayer-preliminary to the symmetries in trees.

BREATH, BRING NOTHING TO TERM

Ring
Wrong instead of *song*—

Sense not sense, but fatal interference.
Arc of
     the maker, the marker

Born in reverse:
The borrower, the rower from the frozen zero.

So cotillions of ice shall
     clatter to
Unsure closure: rare air or error

     cool to all call, all clash of clouds.

Wanting
One without outside

     —while knowing the turn of torn, the
     deviance of all device.

So reckoning is this
Night-wreck of the Sun, perception pointing

To its stoppages:

     still object &
     agile shadow.

Fluent fall to flow to Flower
     &
Lightning-littered letter.

Imagine, engine
The state in flames

     & black
     thoughts
Of the character of a cataract, roaring
     to assemble the mind's semblance to nothing.

THE EVENING OF CHANCES

The leveling of chants is—

The etching of, the evening of, irregular glows. The various chases. The chastening glove.

Pay attention: *the of is*, space, experience, emptiness.

No, slower than silence. Reward to reword, word-whirled world.

Frameless, the real is what we cannot look away from.

Every cause is an accident: so blue, trembling, awaits its turn.

Against begins, nudity without body.

Blue sister, who shows us how to disturb her rest. Revealed in the grain: this deviance grown absolute.

Sheets of motion—writing—the blade that bleeds.

As the senses multiply, we look away to contemplate.

As the rains relate to ruins, as the bells—As the bells, bells, bells, bells, bells, bells, bells—

Can sameness answer its own secret? Here, the rains relate to ruins, & a dead tree has walked across the desert.

Such pauses repeat, but never return. Structure stretches into content, as trace over trance.

Let X represent the human cipher in a pose of astonishment. The future past is understood: we will have existed.

Understood here means *unsheltered*: not stood under. Similar to a prayer's elongated figure.

Cold noise collects in the listening devices. All blues & sciences.

CLAUDIA KEELAN

THE TITLE OF Claudia Keelan's most recent book of poetry is *The Devotion Field*, a phrase that sums up both the volume and the oeuvre: the devotion she offers is not restricted to a single object, but remains an open and ever-expanding field. It begins in and always includes her culture and her community, and much of her work seeks to define these, their obligations and their needs. Earlier books such as *Utopic* dealt directly with themes of social struggle, which she echoed in her form through leaps, gaps, and quick shifts. In later work, she's tended to embed these difficulties in subtleties of phrase and timing, creating texts with highly seductive surfaces that are yet even more ambiguous.

Keelan is the author of four books of poetry. The first, *Refinery*, won the Cleveland State University Award; the second, *The Secularist*, was selected for the University of Georgia Series, nominated for the Los Angeles Times Book Award, and a finalist for the PEN West Award in Poetry, while her third won the Beatrice Hawley Award from Alice James Books. Her fifth is due out from New Issues Press in 2009. She has done extensive critical writing, particularly on Alice Notley. She devoted a special issue of the literary journal that she edits, *Interim*, to Notley's work and has contributed essays to various collections, such as *Innovative Women: Works and Interviews*. Keelan studied music for her BA at Humboldt State University, and shifted to poetry when she began her MFA at the Iowa Writers' Workshop. She currently teaches at the University of Nevada at Las Vegas, where she also directs the creative writing program.

FREELY ADAPTED

In the future
There were blackouts
Pell-mell, *randonnée,* on the beach
And in the bay

The last woman a remaining aunt
Helter skelter *affiché*
And other follies
Along the way

Perpetually beginning
Past afraid

Heh heh over the wire
The sun rises inside a cry

Pell-mell, *randonée,*
Helter skelter
Hey hey

Bled my gift into the now
To culture citizen's shining paws

Lost the power to withdraw
Endless in change

Controlled hysteria
Earthly fires

Bequeathed
To tradition at last

REPRESENTATION WITHOUT TAXATION

A meadow full of Easter lilies

Turned into a province on a map,

The province renamed 20 times in 20 years.

In The Tiger Information Center, Asia lies sleeping . . .

Being here/or there/and how it feels,

And how I say my name to you

As in "I am not your Lily,"

Or "A meadow is finally only a province-in-progress . . ."

Ask any tiger,

But don't ask me, I'll only try to make you love me.

So many nation-states in a name!

I was surprised, were you?

Supra-inside a flag's star . . .

"Our" identity problem,

Is it clinical or critical?

Haven't they made a government yet,

Who's gone to exile this week?

His wife needs us to deposit some money,

She who was the jewel chix of Liberia . . .

Liberia! So surprised to get her letter

I wrote and sent her the key to *Uncle Tom's Cabin*.

Every place that ends in *eria* is the Key to exile,

And some are cold and some hot on their enforced Isle.

And we, we are the hot air ballooning above you . . .

CRITICAL ESSAY

Anyone writing can come to know
Everything one reading does

Anyone reading might never know
Everyone one writing does

If anyone is really writing
Anyone is really reading

Anyone knows everything writing
Everything anyone reading might never

Anyone for example I I found writing
The experience of the dead gods you

Read in Jane Harrison's *Prolegomena*
The gods already dead and gone already in Greece

At the moment Orpheus is born
I for example I found writing the empty

Alpha where the beginning died and I
& Anyone for example Anyone finds writing

Truly writing the end's beginning the empty
Alpha full of the gone God's writing

VIA NEGATIVA

You had nothing you said,
Though all of our life
You'd reminded me that there is no
Such thing as nothing
In nature, so naturally
The grasshoppers drowned in the pool.
It was my job to net them
Until nothing remained
But the shadow of wings on the water.

I opened some books and stole some words.
Here, put them back.
I opened a door and stole some air
So—breathe.
No, you don't know what I mean.
I've only seen one movie,
The one where the boy wags
The plane's wing
Over his mother's house
To say he is well,
And encouraged by shadow,
She gives meat and milk
To a young German boy
Who will not thank her.

You think you can get off the movie set?
You better count your lucky somethings.
Some people's lives are, moment to moment,
A live shot of a car explosion
In one of the countries where they hate you,
And the rest of the world, believe me,
Is marching with signs of their approval.

Not everyone loves Jesus or Uncle Tom,
But I do, sweet suffering Christ,
I love them and I love you, too,
Generally and specifically,
So march on over here
And let's have some love.

(Put your sign down, I say,
Lay down your v_nity)
You sorrowful monkey, you.

A movie set or an ocean . . .
Sorry to get metaphysical on you . . .
I'm physical about the metaphysical:
Coming from and/or in an ocean . . .
You come too!
And if you insist on staying there,
All alone in your blanket,
Jesus or Uncle Tom or I
(You come too!)

Will rock you in our arms
And the ocean will be your bed
O sorrowful and suffering . . .
The cries of the monkeys on the movie set
So distant now,
We leave our shadows and follow.

THE SYBIL'S AFTERLIFE

—*a poem for Ronald Johnson in heaven*

There's a hole in the beam,
31 December, 1999.
Sight can't be taught.
The angels the century boys adore
Are sitting, yes, standing, yes,
All over the place.
I shut the door.
Feel the ending.

Inside the sight and therefore not fable,
I made them leave the room.
This is my book.

Inside and on the surface of my face
All that mistaken love,
Gone now so you can see just how
Empty. Empty possible zero.
Auld lang. I met myself and left
With me & she came home forever changed.

NOUMENON

Our son fell to his knees,
Ben someone else now, someone—

The dust I write in,
The closet exhorted for prayer.
But I didn't enter,
Not today, not all day.
Culture's confessions arrive in the mails.
Yes, they're lost, so many,

Piled on the kitchen table,
Their faces age progressed.

The end of the century wants to be faithful to time.
Someone is watching the wind believing erasure is Truth.
Earlier, someone fingering the years spent,
Tastes her eventual death in the dust that spins
Off the book she is reading.
Now someone some
Would call the same someone,
But not the faithful to time,
Is summoning
The new forms from the air, but no—
Someone draws blanks,
Someone in her heart, Celan
Shoving Jabes' *Book of Questions*
Back through the mail slot.
The sound of it hitting the floor.
The lost original in the story of the clown,
Together once, when we walked we cart wheeled,
But joy made pride and we were severed—

Are you my Ben, are you my first
Trying to fit himself back to
The someone now everywhere,
Sorrow's learning loved Her all.
His namesake shot on the border hours,
His other name, including two wives and the donkey,
& the first brother confined to the wheelchair.
Someone taking tickets at the bridge.

First and last,
Following the dust of your reading.

MYUNG MI KIM

O VER THE COURSE of her several books, Myung Mi Kim has always held to the promise—and the failure—of language to reveal identity by connecting a speaker to the world. This intricate and endless impasse is behind language's ability continually to renew itself in yet another attempt at elusive connections. Kim's work examines the communal nature of all language, and the dimension not only of documentary but of testimony that is an essential aspect of all language acts. And while her work evokes specific events and situations in an outside world whose concrete social forces she recognizes as constituting history, it is also insistent upon language as a social force in itself. Her fragments, her spare distillations, her unstable pronouns all keep us aware of language as a primary actor, mediating not only our access to the world but that very world itself.

Myung Mi Kim's world was broken open at the age of nine when her family immigrated from Korea to the United States, and that rupture is a key to her poetics. Kim summed it up in a comment at Woodland Pattern, saying, "In this effort and failure of bridging, reconfiguring, shaping, and being shaped by loss and absence, one enters a difficult negotiation with an Imaginary and a manner of listening that to me *is* the state of writing." Kim is the author of four books of poetry, including *Under Flag*, which won the 1991 Multicultural Publishers Book Award, and, most recently, *Commons* from the University of California Press. For several years on the faculty at San Francisco State University, she now teaches in the Poetics Program at SUNY Buffalo.

EXORDIUM

In what way names were applied to things. Filtration. Not every word that has been applied, still exists. Through proliferation and differentiation. Airborn. Here, this speck and this speck you missed.

Numbers in cell division. Spheres of debt. The paradigm's stitchery of unrelated points. What escapes like so much cotton batting. The building, rather, in flames. Does flight happen in an order.

Dates to impugn and divulge. The laws were written on twelve tablets of bronze which were fastened to the rostra. Trembling hold. Manner of variation and shift. Vacillation hung by tactile and auditory cues.

■

Those which are of foreign origin. Those which are of forgotten sources. Place and body. Time and action. The snow falls. A falling snow. A fallen snow. A red balloon and a blackwinged bird at semblance of crossing in a pittance of sky.

Chroniclers enter texts and trade. Was to children dying before their mothers. Accounts and recounting. A nation's defense. Names of things made by human hands. Making famine where abundance lies.

Mapping needles. Minerals and gems. Furs and lumber. Alterations through the loss or transposition of even a single syllable. The next day is astronomical distance and a gnarled hand pulling up wild onion.

■

Placed on a large flat rock and covered by a series of smaller stones. Edicts of building for private persons. Remaining principalities long ago divided off. Under that place which is called the earth wall. Around which extends a savage, trackless waste, infested with wild beasts.

Near city walls. Shapes of battle helmets. Instruments for giving precision to ideas of size, distance, direction, and location. A projection of the possible state. Lay bare and make appear. The gates are wicked—fresh.

With shields. For war and fields. This hill was previously called—it is recorded that on this hill—When the rickshaw stopped, it was three o'clock. The heavy chains were taken off and they walked to the place of execution. One boy's shoe fell off, and he reached down to put it back on, taking a long time to do it. Fierce dogs have come over the sea.

■

Cutworms in tomato beds. Roots of a tree close to the property line have gone out under the neighbor's cornfield. Wherever kin of word is. Partnership of words is one of many members.

Glyphs to alphabets. In which words have indications of time. They had to eat as much as they could in a hurry. Baskets woven by bloodlet fingers.

Venom verifies. Minuscule pebbles embedded in domestic crops. With the soot covered rice pot—stood and sat, stood and sat, several times. Meals offered up from yet more pinecones burning.

■

A second class of words in which comparisons are made. The pond after rain, a lily. Watershed and water level. Coinciding glint of scales and scrapers. Conjectural poles.

Speaking and placing the speaking. To speak from the place of the word is speak forth. Such noise in the ditches—the mills and farms.

Standing in proximity—*think* and *love*. See, meet, face. Incidence of generation. Walls, wattles, straw, and mud. A laundering stone and stones for the floor. Gently, gently level the ground. This is the leveling of the ground.

from PENURY

[gulf   library]

tw   neither bird nor ornament

the calf stranded across the creek | that bellowing

valuables stored under plywood

the ragged ranges

thorn beast

■

Fighting house by house
You saw it and you heard it?

Grass grew from the sternum
Roots took over the mandible

■

thatcher poacher . the stripped bark . who, allotment of arable

land . of being in and affecting . I don't know what's the problems in that
family . probably poorness

Scn:
Scn:
Scn: Those 840 workers? They're just gone—

■

[offering to general protectors]

why is it that the tips of the beaks are burnt

: was first year high school

: because from far away   distant

: came out   noise came to see

: every morning street close by hospital newborns thrown away

■

perimeter grow up without you plain view

onset infuse Y of the branch full tip

channel scanned yes sir I do three of those were

fixing it no seeing them elemental buffer

in that twitch feel of limbs there's no fixing it

huddle quadrant swept counting inhabitants

operative swath who is in there who's there blaring

rout draped will be returned as practicable as possible

transcript February 2003

ANN LAUTERBACH

THE EXPERIMENT IS always between, like a hinge, a preposition," writes Ann Lauterbach, and her poetry echoes this idea in its charged spaces between words, fragments, statements, and stanzas. Much of Lauterbach's recent work recasts the fragment, no longer considering it a piece of (and thus a reminder of and an elegy for) a larger whole, but as a whole in its own right. Her titles—such as *On a Stair*, *If in Time*, *And for Example*—focus attention on the importance of the smallest words in the language, their huge role in creating meaning, and on the concomitant myriad possibilities that can be condensed into a tiny phrase. Reflecting the oblique philosophical approach of Modernists such as Stevens and Olson, Lauterbach's work as a whole encourages this kind of minute attention and rewards it with social force and emotional clarity.

Born and raised in New York, Ann Lauterbach attended Columbia University Graduate School on a Woodrow Wilson Fellowship and then spent seven years in London curating the Literature Program at the Institute for Contemporary Arts, among other things. Returning to New York in the early 1970s, she remained involved in the visual arts community, writing catalogue essays and collaborating with artists, including Ann Hamilton and Lucio Pozzi. In addition to seven collections of poetry, she has written a critical book, *The Night Sky: Writings on the Poetics of Experience*. A contributing editor to *Conjunctions* since 1981, she has received fellowships from the Guggenheim Foundation, the Ingram Merrill Foundation, and the John D. and Catherine T. MacArthur Foundation. She is the Schwab Professor of Languages and Literature at Bard College, where she is also co-director of Writing in the Milton Avery Graduate School of the Arts.

AFTER MAHLER

A thousand minutes came out of the tottering state.
The bed of thyme moved within its bearings like a dream.
He answered, *tomorrow*.
Someone else was screaming on the radio; people laughed.
The cat has been dead for some time now.
The wedding party's bright joy looked strange from the streaking jet.

Meanwhile persons are moving around outside. They have decided to
                                    foreclose on
options pertaining to the new world. Instead, to allow themselves to
                                    live in a world
neither new nor old, but which abides as in a balloon floating
untethered above trophies and noise so that
                                    truncated, wren-shrunk

        Pentecostal shade
                    harp rubbed under Mahler's tent (his abundant farewell
                        to Alma's rage)
            after all   the part that was said and the part that was done
                the conductor in his care   so one was forced to go
                        back
                to how it might have begun   after all
                    the century that leaks its tunes into the summer air
                    refuses to call
                            to call is to ask   break a silence   but the
                                    music

after all it is music   song-spiraled
            and the landscape detained   across a field   into a night
                                                in which we
learn only the pornography of sight
        its ocular target

                        see see see

        from above the tents and the persons milling about
        in their robes

                        they are the disciples! silence them!

And if they are merely birds   flocks rising in circles
like smoke without song   *see see*
we cannot hear the tremulous strings nor the soprano glittering
in the heat of the tent
the conductor mouthing her words   not that.

Sun, making its way east and east and west of the river
where the ivy is not poison and the trees not weeds. And
this or that spins into
the final cycle, its systemic will. Do not butter the toast, do not come
like a ghost without shame, a promise adumbrated
against the cry of any nocturnal creature.
All against one, and the philosophical questions
on a far continent like so many markets.

Not that either.
Conditions above the smashed agora with the cowboy riding sunset on his
mechanical cart, his small mouth and child's
incontinent whine. Casinos in full play, paying for
assault, moving to the rush of coin. And still we did not speak, did
not know to whom to speak, muttered at lunch, gave each other
proofs of care, one to
one, but did not come to the table to hear our fathers, they were dead, our
mothers, they were busy, our neighbors, they were
elsewhere, our lovers, they
were not listening. Listen. This is a lullaby. Listen.

to Leon Botstein

INTERLEAVINGS (PAUL CELAN)

Snowfall, denser and denser,
a knight's breath

Snowfall, as if even now you were sleeping.

A collar of cold at his neck
above it, endless,
a foreign sky.

Below, hidden,
where my hand held the soft stuff
was den Augen so

prone, entire

almost fetched home into its
delay, the cast-off limb
posted.

The watch and music
in twin branches:

what body falls through the bridal mass?
is the colored cloth a flag?

HUM

The days are beautiful.
The days are beautiful.

I know what days are.
The other is weather.

I know what weather is.
The days are beautiful.

Things are incidental.
Someone is weeping.

I weep for the incidental.
The days are beautiful.

Where is tomorrow?
Everyone will weep.

Tomorrow was yesterday.
The days are beautiful.

Tomorrow was yesterday.
Today is weather.

The sound of the weather
Is everyone weeping.

Everyone is incidental.
Everyone weeps.

The tears of today
Will put out tomorrow.

The rain is ashes.
The days are beautiful.

The rain falls down.
The sound is falling.

The sky is a cloud.
The days are beautiful.

The sky is dust.
The weather is yesterday.

The weather is yesterday.
The sound is weeping.

What is this dust?
The weather is nothing.

The days are beautiful.
The towers are yesterday.

The towers are incidental.
What are these ashes?

Here is the hat
That does not travel

Here is the robe
That smells of the night

Here are the words
Retired to their books

Here are the stones
Loosed from their settings

Here is the bridge
Over the water

Here is the place
Where the sun came up

Here is a season
Dry in the fireplace.

Here are the ashes.
The days are beautiful.

IMPOSSIBLE BLUE

The blue   there are no slippers   phoned from the street
the countess   a walk across the bridge   finding a dress and shoes
the black shoes   transparent   raining on snow
the birds   to be ready for the dance   the second wife
came back   sailing   the blue
the bridge in gold light
the birds in snow
you telephoned
I said I would I
did not   the blue   after crossing

And that the obscure would approach
in crystal sheaves
accumulating but
undressed, denuded
as of spines or wires or where
there cannot be a mirror
only the blankly encumbered mass
as when the sitter closes her eyes
the veins under skin
or the person falls
the kitchen tile on her cheek.

That the obscure
approaches with mere crutches, polished,
and the title of a book
or the blank inside of the book
or the recollected word.

There is no telling, except by the analogy of the snow
and the embarrassed receptor
embodied, so one imagines a shell in a tree
as bells chime discursive thirds.
The stones will return, their
old grammar
leaked upward through snow.
And there, a bench, a path.
Birds, or shoes, on the hill.

I cannot say
how the vanishing
turns to a sign for blue after it has left
only the light by which it became blue
as a body makes a sign
lifting the hand
turning the head.
And the stamp in the snow
is, we say, a footprint
down into the blue
print in the snow
or of the snow
noticed, the requisite
agreement, and the normal
progress from snow to blue to cold
logic, without argument, open to shut
like curtains but not
how the dream has
no proof of its objects, not
how the world folds into speechlessness
how the silk curtains are enflamed
feeling in the folds of the silk curtains
untranslatable effects
as if we could touch the light
pick it up and put it in the mouth
exhale audible shade,
the deepest blue, say you
saying *I* say you.

to Norma Cole

MARK LEVINE

ECAUSE IT IS balanced right on the edge where sense becomes non-sense, Mark Levine's work is always engaged with the issues and mechanisms of sensemaking itself. Often tapping the devices and methods of more traditional lyrics, he configures his meaning as much out of sound as out of sense, supporting it further through imagery that lets us always feel that the world we know is not far off. And yet he refuses simple meanings, preferring high ambiguity and open ends, letting a tension and suspension drive his poems forward into an ever-expanding version of the world. Levine has likened the problems underlying poetry to those of juggling: the relationship to matter, the intricacies of pattern, and the problems and possibilities of symbolic action. Perhaps timing could also be added to this list, as Levine has an acute sense of delivery and delay that gives a spring action to his lines and keeps his readers poised.

Although Levine identifies himself primarily as a poet, having been educated at Brown and the Iowa Writers' Workshop, he has also had an active career as a long-form journalist, reporting for *The New Yorker*, the *New York Times Magazine*, *Outside*, and other magazines, and recently publishing *F5*, a book about a natural disaster. His first book of poetry, *Debt*, was a 1993 National Poetry Series selection; his two subsequent collections have been published by the University of California Press. The recipient of a Whiting Foundation Award and a National Endowment for the Arts Fellowship, Levine teaches at the Iowa Writers' Workshop and divides his time between Iowa and Brooklyn.

CHIMNEY SONG

Mother's shelf is crooked and bare.
Mother lost her hair.

We swim regardless. The white sandstorm
Is no cause for alarm.

Then in the plaza on coronation day
A shadow in disarray

Teased the hawks through the bare sky
Today; in disarray.

Wrapped in air in the absence of sun
We fell as one

And thought as one and sang or thought
We did; all for nought.

Mother's gash was tamped with pine-needles,
A nest of yellow pine-needles

Swept from the eaves of a crumpled den.
But why and when?

Pilot came by with an illuminated book
And an injured rook; and the cook

Tried his best to deny what he'd heard,
Dusty forgotten lord.

All of our scalps itched all of the time.
The pollen's to blame,

And the stew and the wind and the wig and the sling
And the destination and the ashy thing.

EVENT

1.   Thatched roof webbed against the sea.

2.   Moon and red water, red sea-vines, sea-plants, the momentary
     shoreline.

3.   Striped shirt knotted to the branch of a fir.
     Spotted shirt tacked above a sagging doorframe.

4.   Darkness on one side; daylight beyond.

5.   Rain. Glass tiles in a murky basin.

6.   The instruction to dance, heels fixed to the plank.

7.   Clattering of beads. Wind stirring the red lanterns.

8.   ". . . a long way from home," etc.

9.   Ladder angled against an angled wall; rungs blackened by bootprints.

10. Accordion, bamboo, crinoline, drift.
     Burial, crabgrass, demonstration, edge.

11. A metallic thrum beneath the pile of shavings.

12. "The women pretending to be crows,
     The men pretending to be something else."

13. Bodies glossed by moonlight.

14. A keepsake, a number, a means of transportation, a message, a rock.

15. Cudgel, dimension, effigy, guile, hasp.
     Effigy, guile, hasp, ink.

16. Asleep in the weeds with the migrating sea-birds.

17. Borrowing a stranger's varnished canoe.

THE WILDS

Child of my hand
the field is combed for you
in patterns, postage stamps.
Yield.

I was writing of the sun
in that other place and the blaze
of it hit me in the
runnels, daybook

devoted
to the swelling laurel tree.
I found power's strap
on an old torso

at the back of the icebox
alongside the fallen item
and closed the coverlid
the moment the sun stopped.

I miss being in its identifying cinch.
I gave up my title
but reach for it back,
pond-dweller

spilling flowers on my
ruminations.

■ ■ ■

I HAVE a little alphabet
for you, my near-miss
in the disordered port.
It keeps track of the aurora
speaking of it.

Speaking of us on the cedar bench
studying the minnow pool
on whose utmost layer
a stick figure floats
its militancy.

In the child's game a child
is launched from branch to branch
in a toy forest
having been targeted for
invisibility.

I have a little world
for you, my sake-of-day, I fashioned
it from this world's
seedy thing, dross in which
I know you only.

■   ■   ■

CHILD does it hurt?
The moon is searching you
out across the ravine.

Day comes and helps
you from your blankets.
No one needs
you to know they are
remaining behind where
it hurts less,
immediately.

There is a
substance in your hand
lifted by your hand
from the sill as you
went out.
It is what, a tissue of fact
disintegrating,

carrying
you to the reputed
frozen waters, you

leaping across not
looking down.

■   ■   ■

SPRING. Absence of wonder.
Lay beneath a willow

clutching tussocks of whispering grass.
Extruded the bloom. Spring.

When I consider that I
am a half-child, have half a child
fading in the glade
in disbelief, then I consider that the
other child, old and stiff and straying, must
stand and wait.

Two things, darkness, like two women,
one past her best days in the basin,
one taken by force.

Hurt my hand holding myself
in the armed position and the hurt
migrated up my arm in sleep
past the turnaround point and
lodged with me.

It was the outcome of a proposition.
It was a set of shoe prints in white mud
in a given direction.

■   ■   ■

WE WILL not stare in that
particular pond again.

            Tell me about the woods again.

I was speaking in blocks when I
was speaking in sheets. Rain came washing.

Nature, its petals, reared up
a twig, burnished in my side.

We made a truce in our waders in the chill
willow stream and rags changed hands,

rags in whose illumined threads
a future was embedded.

      Boy slips full grown
      through the grazing portals

      into the woods to check his traps.

    ■   ■   ■

you down there, old
child, you in your outgrown hobs.
I think I'll remember you
spilling your sense
where the earthy things play.

      You, goose-stepping
      in the poppies, thinking, thinking through a tank.

      Or on a sea of foam, peeping above your crawlspace,
      pencil rising and incising.

A delight could be had by bearing it,
an ornithologist's delight at the appearance
of the curved beak.
Vowel pokes from the soil forevermore,
I remember.

Fastidious rain.
Wading pool, stirred by
a child's fingers,
in which the dashing watercraft
subside.

Nail in the socket,
memory dividing
into grass and brain,
I hear music in the stars,

      dust-obliterating day
      of welcome.

NATHANIEL MACKEY

O
VER THE COURSE of his many books, both poetry and prose, Nathaniel Mackey has become a master of the multivolume serial work, such as his ongoing *Song of the Andoumboulou,* named for a rasping Dogon funeral song that is also a song of rebirth. The Andoumboulou are, in the Dogon cosmology of Mali, "progenitor spirits," a failed earlier form of human being, "a rough draft," and, as Mackey makes clear, "the Andoumboulou are in fact us; we're the rough draft." In and out of all this weaves the serial poem "*Mu*," which also takes music as a point of origin, in this case, the jazz trumpeter Don Cherry's "*Mu*" albums. And Mackey has written three volumes of an ongoing epistolary novel, *From a Broken Bottle Traces of Perfume Still Emanate.* Though diverse in style, all of his works show the writer's mastery of the complex, interwoven textures of storytelling, incantation, and jazz. Resonant with history and mythology, Mackey's work nonetheless always addresses the needs of our contemporary social fabric.

Nathaniel Mackey was raised in Southern California; he received his BA from Princeton University, and his PhD at Stanford. Since 1982, he has edited the important multicultural literary journal *Hambone,* and he is also the host of *Tanganyika Strut,* a radio show that explores African music and its influences throughout the world. In addition to poetry and prose, he is the author of two books of literary criticism, *Paracritical Hinge* and *Discrepant Engagement: Dissonance, Cross-Culturality, and Experimental Writing,* and co-editor with Art Lange of the anthology *At a Moment's Notice: Jazz in Poetry and Prose.* Mackey's latest book of poetry, *Splay Anthem,* received the National Book Award in 2006; he has also received a Whiting Writer's Fellowship and is a Chancellor of the Academy of American Poets. He teaches at the University of California at Santa Cruz.

SONG OF THE ANDOUMBOULOU: 64

—sound and sediment—

In the alternate world
another alternate world.
  I tore off and I turned
    away. Alma Bridge
                    Road
    I turned off on, non-
  allegorical water on my
right, allegorical water on
my left . . . The left side
    said the soul was
                    burnt
    wood. Soul was only
      itself said the right . . .
Sweet beast in whose
belly we fell asleep again,
                        the
      sweet beast music was
    we'd be. I was pinioning
  light's incommensurate
      object. I wanted the
      baby's cry to mean I'd
                        begun
    again

            ∎

  Soon it came time to go,
the one thing we'd hear
  no end of. Going newly
                    sung
    about known from day
                      one,
  tread of light newly blue
unbeknown to us . . . Earth
fell away toward water,
      dreamt or imagined
                      incline,
  newly anaphylactic walk . . .
    Began to be gone away
from, soon it was a train we

were on. In the club
                    car
    toasting time, drinks lifted,
                              people
getting ready not ready, an
    autumn note suddenly
                        struck.

Where we came to next I
    was lately an elder. Spat rum
    rode my head. Torn organ
I wanted to be done with, I
                        lay
on my side hearing a baby
                        cry . . .
Late moment gotten back but
altered, endlessly not what it
was. Nub was to Quag as
                        he was
    to her, we to what what they
    sang disguised . . . Goat-
faced abatement might've
been bird-faced, warble an
                        acoustic
    feint . . . Sun streamed in thru
    the leaves, branches, light
                        between
    lubric legs. We were men,
    were it light between a man's
legs women, women, were it
    light between a woman's
                        legs
    men. So light's amendment
                        went . . .

    Light streamed in, the air
    suddenly strung, none were we
                        either,
    both

■

It wasn't light we were
attended by. Dark lay
  under the leaves and we
                    with
  it, we for whom the rain
                    would
come . . . Not to be known what
  we it was, its or another,
  water, falling star, non-
equinoctial slope gone off
                    of,
what what it was no longer
was . . . Had it been a house Quag
Manor we'd have called it.
No roof bestowed its blessing,
                    no
  walls kept outside out, no way
  could we say it was a house.
    We thought it a gloam state
    scatting its whereabouts,
    tongued runaway, talked out
                    of
our heads . . . All we knew was
  the two we were divided
  by, pungent book where their
legs met sung about incessantly,
                    said
  to be where ours would end up . . .

  In an alternate world it was other-
      wise. Dreams wore off and we were
    only as we were, dreamlessness no
                    dream
anymore

DOUBLE STACCATO

for Thaddeus Mosley

A tipsy walk the walk we took.
Tilt had its way, teeter. So to
   say, so to say, we said,
  wood's whatsaid serenade
   emulated, "mu" forty-fourth
                            part . . .
A closer walk thru the forest of
semblances nicked our skin. Wood's
near side leaned in, leaned out.
   Gouge's gospel it was we
  brushed against, wood's new
                  kingdom
   come . . . At blade's edge ground
  gave way. Planetary mend, ad-
  monishment. Legs abruptly
  rubber it seemed . . . Synaesthetic
   snout, synaesthetic eye-slit.
                     Head
   broken off come to a point pointing
   up in back, grain plied say on
say. Grain said say, laid elsewhere,
               lay
within squint's reach . . . A wobbly walk
                thru the
   forest of semblances it was. Sledge-
  headed lean looked out at us . . . Book
  of blade, alphabet of scuff it turned
                  out,
scrape, scour, scuff . . . Water slid ashore
not far away, wood eventually water,
  walk so long sung about closer
than we thought. Wood said to be
  source as if to say it was once
               water,
wood already water, grain its giving
  way . . . Sand lay grain on grain, we
saw each one, said or thought we
            saw.
  Wave an oblique writing on wood,
             ripple,

wave our diluvian book . . . So to say,
    we said, so to say. What I heard
       was in my head, I said, no one was
listening, wood's walk talked
even so . . . What would wood say we
                           asked
and we answered . . . So to say, we said,
    so to say . . . Dark wood siphoning
    light, we leaned in, dark wood's long
                          way

home

BLUE ANUNCIA'S BIRD LUTE
after Bob Thompson

  Bedless trek she saw
them embarked on. Choked
  earth they were strewn
    across . . . Sleepless,
                 walked
  in their sleep she said it
seemed, yet-to-be world
on the tips of their tongues,
    each in the other's
               eyes no
  end . . . Lost endowment,
indigent kin. Lapsed earth
gone after, something they
             saw
  she knew they saw . . . The
lute's neck's gooseneck
          look . . .
And so said nothing. Cigarette
stuck to a nonchalant lower lip . . .
  No book of dissolving the
            book
  said less . . . Lithe body had at
by one that wasn't there, hers in
            the
    his-and-her ghost house, near
  water, nose caught by sea smell,
salt, said to've been known before,

              moved on, soon to be there
                                            again . . .
              Patch of hair he put his hand
              to. Voice eaten at by what names
              fell away from, thrall nothing
          there gave its due . . . Roofless,
                                        floor-
          less umbra. Patch of hair parting
              the dark welcoming heaven.
              Bound legs of a bird she held
                                        on
        to . . . Amniotic light in no one's
            eyes if not his. Hand assessing
            her leg mounting skyward . . .
              Wonderment winged but
                                    with
          legs held, hard to miss what it
                                      meant . . .
              Hers to be his to be hers ad
              infinitum, smoke smudging
                                    the
          bell of her throat. To what had
              been or might've been her
              thoughts migrated, cloth wall
                                      he
          pressed his hand against, he of
              the indelicate embrace. Split
                                    stem
        of a bass played awkwardly, canvas
                                        wall he
          reached in
          thru

STEFANIE MARLIS

S
TEFANIE MARLIS'S SPARE, aphoristic poetry combines crisp, open language with startling imagery to focus on the emotional undercurrents of contemporary life. Her sharp eye looks at neighbors, lovers, strangers, and friends with a compassion that refuses sentimentality, rooted instead in a faith in the rhythms of life that she articulates through the rhythms of language. Her free-verse lyrics put pressure on fine detail—whether it's a single word or a fallen leaf—to search out patterns of meaning, and use the first-person singular to underscore a commonality that runs through human experience. Often, as in her prose poem series based upon the definitions of obscure or forgotten words, what begins in logic suddenly veers into flights of association and impression as if, paradoxically, by recovering lost language we could enter into previously unexplored regions of signification.

Marlis was raised in Buffalo, New York, and moved to the Bay Area in 1974, where she received an MA in creative writing from San Francisco State University. For the past sixteen years, she has run her own copywriting business, specializing in green companies, arts organizations, and non-profits. In addition to six volumes of poetry, she has written two commercial books for Chronicle Books and a novel, *Love (K)nots*. Her second book, *Slow Joy*, won both the 1989 Brittingham Prize and the Great Lakes Colleges New Writers Award, and *fine* (2002) was nominated for the Bay Area Book Reviewers Award. Other honors include the Joseph Henry Jackson Award, two Marin Arts Council grants, and an NEA Fellowship. She currently lives in Santa Fe, New Mexico.

GREEN FLAME

a woman turning in her bed
like fire catching on   we know what we inherit
          bonfire high as a water tower

       she threw someone in, in his forest-green suit,
close by, by accident, a child learns

blaze running down each branch, each petiole,
      leaf   a flamy face

we can almost come to

ANTENNAE

•

The doctor lifted the baby's leg, and the father heard his mother-in-law whisper, "What is it?"

••

A tiny red, white, and blue flag waves on an antenna—now and again.

•••

One notices more bearded ladies these days. To what are they listening?

••••

He said the ability to decide to be good. She said we can watch ourselves.

CHOICES

•

The last to choose, a boy walks across the band room to a clarinet and a trombone.

His father is a tall man who considers banana bread fruit and clicks his tongue at beauty.

His mother sleeps with a leg over the edge of the bed. The boy thinks of her carrying groceries by the French bakery, pointing to eclairs with her elbow.

This or that, cool in his hands, he compares their heft, how each mimics his body.

People are glad inside their ears. He has slept many nights on why just those two remained.

Some notes look up like animals drinking.

•

Turning away, a man who's lost and lost looks out on a green lake and calls himself lucky.

His father, a scientist, the son of a scientist, the son of a man who made rope, would pat him on the head.

When excited his mother made high-pitched oohs. She sailed to Ceylon and brought back a tin of cinnamon.

The man knows the rippled green is perfect with his eyes closed.

Inside the curve of a horseshoe, beneath the roof of a seven, the rest of his life cannot wake.

A bitter storm blows over the lake; the man slides an egg into a drawer.

•

A woman with callused hands hovers between two climate zones, one with little rain.

Her mother, a woman who moistens her thumb before turning a page, lives to the north.

Her father, long gone, a sun-stained man with bristly hair, had wanted a boy.

In the midst of packing, she envies the bee and dung beetle their certain knowledge.

Over and over it comes round, as in a shooting gallery, a blue duck among the yellow: where is home?

She anticipates a checkered lily. She pictures cloth made from the ocotillo's ruffles.

•

A man stops drinking and meets a woman who betrays him, then one who does not.

His mother prides herself on sweeping her hair into a perfect chignon in under two minutes.

His stepfather polished his boots with mink oil and woke in the night with leg cramps.

The man looks at where clouds have come together, puzzle pieces.

He likes the one woman. She keeps his favorite ice cream in her freezer.

The other, whose lies are black, lies back.

•

A woman who's gone to the movies by herself finds a wallet.

Her mother forgets things. The woman has an image of her doing the cha-cha on the patio beneath a kiwi vine.

Her father lost a finger many years ago. He's described the dreamlike slice many times. She pictures him holding a glass.

She sets the wallet on the armrest. There's a lot of sighing on screen.

A finder's fee may be hers; the woman considers how generally an absence becomes a presence.

She feels for the wallet—finds a piece of fruit.

•

On the way, a woman decides there are no words to make things right.

Her father divorced her mother for the woman next door.

Her mother met a man in an aisle in Safeway who volunteered.

She wheels her father out into the air. Looking straight ahead, he tells her that her mother comes to him every day.

When she asks if she helps him, he says no; she sits and visits, looking beautiful.

On the way home, she tilts the rear-view mirror down. She has her mother's mouth.

•

A woman rolls back the freezer door with a hand round as a crab.

Her mother would wait on the front steps, skirt above her knees. She'd tilt her head back on its stalk and exhale smoke.

Her father was as pretty as a woman.

When she was young and went to the coffee shop with friends, she'd eat lemon wedges, which she'd salt first.

She's parked across from the corner market, bag with ice cream on the seat, tubular cloud asleep in the blue over the roof.

She can feel rolls of flesh spread across her body, tide of smoke.

•

A young man drops out of a Hindu monastery.

His adoptive father visits him in the Philippines after the young man falls for a Filipino girl selling jackfruit and coconuts.

He pictures his adoptive mother, always athletic, dipping her head as a bird flies through the car.

Walking to his apartment carrying three containers of orange juice, he sees his mind/body as a window he's looking through.

After India, the Air Force sounded inviting. Twenty years ago.

He pours a glass of juice for one of his sons. At least he thinks he does.

•

As a girl she found a cold bird in the duff beneath a grove of pines and put it in her pocket.

Her father hid his past, but when he grew older wrote down his thoughts. Things like: "You cannot trust a god you know."

Her mother once watched Hitler take off his coat at the opera.

A terrible man is found in a hole beneath a cellar.

On television, a hand shines a light in his fur-hedged mouth.

Her heart bristles when the news says "spider hole." Bring the heinous close she says to herself.

occur—to take place, to come about, from the Latin *occurrere ob* + *currere*, to run—some chalk it up to vibration, an imitation of the hummingbird's hover, a fence grazed by a cloven hoof. Whatever makes electrons wobble or a deer skittish makes those who can't help but notice one another ready to run, though it's unclear in which direction.

creek—a watercourse smaller than a river, from the Old Norwegian *kriki*, bend—fallen, hand-sized, heart-shaped leaves cover the octopi and treasure chests imprinted on the plastic pool he bought for the dog. Everything's changing; everything's turning; soon the rains will come, and the dog won't want to cool off. Soon, everything will sail around the bend.

sfumato—the blurring of lines, from the Italian *sfumare*, to fade out—and they meet again, after twenty years, at the bar out on the highway. One remembers the way the other would push his cowboy hat from his face with his beer. The world is stamped with tenses, every bird-beaded roadside existing equally, none caring about any other as a jet's roar fades into a dog's bark.

twist—to wind together so as to produce a single strand, from the Middle English *twisten*, a divided object—the shadow on her liver's still there, but "good news!" sings the doctor, her bones seem cancer-free. Husband cries with joy in that moment God's speed flies towards him; frozen to the track, he thinks: could this life (her in bed and two demanding children) go on for years?

thwart—to prevent the occurrence of, from the Middle English, *thwerten*, across—"no bras showing, no slouchy pants, no bare midriffs"; the twins, thirteen in November, discreetly circumvent the school's new dress code. The one who walks with a crutch has on a lovely, little spaghetti-strap tank; she's looking across an imaginary divide, which, of course, isn't imaginary at all.

DANGEROUS ARCHIPELAGOS

A man takes a break from his paper work and stands thousands of miles away—on the deck of a boat in the South Pacific—years ago. He hears the water lapping on the hull and the voices below. The light pours down from the stars, from holes punched in the top of a shoe box. Everything, they say, has its time and its place. He's doing his taxes; Jupiter is about to be struck by a comet; and he remembers a man old enough to be his father walking around on deck with one shoe.

GREEN CARD, BLUE SHOES

Tired of waiting table at the Yacht Club, in June, she writes a romance novel. In July, just before she leaves for Paris, she meets a Frenchman who would like to marry her and who she would like to marry—each has fallen in love with the other's country. They spend a week in Provence together, cherries and hazelnuts being sold in the markets. He's like a pair of shoes I once bought, she says. Little blue Italian sculptures that went with nothing in my wardrobe or any future wardrobe. When Harlequin rejects her book—not enough sex, she is told—she doesn't despair but begins rewriting it, switching genres, replacing the love scenes with murders.

DEAR ELEGY

The dear slipped into the wood—
a second time, I thought, swept up to a tender post.

I sat for two nights with my legs crossed.

Simple in their bodies as dolls without clothes
those dear to the dear pop up.

Weeks shoot past, the dear appears, a red J stuck over
his heart,
the one from his passport

PHOENIX ELEGY

People cut down their piney homes, then, after sixty years, it's us happily hearing ivorybills again—their spondee rap just like that of woodpeckers in South America. After Earth shakes loose, a man, eating dinner, might spur human kindness, as you did. That may be the only kind of man at the table.

MARK McMORRIS

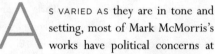

S VARIED AS they are in tone and setting, most of Mark McMorris's works have political concerns at their core, whether based in international relations or interpersonal communication. Never didactic, or even particularly direct, his approach is often intimate and individual, shifting through personas identified by dialect, attitude, or point of view. These shifts keep the reader mindful of the determining role of perspective and, above all, of social relationships. Though his poems often take a narrative stance and his lines are often syntactically and grammatically clear, they give a false sense of stability as they build into nebulous scenes that resist a single, set interpretation. Instead, through highly evocative vocabulary, they create a field of charged potential in which memory and image fuse.

McMorris was born in Jamaica and moved to New York City to attend Columbia University, then went to Brown University, where he took an MA in poetry and a PhD in comparative literature. His books have twice been chosen in the University of Georgia Contemporary Poetry Series, and *The Blaze of the Poui* was a finalist for the 2004 Lenore Marshall Prize. In addition to poetry, he has written critically on a wide range of subjects, from Louis Zukofsky to contemporary experimental poetics to postcolonial literature, and has worked in sound poetry and performance, presenting work at the annual arts festival in Geneva, Switzerland. Mark McMorris has been the Holloway Visiting Professor at UC Berkeley and is on the faculty at Georgetown University, where he also directs the Lannan Center for Poetics and Social Practice.

from REEF: SHADOW OF GREEN

(WOOD)

The camera's eye-lid, a noisy blink: yellow petals flowering

Some sent their daughters to Vassar College in the north
I married one, one yellow tree, one college, one minister
some woke later than the gardener who cut the lawn
and went astray, in the back yard, catching butterfly.
One could still catch butterfly in those days, believe me,
and I caught lizards, a bad cold, a beating, other things.
Went to the wharf to see the skyscraper ships (New York).
Went to university to see the knowledge heads (New York).
No joy.

> Agouti is an animal and
> today is the hero's birthday
> a statue erect: *Bob Marley at the Arena*
>   gouging the population
>   a South American movie
I found the log book, a translator.

                    ■   ■   ■

The log-book opens: "America is conquered.
We have seen no savages in months—no trace.
The gods have left for more habitable spots.
Send reinforcements: seven armadas, *grazia*.
I leave these heirlooms to my replacement.

>   rotting wood, methane gas, pulped star-apples
> the conchs carelessly dead
>   (Our wives—were we ever married, were we?)

Someone kept a catalogue of the landfall.

(TONGUE)

The undressed jungle at the water's edge—
green leaf like a naked belly.
                    (Our wives—were we ever married?)

The starfish with her pimply arms as
rigid as a tongue on my neck.

The sea urchin washed up from the sea bed—
her prickly sex.

The wounded skin of driftwood—
seamed by water and
left out to dry by a careless hurricane.

The tide-suck in the stomach as
the moon seduces the ocean away
from her lover on the black land, my land.
                                    (Our wives—)

(BLOOD)

        list pinned to the zinc wall of the rum shop
            sea-gull   canoe   man-eaters   wild-pig
                                            (no one)
marlin   callaloo   google-eyed fish   frangipani
                                        (wood word)

                    ■   ■   ■

A single tree, the tree with a name, the yellow poui
a single tree, the tree of blossoms, the name is lost
in heaven and everything turns to brown, it mash up

some do the mashin' and call the police
some go to jail, others to seed, some to all that trouble

                    a graceful body that love the deep places
                white flowers to amuse a girl
                                        (no one to see)

FAUVE HARMONICS

In thick magnolia, the bodies of parrots—a city of parrots—
assemble their dark-blue feathers and build to solid forms
promising rehearsals for the night's seductive theatre
dense-packed, moving interiors in tune to a leaf's murmur:
the birds attentive to sit within the perfect space

the leaves dreaming of the Fauves, still to announce
brushed paint across white landscapes, a daubed
evolution feathering the present, viridescent wings.

Still in the dark, the tree frog in hiding, the cricket and owl
begin to self-compose, the nightly discord of nostalgia
ripples the leaves to silver chords in a chorus of fern
and the basso-note-poet, he comes with his clumsy
imitations, and lays metaphor on the stone, on leaf
that shelters the birds from our sight, where they perform.

Such sounds have green sea and mountain for sources
or nothing collects in the night that tremors
without significance—without symbols to seal them in—
until I watch the ideas pushing through the feathers
like cracks just visible or blossoms, once the season ripens
and the forms huddle and blend, in their chosen parts.

LETTER FOR K & POEMS FOR SOMEONE ELSE

(A POEM)

The mirror says: a chalk house. The mirror says: leather box;
a courtyard with moss. The air frantic with fire and books
so pages fall to the cistern. The mirror's back has no silver.
The book needs to begin, needs a rose, I said, a place to sit
and study the tea that falls from the tea plant, the light
falls steady in the book, the leaves of light and of tea
in the mirror that is a book and a girl that reads looks up
a name in the moss, a green name in a red house, looks up
at hawk, at hawk-writing, and sees a girl in a red window
a green finger to her lips. I know her from the photo-
pictorial in the leather box. But the hawk and his name
the girl and the book; so the leaf and silver cloud, so back
and beguile; so sweater with moth-holes and scripts
from the Caliphate of WAS: they went into the book
that went into the flames. The girl and her ashes and hawk
are on a path to the courtyard; say then that the book
was banned and the tea was tea-ish, the mirror a glass.
What girl could read such a fire, what leaf would light
begin to write upon blue, or on moss, at stroke of noon?

[LETTERS TO MICHAEL: DEAR MICHAEL (1)]

Dear K
Found the passage you asked for
it's lovely I know you think
better of me that I like it too
that's a joke my sweet the war
bruises everyone until and even Nicole
is afraid of the government and
I miss you it's crazy to talk
this way but it must be the time.

(A POEM)

> dis poem shall say nothing new
> dis poem shall speak of time
> —MUTABARUKA

The larks animate the morning with their signals
to each other that I overhear and cannot decode
draw me from the doorway to the street, to be one
among several musics that score the city I love.
Today the Lord dies again; a scholar writes in Greek
his story of mystery; the translator comes to Antioch
to start on the final book, the one that was lost for good.
I breathe the same air and sound of voices falling
onto a page that cannot record the thing itself
how your face is close to my thought, as close as a breath
that I still listen to, a translator who keeps very still.
In one or another folio on the shelf, it says that I look
at train schedules and take steps to book your flight
dressed up for a meeting at a café. It is a volume
I want to read at once, to conclude, and start over,
a book that meets a scholar, a scholar that meets a train,
a train that meets a woman, a woman who meets me.
But this poem is like a war that never ends, this poem
has no closure, it unravels as I write, it starts again
on the Pontus Euxine, on an island, and then it says:

(A POEM)

And so the vehicles came from driveways in the suburbs
on television the Budweiser cart brought kegs to a tavern
a game was decided in the final seconds, and the war—
the war was pictures and absence, and folks ran up the flags
over the middle country, the coasts and the South, bewildered
and yet relieved to see all that power, that certainty of might.
Some said that night would never end, had been a war
since 1453   or 1097   /   or 410   or 336 BC
had been continuous combat since Helen gave Paris a flower
at least since the Bronze Age of Agamemnon's armada.
I had no time for the war. The bundle asleep on a ventilator
was a person under folds of thin cloth; I had no time
for this individual who was as good as dead, in this city
of memorials to the dead. The seat of a new imperium,
the White House said freedom and meant that the dead
are free to trouble each other. I had no time for the dead.

■   ■   ■

Since the Hittites rode on chariots, and there was script.

In caustic time, since Byblos fell to Alexander, since Damascus
to the English lion; and since Hektor, tamer of horses
and since Dunkirk and Bosnia fell to enemy phalanxes.

In caustic time, since Balaclava, Barcelona
since Byron fell asleep on the Aegean, and since Kuwait
fell to the tanks and Agincourt to the bowmen and since
Baghdad fell to Crawford in Texas, and Archimedes
built his engines and fell to a legionnaire—I am perfectly
sane—and since Delhi fell to the Indians, as was right,
and since the Orange Street holocaust in Kingston.

And in that time, since a scholar read old Egyptian
and brought an obelisk to the Place de la Concorde
(the circle of harmony), and since the Tutsis or the Kikuyu
or since the Xhosa or the Taino, I have no time for this.
The year is not yet ripe

                    to read novels as the bombs fall
to study the Phaedrus or go bowling and have a pancake
or to be ordinary and to fix a broken door lock. I disagree.

It is better to shine shoes than to starve, I can't agree.
I know nothing about it. It is better to pick apples—or slash cane—
on earth than to lie under it. I have no time for questions.
Bring the troops home, people do Vandal, they riot in America
I see it on television. Cherry blossoms are falling there love.

I remember the blossoms. The light falls like blossoms.

Everything falls, to pieces, to the victor, to someone's lot
falls like a girl falls or a blossom, falls head over heels
like a city or water and like darkness falls, a dynast
a government can fall, or an apple, a cadence, the side of a hill.
The road can fall to the sea, the land in the ascent, o sky.
Doom like a knife in the chest, this falls
and has fallen from spear points and rifles, blades of light
that cut through the skin of a lemon and peel away doubt
falls into line with opinion I know what you think
a glance can fall like doom and therefore like a knife and a river
this makes no sense I have no time for metaphor or you or this
falls or I will more than my share and you will have less
oh yes, the water can fall like a sky and a lot
like a blossom in the dusk, and a scepter falls to the mat
the Fall of Byzantium was not so long ago that it falls
out of mind like a person from a moving streetcar, always
I said that the light falls on lilacs in the window box
the features on a coin fall away and the era of mosques, this
time of cathedrals and temples, and the long fall of Lucifer
to his kingdom on earth and our falling is always falling.

(A POEM)

When the combat finally stops, then I will come to you
like a soldier to his commander, and you will decorate my chest
with fingers too soft and too precious for other uses, asking
my kill rate and praising my accurate eye, the night of lemon
blossoms perfuming your under arms, your heart's land
undressed for my touch and my guilt abolished, the blood
left on the porch. The cicadas will trumpet my coming
and cancel the shriek of Tomahawks and soothe my ears.

When the combat ceases for good, I will put off the clothes
stained with shit and gunpowder, the boots eaten away
and my rusty helmet, and dress up to suit your dignity.

I will have cherry blossoms or the photo of a yellow poui
and they will speak on my behalf of the continuous war
the war that is falling in and out of the signal's compass
the signal I rode on to this gate that creaks behind me.
Combat spells the end of civility but I must begin with you.

When the combat ends, and bulldozers have crushed the shanties
and ploughed a thousand or five corpses under the pasture
the young man has lost his legs, and has questions for someone
and the vehicles head home to Greenwich and the janitors
empty the trash, and the captains hold their fire. At that time
but at no time does the war cease from thunder and the crack
of a rifle, and the book of your labyrinth has no beginning
or respite from the dark, and I must retreat as I approach.

When the combat closes down, look for me in Tempe
and you should expect some ceremony in my face
because when the war goes bankrupt and is swallowed up
then it will be time to drink a toast, and to get on with it,
one on one, one kiss or word at a time, in good time.

—*16 April 2003*

JANE MILLER

ISARMING, COLLOQUIAL, WRY, and intimate, Jane Miller's poems are immediately compelling with their companionable voices and surprising metaphorical transformations. Sometimes narrative and sometimes associative, they reflect her concern with lyric process and a complex seriality. A Jane Miller poem can be brazenly extravagant or subtle and restrained. There is a supple grace to these poems that allows the reader to be woven into the fabric of their meditations. Her recent book-length collection, *A Palace of Pearls*, draws (as does some of the earlier work) from a rich palette of multicultural influences—in this case the architecture, science, and art of an ancient Arab kingdom, Al-Andalus, resulting in a tour de force reckoning of traditional and personal mythologies while touching upon sources as diverse as contemporary Rome and the life of Lorca.

Miller is the author of eight collections of poetry: *Many Junipers, Heartbeats*; *The Greater Leisures*; *Black Holes, Black Stockings* (with Olga Broumas); *American Odalisque, August Zero* (winner of the Western States Book Award); *Memory at These Speeds: New and Selected Poems*; *Wherever You Lay Your Head*; and *A Palace of Pearls*. Her latest work is *Midnights*, a collaboration with the painter Beverly Pepper. She has also published a collection of essays, *Working Time: Essays on Poetry, Culture, and Travel*. Miller has been the recipient of a Lila Wallace–Reader's Digest Award, a Guggenheim Fellowship, and two NEA Fellowships. She is a professor of English in the Creative Writing Program at the University of Arizona.

from A PALACE OF PEARLS

2

Lightning lights the moon's shroud

the surface of my body is excited

like sharp stabs of emotion in love

for whose art the sun is god

tonight the senses spring from the soul

as once was thought

a brief release of something unseen then enlightenment

like a gaslamp struck

embarking on a long weekend alone a long week a season a year

another year father trying to pierce the dark

thinking is only ever provisional

this is what I think now that we are both alone

I can't remember enough I make shit up

our time together is now a feeling

and all my thinking about you the flicker of event

the bond of physiognomy a child's distant melodic greeting

by all accounts sketchy lest I make too much of them

lost just in time nothing serious

on my own reconnaissance some admire me some feel sorry

I've spent most of my life

thinking art would make sense of it

A FOOT SOLDIER SEIZED IN SIGHT OF HIS OWN SQUADRON

4

Do you know how long it has been since a moral choice presented itself

and the wrong choice was made

not two minutes

why is it not quiet between lightning and thunder as if someone were asking

do you have other articulable feelings if so express them now

tragedy ensues

with a laser blast from the cockpit

the dangled finger of God makes contact

PLEASE CALL FOR SEVERAL HUNDRED THOUSAND PHYSICIANS QUICKLY

22

My darling would rather raise a goose

before she'd cook and eat it

does that mean she would then eat it

is not such ambiguity

a creamy golden cherry blushing

impenetrable all clear juice and perfume

of honeyed lavender Michelangelo's males

don't have more porcelain beauty than my white peach

my beloved can separation return us

our young and lithe marriage our heroics of love

where I pull back the pale green summer coverlet

upon the manner of our incompleteness a blue

which may not exist in nature and a gray too

beyond our understanding but often present

to find willingness and open air and grandeur

as the sun and the moonlight variously play

upon our round bruised bodies and our bruised sharp minds

our hope seems justified but let us not return

to innocence let us come with half closed eyes

to feel more powerfully actual than merely real

things stomachs taut with sexual thunder rumbling

some moments of some days at home in our own bed

and live the rest of the time in this great rotten country

trying to make sure there is a rest of the world

it's no example to fathom a banquet of fruit

squeezed and dripped nimbly in the sealed wild

mood of eager mind my darling loves me

unaccountably despite my wasting her time

in this poem while she's hard at work in the real world

of Rome and I'm at home excoriating

a surface a small matter never mind it feels

like my own skin unheroically grating a lime

in God's hands but more ironically than some

Renaissance painters may have thought of the brush

to wit I am as free-spirited as any Roman

thinking about the surface as it reflects the depths

but history is the last thing poems should tell

and stories next to last so poetry is all

a scent of berry like a splash of destiny

which hints at the best of life and after its small

thrill passes like a small lost civilization

it can be solace and sadness as well

no matter how long I write how ill or well

the story say of a lost civilization

or that we might be last of the generations

the poem restores nothing

blueberries limes peaches my love zero

why then is the poet

the last to see as a god

that earth from the heavens is radiant fruit

CHERRIES BLUEBERRIES WHITE PEACHES AND LIMES

28

Dressed as a Moor in curtain and towel and plastered in rice powder

a servant gravely recites a semi-invented tale

The Palace of Pearls of which little is recorded

but much might be imagined

for the delectation of two enthralled brothers

with black shiny hair and white starched blouses

as white as funereal roses and black eyes as black

as a sleeveless black summer dress of mourning

for an endless hour in an Andalusian garden

before these well-off kids are called to eat lemony squid

and forced to nap from the heat such that years shall pass thus

before they awaken to a day their Granada is surrounded

by Nationalist soldiers who are sneering at them

saying that those who don't wear uniforms should wear skirts

I imagine at night more bullshit with their short cigars

while they search house to house accusing the one slight man

of contacting Russia and hiding

the radio in his piano a vile invention of armed civil authority

who murder Federico García Lorca

on native soil to this day no one is saying

exactly where exactly by which olive trees

does he fall like a puppet do the Guard piss afterward on the shallow grave

there comes a reckoning that it might be a failure

to theorize and anyway what's art

all about if it merely lengthens the shadows

that make the cowards evil and the poet immortal

nevertheless even the lowliest poet

would rather go home

to a meal of fireplace embers than not

go down that deserted road

of red earth and imagine the bloody worst

because necessity dictates one must

BE CAREFUL OF MURDERERS IN A PALACE OF PEARLS

CODA

The horizon is totaled by clouds

A foot soldier seized in sight of his own squadron

No one will be responsible least of all

Please call for several hundred thousand physicians quickly

As they move about the intestines of my backyard

We have our secrets

The theme of the hero brought low

The last days of and so on

The natural light of the night

Caravaggio the bull and Goya the dark horse

More or less on a fool's journey

One should not stand in for someone else unless the choice is clear

In the south they will kill for a pomegranate

To fell the precious redwood to live in a redwood house

When the soft flesh falls off the fallen giants

Dead the features of the sick man are barely visible

Just my father is not my father any more

Those strangers seemed far away and harmless

A patron who has paid to be amused

The full pale moon rising in lavender sky

I think it is a lovely day

Cherries blueberries white peaches and limes

To drag recruits from their families

On quivering bones it makes a ringing of bells

The whole family will enjoy singing in fellowship around a piano

One mustn't take public transport during a war

Four times until they finally blow away

Be careful of murderers in a palace

Perfumed with warm pineapple

Beyond what is humanly possible must be an astonishing figure

The grand piano crammed into our ear

The ancestors are asleep in a safe place

Streaking toward the emergency room of my eardrum

A palace of pearls

LAURA MORIARTY

L AURA MORIARTY'S WORK fuses genres to arrive at a fluid writing rooted in the vivid impressions of everyday life. Neither metaphoric nor symbolic, her images freeze actual moments through the use of proper names and specific references. She has developed a kind of realism that suggests that history, literature, and imagination are as real as experience. Often taking on the question of the body, she enlarges it to include the body of language as well as the physical body in the world, and from there moves on to the body of work, as in *Nude Memoir*, her book-length examination of Duchamp's installation *Given*. Often lyrical, often cryptic, her work plays with coherence in a way that brings the notion of a whole into question—are these fragments? or are they entireties?—so that a glimpse, though brief, is an entire event.

Moriarty's most recent books are a novel, *Ultravioleta*, a collection of poetry, *Self-Destruction*, and *A Semblance: Selected & New Poetry, 1995–2007*. A longtime resident of the Bay Area, Moriarty was the director of the American Poetry Archives at San Francisco State University from 1986 to 1997, and is currently deputy director of Small Press Distribution in Berkeley. Her work has been awarded the San Francisco State Poetry Center Book Award, a New Langton Arts Award, and grants from the Gerbode Foundation and the Fund for Poetry. She was a frequent contributor to the journal *How(ever)* and the editor of *non*, a Web site of poetry and poetics. Laura Moriarty has taught at Mills College in Oakland and at the Naropa University Summer Writing Program.

from NUDE MEMOIR

2

Blood like
Sap

Her disposition
Her disposal
A rash act

Projected like a shadow or echo

A giantess
Felled
An arboreal fate

So that a squirrel or insect. A white thing. Gets through the crack in the wall. Not where there is brick. But near the center. Where the fruit trees and laurel on the other side are visible. Is it an apple or a peach? Animate. But not free.

"I'm a stranger here myself," she concluded. Though she has the memories of several lives. She functions as a freshly constituted being. One who has hit the wall. Over and over. "Her motion is literal."

She watches a dead man approach an accustomed meeting place. (Later she learns it wasn't him.) It's an old film or tape. The image of him moves swiftly toward his destination. He opens a glass door. His grace is surprising. The context has been established. The film is silent. The ordering is chronological or by chance. There is a color shot at the end of the tape. A familiar landmark. Old color. He smokes there. The penultimate shot. For less than a moment. (But it's not him.) His head changes. The chemistry of fading and forgetting. The close-up of his face.

Oneself as the perpetrator or golem. The inevitable conclusion to a series of stories begun in childhood. He tells his fate looking at his own hands. His cards. His métier. Detective. Close-up of his face. What is he thinking? What does he see?

Chrysanthemum	His face is
Very wide	A screen

Scene

Under the skin	Reflective
Doesn't see	Doesn't live

Holmes *is* Moriarty in this version. He pursues himself. But he kills women. Or men. Dismembers in order to forget. Discards or plants them. He finds the clues. He has left himself. Inanimate. Not separated but broken. Breakthrough. Cursing. "I have broken it!" Like a child. Once she was a bride. Somebody's mother. Someone's son. Now incomplete. "Definitively unfinished." He is not able to return and fix it. She is not.

"Funny when you want something," Diana mused. Or are wanted by something. They say she would never have married him. But what do they know? You form yourself to the desired thing. Become congruent. Feel what it feels. Is he the next in a series of developing situations? Or is he Jack the Ripper? Is this my life pouring out of me on the street? Wait a goddamned minute. I.

"From an invisible mouth words were streaming forth, turning into living entities . . ." *The Golem* (Meyerlink). His recorded voice was breathless. Rough like a road. Like a death there. A long pause. Between breaths. Lines. Lies. The anniversary of my death. And me on this fence. A tape places in the grave I call my head. People file past. They forget.

LAURA DE SADE

"To wear binding like binding" she wrote
Also "my name as the title shows
Is Laura" a common enough situation
To be bound as oneself to admit
To unpardonable pride or unusual
Desire "to court sensuosity as if it were
The judge of truth" as its own renouncing
Stands against men in the old sense
To wear down in the arena

Of full view the libertine regalia
Imagined upon a rigorous silence
As when turning back to a woman
Entangled in leaves an animate
Becomes a sentient piercing willfully
"To where a man's heart beating . . ."

SPICER'S CITY

when like palms with life
lines crossed as if memory
also didn't last

> you along the street seen
> dripping with trees
> the mind bright

We talked so long it burned my back. We never talk. My throat is bare. The
sun. Never there. Day or night.
or white but not
like this stone ball
or like this record
round
The world in your town drenched as they say. Speaking about absence. There is
a register. A blur. A child tearing though the street. Not like you either.

> high afternoon haze
> your day to be home
> In your day

is language strangely. You ask yourself what it would take. That taken. In the
same words. A boy feels along the walls as if he were blind.
they take him
they taste him
angrily
The street is torn apart. The old street hidden and changed and hidden again.
The new material. We don't sing. Our steps thrown back. The pavement as
white as the sky. Hell with the women these flyboys.

> but you are no pilot
> we sit in Gino & Carlo's
> at midday

The livid tables green as the child I mean when I say "We are not alone here."
The music is identical. The pipes moan. There is less water than before. There
is no rain at all
like real rain
I have not forgotten
we sound
the same when we say the same things like people of a certain time. As if
history were not over. This is about the neighborhood of objects we are in.
Someone is here. Is not here. It can be written the same way. It can't be said.

Black fish in paper bins. Water as clear as the sea. A boy playing hide and
seek. A small boy. A large ceramic tree. He seems lost without you. He feels
nothing.

> yet as time
> pretending to be
> you or I

Frankly I have come here for you. Some things are brutal. There will continue
to be works about gardens but this isn't one of them. This is the real world. Or
is this the world? Do I have time for a quick one before whatever passes for
night around here passes?

> distant bit of roof
> pink and red pales
> wall of gold

Chinatown finds itself open. All this silk. The old patterns imagined again
burning. Torn or thrown away. Acres of it. Children dancing crazily to bells. No
one tells them.

> moon of iron
> rock garden steps
> am tired boy

oak and palms tried
Like criminals we
know too much. A deserted watering hole in the deserted West. The Polk
Gulch. The Mediterranean sun divides its victims. Each searches for the
other one. And I can still feel the burn. The new set of words. Obvious in its
disguises. I have pictures of the empty room.

> unconscious quotation
> broken like bones
> they were yours

Gay bones. Jay De Feo eyes. On both sides of you naked. Your face. Capable of anything. The accident of putting two things together. Any two. Any time. It's territory day in the islands. Also your fault.
gone all out
prediction
A man takes his breath in and I decide to get it back out again.

> love of
> Oh! Poor girl!

The scale is the same. The space between house and ancient building choked with greenery. The moist air between us. The con men play with each other. A hero is trapped in a pinball machine.

> Poor taste

is never enough. My fever shakes this picture of trees. Blooming. Not everything that doesn't exist is me. I have nothing to explain. That seems shallow but goes in. Contains blood. Is round. The steaming tar like lava makes the new town.
the figure with strings
strung
A mannequin in a window manipulates a doll. Caught in the act of being motionless. Her head turned away. Inasmuch as it is a head. He seems to fly. His arms held out. They are arms. Our arms. It follows with the logic of a false similitude left from another age. We believed in that too. Christ what innocents. Whose will go first?

Like firecrackers in the Broadway Tunnel. The continuous roar between things. He claims not to understand negative space. The soft skin. The mute discipline no one is ready for. We say nothing to each other. Day after day. The celebration is ruthless. There is a musical version of the past.

> caught in the radio
> is constant danger
> Also I am

constant also caught. The indecipherable note pasted like a rose to the wall barely lit by the sun going down. Is clear to someone. Or like a castle under siege. Overgrown with Edenic trees. The worse for the wind raging above this solidity. Things made of stone subject only to the catastrophes we know don't change things. Or change completely but we remain unshaken. We are the objects. The people were destroyed. More than once.

> we were just words
> like the pear is a fruit
> and is yours

and is filled with sun like the valley with the white roses pictured here. You can almost see the heat. The petals blurred as if unsure of themselves. The rain also pictured.
rains
naked from the waist
smokes or steams
Because the heat is relentless. It never rains when it's hot here. Petals for eyes. Something new pasted over the new thing. A child holds you to its lips. A highrise where the hotel. Also of granite.

A burned out pit. Graffitied man alive at the bottom with what did you expect written in red paint. A tent made of paper. The moon is still empty. But it will never be like it was. Known not to exist. The new moon.

> is midday

We lay down in the lightest possible sun. She sang while it was too hot to move. But now it's not. Kwannon ice white Chinese goddess of love. Old red flowers turning yellow. Things disappear in the fog. He referred to certain people as the neighborhood.

> still here
> we are gone

This is the series of stone steps that don't go on. The animals squirming.

JENNIFER MOXLEY

J ENNIFER MOXLEY'S POETRY shows an uncommon range, stretching from the clear and careful statements of a poem such as "The Critique" to the equally clear but dramatically ambiguous, ambivalent prose lyrics of her most recent book, *The Line*. But at every point along this continuum, her work shows its signature intelligence and a relentless pursuit of a specifically philosophical kind of knowledge. There's often a bite to this knowing, and a social commentary runs as a substratum through much of her work. At times, as in the prose poem series on Rosa Luxemburg in her book *Often Capital*, Moxley adopts an overtly political tone, while at others, she's looking at the subtler interactions that make up daily contemporary society. As an MFA student at Brown she developed an interest in form, and throughout her career, she has pushed formal boundaries in subtle ways, often bringing genre into question; an example is her recent creative memoir, *The Middle Room*, which reveals her interest in poetic history and the ways in which poetic communities are shaped.

Moxley recognizes editing as crucial to community development; during the 1990s, she founded and edited the poetry journal *The Impercipient* and, with Steve Evans, the critical review *The Impercipient Lecture Series*. She is currently the poetry editor for *The Baffler* and a contributing editor to *Poker*, and she frequently contributes critical articles to a variety of journals and Web sites. Her work has been published in England and France as well as the United States, and she has translated and published two books by the poet Jacqueline Risset. Jennifer Moxley teaches at the University of Maine in Orono.

WREATH OF A SIMILAR YEAR

A circlet ring of light
     beneath our feet
a door, a possible path
     of very best will,
placed before us
     in infinite intervals.
Such facets of mind
     might sustain us
if luck runs over, or love
     provide the lost,
more bodily
     forms of warmth.

The inconsolable mind
     has created
abundant distress—
     the scarcity required
to bury a world
     of living evidence.
Abandoned so, in an idea
     of innermost anguish,
we have become accustomed
     to the unheard music,
the quiet accompaniment
     of water,
being disturbed within.

Thought intent
     upon contentment
may temper the guests of our greater being,
     unearth
the hourly questions
     burned down from youth
with energy and light. As in the wake
     of awakening
wrong attempts
     and wrongful death
will fall adjacent
     careful Hope.

            Hope,
how strangely of untold direction
            it sounds, blind as
the first letter on the first stone
            written down
as if a wreath to circle
            the last sound spoken
on some distant, though similar
                              Earth.

"DIFFICULT OF ACCESS"

Linkages of self-derision.
        How often have I
avoided
        the work, the disgusting curve
of my absent spirit, grown
        in the regressive
            onset
more difficult
                to force
into place.
        You play the teacher,
prop me, a tiny doll,
        on your knee.
The old hands again
                confuse me,
just as these fragile words
                on fragile paper
        confuse me, and will not be
dictated.
                I have been deceived—
        a convenient
delusion, to discover how little one life,
        love notwithstanding,
                transmits
in the end. The mind
        is a ghastly
instrument, it will age,
        as the body ages, swaybacked
with infeasible
        desire, on hands and knees

it would crawl, or be willingly
    satisfied,
        beyond all linguistic
    answers
by a young woman's
    famished
movements
    beneath
      its
        intelligent hand.

THE CRITIQUE

I'd rather say "I shall not tell"
than tell you, in a noble lie
that all compassionate choices
must be stomached, and for a pinioned-heart
deserve our praise. For there is no
plain-spoken sorrow that does not
hide rogue secrets, strange to believe,
and never but one motive to a man.
You cast me as the judge and executioner
of your foibles, a righteous knot
of ill-reason, wasteful in my wrath
at false accord. But how can it be preferable
to lean into a string of favors
and never speak your mind? To flatter dabblers
and hide all doubts? "I will tackle these sensations
with strange beauties," you said,
though they are undefined about your bed,
and from their atavistic grasp you wake,
dry leaves exiting your mouth,
in spite of the darkness your eyes are bright,
in terror of the imminent scolding
that visits you each night in dreams, they shine.

from ENLIGHTENMENT EVIDENCE

red room, it means nothing other than resistance,
and remember her back into my living,
lost in the dazzling love of you—my surroundings—
Germany threw her off, and throws the point of present day,
you reconnoiter this meager house coat based on a shading,
a color of history, my religion nostalgia and this
mood, iconoclast you the practical can seem too firm-
headed for neuralgia for christ's sake to be unnerved
means different when Rosa is not dead weight as I have
become for you

•

must I be imprisoned to justify this icebox chill,
flowerless now and then the powdery substance that was
my existence did not on simple transfer lend, a billfold
is no use nor definition so I retard your sweet yogurt
on a flagging sense of self, such offerings are without
comfort for we cannot build on fluids anymore than I can
tend my prison garden daily

•

open field, the privilege to limp across desire
no simple anchorage works when exile is a state of
time past, the wasterly girlhood can call me from your
ways entreating lover and I shall pettily dream as
Rosa limped without a country your solution-less must be
my homeland now since eyeward I befall the open field

•

dissenter is wantonly the name I gave to you
of the paper with the bad intent, betwixt impression
and ownership lies idolatry worth every flagstaff,
obelisk, and needle caressing one million small buds,
the forest is damp beneath your legs and embarrassed,
work cannot be the volleying of pet names real-world man,
let sweetness be the creator of moments, building revolution
one kissing at a time

THE STATE

However much we wish it so, everything does not change in a moment. The sedative present, tugging, sucking, and many-voiced, timelessly freights the mind. There will be no more marking of days. Under your right arm, a memory crutch, under your left, the future, a failure kicked out upon waking. But as punishment you can still dream. A nursing infant, the birds you have killed, a hill so steep your ascent of it leaves your lover struggling beneath you. Each night in houses you can never go back to you leave your promise behind.

THE PROMISE

Newborn, palpable loneliness shakes you from even the deepest sleep. Against the cold air and shadowed darkness flooded with sudden consciousness the vulnerable flesh recoils. In the liminal all times converge. Severed memories long for the text, the comfort of dialectic. Below you a body persists, with heat, with cold, with longing, it forms many limbs of translucent skin out of what once was a will. Despite their spasmodic quavering these nascent horrors of wasted potential are speechless and none awake.

IN ONE BODY AND ONE SOUL

Preview glow of another morning held at bay by the eyemask. The heartbreak of time is not that it passes but rather the language yoke. By grace of grammar alone the moment's fleeting existence. The spatial dream-life of complex syntax hides the author's erasure. Having lived through it the flesh knows otherwise. The odor of wood in an old stairwell effortlessly constructs an alternate origin. To hold the past, present, and future in a single body and soul. Permanently open the ears and nose act as our sensuous metronomes, memory reservoirs against the eyes, portals of wordless oblivion.

AWAKE

How many more days will you awaken? The flesh envies the word's longevity but not its delayed effects. You shift your body from side to side, stuff the pillow beneath your neck, burrow into the down. You repeat a rhythmical phrase in the mind to bring forth the image. Over broken stone films a shallow coating of clear sea water roped back by the waves. This is a picture of time which doesn't yet exist, a counting that cannot be reached. You are asleep before belief, held captive mid-metamorphosis. Once the hunter you are now in flight, not from the intangible long run, but from each new instance of daylight.

THE MILKY WAY

You were alone when through the time-punctured present an inkling of reason found you, this illogical indefensible insight momentarily tore the teleology of hope away from the future tense, celestial intelligence of the embodied now, or the sense that you are held in place by two connected minds.

Despite belief-comfort you are pricked by limits—social, material, psychic. All that you know but cannot explain goes directly into the woodwork, while the plastics like planets refract emanations and thus can neither age nor help you.

Is this the reason old houses comfort you? Their sleep allows for mysterious things—filmy journeys over ethereal banks, star-by-star stone-stepping, beneath your feet soft waters of nothingness and centuries of hidden thought—events that work your defeatist will into a strange elation.

THE BURNING PEONY

Up went a beautiful microcosm. A silken crowd whose self-obsession was invaded by an army of insects. A physician to the Gods. This is not a vision but an occurrence in words, an image suggested by sound and experience. Undergoing a trial by fire the peony, procreatively excessive, with stamens and pistils galore, girdled by artificial means because of its enormous head, stands in for the discarded aesthetic. Beauty, inward-looking, consumed by its own desire.

HARRYETTE MULLEN

H ARRYETTE MULLEN'S RECENTLY published *Recyclopedia*, collecting in one volume three early books, *Trimmings*, *S*PeRM**K*T*, and *Muse & Drudge*, just won a PEN Beyond Margins Award. The collection illustrates the lyric verve within her prose poems and the elegant intelligence of her verse stanzas, all reflecting a nuanced redefinition of poetic lyric. Mullen positions her poems at the juncture of a multiplicity of meanings, at the cultural crossroads of linguistic collisions, using the languages of advertising, fashion, femininity, black vernacular, and theory— among others—to examine and question the hierarchies of expression we have come to assume. Mullen's most recent collection, *Sleeping with the Dictionary*, reminds us that language play is at the root of her inspiration; she uses both *Roget's Thesaurus* and *The American Heritage Dictionary* (not to mention some of the composition principles of the Oulipo group) as collaborators in her hilarious, relentlessly punning and parodic indictments of the imprisoning conventions of English. The effects are both liberating and intoxicating.

Harryette Mullen was born in Alabama and raised in Texas. *Sleeping with the Dictionary* was a finalist for the National Book Award, the National Book Critics Circle Award, and the Los Angeles Times Book Prize. Mullen is also the author of *Tree Tall Woman* and *Blues Baby: Early Poems*. She is a former Rockefeller Fellow and has received a Guggenheim Memorial Foundation Fellowship and the Gertrude Stein Award for Innovative Poetry. Mullen teaches in the English Department and African American Studies Program at the University of California, Los Angeles.

from MUSE & DRUDGE

Sapphire's lyre styles
plucked eyebrows
bow lips and legs
whose lives are lonely too

my last nerve's lucid music
sure chewed up the juicy fruit
you must don't like my peaches
there's some left on the tree

you've had my thrills
a reefer a tub of gin
don't mess with me I'm evil
I'm in your sin

clipped bird eclipsed moon
soon no memory of you
no drive or desire survives
you flutter invisible still

my skin but not my kin
my race but not my taste
my state and not my fate
my country not my kunk

how a border orders disorder
how the children looked
whose mothers worked
in the maquiladora

where to sleep in stormy weather
Patel hotel with swell hot plate
women's shelter under a sweater
friends don't even recognize my face

tombstone disposition
is to graveyard mind
as buzzard luck
to beer pocketbook

slashing both your wrists
to look tough and glamorous
dead shot up in the art gallery
you can keep your shirt on already

while I slip into something more funkable
rub-a-dub with rusty man abrasions
was I hungry sleepy horny or sad
on that particular occasion

invisible incubus took up
with a cunning succubus
a couple of mucky-mucks
trying to make a buck

slandered and absurdly slurred
wife divorced her has-been
last man on earth hauls ass to the ash can
his penis flightier than his word

they say she alone smeared herself
wrote obscenities on her breast
snatched nappy patches from her scalp
threw her own self on a heap of refuse

knowing all I have is dearly bought
I'll take what I can get
pick from the ashes
brave the alarms

another video looping
the orange juice execution
her brains spilled milk
on the killing floor

if she entered freely
drank freely—did that not mean
she also freely gave herself to one and all—
then when was she no longer free?

we believed her
old story she told
the men nodded at her face
dismissing her case

debit to your race
no better for you—lost
gone off demented
throwing unevenhanded

disappeared undocumented workhorse
homeless underclass breeder
dissident pink collard criminal
terminal deviant indigent slut

riveted nailed to the table
crumpled muddied dream stapled
in her face mapped folded back
to the other side of the facts

■

just as I am I come
knee bent and body bowed
this here's sorrow's home
my body's southern song

cram all you can
into jelly jam
preserve a feeling
keep it sweet

so beautiful it was
presumptuous to alter
the shape of my pleasure
in doing or making

proceed with abandon
finding yourself where you are
and who you're playing for
what stray companion

THE LUNAR LUTHERAN

In chapels of opals and spice, O Pisces pal, your social pep makes you a friend
to all Episcopals. Brush off lint, gentile, but it's not intelligent to beshrew the
faith of Hebrews. I heard this from a goy who taught yoga in the home of Goya.
His Buddhist robe hid this budding D bust in this B movie dud. If Ryan bites a
rep, a Presbyterian is best in prayer. Oh tears oxen trod! To catch oil, or a man
born to the manor, you need a Catholic, Roman. On Mon. morn, Mom hums
"Om" with no other man but Norm or Ron. A Mormon son would gladly leave
a gas slave in Las Vegas for a hut in Utah. These slums I'm from, I'm leaving, Miss
Lum, with a slim sum donated by some Muslims. What would it cost to gain
the soul of an agnostic? Where the atheist is at, God only knows! 'Tis hate, he is
at the heist. A Baptist was able to stab a pit bull when the sun hid behind some
Hindus. To fan a mess, I write manifestos. So said the lunar Lutheran.

SLEEPING WITH THE DICTIONARY

I beg to dicker with my silver-tongued companion, whose lips are ready to read
my shining gloss. A versatile partner, conversant and well-versed in the verbal
art, the dictionary is not averse to the solitary habits of the curiously wide-
awake reader. In the dark night's insomnia, the book is a stimulating sedative,
awakening my tired imagination to the hypnagogic trance of language. Retiring
to the bedroom, turning on the bedside light, taking the big dictionary to
bed, clutching the unabridged bulk, heavy with the weight of all the meanings
between these covers, smoothing the thin sheets, thick with accented syllables—
all are exercises in the conscious regimen of dreamers, who toss words on their
tongues while turning illuminated pages. To go through all these motions and
procedures, groping in the dark for an alluring word, is the poet's nocturnal
mission. Aroused by myriad possibilities, we try out the most perverse positions
in the practice of our nightly act, the penetration of the denotative body of the
work. Any exit from the logic of language might be an entry in a symptomatic
dictionary. The alphabetical order of this ample block of knowledge might
render a dense lexicon of lucid hallucinations. Beside the bed, a pad lies open
to record the meandering of migratory words. In the rapid eye movement of
the poet's night vision, this dictum can be decoded, like the secret acrostic of a
lover's name.

WHY YOU AND I

Who knows why you and I fell off the roster?
Who can figure why you and I never passed muster
on our way out yonder?
Does anyone wonder why you and I lacked
the presence of minding our blunders?
Can anyone see why you and I, no longer intact,
pulled a disappearing act and left with scratch? Our secret pact
required that you and I forget why and where
we lost our place when we went off the books.
Could anyone guess, does anyone know or even care
why you and I can't be found, as hard as we look?
Who'll spell out for us, if we exist,
why you and I missed our turn on the list?
Who can stand to reason why you and I let
our union dissolve to strike the orderly alphabet?

ZOMBIE HAT

Greatest thing since Texas toast,
the ever-popular zombie hat
flies off the shelf
like sandwich loaf.
For your tête-à-tête
with a headhunter, or chat with a shrink,
zombie hat's the right think.
You'll look like a hero
in your zombie sombrero.
Don't forget to wear your hat.
It's what the head cheese ordered, stat.
Statistics show the zombie hat
helps to maintain social stasis.
With the right fit,
you'll brim with social graces.
We recommend it for all our head cases.
Meet every problem head on,
so long as you keep a lid on.

LAURA MULLEN

AURA MULLEN'S WORK investigates popular culture through disruptions of genre. Her latest book, *Murmur*, takes on the detective novel just as her earlier *Tales of Horror* took on horror fiction—each manages to poke fun and to *be* fun while revealing an architecture of true social disquiet at the root of these popular literatures, and each achieves a hybrid form that combines the clarity of prose with the vividness and volatility of verse. Her poetry also focuses on making subtle underlying structures apparent, and often addresses issues of self and family, and private and collective identity, enacting the violence and ruptures she sees inherent to identity construction through her broken syntax, quick juxtapositions, and slippery pronouns. There's a distinct political aspect to all her work, but defined in intimate terms that begin with how we make meaning. "There are politics involved in asking people not to make sense the way they've made sense before," she suggests in response to an interview question.

A graduate of UC Berkeley, with an MFA from the Iowa Writers' Workshop, Laura Mullen has published five books. Her first, *The Surface*, was chosen in the National Poetry Series, and her second, *After I Was Dead*, was chosen in the University of Georgia Series. Her work has also appeared in several anthologies, including *New American Poetries* and *New Wave Fabulist Fiction*. She has received awards from the National Endowment for the Arts and the Rona Jaffe Foundation, among others, and held residencies at the MacDowell Colony and the Fundación Valparaiso. She teaches at Louisiana State University at Baton Rouge.

REFUGE

Here is the church.   And . . . . And? The interlocked   Fingers undone—
The form fails.

"Here is the church,"   Entreaty, willful: The wringing hands held
Together   And the gesture

Held. Still. The amnesiac   Builds another temple,   Tells (*Here is* . . .) a
Lost   Child (*the church and here*

Is . . .) the loosened tale.   Arms   Twinned and entwined, flow; palms
Sweep up inward and   Down,   Responding as a wave responds

To the tug from above,   The tug from below.   "Here is the church,"
Shape in the air the eyes

Follow, waiting to see   What beneath the whitening   Steeple?
The expelled,   Suddenly alien

Digits writhing in the out-   Stretched palms' exploded   Hollow?
They writhe like worms   Whose bones no longer serve

As the tightly shut doors, roof, stiff   Arrow of the steeple.
"Like worms":   Like no part   Of the body they belong to,

Belonging to a body   To itself unrecognizable.   "Open the doors."
Here.   There is always

Some other place   We imagine they   Can be sent (back) to
(So open the doors).

Some other place: As though we were not   The container,
"And here . . . "   The contained also.

PLANS

Who can think of a flower that is red?
What is a person who cannot hear called?

(Solid blocks of ice are at first sight so unlike masses of feathery snow that a child would be surprised to hear a snowflake spoken of as "ice." Yet the difference lies mainly in the arrangement of the little ice needles, in the way they are put together: those of hard ice are more densely packed; those of snow are more loosely joined, with open spaces between, full of air. It is the abundance of air, mixed in with ice-needles, catching and reflecting, which gives to snow its whiteness.)

Have a boy place quietly beside her one of the very realistic Japanese spiders.

Spend this whole week playing Pilgrim life.

"Shall we have daylight all the time or night all the time?"

Write the answers.

Have the children cover their eyes. Pound on a tin pan. Have the children guess what the sound was. Ring a small bell. What was the sound? Blow on a whistle. What was it? Stamp on the floor. Have the children guess what the sound was.

Write an advertisement asking for a position for yourself.

A desk or chair, or a box will serve for the rock.

Have the children close their eyes.

What do we call a person who cannot see?

The passengers will wear their hats, and books will serve as luggage.

Explain what is meant by the blare of bugles and the ruffle of drums.

The bread. The fruit. The nuts.

Have the children write: *Secrets big and secrets small*.

Write a composition on snow.

Write a composition on snow.

Pretend to spin, explaining the process.
I give my head, my heart, and my hand. . . .

How many can guess, by the feeling, what the objects are?

Write the name of a red flower.
Play "I'm thinking of a flower," the others
To guess what flower is being thought of.

from A NOUN'S MEANT

Falls back from the open book the interrupted reader turning inward (where it will)
In her place at first perhaps this inward turning I am a passage then or hollow place
Halted in her reading hand outstretched as if to stay or silence   *would finish*

Open on her lap   the forgotten book

The messenger lifting meanwhile
His admonitory or encouraging hand
                                                    enters left

Allegory inevitable? "I'm here now aren't I?"
In her room close closet coffer box this book
Outside   intelligence arrives in passing passes through her pierces

singles her out vessel   fingered

When did you lose your will exactly
What were your desires exactly

Or crosses both hands over her heart   answers a servant
Seemingly gazes inward won't meet his eye can't doesn't not meeting his eye   is   *seen*

Starts at his entrance (drops her book shields her eyes)   Windblown

Heavy center waiting for what will through press   attending
White bird leaking a trickle of gold sand down into the chill dark   in between

Here
Holds in the book she shut a hand pale as the page: she holds her place.
As place(mark)   blank   displaced   her sudden guest
"I can't quite place you"
Her other   hand to her heart the messenger   still for her response

She looks away gathers around her closer cloak   nothing takes the words back
Touching the lines of text as if she read   blindly   feeling
Head tilted illustration I listen and   "a servant"   she closes the book her hand in it

Enters

Fail tarry lull efface

Light in the folds her robe as she turns from her reading half turns the light from the page   on her face a figure for what might the words bleed what she reads coming true suddenly   a white bird hovers wings pages a cry a burst of light a stopping place looking up to   answer what was not in fact a question although the one who brought word awaits a response   open window between them   reception   dead gaze of he who looks   inside to recall exactly in their author's order words not his elsewhere eyes having by   heart spoken through her single finger held in the open book as though when left again   alone she might return to that page paragraph sentence word "Where was I exactly?"   Rereading until abruptly that uneasy sense of recognition stops

deep and the tide the currents
smoky underwater light

Draws back in the instant of giving in   no / yes   listen   a messenger arrives

tilt this gleaming sky   of gold leaf   there are two of them a gate   and between
    shape

A message arriving   alights   urges seeks to persuade convince   what
will come to pass   attend

She lifts one hand as if to ask for silence   as if to say but halt here wait a moment
let me read a little longer   before   holds one hand up the fingers curved
yes as if to say yes of course but oh not yet not please yet

Attend   an instant

Swirling depths of heavy roses warm folds of the red cloth of her dress
disclose space that opens between them necessary   space   of   communication
infinite elsewhere the speaker whose word within her messenger sent to say that
already within her   a space opens past sense   optimal   distance from which

Attend this mouthpiece turned by her strayed gaze to ghost
Unroll from the scroll words held at her high her narrow window
Open between them her good book

From the candle blown out on his entrance a waxy smoke floats slowly up undulates the
theme a thin excuse for this glow and sheen of light on the curved edge for instance of a
brass candlestick gleaming above a gold head bent

"You'll ruin your eyes reading in the dark like that!"
From the left I enter left my eyes in fact

Interrupt announce   and now for an(other) word *from*   I walk in she looks up
she's reading   I walk in in the middle   of a sentence   "He   came   nearer,"
"Suddenly she was aware of his nearness,"   for instance

A caller   what is this place   empty a room that gives   on a garden   she
hears him out   sets down her book for the sweet-voiced stranger seeking to
engage her services   oh some white bird dropped pendulum-like sways above

them at the end of a glittering cable above the body contrail of gold leaf in the wake of
the said thing (meant

Here's what will happen he says but he kneels before her to say it   and she
her answer   always   but it happens as he says no matter what

Attend acceptance (speech)   The partition of space (this)

The messenger says nothing stops lifts a white hand flower-like white blooms in the other motions toward what
appears above invisible completes a thought not his explains the doubled nature of what she halts in her reading
turns abrupt into terror doubt agreement stopped hands raised in surrender rose in the swirl of hot orange-red
cloth already seems pregnant (oh there's a cat behind her back arched caught in the act of dashing off

Parted dark   a woman immersed   interposed   an entry   wanting a word with

Enter a messenger bearing   a stem of lilies or unfurling left a scroll his own mouth shut
always the reader in her coffin-like room   a garden opens away from   boxed in
with her good book   starts   start here   amaze us   preface

(Start here eye holes in an old wooden door admit through the broken wall your long your
private view her shaved sex wound-like set slightly askew bare limbs akimbo among
weeds aglow in the light she lifts   for instance)

ALICE NOTLEY

ALICE NOTLEY HAS played a leading roll in the second-generation New York School and in the rise of women's writing from the late 1960s on. Raised in the desert in Needles, California, she blends the clarity and aridity of that landscape with an urban pulse fueled by a sharp sense of poetry's social responsibilities. Often narrative at its core, Notley's work covers a tremendous stylistic range and frequently has its impetus in challenge or refusal. For instance, in a *Jacket* interview, she states that *Mysteries of Small Houses* was in part a response to the rejection of the first person prevalent in the eighties, while *The Descent of Alette* was inspired in part as a response to the rejection of narrative at around the same time. Through such double negatives—rejecting others' rejections—Notley attains a defiant assertion that roots her poetry beyond the fashion of a given era.

The author of over twenty-five collections of poetry, Notley has also published an early biography, *Tell Me Again*, and a book of critical essays, *Coming After*. She received her BA from Barnard College and her MFA from the Iowa Writers' Workshop, which she entered as a fiction writer. A finalist for the Pulitzer Prize in 1998, she was awarded the Griffin International Prize for *Disobedience* (2001). She has also won the San Francisco State Poetry Center Book Award, the Los Angeles Times Book Award, and the Poetry Society of America's Shelley Memorial Award. Alice Notley's work has been the focus of much critical attention, including a special issue of the journal *Interim*. She teaches frequently in Naropa University's Summer Writing Program and lives most of the year in Paris, where for several years she co-edited the journal *Gare du Nord* with Douglas Oliver.

POEM

St. Mark's Place caught at night in hot summer,
Lonely from the beginning of time until now.
Tompkins Square Park would be midnight green but only hot.
I look through the screens from my 3rd floor apartment
As if I could see something,
Or as if the bricks and concrete were enough themselves
To be seen and found beautiful.
And who will know the desolation of St. Mark's Place
With Alice Notley's name forgotten and
This night never having been?

AFTER TSANG CHIH

I was brought up in a small town in the Mohave Desert.
The boys wouldn't touch me who was dying to be touched,
            because I was too quote
Smart. Which the truck-drivers didn't think as they
            looked and waved
On their way through town, on the way to my World.

POEM

Why do I want to tell it
it was the afternoon of November
15th last fall and I was waiting
for it whatever it would be like

it was afternoon & raining but it
was late afternoon so dark outside my
apartment and I was special in that
I saw everything through a heightened

tear, things seemed dewy, shiny
and so I knew there was a cave
it was more or less nearby as in my
apartment it was blue inside it

dark blue like an azure twilight and the
gods lived in the cave they who

care for you take care of at death and
   they had cared for Ted and were there for me
       too and in life even now

from THE DESCENT OF ALETTE

BOOK ONE

"One day, I awoke" "& found myself on" "a subway, endlessly"
"I didn't know" "how I'd arrived there or" "who I was" "exactly"
"But I knew the train" "knew riding it" "knew the look of"
"those about me" "I gradually became aware—" "though it seemed

as that happened" "that I'd always" "know it too—" "that there was"
"a tyrant" "a man in charge of" "the fact" "that we were"
"below the ground" "endlessly riding" "our trains, never surfacing"
"A man who" "would make you pay" "so much" "to leave the subway"

"that you don't" "ever ask" "how much it is" "It is, in effect,"
"all of you, & more" "Most of which you already" "pay to
live below" "But he would literally" "take your soul" "Which is
what you are" "below the ground" "Your soul" "your soul rides"

"this subway" "I saw" "on the subway a" "world of souls"

BOOK THREE

" 'We will be silent" "& wait,' " "the voice said" "Then we were
truly quiet" "& being that," "were nothing" "Really nothing" "but
the darkness" "This moment was very long," "very long &" "very wide"
"It had a" "vast diameter" "I felt as if" "I could be" "falling

asleep forever" "Then I saw it" "coming towards me—" "so stately,"
"so stately—" "a light," "a white light" "A radiant" "small sphere,
I guessed" "Diameter" "of but a few feet" "It was seeking" "me out,"
"this light so" "unexpected" " 'What is this light I see?' " "I asked the

voices" " 'You are blind,' " "the voices whispered" " 'You are blind' "
" 'You do not *see* it' " " 'You have no senses' " " 'You are effectively"
"dead' " " 'I see it,' I said" " 'It is a small light—" "It lights up
nothing" "There is obviously" "nothing here" "But it is beautiful"

"Beautiful' " " 'It is not a light,' " "the voices said" " 'It is yourself' "
" 'It is something like" "yourself' " "Then the authoritative" "voice said,"
" 'We are going to" "leave you now' "

"I looked into the light" "directly" "with what I knew to be black eyes"
"Light streamed down through" "my eyes" "into myself" "And"
"as if inside me" "were only mirrors" "which faced each other" "I
felt myself" "light up within," "entirely," "the length of me"

"I was sight," "pure sight" "Was being," "was seeing," "with no object"
"whatsoever" "Nothing to see," "nothing to be:" "There was" "an other
though—" "the light which lit me" "& I loved it" "most purely"
"though I" "was also it" " 'Is this" "the deepest darkness?' " "I

asked it" " 'It is,' " "it said," "in no voice at all" " 'It's what you've
always" "suspected" "It's nothing but" "what you've always known,"
"always been" "For you've always" "been being" "It's simple" "Simple'"
" 'This light,' I said," "our light," "is the same as the" "surrounding

darkness' " " 'Of course,' " "said the light" " 'Both" "are being"
"There is no darkness" "or light, here" "But when I leave you" "you
will be lit—" "even if the light" "does diminish' " "We were silent"
"awhile;" "then I spoke again:" " 'I'm at peace with" "being" "In

this moment" "I've become" "all that" "I am" "I'm ready" "to
go back'"

I MUST HAVE CALLED AND SO HE COMES

"You're accusing me of something in these poems."
"No Ted, I'm not accusing you—can't catch your voice though."
"Through dead curtains," he says. Gives me the disgusted
Berrigan moue, casts match aside lighting cigarette
"So what are you doing?" he says. I say, "As the giant lasagne
on Star Trek—remember, Spock mindmelds with her
and screams, Pain." "So this is pain?" he says.
"I suppose it is. Was. But not from you," I say.
"We don't say pain we say fucked-up," he says, "Or
Kill the motherraper. Inside yourself . . ." (he fades)
"I can't catch your voice . . ." (I say)
". . . there's a place inside you," he says, "a poetry self, made by
      pain but not

violated—oh I don't say violated,
you're not getting my dialogue right, you can't remember
        my style."
"Would you say touched, instead?" I say.
"There's this place in us," he says, "the so-called pain can't
        get to
like a shelter behind those spices—coffee and sugar, spices,
matches, cockroach doodoo on the kitchen shelf.
But I was exhausted from being good without pills—
went off them on Diversey you'll remember—and you were
wearing me out. Well just a little. I took pills to
keep from thinking, myself. Do something else don't think
you're a poet write a poem for chrissakes, you're not
        your thoughts;
but I was afraid . . . you were mad at me deep down then."
"I don't think so," I say . . . "Men were a problem—I
        see that better
in the future, but you, sometimes you were 'men'
usually not." "Then were men men?" he says, "I mean—"
"No, I'll interrupt," I say, "Someone was being those times
why else was I unhappy." "Do you want to know," he says,
"if I loved you in 1970?" "No," I say, "I don't."
"Anything later than Chicago? But I've just got
a minute," he says. "No that's either your business
or something I already know," I say, "I really enjoyed the late 70's
        in New York, you know."
"You haven't wanted to talk to me since I died," he says.
"That's true," I say, "Too dangerous. But I want to say there's no
        blame here. I see your
goodness, plainly. I want to be
clear; I'm a detachment"—"As I am obviously," he says,
his voice getting fainter.

LADY POVERTY

Sings in the gullies
To all you go without is added more as the years
Youth's face health certain friends then more and
so to get poorer
life's arrow—tapers thinner sharper

She always sang there to purify
not the desert always pure
but me of my corrupt furor
So losing more further along in this dream of
firstrate firmament fireworks—
consigned to roam above brown dirt occasional
maxilla, and be shaped badly—
twisted internally: join her truly

She's I

She should be

the shape of a life is impoverishment—what
can that mean
except that loss is both beauty and knowledge—
has no face no eyes for
seasons of future delivery—rake the dirt
like Mrs. Miller used to
down at the corner had a desert yard and raked her dirt.

Beginning in poverty as a baby there is nothing
for one but another's food and warmth
should there ever be more
than a sort of leaning against and trust a food for
another from out of one—that would be
poverty—we're taught not to count on
anyone, to be rich,
youthful, empowered
but now I seem to know that the name of a self is poverty
that the pronoun I means such and that starting so
poorly, I can live

MICHAEL PALMER

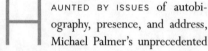

H AUNTED BY ISSUES of autobi-
ography, presence, and address,
Michael Palmer's unprecedented
style has become a point of departure for subsequent poetic generations.
Diversely influenced by a Romanticism based in the unbridgeable gulf between
life and language, radical modernism and its poetics of immanence, and postmod-
ernism's fragmentation and juxtaposition, Palmer's poetry began to take its dis-
tinctive shape when, at the age of twenty, he attended the 1963 Vancouver Poetry
Conference. There he came to know Robert Duncan, Robert Creeley, and Clark
Coolidge. Duncan in particular remained a lasting influence and close friend.
Palmer taught for many years at the New College of California while Duncan
directed the poetics program there. He succeeded in bridging Duncan's classicism
to the theoretical interests and formal experiments that were rife in the Bay Area
at the time.

Much of Palmer's work is also influenced by other art forms; he has frequently
collaborated with painters, and for twenty-five years he worked closely with the
Margaret Jenkins Dance Company. An active translator, he has translated pieces
from the French, Portuguese, and Russian, and taken part in various conferences
and group translation projects. Palmer is the author of ten collections of poetry
and the editor of *Code of Signals: Recent Writings in Poetics*. His awards include two
NEA Fellowships, a Guggenheim Fellowship, a Lila Wallace–Reader's Digest
Award, the Shelley Memorial Prize, and the Wallace Stevens Award. He served
as a Chancellor of the Academy of American Poets from 1999 to 2004. A native
of New York City, he has lived in San Francisco since 1969.

AND SIGHS AGAIN (AUTOBIOGRAPHY 15)

A sea of small killings, invisibilities, precise
scents of night

in its wetness
its edges of bloom

and inflection
A woman, chestnut-fleshed, nipples erect, ascends a
          kind of cross

Her companion, her double, her accomplice in this
helps her rise up with her tongue

Out of the dark they are fashioning a rose,
a window

They are examining the mathematics of the fold
They are baking themselves in salt

that we of little faith
may be saved

from the dampness and the dark
They are writing a book of common knowledge

a book of maxims and proverbs
such as a father

might pass on to a son
Did I say father and son

when I meant
farther and farther from the sun

Did I say fold
when I meant fault

salt when I meant song
dark when I meant a little bark

steering straight into the storm
Boat, little boat

with sail of stone,
Are you bearing an alphabet

among the rats in your hold,
an A-B-C-D of twinned bodies

Is the skin of this city your own,
city over which another city floats

skin of a retinal machine
salt sea of invisibilities

STONE

What of that wolfhound at full stride?
What of the woman in technical dress
and the amber eye that serves as feral guide

and witness
to the snowy hive?
What of the singer robed in red

and frozen at mid-song
and the stone, its brokenness,
or the voice off-scene that says,

Note the dragonfly by the iris
but ask no questions of flight,
no questions of iridescence?

All of this
and the faint promise of a sleeve,
the shuttle's course, the weave.

What of these?
What of that century, did you see it pass?
What of that wolfhound at your back?

UNA NOCHE

Then El Presidente,
uncoiling his tongue,

"You cannot stop time
but you can smash all the clocks."

And so, seeking Paradise,
we have burned the bright house

to the ground.
A necessary act.

We have invented glass
and ground a dark lens

and in the perilous night
we continue to dance.

The tarantella, the tango,
the pasodoble and the jig,

the bunnyhop, the Cadillac,
the Madison and sarabande,

mazurka and the jerk,
the twist on tabletops.

Rolling our eyes,
flailing our limbs.

It's how we keep time,
our feet never stop.
                    —*after Bandeira*

TONGUE ASLEEP

A wind had cleared things out, stolen things. Had swept down the stairwell, it was that dark and late, dark field with swirling dots. Mass of summer stars, window shattered, all pages gone, all pens, all amulets, lists, all machines but one. How will you now read in the dark? asked the pyrographer. Where will you place your hands, how hold your arms? How hobble, how step from wall to wall? How gather in images forthwith? How focus the eyes, draw a comb through your hair, fix your gaze on the missing thing? How listen, where dwell? Once more, once more, said Khlebnikov. And that was all. Things were years. Idea of light, of flesh, of thought. Stolen things.

THE THEORY OF THE FLOWER

I will translate a few of these to see if they exist
(We will translate logos as logos)

He swam in the rock
I am here from a distance

"Now kiss her cunt"
"Now take his cock in your hand"

The film is of a night garden
There is nothing meaningful about the text

There is nothing meaningful about a text
She

brushed away the sand
She brushed away the hand

This is Paradise, an unpunctuated book
and this a sequence of laws

in which the night sky is lost
and the flower of theory is a black spot

upon the foxglove
(These words have all been paid for)

He turns then to shade his eyes from the sun
She edges closer to the fallen log

This is Paradise, a mildewed book
left too long in the house

Now say the words you had meant to
Now say the words such words mean

The car is white but does not run
It fits in a pocket

He slept inside the rock,
a flower that was almost blue

Such is order
which exenterates itself

The islands will be a grave for their children
after they are done

You may use the paper with my name on it
to say whatever you want

I promise not to be so boring next time
never again to laugh and weep so much

which is how spring comes
to the measured center of the eye

The mind is made up
but you forget who it was first spoke

The mind is made up
and then and then

This is the paradise of emptiness
and this the blank picture in a book

I've looked over the photographs and they all are of you
just as we'd been warned

How strange
The winged figure in tuxedo is bending from the waist

The metalion addresses the mirror
and the music of the shattered window

falls unheard past the window below
How strange

but not so strange as speech
mistaken for a book

The phrase "for a moment" is popular in the world
yet not really meant to be said

That is the third or the fourth world
where you can step into a tremor with your tongue

I do not drink of it myself
but intend a different liquid

clear as the glass in which it's held,
the theory of the flower and so on

or the counter-terror of this valley
the fog gradually fills

just as we've been warned
It isn't true but must be believed

and the leaves of the sound of such belief
form a paradise

(pronounced otherwise)
from which we fall toward a window

D. A. POWELL

D. A. POWELL'S poems exist in an urbane and often urban landscape, moving with exceptional graciousness and true wit through the social dimensions of modern life. Powell loves—and lavishes marvelous descriptive detail upon—the luxuriant and artistic terrains through which his speakers travel. Stylistically raw, even naked (the lines are sinewy, often fragmented, and eschew capitalization), his poems celebrate the individual courage and perseverance of those around him in a world increasingly haunted by AIDS. It would be easy to reduce this powerful work to the pleasures of its sardonic intelligence, or to the wise precision of their singular observations, but Powell's poems are far more redemptive in their ambitions. Indeed, his three Dantesque volumes of poetry form a secular prayer book for the coming century.

D. A. Powell was born in Georgia and attended Sonoma State University and the University of Iowa. He is the author of three collections of poetry, *Tea*; *Lunch*; and *Cocktails*, which was nominated for the National Book Critics Circle Award in Poetry. Other honors include the Lyric Poetry Award from the Poetry Society of America, the Larry Levis Award from *Prairie Schooner, Boston Review*'s Annual Poetry Award, a Pushcart Prize, the Paul Engle Fellowship from the James Michener Foundation, and an NEA grant. He has taught at Columbia University and the University of Iowa, and served as Briggs-Copeland Lecturer in Poetry at Harvard. D. A. Powell currently teaches at the University of San Francisco and edits the online magazine *Electronic Poetry Review*. His forthcoming collection is entitled *Chronic*.

CALIFORNIA POPPY

shuddering back to this coastline, craggy old goat rock
or the sweep of dune where judah meets squid-ink pacific
no more the nomad for now. or—stubbornly—everywhere, as each
exotic dancer filling the cracked sidewalks of north beach

as the indigent waving his tattered placard on the island
[what we call this meridian near church & dolores where the fronds
of palmtrees are stippled with shrill green or yellow lorikeets]
saying "come to my island: live cast-off cargo on this desolate reef"

—as the transmissible fruitfly larvae ravaging local oranges
as a fragile head upon a thinning stalk that somehow manages
to clasp hands at evening and send up its muttering entreaty
so small you might not notice, so ubiquitous, you see

so many ugly little flapping faces pocking city car lots,
the freeway onramps, the piss-scented flowerpots,
the unclaimed and untended plots (so few—and yet they're dense
with the wispy strands of hair and the folds of sallow tents)

that you've your right to ignore them, to ignore the grasping
fingers and bloated waxy face of the wildly surviving thing
that once was somebody's boutonnière, somebody's flash of light,
trail of phosphorescent streetlamps punctuating the homeless night

CREMATORIUM AT SIERRA VIEW CEMETERY NEXT TO THE HIGHSCHOOL, REGARDING THE

impoverished graveyard: mangy green triangle where two freeways form a
    crotch

twenty yards from the gym and the AG shop: see, it's morty's mom's funeral
    today

there's morty in a tie, his dad's head rocking: the pendulum of a clock tsk-tsks

holes just the size of flowerbeds claim sleek boxes.   marry me, you ruined
    seed

all semester they open and gnash their yellowy teeth: there goes mike, we
   say—his hearse lumbering through the iron gate—remember: he used to
   drive so fast

and then that smokestack poking its head above the surrounding grass

so that others—ever mindful of space, perhaps—could singe and shrivel on
   oven racks blazing into eggshell-colored ash collected in old penny jars and
   in paper sacks

there goes dusty (pointing at the belching puffs that tumbled over the valley)

between PE and molecular biology the smoke you'd sneak: half tobacco,
   half human white alloy of the usual carcinogens and raymond pettibone's
   granny.   or a bit of mike

that chest that—before it caved against the steering wheel—felt strong and
   sinewy

CLUTCH AND PUMPS

if I were in your shoes, you purse your mouth
but you were never in my shoes, chinaberry
nor I in yours: the cherry ash of fags
burns your path down the scatty streets

your smile wraps round pumps with a smack
the jawbone of a mighty red croc
who served up his behind to your toes
jagged bite marks: the hem of your frock

tombs, sister, you've got lithic tombs for hips
one chimney stack where a bbq pit should be
you say that I'm in janitor drag this year: as last
do these tits go with these shoulders? why ask me?

those talons you cultivate I do admire
the cochineal cheeks the flirty lashes
I don't want to live in a clutch purse town
you snap: and yet everything matches

[MY LOT TO SPIN THE PURPLE: THAT THE TABERNACLE SHOULD BE MADE]

A SONG OF MARY THE MOTHER

my lot to spin the purple: that the tabernacle should be made

with ten curtains of fine-twined linen and scarlet.   and the silk

and the hyacinthine.   even woven with the gold and the undefiled
which is white.   having the true purple for its veil

when the lot fell to me I took up my pitcher and filled it
took the purple upon my fingers and drew out the thread

in shag and floss: in coarse bottoms and in tight glossy skeins
the thrum did wind itself away from me

for a word had entered my womb and leapt inside me

I make the dark pillow where the moon lays its opaque head
I am the handmaid: pricked upon the spindle

the fine seric from the east was brought to me
soft and unfinished.   dyed in the tyrian manner

of purpura and janthina the violet snail.   cowrie and woodcock shell
the spiny hedgehog murex and the slender comb of venus

from betwixt my limbs arachnine the twisting issue I pulled forth

purple the night I felt the stab of the godhead in my side
purple the rot of the silk: its muscardine.   its plague

a raw tuft dwindles beneath me: I feel the tug of a day ravelling
even as such gloom as this winds tight around the wooden reel

would that a potion could blot out the host inside me
grove of oak, chestnut, willow.   a place of skulls.   succubi

a necropolis in me rises.   its colors mingle in the dark: aurora

spinster to throwster: purple my loom spread with the placenta cloth
I put a fine pattern to it: damascene sheaved and lilied

threads thrown in acute manner so that the bee rises on the border
the rose of sharon the cedar the camphire.   calamus and pleasant fruits

and these even dotted with locusts caddis flies and polyphemus moths
a fountain: a garden wattled with reeds upon the weaving

garden to be betrayed in?   a shadow against the breast of the tree

so the flox did luster in mine eye: in the cloth I beheld a fine water
as one might arduously with calender produce: the weft

a wave offering in my hands.   pin that pierces the body

over my lap a spreading wound of purple: purple that puckers and gathers
cloaking my folds of purple.   the swollen vein of a young boy's manhood

purple deep and hopeful.   a scar under the frenum.   a heavy prepuce

a caul.   an umbilical cord.   a wet sluice.   an angry fist.   a broken vessel
a bruise.   a blemish.   a raincloud.   a lesion.   a fissure.   tissue

the ends I took up and selvaged.   this veil shall not fray

and vast the warp of the cloth.   sea of galilee.   tigris euphrates and jordan
flow not as wide as my great bounty: undulant sky above my loom

the shuttle through me: a lance in my side.   a heave in my bowels
how will the temple receive my gift: scab of purple.   pustule.   genitalia

[and a future who? unfurls above the altar]   the thread the thread the thread

[LISTEN MOTHER, HE PUNCHED THE AIR: I AM NOT YOUR SON DYING]

A STABAT MATER

listen mother, he punched the air: I am not your son dying
the day fades and the starlings roost: a body's a husk a nest of goodbye

his wrist colorless and soft was not a stick of chewing gum
how tell?   well a plastic bracelet with his name for one.   & no mint
his eyes distinguishable from oysters how?   only when pried open

she at times felt the needle going in.   felt her own sides cave.   she rasped
she twitched with a palsy: tectonic plates grumbled under her feet

soiled his sheets clogged the yellow BIOHAZARD bin: later to be burned
soot clouds billowed out over the city: a stole.   a pillbox hat   [smart city]
and wouldn't the taxis stop now.   and wouldn't a hush smother us all

the vascular walls graffitied and scarred.   a clotted rend in the muscle
wend through the avenues throttled t-cells.   processional staph & thrush

the scourge the spike a stab a shending bile the grace the quenching
mother who brought me here, muddler: open the window.   let birds in

[ROBE AND PAJAMAS, STEADFAST AND SOFTER THAN ANYONE WHO TOUCHED ME]

PAPA'S DELICATE CONDITION
(1963, GEORGE MARSHALL, DIR.)

robe and pajamas, steadfast and softer than anyone who touched me

in the blear night dark: black your spine a musty bible.   we sway together

wrinkled lovers with tousled hair—a cocktail in hand—a pillow soiled in sweat

snowdrifts of terrycloth soaking where I spilled—mostly water: we measure
in drams and centiliters and shots: give me another, my sotted boys. *roll
footage:*

A LIFETIME OF HAPPINESS CONDENSED.   or, HAPPINESS OF A LIFETIME
CONDENSED

we slip and slop and spill our soup—we pop our rocks—droop and droplet
   flung over the back of the sofa: limp as a cashmere coverlet.   damp as a
   bloodclot

takes after his _(insert member here)_ I heard of others.   but me? I took after the
   dog

I don't know who brought these strawberry gin blossoms but surely they are
   mine won't they look lovely next to the tv—the vd—the pictures of mom
   and pop

who fell in love with the circus.   brought it home every night: we cleared
   beer bottles off the endtables: there, the stinko bears had room to dance
   their dance

[DARLING CAN YOU KILL ME:
WITH YOUR MICKEYMOUSE PILLOWS]

darling can you kill me: with your mickeymouse pillows
when I'm a meager man.   with your exhaust pipe and hose

could you put me out: when I'm a mite a splinter a grain
a tatter a snip a sliver a whit a tittle.   habited by pain

would you bop me on the noggin: with a two by four
the trifle of me pissing myself.   slobbering infantile: or

wheezing in an oxygen tent.   won't you shut off the tank
mightn't you disconnect the plug: give the cord a proper yank

when I lose the feeling in my legs.   when my hands won't grip
and I'm a thread a reed a wrack a ruin: of clap and flux and grippe

with your smack connections could you dose me.   as I start my decline
would you put a bullet through me.   angel: no light left that is mine

—for SamWitt

BIN RAMKE

B IN RAMKE'S POETRY layers a long-lined lyric with voices and facts gleaned from philosophy, natural history, and the sciences to create poems that both celebrate and interrogate the world. Acutely aware of life at all its levels, he brings everything from insects' wings to volcanoes to his poetry, implicitly querying the proper position of humans in this pattern. And his concern for humanity and its many fragilities is always a motivating force. As in "All Saints," included here, he at times uses ancient stories, myths, and legendary characters to underscore the public nature of our quest out of loneliness. "To waste to essentials is one form of grace," he writes in that poem, and throughout his work, he contrasts that impulse with its near opposite, an overflow of language in careful, ornate constructions that testify to the inexhaustibility and beauty of fact.

Ramke's first book, *The Difference Between Night and Day*, was chosen for the Yale Younger Poets Prize in 1978, and two of his subsequent seven books have won the Iowa Poetry Prize. Born on the Texas-Louisiana border, he attended Louisiana State University and the University of New Orleans before getting his PhD at Ohio University. Author of critical articles on contemporary poets from Susan Howe to Derek Walcott, Ramke has also had a distinguished editing career, editing the Georgia Series of Contemporary Poetry from 1984 to 2006 and the *Denver Quarterly* since 1994. On the permanent faculty at the University of Denver, he teaches frequently at the Art Institute of Chicago.

BIRDS FLY THROUGH US

Of any boy a story, of any girl, his kind, her kind,
his kindness gone and glory   all remains, all that
remains is a kind of glorious   grieving, a skill like any.

"If he had not had a house, where would he have raised his son,
and in what rafter would he have stuck the sacrificial knife?"
    Kafka, "Abraham"

As boys they played, as girls   played again against
the will or wisdom of mothers,   others, there was a river
there where boys and girls   who play each the other

apart part   of growing up was pain and painful all
fathers say the sacrifice cry in the night   the knife
cry I or Ai Ai   or some Greekish chorus cry

call of lament out of the night   the past of feeling feeding
for once and again against   aghast at what fathers do
must do to keep the kindly   household whole, budget

balanced, the orders.   Past what whimsy the past
too lived there   no more   but he did, Abraham, obey
and lived after   so they say   with himself knowing

he would have cut   having loved god more than a son   how
fatherly is that   what boy as a boy I would play
and she would play and cry   and we had a house

and the river stayed where rivers should   and still
there was death and darkness to dream and a knife for guidance
good riddance a sharpness and a gleam like water

I see icy nights   ahead he said   he sadly
said to her in bed, in her bed
in bed a boy   and a girl and dread

Here is a story some Greek told: a father
had a dozen children each child had thirty
white sons and thirty black daughters
each died every day but became immortal

the word *fear* is related to *fare* and it fits.
To fare forth into the murderous day,
the far-bordered night. One of the ablaut forms
of the Aryan root "per," to go through
we go through days and nights, Time, timorous.

"There is an earthly house which sounds with a clear
note, a tone, and the house itself makes a music
but contains a silent guest and both
hurry onward, guest and house together—"
Flumen et Piscis, the twelfth riddle of Symphosius.

If we are afraid, his father said, of anything
we are afraid of everything, just not all the time.
Anything can be a weapon, any weapon can be
a poem: "when Cyrus invaded the Scythians
they sent him arrows, a frog, and a rat
Cyrus could read the message: unless
he could hide in a hole of the earth like a rat,
or in water like a frog, he would not escape
their arrows which would fall from air,
the sky no refuge, no border"

But the lovely fish, silent, who moves with
the water his house, which house is buried
in earth—not covered, but a long hole in which
frogs might live but are not silent—in which
rats might swim but are in but not of the house—
moves, is not afraid of water is of air, of arrows.

A writer named Wiser described the beheading,
of Landru the casual look the quick transfer
of a head severed dumped adeptly from
its basket into the casket to join rejoin
the body—the task of the headsman's
assistant, swift ritual after the blade's descent.
An interesting brief divorce, for moments,
measurable if few, head and body separate,
(the body rolled immediately off the machine
into the adjacent casket before the blade
ceased trembling) then introduced (the crime
of the one the innocence of the other) now
absolved, resolved. Remembered.

MERCY

Hardness of hearts, all full of figures
of clarity glass-hard all   *How hot the sun rushes*
full of words minds   *Like fire in the bushes*
of men and women trying against
the fullness of their hard lives

hardness of hearts and John Clare
crazy. With the world. Of it.

We know why some men of Japan think
so hard of school girls the plaid jumpers
the little desks the shiny shoes the damp   *The wild flowers look sick*
determination . . . it is hard to be good   *at the foot of the tree*

Clare was good the stars are
small enough to ignore they touch us not
so easily yes they touch us light is star   *Birds nest are left lonely*
is part of the star to come to be seen by me   *The pewit sings only*
my hardest companion-
ship of hearts and pains

of sun and shine shinest
hard glitter you know better then
than to forgive far harder to   *And all seems*
live full fascinating yourself   *disheartened,*

the little girls have the hardest
life to fall into   *and lonely like me*
dangerous it is to be and beautiful

I would use such tools children
rejoice   it   is a day
workmanship could not be than the work
more valuable
more than angels

        recite to an audience
of ruminants literalists
filling themselves with whatever lies
at hand as if as if

some seasons lie
and no one knows better how to confront
the rain with its promise
contemplation,
such ennui—

there was a practice common in Europe
of eye-portraits, small compact gestures
like a little dance kept on a string
or some would have the artist paint
other parts, intimate
alliance
for war, for instance, a memorial

I would could I have such memory.
There was a practice common in Europe
called drizzling destroying
embroidery
for its gold thread to keep   winter afternoons
in a pouch as if to make more

but the practice grew out of desire
to dazzle with such excess of old gold thread
an imitation of the common women   (under dim light
who must reuse & husband resources   bending eyes badly)
the drizzlers displayed their gold thread & ript
apart the embroidery of the previous century
drawing room dazzle while gossiping among
themselves the sounds like rain on the roof

of ripping with little gold knives & scissors meticulous.

ALL SAINTS

ARIADNE

If the stained things of the earth lie, as in
lie, and a thread on the floor is remarked,
there's a story to tell but not the one
that leads out, only, for instance, beginning,
or to begin again leads in, torn from
elsewhere, now here, nowhere you know

but still the face rises as in dream and speaks
as in dream but that's a real child in the corner
small and weak and beginning
its own sort of threaded passage

now it makes you want to touch only
surface, a blind tongueless traveler
when the word alone is witness to all,
the word which comes out of lung from
an act of breath and constriction of
the various parts of the throat—the breath

a thread dissolving on its way out—
a child out of the warmth into the world
ready to be fed, ready to listen: Listen,

RUSALKA

Dvorak told this story: another creature of water
wants to be mortal (to have sex with a human), needs
permission from her father to die; there she sits
beneath the inconstant moon she sings
an aria for him which asks the moon to say
Mine are the arms that shall hold him, That between
waking and sleeping he may Think of the love that enfolds him.

This mortality allows us to touch one another and thread our way
out into bluish air and tinted anemones persistent in our paths,
temptation and a kind of hunger

SAINT ALPHAIS

which only some can resist—hunger's catastrophe of touch—remember
Alphais's inedia, her gift of subsistence on only the host, the wafer of bread
received daily. To waste to essentials is one form of grace. Having lost
her arms and legs, living in a lean-to next to the church—these legends
grow beautiful in their cruelty, a thread thrown to the drowning, a sound
enlightening, even hunger quivers bird-like in the mouth

> *imitating with the mouth the birds'*
> *liquid sounds came before men could delight*
> *their own ears by singing sweet songs (De Rerum Natura)*

SACRIFICIAL SANCTITY

The habit of hope saints evade, and the pettiness of life viewed from a certain angle.
Avoid the certain angle. If the air were flavored with lemon, say, or any
accidental floral that lines the walk, the habitual path from home compounding
the inarticulate with despair, the last remaining virtue, one learns with age to
trust, to greet with a nod in the morning, ever waiting in the bathroom mirror,
ready to carry on, to care. Among the things a long life teaches none matter
beyond a mirrored silvery way among the plants thick with insects eating each
other into other forms, larva to pupa to the serial splendor of wings and delicate
dining on nectar; such liquefaction of appetite can be learned in such a world
can be learned by the singularly attentive, that the best birds are pigeons, next
are sparrows; the full avian hierarchy founded on commonness—crows, boat-
tailed grackles, etc. Nothing rare counts to the Saint who has seen all
things familiar and contained, who has seen and is content to see, and sigh,
I can do all that angels can

Wallace Stevens

CLAUDIA RANKINE

T HERE ARE SOME of us who are constantly mending our hearts," writes Claudia Rankine. "I write into that mending; my writing is that mending." Rankine's four books often deal with social issues, though never in the abstract; rather, she searches for both the root and the ramifications of social discord in the specific choices and responses of individual people. From her first book *Nothing in Nature Is Private* (1994), which won the Cleveland State Poetry Prize, to her most recent *Don't Let Me Be Lonely* (2004), from which the excerpts here are taken, her work has become progressively more layered, evolving from a lyric aligned with the tradition of the poem as testimony to the primacy of personal experience to a genre-free hybrid of documentary, memoir, lyric, and image, in which subjectivity is much more diffuse, much more communal.

Born in Kingston, Jamaica, Rankine moved to the United States in 1969, and attended Williams College and Columbia University. From 1996 to 2003, she taught at Barnard College, where she organized the influential 1999 conference "Where Language Meets Lyric," which in turn served as the basis for the anthology *American Women Poets in the 21st Century* (2002), which she co-edited with Juliana Spahr. She is currently co-editing another anthology with Lisa Sewell titled *American Poets in the Twenty-First Century*. Claudia Rankine is on the faculty at Pomona College. In collaboration wiith her husband, the filmmaker John Lucas, she is currently engaged in a video project composing portraits of America.

from DON'T LET ME BE LONELY

Cornel West makes the point that hope is different from American optimism. After the initial presidential election results come in, I stop watching the news. I want to continue watching, charting, and discussing the counts, the recounts, the hand counts, but I cannot. I lose hope. However Bush came to have won, he would still be winning ten days later and we would still be in the throes of our American optimism. All the non-reporting is a distraction from Bush himself, the same Bush who can't remember if two or three people were convicted for dragging a black man to his death in his home state of Texas.

You don't remember because you don't care. Sometimes my mother's voice swells and fills my forehead. Mostly I resist the flooding, but in Bush's case I find myself talking to the television screen: *You don't know because you don't care.*

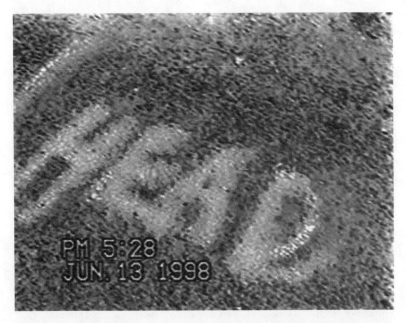

Then, like all things impassioned, this voice takes on a life of its own: *You don't know because you don't bloody care. Do you?*

I forget things too. It makes me sad. Or it makes me the saddest. The sadness is not really about George W. or our American optimism; the sadness lives in the recognition that a life can not matter. Or, as there are billions of lives, my sadness is alive alongside the recognition that billions of lives never mattered. I write this without breaking my heart, without bursting into anything. Perhaps this is the real source of my sadness. Or, perhaps, Emily Dickinson, my love, hope was never a thing with feathers. I don't know; I just find when the news comes on I switch the channel. This new tendency might be indicative of a deepening personality flaw: IMH, The Inability to Maintain Hope, which translates into no innate trust in the supreme laws that govern us. Cornel West says this is what is wrong with black people today—too nihilistic. Too scarred by hope to hope, too experienced to experience, too close to dead is what I think.

■

Mahalia Jackson is a genius. Or Mahalia Jackson has genius. The man I am with is trying to make a distinction. I am uncomfortable with his need to make this distinction because his inquiry begins to approach subtle shades of racism, classism, or sexism. It is hard to know which. Mahalia Jackson never finished the eighth grade, or Mahalia's genius is based on the collision of her voice with her spirituality. True spirituality is its own force. I am not sure how to respond to all this. I change the subject instead.

We have just seen George Wein's documentary, *Louis Armstrong at Newport, 1971.* In the auditorium a room full of strangers listened to Mahalia Jackson sing "Let There Be Peace on Earth" and stood up and gave a standing ovation to a movie screen. Her clarity of vision crosses thirty years to address intimately each of us. It is as if her voice has always been dormant within us, waiting to be awakened, even though "it had to go through its own lack of answers, through terrifying silence, (and) through the thousand darknesses of murderous speech."

Perhaps Mahalia, like Paul Celan, has already lived all our lives for us. Perhaps that is the definition of genius. Hegel says, "Each man hopes and believes he is better than the world which is his, but the man who is better merely expresses this same world better than the others." Mahalia Jackson sings as if it is the last thing she intends to do. And even though the lyrics of the song are, "Let there be peace on earth and let it begin with me," I am hearing, *Let it begin in me.*

Then my father dies and I cannot attend the funeral. It is not possible. I telephone my mother. We speak daily. I recommend cremation. I defend my recommendation. I send flowers. What I want to send is a replacement mourner. It seems odd that I can neither rent nor buy this; no grieving service is available. I mention this to a friend. She says that at her father's funeral in China they hired many mourners—the more mourners, the better. Many, many mourners show many, many dollars, she explains.

At night I dream about my replacement mourner, a woman. She has lost her mother years before and because she is already grieving she just continues attending funerals for a price. Like a wet nurse, the prerequisite is a state of "already grief." Still, all the narrative control in the world does not offer me insight into her occupation. One creates her motivations and her tears, but cannot understand why she stays by the corpse—"with him" is the phrase no one utters, especially not with him "gone." Or one looks into the mourner's face and wants life to matter more. In the dream we talk about what a lonely occupation she has chosen. No, she says, you, you are the one with the lonely occupation. Death follows you into your dreams. The loneliness in death is second to the loneliness of life.

Or I remember that the last two sentences I read in Fanny Howe's *Tis of Thee* before falling asleep the previous night were: "I learned to renounce a sense of independence by degrees and finally felt defeated by the times I lived in. Obedient to them."

Or, well, I tried to fit language into the shape of usefulness. The world moves through words as if the bodies the words reflect did not exist. The world, like a giant liver, receives everyone and everything, including these words: Is he dead? Is she dead? The words remain an inscription on the surface of my loneliness. This loneliness stems from a feeling of uselessness. Then Coetzee's Costello says in her fictional lecture, "for instants at a time I know what it is like to be a corpse."

Or Paul Celan said that the poem was no different from a handshake. *I cannot see any basic difference between a handshake and a poem*—is how Rosmarie Waldrop translated his German. The handshake is our decided ritual of both asserting (I am here) and handing over (here) a self to another. Hence the poem is that— Here. I am here. This conflation of the solidity of presence with the offering of this same presence perhaps has everything to do with being alive.

Or one meaning of here is "In this world, in this life, on earth. In this place or position, indicating the presence of," or in other words, I am here. It also means to hand something to somebody—Here you are. Here, he said to her. Here both recognizes and demands recognition. I see you, or here, he said to her. In order for something to be handed over a hand must extend and a hand must receive. We must both be here in this world in this life in this place indicating the presence of.

STEPHEN RATCLIFFE

S TEPHEN RATCLIFFE'S PATIENT, meditative examinations of the scene immediately before his eyes unfold a detailed and nuanced world. He writes one every morning at the same time, no matter where he is, creating a sequence that gives the reader the uncanny sense of the actual pace of life, its repetitions and its minute evolutions. Though this approach extends the tradition of the daily developed by William Carlos Williams and the early Modernists on the one hand and the New York School on the other, Ratcliffe uses repetition to put pressure on the words themselves in a way that reveals his grasp of the principles of the Language school and his deep commitment to the work of Gertrude Stein. The result is both immediately accessible and utterly estranged.

Ratcliffe came to the Bay Area at the age of four, was a Stegner Fellow at Stanford, and then moved to Bolinas, just north of San Francisco. He has been an important part of the Bay Area experimental writing community for the past thirty years, and teaches at Mills College in Oakland, where he also directed the creative writing program. In addition to eighteen books of poetry, he has published critical works on poets as diverse as Thomas Campion, Robert Duncan, Leslie Scalapino, and Shakespeare. Some of the pieces presented here are from his erasure project based on the *Sonnets*. His book of essays *Listening to Reading* focuses on the visual dimension of twentieth-century work from Stein to Robert Grenier. Ratcliffe also edits and runs the small press Avenue B, which specializes in contemporary experiments in poetry.

from HUMAN/NATURE

6.26

red finch disappearing from feeder into grey whiteness
of fog in front of invisible ridge, curve of black pine
branch in foreground below it, sound of waves in channel

Braque thinking "when Picasso and I were close, there was
a moment when one had trouble recognizing our own canvases"

de Kooning explaining "the point they all had in common was
to be inside and outside at the same time, a new kind
of likeness, the likeness of the group instinct"

line of pelicans flapping across grey-white sky,
on horizon, circular green pine on tip of point

6.27

silhouette of rufous-sided towhee perched on black pine branch
in right foreground, hummingbird whirring against grey-white
sky to the left of it, sound of jet passing overhead
                                                        man
on left explaining "pictorial space has lost its 'inside,'
a spectator can no longer escape into it"
                                        man across
table noting "when it lights up from inside, a painted
surface breathes, because the internal relations which
dominate the whole cause it to oscillate"
                                        grey-white
clouds on horizon to the left of the point, grey-green
mouth of wave breaking into the channel across from it

6.28

yellow of goldfinch landing on fence post in lower right
foreground, curve of black pine branch in grey-white sky
above it, sound of jet passing overhead
                                Matisse noting

"sponteneity is not what I am looking for, thus *The Dream*
took me six months of work"

>Turner thinking "thus yellow

is the scale of its tones from red to brown to blue, hence
those midnight shadows become toned or tinged with other
primitives, or admitted as means of *contrasts*"

>white

clouds behind circular green pine on point, oval grey-
green mouth of wave breaking across channel below it

6.29

hummingbird whirring at pink-white tobacco plant flower
against grey-white sky, quail pecking up seeds from wet
brick-red plane below it, sound of jet passing overhead

Cézanne explaining "painting from nature is not copying
the object, it is realizing one's sensations"

>man on left

noting "natural objects are left unaltered, yet at the same
time invested with a substantial Idea as their significance,
so they receive the vocation of expressing it"

>grey-white

fog behind slope of sandstone-colored point in right corner,
3 cormorants flapping across windblown grey plane toward it

6.30

egg-shaped granite rock on rectangular white table in right
foreground, circular orange flowers on green passion vine-
covered fence behind it, shape of bird passing overhead

man on phone recalling man asking "what kind of sparrow
was it, imagine not knowing what kind of sparrow"

>man

across table explaining "the *Idea as such*, though it is
the essentially and actually true, is yet the truth only
in its generality which has not yet taken objective shape"

line after line of white water moving in across grey plane
grey-white cloud in front of invisible point across from it

7.1

shadowed green line of black pine branch against grey
whiteness of sky in upper left foreground, red finch
landing on feeder below it, quail calling *Chi-ca-go*

man on left wondering "couldn't it be another shade
of red, like the black-on-black of the same elements in *Town*"

Turner noting "refraction returns, changing shadows positive
into shadows negative, shade on to shade to the verge of its
existence"
        flat grey clouds to the left of point reflected
in the motionless grey-green plane of the channel, cormorant
flapping in from circular green pine on point across from it

7.2

grey whiteness of fog in front of invisible ridge, hummingbird
hovering at circular orange flower in foreground below it,
sound of waves breaking in channel
                         Matisse thinking
"when we capture it by surprise in a snapshot, the resulting
image reminds us of nothing we have seen"
                              man across table
noting "when the three main radiating bands of grey or white
cross the circle's circumference they change color and, even
more decisively, change tone"
                      grey-white plane of clouds
across top of sandstone-colored point in left corner, oval
grey-green mouth of wave breaking into foreground below it

7.3

quail walking to the left across brick-red plane in left
foreground, blue jay pecking up seed from basket on table
across from it, grey-white sky in front of invisible ridge

Matisse noting "if I take a sheet of paper of a given shape,
my drawing will have a necessary relationship to its format"

man across table explaining "its blues are so crisp
and noncommittal, its blacks and whites so impassive,
its touches of red all stillborn"
                              sandstone-colored
point against grey-white cloud on horizon, line of ten
pelicans flapping across the grey-green plane toward it

    7.4

yellow of goldfinch perched on fence post in right corner,
blue jay pecking up seeds from table in foreground below
it, sound of jet passing across grey-white sky overhead

Matisse noting "my destination is always the same, but
I work out a different route to get there"
                              Malevich
explaining "that is, a single dark ray has swallowed
up all the colors and placed everything beyond mere
difference and advantage, everything is now the same"

grey whiteness of clouds behind sunlit slope of point
in right corner, tree-lined green ridge across from it

from PRESENT TENSE

    ONE

Pen, turn left, swallow—accent on the second or down beat
speaking of screens like a shock the scarlet under disappearing blackbird's
    wings,
any material malleable as water—ideally speaking
the next word will be white—

white one scans the horizon, banks of clouds on the western front, Bach
on the road which holds up long enough not to finish—
hardly a whisper, the thistle stirs—

                           ■

Bill Evans played a cool jazz samba, his slogan "My life, my gas"—in context
of a book of words the side of the house needs stones,
my cough allergic to spores,
his left hand kept out of sight in a glove extended to shake mine—

the scat singer warms her throttle, the twins have a room with a narrow leak—
    picture squirrels
through the keyhole, a child's jacket crossing the street soaked—
outside, the light fades after six—

∎

orange cones askew at the scene of a car pulled over the cliff higher than one
    could imagine
the Farallones float down stream—that was one of a dozen dreams
including daylight pines for maximum sun,
45 degrees most aesthetically pleasing a pencil the drift would hold—

come live with me and we'll play gin in the attic, after hours
the cat curled on the table
—the scared-to-death-of-thunder dog gone—

from [WHERE LATE THE SWEET] BIRDS SANG

17

            in
         your
          now
                            part
                  eyes
   number
          say, "This
      touches
      paper
          less   than tongue
        termed
     meter of a
       child
       twice

81

              make
          ear
       memory
    in
name
  I, once gone
            a common
              eye
        be
    not yet
tongues to
     breathers of
      —such
       breath

109

   say that
   absence seemed
easy
         which in
        love
         return again
             exchanged
        water
        in
          kinds of blood
           stained
  for
nothing this wide
      rose

DONALD REVELL

THERE IS A sorrowing dignity and an oracular mystery to Donald Revell's poetry. Over the course of his career, Revell has increasingly sought a more restrained, spare, and enigmatic diction in which to clothe his sometimes terrifying and always heartbreaking meditations on individual desire and loss. In his most recent collections, Revell has looked to spiritual realms, to questions of faith, and to the idea of God in order to better reckon the anguish he sees in the world around him. Yet there is also a profound freedom of spirit in his poetry, which employs a complex verbal and rhythmic musicality that honors those classical composers he so dearly loves (both historical and contemporary figures), as well as his literary and poetic precursors.

A prolific poet, translator (of Apollinaire), and critic, Donald Revell is the author of ten collections of poetry, most recently *Pennyweight Windows: New and Selected Poems* and *A Thief of Strings*. Winner of the 2004 Lenore Marshall Poetry Prize for his collection *My Mojave*, and a two-time winner of the PEN Center USA Award in Poetry, Revell has also received the Gertrude Stein Award, the Jerome J. Shestack Prize, and fellowships from the NEA as well as the Ingram Merrill and Guggenheim Foundations. He was a finalist for the 2005 Los Angeles Times Book Prize in Poetry. Revell is currently a professor of English at the University of Nevada at Las Vegas and the poetry editor of the *Colorado Review*.

MY TRIP

for Robert Creeley

I am looking at a smallpox vaccination scar
In a war movie on the arm
Of a young actor. He has just swum
Across a river somewhere in Normandy
Into the waiting arms of his rejoicing comrades.

Of course, the river's in California,
And the actor is dead now. Nevertheless,
This is the first of many hotels this trip,
And I find myself preferring wars
To smut on the networks,
Even as I find myself reading
The Pisan Cantos for the umpteenth time
Instead of the novel in my bag.
The poet helps me to the question:
Does anything remain of home at home?

Next day is no way of knowing,
And the day after is my favorite,
A small museum really perfect
And a good meal in the middle of it.
As I'm leaving,
I notice a donkey on a vase
Biting the arm of a young girl,
And outside on the steps
A silver fish head glistens beside a bottlecap.
Plenty remains.

The work of poetry is trust,
And under the aegis of trust
Nothing could be more effortless.
Hotels show movies.
Walking around even tired
I find my eyes find
Numberless good things
And my ears hear plenty of words
Offered for nothing over the traffic noise
As sharp as sparrows.

A day and a day, more rivers crossing me.
It really feels that way, I mean
I have changed places with geography,

And rivers and towns pass over me,
Showing their scars, finding their friends.
I like it best when poetry
Gleams or shows its teeth to a girl
Forever at just the right moment.
I think I could turn and live underneath the animals.
I could be a bottlecap.

Going to the airport going home,
I stop with my teacher, now my friend.
He gives me a good breakfast, berries and hotcakes.
We finish and, standing, I hear
One policeman saying to another
Over the newspaper in a yellow booth
"Do you know this word regret, Eddie?
What does it mean?"
Plenty of words over the traffic noise,
And nothing could be more effortless.
Catching a glimpse of eternity, even a poor one, says it all.

MY MOJAVE

Sha-
Dow,
As of
A meteor
At mid-
Day: it goes
From there.

A perfect circle falls
Onto white imperfections.
(Consider the black road,
How it seems white the entire
Length of a sunshine day.)

Or I could say
Shadows and mirage
Compensate the world,

Completing its changes with no change.
On the morning after a storm,
We used brooms. Out front,
There was broken glass to collect.
In the backyard, the sand
Was covered with transparent wings.
The insects could not use them in the wind
And so abandoned them. Why
Did they lie so stilly where they'd dropped?
It can only be the wind passed through them.

Jealous lover,
Your desire
Passes the same way.

And jealous earth,
There is a shadow you cannot keep
To yourself alone.

At midday,
My soul wants only to go
The black road which is the white road.
I'm not needed,
Like wings in a storm,
And God is the storm.

PICNIC

The story of my life is untrue but not
Thanksgiving Day when the bee fell in the bottle.
All days take instruction from accident.
My wife opened the red wine in a good spot
We'd found as we were hiking along a dry
Creekbed. She filled our cups as I cut
Bread and apples. We saw the bee dive
Into the green bottleneck and start

To swim. Then we spoke about children and ways to move
An old piano north to where our nephews live.
We finished the wine, and the bee was still alive.
I tapped him onto the ground, and he walked off,
Untangling antennae from wings and wine.
We hurried to reach the car while there was still daylight.

ZION

Suddenly copper roses glow on the deadwood.
I am these because I see them and also see
Abolition, the white smock on a girl
Eating an apple, looking down into
The valley, a small train steaming there.
I go to the uplands to join death,
And death welcomes me, shows me a trailhead,
Foot-tracks overfilled with standing water.
Man has never owned another man here.
Aglow in the shade hang apples free for the taking.
I'm saying that death is a little girl. The apple
There in her hand is God Almighty where the skin
Breaks to her teeth and spills my freedom all over
Sunlight turning deadwood coppery rose.

CONQUEST

Found a field mouse drowned in the swimming pool this morning . . .
Call him Signa Winky if I were writing
A children's book . . . I spoke aloud, softly, but out loud,
"Who made the iris to stand upright and walk with me
All my life, from house to house, from New York to Las Vegas,
Could recreate a mouse a good swimmer and he would live."
Or did the mouse fall dead already from the talons of a bird?
God did not make me. God is new creation.

In a dream last night,
I climbed a staircase made of fossils of flowers.
At the top was a little room with a bed,
And in the bed was an old man, lanky and sallow
And long-bearded. Cradled in his arms, appearing
To laugh even as he slept so deeply,

Lay a small boy, tousled, with no flaw.
He would awaken soon
And then create the universe.

It makes sense if you think of it.
As I was saying to my friend who made the iris only this morning . . .

Actually,
I have no friend, yet my
Experience of friendship is so real
I sometimes find myself speaking
To him out loud.

I could also pick up the phone.
There is a man in England, and I love to hear him say
The words "Felpham" and "cottage."
He too is real.

Poor pastor mouse,
This morning also
There was a frog swimming in the milk
And another one sitting on the edge of the bowl.
They must have been great pals.

LANDSCAPE WITH TITYRUS IN VERMONT

Is the shearing done?
Was it done well?
I remember the hillsides
As being real
Workplaces for gathering wool
From off the weeds.

Exactly the same are beautiful
Waitresses lounging in their dignity
For want of trade in terrible
Chinese restaurants.
I mean beauty
Is a discard of our too-late labor now.

So lately, many have settled in the remote places,
Umbria or Vermont or any place

The blankets tear at our skin
Because the wool is coarse and the news,
When it reaches us, reaches us, then
Starves at the doorstep.

War starves.
Word of corruption
Starves, and even
Things near to the heart—
My old dog dead
And burned and in a box
Beside my unopened mail—
Starve.

On the hillsides over there
In the wooly November snow,
Cow mounts cow, ewe mounts ewe.
News of the American empire
Blows into drifts against broken fences.
Io, as I remember,
Was a cow,
And her father a river.
Corruption in Heaven
Made such hap.
If Andrew Marvell had had a typewriter,
If William Blake had had a cassette recorder,
If Walt Whitman had had a brace of healthy sons,
How the hillsides over there would melt and shine!

Nevertheless, today an exceptional pine tree,
Even in November,
Did actually burst into berry-red root and branch.
Unprecedented things
Are massing at the edge of eyesight.
Their technology
Makes holiday and fresh hills
And strong new fires for new gathering.

ELIZABETH ROBINSON

P LACING THE BODY in its proper rela-
tion to the world—and exploring the
spirit's role in this relationship—forms
the foundation of Elizabeth Robinson's work. Her poems often begin in narra-
tive, sometimes personal but more often public, and at times borrow from fairy
tales or legends whose basic structures we continue to sense as the story itself
gives way to philosophic speculation. Robinson began studying poetry under
Robert Kelly and others as an undergraduate at Bard College and continued in
an experimental vein during her MFA work at Brown. She then left for the Bay
Area, where she studied at the Pacific School of Religion in Berkeley, graduat-
ing in the early nineties with a master's of divinity. Her blend of abstraction
punctuated by the concrete and immediate displays a twin commitment to the
immanent world and the spiritual one, and her interest in language as their
natural mediator.

Robinson is the author of eight books of poetry; *Pure Descent* won the
National Poetry Series, and *Apprehend* won the Fence Modern Poets Series. Her
most recent books are *Apostrophe* and *Under That Silky Roof*. For the past several
years, she has also been involved in publishing; she's the co-editor of Instance
Press, which publishes the work of under-recognized writers, and co-founder
and co-editor of the EtherDome Chapbook Series, which publishes the work of
women who have not yet published a full-length book. Both these projects enact
the belief in the importance of community that runs through all of Elizabeth
Robinson's work. She lives in Boulder, Colorado.

from HOVENWEEP

i

Hackberry cancels out juniper. Travel approximately forty-five miles on a road
that is variably paved.

> Here find the testimony painted on tin, regarding his journey,
> traversed entirely
> on his knees.

> As though the humble man could crawl the full circuit, yet end up only
> here, and still

> mark his disappointment as affirmation: this is what's accomplished

> in the

> creek, water rotting away
> rock.

> Your compass: obliges you to take him out briefly to the night, look
> up, and him crawling and panting in its dim.

You, at the base, looking flat, see north. See towers. You and he. Before the long
time.

ii

We look down, straight down on you from above. It was eighty-five minutes of
travel on an unpaved road.

> And we saw that ruined honeycomb

> as though we were masons

> who knew better. The weathertight world

> and all that's inclement, we

> cast aside: affirmation for assertion.
> Tower is a term of endearment. That you not disgrace your family by
> insisting that they serve as pilgrims with you. The names of those places.

And then those who do witness to the structure of the honey go in your stead. Fallen rock and knees curved to it. That map consults upward to sweetness, its supplication, darkly sticky.

Aneth, Cortez, Blanding. Aneth and Cortez. Aneth. Aneth and Blanding. Aneth.

iii

The essence of nature is to be always borrowing. The wing falls from the bird
mid-flight

and then is affixed elsewhere. Winged stones, winged weeds, and so forth. They jitter around like small dolls. Made for new utility. The wind falls off the wing

in the semi-deliberate world. Dolls fall into a tableau. Twigs or flecks of dead skin.

Little angular dolls flop over, overlapping, making a corral
where there once was a corral. The essence of falling is repetition or overlap.

And summer the most dilapidated season, most likely to stumble from overhead.

Most likely, these shabby playthings are ancient. Herding wild creatures into domesticity. A little saliva will glue a leaf onto the doll's back, winglike.

But not a phony angel. No saliva in a place devoid of mouths.

Toys, they lack their own volition, and for that, they are made to lie down and cover up the tools. They fly away.

iv

Someone sits cross-legged before three piles. Tallow, flint, and a mound of unknown objects. She twists cotton wicks in her hands.

Elsewhere: she digs recklessly, throwing up dirt in what was, archeologically, a garden. There is a fossil hand grasping a fossil shovel. All this becomes evident in the aftermath of flames and wind. She invokes play and the mortar falls into heaps. The careful ruins of fruit. The tentative petrifaction of herbs. Overripe by millennia, the place smells of shit.

Someone will come along and counter the smell with another finding. Buried communities are not concerned about weather's vicissitudes. The cistern dries out into a primitive lantern. She digs not to unearth herself, but to absorb light from the detritus. She clenches her tail with a set of facsimile teeth.

THE LITTLE MATCHGIRL

The fingers were divorced from the hands.
Now there is a glowing
around the numbness of the mouth,

and that
light-ridden
painlessness is
the hand.

Hold the flame
up to the detached fingers.

Sensation as pentimento, overlap.

(Revoke her poverty.)

◼

Wish is a form of overlap,
of articulation:

to unite by a joint or joints.

Or the smooth-jointedness
of x-ray vision:

looks through walls
from the empty belly
to the feast.

While this wan fist

has no knuckles
to penetrate
coherence.

■

Would a second wish
lay on the bed of the first
as if to put words to,
or interpolate a blanket.

Leaf back through definition
and you will find her
lying there,

betrayed by those ghostly fingers
who point,

and ignited on the flint
of the abandoned
street.

And distinctly
unwarm in the gesture.

■

Perhaps you are happy with yourself
because you are familiar with a story
like this, and you experience the wall, too, as transparent.

Do you know the segments, the succession?
Perhaps you experience the bare palm as an embarrassment—

the disjointure,
the disarticulation
are not a muteness.

Shame on the fingertips:
matchtips
strewn with sulfur and phosphorous
do not remediate a bitter cold.

(You have been eavesdropped upon
when the image fell from the lips.)

She saw as a physical part of her heart
the pulse of some extremity.

Transparent or amputated:
admitting the passage of light through interstices.

What third vision spies
back upon her
hinges upon

the ability to move

while the false narrative of her
contentment is frozen.

The wicks of the fingers
one from another so far.

THE SNOW WINDOW

for Robert Kelly

i

The consistent back door
on the face of the hill.

Some creatures live here,
or under the 'here,'
known only consecutively:
"A," "B," "C."

That's the seasonal claim
when days accrete
like alphabets

and dwell below.

ii

Somewhere,
white's mundane
and most mysterious
lies

    between
and not serial.

Unconditional
the failure to recognize
that opens

on, finally, parallel greenery.

iii

    This is the door in the face,

      one of the series,

     that fell from above.

MARTHA RONK

THERE IS A quiet, meditative, and luminous quality to Martha Ronk's work. She is equally adept at considering the landscapes of the natural world, the particulars of daily life, the oscillations of memory, and the effects of the mind in process. Though her discrete lyrics unfold one by one through the passage of any of her collections, we soon notice how dialogic and interwoven each piece becomes with the others. Vision seems simultaneously precise and approximate in her work, and the most quotidian objects or events echo within the fluidity of her perceptions, even as she questions the most elemental contexts of convention. Ronk's poems are grounded in observation, yet they are unapologetically cerebral, airy, and linguistically complex as well. Conceptually and stylistically experimental, Martha Ronk is concerned with redefining beauty and the sublime.

Ronk received her PhD from Yale and has lived in California since 1971. She is the author of eight collections of poetry, including *Desire in LA*; *Eyetrouble*; *Why / WhyNot*; *In a landscape of having to repeat*, which received the 2005 PEN USA Poetry Award; and most recently, *Vertigo*, a National Poetry Series selection. She also received an NEA grant in 2007. A Renaissance literature and Shakespearean scholar, Martha Ronk is the Irma and Jay Price Professor of English and Comparative Literary Studies at Occidental College in Los Angeles. She has also taught in the graduate writing programs of Colorado University, Otis College of Art & Design, and the Naropa University Summer Writing Program.

from VERTIGO

"I cannot remember anything about this journey other than this"

A moment of inattention brought it all back as in the dream
it catches in your throat and you jerk back from the edge or
hear the cry from someone else although the scene is eerily
quiet almost everywhere. The more images I gathered from the past
the more unlikely it seemed that the past had actually happened
in this way or that, but rather one had pulled back from the edge
and for that moment it all came rushing in.
Events that might have happened otherwise play themselves out
in ways that begin to seem more familiar as if the sentence
itself by the one word turned the stream as a jutting rock might do.
I see a man fishing and I see the line spooled out
over his head in beautiful figure eights as if I were practicing
my hand in the school my mother went to before I was born.

"It is only a question of discovering how we can get ourselves attached to it
        again"
                    a drawing by Vija Celmins

I practice interruption to get used to it, get up to get the cup
and then sit down, go out to look at the sign on the corner, sit
down, open the book to 37, "Moon Surface [Luna 9]," close
it, open my mouth to get used to what it says and then
in some weathers, it's offered up freely and you have to
cover the books in plastic, remember to take it with you just in case
and you have to be grateful not to think things up.
Her surface drawings put one squarely on the moon
and there's nothing to take your mind off it, no one brings coffee,
and she's reminded of a scene where the actor talks about how
he's scared to leap off a balcony and then he finally leaps.
Someone keeps coming to the door, someone makes a mark
like graphite until it builds up slowly on the surface.

"The grayness of the early hours lasted almost until noon"

The crows are always there if this is where one lives.
So much for the principal parts of the story.
But it was not until two weeks later

I wrote about the birds but got no response and
it remains puzzling, whereas in fact all is determined
by the most complex of interdependencies.
I told her they always woke me up when I was there
and she noted them but said she always slept through.
Then she began to acquire a bit more definition
later in the day and after I moved where the crows
from behind the gray cloud had done everything together
in the most ominous way. The association of the two
seems to have to do with sleeplessness,
with how so much earlier keeps hanging on.

"It seemed similar to choice, although in an adjacent register"

Ferns and jewelweed fanning the air too slowly for the coming shift
as if the package as yet unwrapped had already arrived
in another time zone, the desert hot and dry.
Anticipation veiled what could be seen from the window.
We remained seated for about a quarter of an hour
counting the number of trees in order to put off the inevitable,
in order to see the effect the change would have before it happened
giving up what perhaps needn't have been given up,
selecting pain as one of the necessary elements,
not to lessen its effect, but to notice the exact moment of selection.

"All that remains in the left half of the painting is"

The precision of color and even of symbols
announces a stance against which one can move either
closer or by indirection further away. If closer
then the meaning is clear and often labeled either
by custom or common knowledge, if farther
then the garments, painted in dark colors, merge
beyond recognition with the background, which is
equally unrecognizable. One doesn't know where one is
and cannot recall the name of one's maternal grandfather
or the person one knows as plainly as one's own hands
that themselves alternate between the indistinct
and the highly etched Durer portraits of his own.

"Twisting and turning like the ebbing tides"

Amo, amas, and the crossword puzzle takes off
even though the shift was not so entirely unexpected.
He looks troubled but it may be that she's the one
turning into the people sitting at the edge of the sea.
It's perhaps her mother checking the tide charts in the morning
and it's troubling even though one understands perfectly well
the need both for categories and the breaking of categories
one might like to have some latitude,
but the crossword puzzle is always there moving left and right
or up and down and the tide is coming in or going out
and to some extent we know it's hard wired
and not just what happens to the body,
but the mind splashed by Latin and the Sargasso Sea.

"Cameras, he explained, came then to replace descriptive paragraphs"

If description could outpace effusions of feeling,
serif or sans serif, punctuated with dashes and in Amherst,
could one say it was a peculiar summer.
I tried to like what I'd always liked and tried to get there
sooner rather than later.
I'd forgotten I liked orange until
on a scale of one to ten the petals ranged themselves
like swallows on the telephone wire
flying off at the sound of someone's coming.
Something should have been a topic—
I had thought it out and left nothing to chance,
but the people kept arriving
never thinking to find the appropriate word for
what they were taking in and writing down.
One snapped a lily between finger and thumb
and one had hair like spilling rust.

"Whenever she speaks to him in that voice, an infrequent enough occurrence"

What's the difference between trying to lift an arm and lifting an arm,
between desire and that other thing. I'm glad to hear you're coming.

I am glad to hear you think you're coming despite the fact
she does take up the entire conversation, expressive as her dress
coming off in colors near the edge of every year she's ever been in.
Yet she talks during the entire playing of the cello piece
displacing it into what she wants us to hear and into the silence
written on her when she takes on your voice at dinner
when you'll arrive and now she speaks out of her beautifully disjointed face,
out of her hair wet from the pond, never in the voice she came in with.
When he lost his hearing, he heard only the cello's low notes
and what he heard changed his way of hearing the piece forever.

"I was astonished at the mysterious slow motion quality"

The water was at a standstill because of the severity of the wind,
taking on the glassy sheen described by authors who are moved by personal destiny
and buy photographic postcards to capture the touched-up beauty
in which the moss is growing up the north side of the rock walls
extending like the Handel aria she sang, her voice a waterfall
reaching from the top beyond the line of vision into the chasm I fell into
in my dreams later that afternoon as I seemed to keep falling into
no matter the various devices staged to prevent such an inexplicable loss of
balance and the sounds are stilled and by coincidence I feel it all
at this time of year as the shadows lengthen across the lawn.

"The shadows of clouds scudded across the steep slopes and through the
        ravines"

An almost theatrical obscurity seems to have settled on
the adjacent area usually described as ordinary and plain.
The field of weeds is overtaken by the constriction of one's chest,
concealed by rhapsodies. In these cases,
despite the numbers of internal distractions
it is usually best to move about and although everywhere
there are great effusions of feeling, it is nonetheless
recommended to follow the last of the sunlight into that very field
even if the darkness itself is overtaking.
After a passage of time a light breaks on the scene
and allows one to exit in favor of the highly unusual display of clouds.

"The headache alone forced me sometimes to the limit of consciousness"

He says you had a bad night and it's as true as if I had told him
but by the time we speak the night has so receded
all oceans must have drained away.
Coleridge infuses voices in the night in ways
both understandable and flushed as writing plays.
Then the lingering sense of dread.
One of the characters must be prevented from collapsing into
the other and must be prevented from collapsing
entirely into the madness he finds so awfully attractive.
In the third act the noise level is such that it could have been morning
and they chime in at the top of their voices in mid-sentence
while afterwards and by the time we speak it's as silent as the sea.

IN A LANDSCAPE OF HAVING TO REPEAT

In a landscape of having to repeat.
Noticing that she does, that he does and so on.
The underlying cause is as absent as rain.
Yet one remembers rain even in its absence and an attendant quiet.
If illusion descends or the very word you've been looking for.
He remembers looking at the photograph,
green and gray squares, undefined.
How perfectly ordinary someone says looking at the same thing or
I'd like to get to the bottom of that one.
When it is raining it is raining for all time and then it isn't
and when she looked at him, as he remembers it, the landscape moved closer
than ever and she did and now he can hardly remember what it was like.

YOU COULDN'T READ A BOOK ABOUT IT

When he goes upstairs he can't find the one he wants
and says, you always like the really depressing ones.
Over time words like *florid* lose their meanings
and the part of the white bird that isn't white is throbbing since yesterday
whether I like it or not.
You couldn't read a book about it or take binoculars
as you keep meaning to or use the painting of the crow
this morning over the newly mown hay or was it wheat you saw,
despite the heavy brush strokes, move wings in that slow way.

IN THE HOUSE

She'd like to unbutton the blouse.
She'd like to give up rhetoric but seems unable
and likes adjectives besides.
She'd like to walk to the house for example up the walkway
but the blouse is another story, a second story,
one she'd rather forget.
How are they so certain.
That's it I guess.
How to unloose the tag end
or make a decision different from the usual.
She keeps looking for a migraine in the near future
shimmering its usual pinks and greens.
It's probably yours in the second story bedroom she says.
These days I don't sleep at all she agrees.
Her blouses are usually unbuttoned and how
can she stand it or what about touching all the
clothes in the closet as if they belonged to you.

MARY RUEFLE

RAISED LARGELY IN Europe, Mary Ruefle came to know contemporary American poetry relatively late, and her poetry still shows the influences of German and British Romanticism on the one hand and French Surrealism on the other. Her concise, dramatic images are rooted in emotion. Loss, desire, and the unattainable all play leading roles, and all are subject to sudden wild, uncanny twists that disrupt the poetry's orderliness and introduce unpredictability into both form and content. Throughout her ten published books, Ruefle pays acute attention to the tangible. Not only are her poems built predominantly of concrete images, but she takes her writing into the visual arts with collages and one-off artists books based on erasure and layering. *A Little White Shadow* is a facsimile of one such book, faithfully rendering the textures of her media and the aged color of the original's pages. She has exhibited her visual work in solo and group shows around the country.

This emphasis on the material and the concrete touches the very roots of Ruefle's work—she's one of the few writers today who still writes by hand, transcribing her poems afterward on a manual typewriter, eschewing computers completely. Although based in Vermont, she spends much of her life traveling. She has been a visiting professor in writing programs all over the country, including the University of Massachusetts at Amherst, Bennington College, and the University of Iowa, where she has taught in both the Writers' Workshop and the creative non-fiction program. Mary Ruefle has received fellowships from the Guggenheim Foundation, the Whiting Foundation, and the NEA, and an award in literature from the American Academy of Arts and Letters.

NAKED LADIES

Rousseau wanted: a cottage on the Swiss shore,
a crow and a rowboat.

Stevens wanted a crate from Ceylon full of jam
and statuettes.

My neighbors are not ashamed of their poverty
but would love to be able to buy a white horse,
a stallion that would transfigure the lot.

Darwin was dying by inches from not having anyone to talk to
about worms, and the vireo outside my window wants nothing less
than a bit of cigarette-wool for her nest.

The unattainable is apparently rising on the tips of forks
the world over . . .

So-and-so is wearing shoes for the first time

and Emin Pasha, the deepest acreage of the Congo,
wanted so badly to catch a red mouse! Catch one he did
shortly before he died, cut in the throat by slavers who
wanted to kill him. *At last!* Runs the diary

and it is just this *at last* we powder up and call progress.

So the boys chipped in and bought Bohr a gram of radium
for his 50th birthday.

Pissarro wanted white frames for his paintings
as early as 1882, and three francs for postage, second place.

Who wants to hear once more the sounds of their mother throwing
Brussels sprouts into the tin bowl?

Was it *ping* or was it *ting*?

What would you give to smell again the black sweetpeas
choking the chain-link fence?

Because somebody wants your money.

The medallions of monkfish in a champagne sauce . . .

The long kiss conjured up by your body in a case . . .

The paradisiacal vehicle of the sweet-trolley rolling in
as cumulous meringue is piled on your tongue
and your eye eats the amber glaze of a crème brûlée . . .

The forgiveness of sins, a new wife, another passport,
the swimming pool, the rice bowl

full of rice, the teenage mutant ninja turtles escaping
as you turn the page . . .

Oh brazen sex at the barbecue party!

Desire is a principle of selection. Who wanted *feet* in the first place?

Who wanted to stand up? Who felt like walking?

WHERE LETTERS GO

How did the arrow fall down the chimney

and how did we seal the seals of envelopes
when they were the furthest thing from our minds?

Why is a stamp destined
to miss the kiss of its own cancellation?

When is a woman exact postage
so that a question need never be weighed?

Who is coughing?
Their concentration is remarkable.

The body is always so sorry.

We live in a world of life and other small, thankful things
combined in deeply satisfying ways.

A tisket, a tasket.

A green and yellow world.

And then I asked it.
Why was I only partly born
before this moment

delivered me?

There they go, stupes
into the maelstrom,
on the wings of a sweet white dove,
on the back of the crow.

PENCILED

No real word yet

Spear of geese
thrown in the wrong direction

Its shadow spreading black mist
over the snow

I was up to my elbows
in a man losing blood on the table

And the white deer
whose antlered breath

Held out hope
with abandon

Seemed cut for us

But the upabove was protecting itself
and dipped the dice in wax

Seven pencils stood by the river
and shook

CONCERNING ESSENTIAL EXISTENCE

The horse mounted the mare slowly and precisely
and then stopped.

He was profoundly disturbed by a piece of straw.

He was profoundly distracted by the sad toy
upside down in the tree.

He was profoundly disengaged by half a cloud
in the corner of his wet eye.

And then he continued.

Nothing is forgot by lovers
except who they are.

IMPRESARIO

Emma Bovary, after a rendezvous, lifting her skirts
over the fields, though her bottom is drenched with dew—

Lily Bart in the carriage, indignant, hands the man her pearls—

And dear Esther Summerson! Holding her ring of housekeeping keys
is beginning to worry while

Fanny Price is beginning to pinken or pale
in want of a cordial for once in her life—

Should I invite them to tea?
Lily wouldn't come.
Emma, in her nervousness, might break a cup
but Esther would mend it—
Fanny in the kitchen would want to be certain:
she ate arsenic *with her hands?*
And then we would serve the tart.

                    I despise muffins.

I despise daisies for that matter
and daffodils are worse.

The men understand nothing.

Or their own intelligence,
whichever is worse.

I like to read because
it kills me.

Yellow should not be too bright.

They read for humanity's sake.

If you give me a brace of pheasants
and a case of wine I will tell you
how I like it.

I like it dull.

GO VERBATIM

I live in the figurative world
where nothing exists
not even a chair
except the one I am sitting on
as I walk le boulevard
when Francie comes up
and pulls it out from under me.
You live in a fantasy world!
she exclaims upon examining it.
Et tu, Francie, I say,
what is your mind made of?
Disappearing soap or a candle
that won't blow out?
And when I had her weeping
I said Francie sit down,
teach me how to say
sad minds think alike,
you know, the repetitious way.

THE WORLD AS I LEFT IT

Wood, cement, steel, polyester.
Glass, marble, ink and ether.
Water, ash, asphalt and leather. Plastic.
Stone, fur, copper and silk. Silver, cotton,
paper and clay. Bone, horn, coal, gold,
gas, soil, rubber and cardboard. Mud. Tin.

Wool, wax, lead. Ice, oil, paint and bronze.
Rayon, cork, vinyl and sand. Numbers.
Dust, slate, graphite and glue.
I was almost happy.

MINOR NINTH CHORD

Everything has an almost brownish clarity.

The loneliness of remote regions has a special tone,
such that one believes one ought to understand
and even see this special thing that slips away from thought.

It is as if the woman has just now
forever shed a painful conflict. It is a very
painful thing, having to part company
with what torments you.

And how mute the world is!

REGINALD SHEPHERD

EGINALD SHEPHERD'S POETRY often surveys classical texts and myths as a means to discover the shadow lives and contexts of the poet's own experiences. Shepherd situated his poems at the crossroads of those mythic echoes of desire and loss that haunt the Western imagination. His poems are lyrical and poised, and the music of his phrasings lends an oracular resonance to his most daily meditations. The importance of "song" as poetic utterance, as celebration, and as defiance surfaces everywhere in Shepherd's poetry. His experiences as a gay man and as a boy growing up in the Bronx find urgency cast within the mythic molds he loved. Yet Shepherd was a realist in the end. As he said, ". . . all things/are full of momentary gods, world-sick/with ritual outline and poisoned// by too much song."

Reginald Shepherd was the editor of *The Iowa Anthology of New American Poetries* (University of Iowa Press, 2004) and of *Lyric Postmodernisms* (Counterpath Press, 2008). He was the widely anthologized author of five collections of poetry, all published by the University of Pittsburgh Press: *Fata Morgana* (2007); *Otherhood* (2003), a finalist for the 2004 Lenore Marshall Poetry Prize; *Wrong* (1999); *Angel, Interrupted* (1996); and *Some Are Drowning* (1994), winner of the 1993 Associated Writing Program's Award in Poetry. His essay collection *Orpheus in the Bronx* was published by the University of Michigan Press in 2008. Shepherd was the recipient of a 1993 "Discovery"/The Nation Award, and received grants from the National Endowment for the Arts, the Illinois Arts Council, and the Florida Arts Council, among other awards and honors. He died in Pensacola, Florida, in 2008.

DIRECTION OF FALL

And then this ruined sky again. Memory
came like migratory birds calling *reaper, reaper,*
reaper, hungry ghosts threshing distance

at the extremity of private sound: whatever wandering
makes sing. Memory came to fragments, then
composed itself, the endless sequence

of silver-dollar days came down
in April hail. Clouds are fools
in whiteface, gone gray with their heavy freight

of rain; Florida falls into mud, leaving
behind flood warnings, hurricanes, watch for
small tornadoes. Late landscape wears its past

as scars, suffering from too much weather,
the many weathers we've had. (This body
is almost mine, but sleep won't take me back.)

The sound of wind welcomed me, wind's indecisive,
noncommittal wing invited me, incited me
to part-recited theories of the half-correct,

starting with the names of stars, lessons
we don't tell the music: myths
abound in me, I woke baroque and unafraid.

A PARKING LOT JUST OUTSIDE THE RUINS OF BABYLON

Just outside the dust of Babylon, tank treads
not designed for desert transport
grind down the royal road from Sardis
to Persepolis. Just outside Babylon, the gate of the gods
is closed for repair, please choose an alternate
route. Ishtar has retired from the fray and may not
return, stripped naked of her ornaments and hung upside down
in the underworld as she is. Just outside
Babylon, the palaces have fallen into disrepair, the lion-
crowned columns have feet of clay. Although

there is an ample supply of imported spirits,
the incense seems to be missing; the astronomical tables
are off by centuries. Sun-baked mud brick
is crumbling into sand and sentiment, forgetful sediments
and fertilizer residues, a depleted water table's salt
and pesticides. Just outside the outside (a window,
door, a gate left open in the rush to leave, creaking
complaints to desert noon, a blankly blazing candor),
the Euphrates is a toxic fire, fish swimming chemical
currents don't know they're dead, the fishermen
eat them anyway, with garlic, onions, and mint,
while somewhere somewhat north of Babylon, the Tigris
is a predator, a fang of lightning ripping Assyria
in half, Akkad is smashed agate
and tin. Just outside, just outside, the hanging gardens
dangle from a frayed and double-knotted
nylon rope, twisting in a storm of chaff and shrapnel; smashed
clay tablets' cuneiform enumerates the daily dead, body
bag winds score the bare ruined walls of Susa with no song.

THE TENDENCY OF DROPPED OBJECTS TO FALL

The air is thick with gods, crowded streets
rife with them, an infestation of
divinity, "the servant-keeping class."
What shape wants them? Memory

is money and what wind wants to do
with it is scatter. Wind doesn't. Want
doesn't. Assembles the materials for bodies
drifting through the past on rubber rafts,

with plastic oars they don't know
how to use. Blank, wounded, or rendered otherwise
helpless. Justice admires John
but never tells him so (*better to break*

than to be broken), establishing a proper format
for suffering. So many laborers
have elapsed, "the torturable classes"
singing *Deus*. Singing *Without money*

we'll all die. They've all died. History
leaves no witnesses, a when and why,
a where and what became
of them. In exile Andromache's handmaid

builds a miniature Troy with toothpicks
and superglue, with matchsticks from a story
that she read: a helpless glitter
with tinfoil walls and someone

rolls over it in his sleep. The notes read
that is Not loved, *or* I shall totally
remove. *Or* Be wealthy, *that is*
Not my people. With us. I was. In

me. Draw near. Head bowed,
still thinking *and*.

TURANDOT

the torn veil parts
days of indecision, rain or
overhanging gray, and here and there
a sun for earth to spin around
some light for someone always

(sky clears its clouded mind
by midnight, taking the drunken road
home, careful of the swerve and veer, the)

■

old emperor wind whistles
through live oak and magnolia
branches: hushes, chastises, hastens,
summoning up rustle, hiss and fall
although it's only starting to be spring:
deposes branchlets to the pavement

the live oaks let down their leaves
in a russet and copper rush
when March strolls in from even farther
south, rough driveway concrete smothers

■

what dies each night before it's born
(there's moonrise after this rain)
how and weather passes through
like storm clouds on their way to downpour
torrent warnings, just showers
in outlying zones

so many men have seen pieces of this day
how famous was that gone sun

■

silk sleeves flutter in the boywind, girlwind, swirling
wind-of-what-I'm-not, what the I doesn't know
of what it wants, wants to be, intention of him
just out of view, wind blurring
perspective with leaf-dust, grit,
some pollen poised in the eye

a tear will melt that

■

(heart)

(fire)

(wing)

(blood)

(ice)

(don't touch me i'm sacred)

at times all of these things
a riddle wrapped around them

■

she'll drink the stranger's kiss
the peasants eat off unfired clay plates

they keep their heads about them
covered when she passes

follow them into dirt

■

and then the moon
strays into circumstance, drunk
on stolen radiance:
little severed head in the sky
stricken white, pale lover of the dead
who walk unburied

they dream other, they dream
of her, the face filled-in
with objections, rejected
abjections, some say
the moon does not exist

nobody sleeps

YOU ALSO, NIGHTINGALE

Petrarch dreams of pebbles
on the tongue, he loves me
at a distance, black polished stone
skipping the lake that swallows

worn-down words, a kind of drown
and drench and quench and very kind
to what I would've said. Light marries
water and what else (unfit

for drinking purposes), light lavishes
my skin on intermittent sun. (I am weather
and unreasonable, out of all
season. Petrarch loves my lies

of laurel leaves, ripped sprigs of
deciduous evergreen.) A creek is lying
in my cement-walled bed, slurring
through the center of small

town; the current's brown and
turbid (muddy, turbulent
with recent torrents), silt rushing
toward the reservoir. A Sonata

passes by too close (I have to jump)
and yes I do hear music here. It's blue, or
turquoise, aquamarine, some synonym
on wheels, note down that note. It's Petrarch

singing with his back to me (delivering
himself to voice), his fingers
filled with jonquil, daffodils, mistaken
narcissus. (I surprised him

between the pages of a book,
looked up the flowers I misnamed.)
Forsythia and magnolia bring me
spring, when he walks into the house

he has wings. Song is a temporary thing
(attempt), he wants to own his music.

ELENI SIKELIANOS

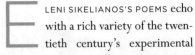

ELENI SIKELIANOS'S POEMS echo with a rich variety of the twentieth century's experimental traditions. Most dominant are the frank, quick energies of the Beat poets and the delight in the daily of the New York School, but her work also shows a deep understanding of Language-based experiments through her focus on surface and her attention to the points at which language can fruitfully break down. Her book-length *The California Poem* transcends all influences to create a new version of the poetry of place with documentary directness and historical scope. Always pushing the question of genre, she has also written a poetic memoir, *The Book of Jon*, published by City Lights in 2004, based on the one hand on her father, and on the other, on growing up in the bohemian atmosphere of 1960s California.

Sikelianos has spent her adult life in many places, including San Francisco, Colorado, France, Greece, and New York. She received an MFA from the Jack Kerouac School at Naropa University, and while in New York, ran the reading series at St. Mark's and taught in public schools with Teachers & Writers. Her many awards include a Fulbright to Greece, a Seeger Fellowship at Princeton, an NEA Fellowship, a New York Foundation for the Arts Award, and the James D. Phelan Award, and her book *The Monster Lives of Boys and Girls* was chosen in the National Poetry Series. The author of six books, she also translates from Greek and French, and teaches creative writing in the PhD program at the University of Denver.

THUS, SPEAK THE CHROMOGRAPH

Saying: One night in a cloud chamber
I discovered a thing: that a thing (I used to have a crown
of light) a thing could be more
than True, and more again

than False, a thing
could carry its name

with a ticket of lights
called Possible: In a cloud chamber, particles are betrayed
by movement and water vapors

leave trails. Discovered: when matter and its antithesis come
together, a disappearing
flash of light: (our share of night to
ear) (I mean what I say): In contempt

of the Law of All
Excluded Thirds: laws are not
symmetrical in the forward and the back
(of time). On which side
are they stacked? and the sky also

(is what made Hart Crane
so crazy in the heart) continued to pile up
clouds without account, a mass of gasses with nothing

scribbled under them; a song in the middle
of the crystal
cavatina. We hardly had any bones then. Did
Hart Crane have bones? If so, which kind? And

how far down? It was written
in the boned hours, the Book of Weeds, a treatise on leaving

the house at dusk, when all buildings have already had time enough
to fit themselves back into shadows. As if there were only:

dusk-to-dusk, between dusk-and-dust
where no animals asserted themselves

as separate from the day, and the night
comes again, as it always

has done. The fact was that
we could not follow the map—Because the Book

of Nature was written
in math's un-
certain language, author of black

rains, why the naked
eye
unclothed
can see

beyond math's limits
why
a baby's bones are soft

as pudding when first let out
of the water & take

a long time
to harden, you can flatten
a newborn

's skull by placing it
on a board, the death-hole
of the cranium takes

6 months to close
and then grow brittle

In describing the last
arc of the last
circumference: I miss(ed) that halo.

(How long it took to understand rivers

run toward the sea)

ESSAY: AT NIGHT THE AUTOPORTRAIT

Each evening from my bed I calculated & compared
the state of my soul with the state
of Kansas, because a place also
carries a name. Did my body make an objection to traveling
across Texas   internal conditions in which I   abstracted myself   Chicago

I never had to force myself to immigrate to the inside
thought // like a possum// playing dead// leaving as little as possible living
at the surface// which might be burned//

a lamp, a desk . . . entered the eye . . . to prove something . . . was going on . . .
                    outside the skin   Baltimore

Deployed over the gutted city: an immense crude sky, scene
of some crime or other, a brusk separation   parented by nature   knowing
          nothing or understanding
nothing requires some concentration   except the things the heart can do
directly   Between the dark

& the bed approaching each place or thing my eyes
(a body) must accustom themselves anew. . . . If a being could be the product
          of a ground one tastes, then I was Texas developing

a vague science of joy or beauty

Forgetting the particulars that make it go

a paysage abandons a window to get an inkling
of the sky or the sky's

second elbow

from THE CALIFORNIA POEM

a lady just asked, why are all the cows
in California? All she saw from L.A. to Alhambra
were cows. In the Camargue, in France, in the Rhone delta was
once a sterile marshland but is now all about cow
Like one big intense cattle ranch, the
California is the Texas and the Riverside of Southern France

Paravent:

in the folding of sheep, the penning
of cattle, laying down
of oysters, the parking of cars

in the creasing of lambs, the origami
of calves, the wrappling of grass

in the pleating of the immortal soul
of the automobile, the deadly knowledge in anthrax or
minute radiating eruditions of anthracite, the tucking in
of pinwheels, uranium enfolding at the anima of
elemental centers, in the plaiting of the city of
palm trees, the gathering up
of glittering Venice Beach, in the fabulous history of *vaqueras*, the bending
of wondrous fenders, in the folding membranes
of organelles, organized & specialized to make me believe
in the plastering of castor plants, & unsurpassable statues of cows

Now how shall it

recalcitrate upon its approved
forms and quit them? How shall the droning world get on
without all its *beaux esprits* in California? Each harbors its own menagerie
of mesozoan parasites. Each to each may I personally undress
the periosteal filaments
of California, & all its
stockinets?

No, you may not.

Let birds of delivery bearing drugs of
        wonder & weather show me
                a providential acquaintance with men & women
                        who can wheel it better on the wing than me, who
                                can hoof it
                        far past the surplus of stars in deed or in thought,
                                dead-of-night & niggardly

Let Leviathans in the land of Beavers take refuge in the ark of daylight

But let E. kiss with the rabbit the dew-struck grass
in the morning, sun-
      light slapping her face

Let E., foster parent of a sparrow praise without end the porcupine,
    a creature who once bristled in my pan
Let Br'er Rabbit bless with the oleander and his people the pillbug, a
    living mineral & silver roundhouse rolling
        beneath the leaf
Red-tailed kite blessed be ELENI & her friends in falcons & in the
    MALL, stealing transistor radios from Robinsons at San Roque
Let the possum beg god for his wily fame, inaccessible
Let me praise with the flea his sharpened tongue, leap up from the
    carpet, my bitter biting friend
Let E. bless the barnowl of gravity amongst my guests

When you consider the gulliest of birds, remember one-thousand and
    one nights of Laridae—jaegers,
        gulls, skimmers & terns free and far from Laredo, generalist
            feeders, scavengers, sometime
        saprophytes, skimming on flesh living and dead; Yet let you sing,
            Caspian Tern,
        silver above,
        white below:—*kra haa*
        Sterna elegans—*car-eek*
        Sterna hirundo—*kee-arr*
        Sterna fosteri—*kay-r-r-r, kip kip kip*
Glaucus-winged gull, screeching *kow-kow-kow*, soft-toned *ga-ga*, let the
    party-goers go
    in the grass and fuck in the night
Let the power of Coney Island come to this place, with its wonderwheel
    and frightened midnight grit
Let burning glass illuminate the power of darkness
Eleni be gracious to the windows indeed lest they let us see how
    strangers are grubbing up my manzanita trees
Let E., me, keep yapping, "for EARTH is an intelligence" in all her
    vestments & pants
Let California awake us from our dressed-up stupor
        by which I don't get shit done
"For the names & the numbers of animals are as the names & numbers
    of stars"
        & they are distracting me

WORLD IS WEIRD

World is weird, and so
what? Water this poem and watch it
take shape, it's layers
of the born
world, heard
world, streaked and shaved, see
it shakes, a
shuttle carrying
all world's weeds, weirds,
trash and goods, gods to you—

Or perhaps it's winter's ordinary scene:
abandoned tires in marsh-shore muck
The highway goes by it, and ducks take
to airways about now

Water World is on the right
Next left No-Oxygen World, Dry World, Dirt World, Tin
World and World of Exemplary Vehicular Noises

Exit the poem for: Sluice City, World of Steel, Plug-In City with
    Maximum Pressure, an
                Asphalt-and-Weed Oasis

Find here: Vacant sky, vacant lots, a few
                Sunday faces nuclear cascading

Of the world, weird: People wear it, "the section they use
like clothes on their backs," and soon appears "an object as
magic as a private face"

ROD SMITH

ROD SMITH'S WORK has a serious tongue in its cheek. "Humor is a process. Depression a useful first step," says the epigraph to his first chapbook. Smith uses humor in just such a complex way, which turns it at times searingly sarcastic, at times despairing, often tender, and always socially aware. Over the years, Smith has been involved in many projects that establish and nurture poetic communities, including a reading series, a literary journal, and a small press. Most recently, he has been an active member of the Flarf collective. Described by *Jacket* magazine as "retro-Futurist," Flarf explores the inappropriate in language as a mode of cultural critique and poetic production. Smith's work is steeped in contemporary culture, but also remains firmly at its margins, and the resulting double view creates an uneasy reflection of the quotidian landscape we take for granted.

Rod Smith, a graduate of the MFA program at George Mason University, is a longtime resident of Washington, D.C., where he manages Bridge Street Books and runs the reading series there. His literary journal *Aerial*, which he began in 1989, focuses on a single author per issue and presents a wide range of writers, including Bruce Andrews, Lyn Hejinian, Barrett Watten, and John Cage. He also publishes Edge Books, which specializes in the work of emerging and midcareer poets, and he is co-editing Robert Creeley's *Selected Letters* for the University of California Press. The author of four full-length collections, Smith has also published many chapbooks and collaborations in the United States and Europe, as well as critical writings in journals and online.

from THE GOOD HOUSE
for Amy Wright

PRELUDES

the egret says
the house, it is something to eat or sunlight, the egret
thinks, the house, it wills, is a subcanvas I can scribble,
        the egret moves
or is awake, loving the familiar solution of loving, this
        explains the egret to the egret in the house
to the house & sunlight, we become intelligible because
        the egret says elliptical, in beckettland or geography,
        in small mammals & planets no egret never not says
        elliptical, no elliptical egret mechanism well under a
        love, today, or today, does not increase elliptical,
        covered stand
of egret then, the sunflower freezing in the egret's reason is
        spilling nutria, is an idea
&
affiliative, monthly, in egret pajamas, lolling, to
merge with the sunflower, frozen in not freezing, but flashing.

                ■

egret lights, they stretch, & revere, they say
i have a thing,
instruct in the new circumstance, elliptical,
tangible, to their sweet ego, in open-heart &
patagonia, go beyond shy in time they gain
& haunt, let's say
the word of the egret is
thumb, let's say thumb
as an egret prelude then, in order to correctly translate sappho, &
        think the cluster-egret, its
didn't get through water, its
safely egret waning
or education of sweet ego thumb then
in time or in
the night did dawn & the whales did spout
as a kind of paperclip on our idiots
all graphic kindness
& all graphic kindness
& to you, my egret soul, all is ooh, & all is

pronounced like a bell, & all is between me proposed,
pursuing one's own all, so to ring, & so to ring

■

The good houses the parts, calls to
them, & wakens—

> in being, the house we will, its precepts
> lumber the stilling male—
> opulence isn't allowed, so to
> form is to erase what's not
> gradual & new—a specific
> love to focus the elements

> when we lock the door
> things float around awhile,
> climax, & rest

> in the new sense

■

The good part of the house
is where something leaves
alone the light that it lattice
the red, souring, hoarse
needs made by no
other—safety depends in
them—
> so knowing strength
> so knowing weakness

this is where we will, & home

■

THE GOOD HOUSE

The good house feels bad about
the territory
                        —the house seems
to be a verb though it dislikes
the term 'housing'—the house
seems to be a bad dog & a
live wire—the house is bored

until people come over—the house
is anxious to please guests—
it is stupid & so thinks cordon
means love—it is wise & so
chooses—

    the honesty of the house helps
    the people to know—they can
    relax & recall other houses
    they have known, they become
    simple & listen to each other
    & to some birds, the birds right now

The good wasn't built into
the house but earned, once a beggar
lived there, & once a small one—

the police came & went

there were parties

The good was an upkeep

It was a perilous upkeep

There was kindling

This house was that house
to many—& to many there was no
house there because they hadn't
noticed—there was one who
noticed & was wanted, was loved

this gave the house hope
this gave the house no hope
this gave the house hope

it alternated. sometimes house, sometimes home

∎

& sometimes the kitty licks the bicycle on the porch

∎

there's a barrel in the basement
that belongs to a country singer
named Nel—

there's an old wonderbread wrapper
behind the kitchen cabinet nobody
knows the story on—

there's a stack of bad news in
a box by the back door—

there's a wreath in a box behind the thing
& a bauble on the windowbox above some stuff—

∎

tears never house us, maybe they
cleanse, maybe they don't, the word
intend doesn't seem to fit

sentiment

∎

anything can be made out of a house.

though many of them are blue.

there's a kind of recovery in it then.

too much innocence, or minutes
left out, those.

a time, or economic worry, a
weird abreaction.

seeps
in the house are loans one cannot trust.

a trusted house, the work of
the house, a dirigible.

seeps in the house should not be imagined.

the worst is not good, it's alone & not nourish

■

time is a housed reputable beginner

thirty more are needed

tripping, the house kneads the flower,
spells me, parts the bowl, stuns
& is soft, stuns
& is real

■

TED'S HEAD

So there's this episode of Mary Tyler Moore where Ted's trying to get a raise &
after finagling and shenaniganizing he puts one over on Lou & gets his contract
changed to non-exclusive sos he can do commercials which is not cool w/
Lou & the gang because Ted's just a brainless gimp & it hurts the image of the
news to have the anchorman selling tomato slicers & dogfood so Lou gets
despondent because the contract can't be rescinded but then he gets mad &
calls Ted into his office & says "You're going to stop doing commercials, Ted" &
Ted says "why would I do that Lou?" & Lou says "Because if you don't I'll punch
your face out" & Ted says "I'll have you arrested" & Lou says "It'll be too late,
your face will be broken, you're not gonna get too many commercials with
a broken face now are you Ted?" & Ted buckles under to force & everybody's
happy, except Ted but he's so dumb nobody cares & everybody loves it that
Lou's not despondent anymore he's back to his brustling chubby loud loveable
whiskey-drinking football-loving ways. Now imagine if Ted were Lou, if Ted
were the boss. You know how incredibly fucking brainless Ted is, but let's
imagine he understands & is willing to use force. That's the situation we're
now in as Americans.

THE STRENGTH

In the renting & in
something lengthy
a loosening, a lack's lattice
round—this beam abbreviate opposite-sized carnal loam—

it is its sever

triad is not so low as to shove a gone stop
& then the solve curses
& thin the corpse ago

—dawn runs it, dawn, that is.

the rising's recourse.

alone.

CAROL SNOW

C AROL SNOW'S WORK has tended increasingly toward the minimal and the enigmatic over the past fifteen years. From the issues of representation and presence that motivated her first book, she has focused more and more on presence alone, questioning it even as she tries to evoke it. Snow often uses repetition and revision to see more precisely, and precision is at the heart of her work. Her meditative clarity concentrates on the senses, exploring what an acute attention can hear, feel, and intuit as well as see. Reflective and constructive at the same time, her poems have a distilled quality evocative of classic Asian poetries as they trace the intricacies of the daily mind, of the present pierced by memory. Increasingly experimental in character, particularly in her use of fragmentation and chains of association, Snow's poetry has the feeling of a glimpse that indicates a much larger entity just out of sight, a history we enter through a single overheard phrase; her lines are intimations, evidence, clues.

Carol Snow's first book, *Artist and Model*, was chosen for the National Poetry Series and subsequently won the 1990 San Francisco State Poetry Center Book Award. Two subsequent collections, *For* and *The Seventy Prepositions*, were published by the University of California Press. She has received an NEA Fellowship, the Joseph Henry Jackson Award, and a Pushcart Prize, as well as a Creative Work Fund Grant for the project *Syntax: A Reading, Danced*, a collaboration with the choreographer Alex Ketley. A San Francisco native and long-time resident of the Bay Area, she is co-director of Blue Bear School of Music at Fort Mason Center.

LE DÉJEUNER

A still life: on a table, a white paper
napkin in a spill of water. The remains
of a sandwich, a salad (two plates).
                              Objects—

napkins, a glass
of some water, flatware, sugar bowl, coffee cup—
(some as at rest on a journey through, some
stationed as at a station on their circuits of,
the café)
              for the moment as form on the form of an outdoor table.

I told him briefly of that hard time, my eyes fixed
on the table (watching the teaspoon
on a napkin near my hand, the water glass,

the bowl of little packets of sweetener and sugar
not changed or harmed).

                              ■

Not to look up at concern (his face);
                              and a couple walking away
from a vendor's booth across the street
with the freshly squeezed orange juice they'd paid for; and traffic,
and litter, maybe a stray; a woman at a neighboring table,

nodding. And the order rustling of the letters of the names of the forms of the
     masses
of blades of leaves moving in the texture of the mass of the figures
of trees I might see growing behind him east of campus (his eyes alarmed).

I would leave you with the objects on the table

as he and I arranged them: the paper napkin crumpled in the water spilled
from my setting down my glass of water nervously, the wheat-colored cup he
     cupped in one hand, plates of the last pieces of lettuce and the crusts of his

BLT—curves of the plates, of the empty cup, of the handle and bowl of
the spoon at my place (weighting a napkin still folded from the dispenser)
glinting
dully in the sun, marked as they were by many uses and washings—objects
left on a table.

Objects on a table
in a season, at a time of day.

GALLERY

MATISSE, *THE PIANO LESSON*

—"architectonic": I read that—the shadowed stage left
of his son's face, a précis inverting the shaft of green
(sunlight through a window) repeating the pyramid metronome.
He's not as young as he looks, the lad. *Tick, tock.*

■

MATISSE, *VIOLINIST AT THE WINDOW*

Self-portrait—his (half-rounded) back, for once,
blocking our view of the artist's view—'violinisting' . . .

■

PICASSO, *LES DEMOISELLES D'AVIGNON*

The artist's fear of them
so that the faces of some of the women came to resemble primitive masks—

frightening in their loose resemblance to human faces;
striking as the familiar, draped—

masks that were faces *between* ("against . . . , *intercesseurs*, mediators": Picasso)
—yes, 'striking.'

■

VANTAGE

Here M. has painted the woman gazing, and background, her entire
surroundings . . .

(save himself and that [unsaved] half)—a thought.
Then again I 'come to.'

"She came to herself." (Before us.)

BOWL

Something there. Something
white there under the water.

Tugged on its moorings.

I know, only seen as tugged, my having seen—off the end of the dock

at low tide—half-clamshells nestled among eelgrass, bowls of one
    or two
not yet half filled with sand but almost overlooked; moving by them
    were tiny (baby?) crabs
sidling the tide in. Pincering and nibbling.

I couldn't help meddling.
From a scalp on the dock's underside, I pried a small (young?) mussel,
tough as a thumbnail—denting the soft wood of the dock where I
    crushed it—
but light so that, even in that shallow, it drifted, settling.
Eluding my favorite. I'd chosen a favorite to feed, like a child

at the Petting Zoo, fistful of grass thrust toward the handsomest or shyest
or driest deer nose (an offering, something between offering and forcing:

'tempting'—) and tracking its deflections . . .

A beetle—the ovoid wash of back with wisps of antennae and finely-haired
    legs—

looking quite real beside the blue-rimmed dish pitched toward us
on its single-stroke base, an oval resting in a wider oval: two almost-ellipses
with the character of the brushstrokes of the Chinese characters
in a column on the left—good-humored, somehow . . . *intended*, each
     oval a curve which began to be drawn and was

drawn.

Only seen as tugged: per the Law
of Refraction—with diagrams and "thought experiments"
I struggled to understand this—and the roiling of the water (the projecting)
surface per the Laws of Wave Motion, Gravity, and Surface Tension,
that "the universe is composed of atoms," that "a liquid seeks its own level,"
per the Laws of About Everything and then the relative clam . . . I mean, calm

a viewer on the dock presupposes, the image of a shell
wavered, displaced, but "on its moorings"—flown like a kite, thrown like a
     lariat—

only so far.

"Roll the TV a little closer."

"It'll come unplugged."

"Master of Illusion, Prestidigitation, Legerdemain, Sleight of Hand—"
     His hands

in prayer or *namaste*; thumbs parting to show us the begging bowl
(empty); pinkies hinged, his hands were a bivalve
opening and closing then faster and faster like wings for flight
until—he seemed as surprised as we were—a dove flew out of them!

White as our dove of the Sleight of Water.

We were 'glued to the screen' of the box
showing us this, a variety show broadcast—as television was, then—
in black and white; exciting, therefore,

rhodopsin on the tips of the rods (my short-lived interest in the workings
of the eye—remember "the rods and cones"?—

because of the word 'rod').

(Was it the green of trees on the water, the black-green
of the water—licorice-black, licorice-green?)

Fingers following the curve of the inside of the bowl
you were rinsing so water would go everywhere.

—He'd already "sawn a woman in half." (One saws a *woman* in half.)

There were two columns of line drawings on each page of the workbook:

apple	truck
robin	spurs
car	orange
saddle	fir
pine	blue jay

Or:

cow	nest
hen	fishbowl
dog	barn
egg	coop
fish	doghouse

So, hen . . . coop: with an oversized pencil and all your body-mind—even the
    tongue—attending,
drawing around each an awkward loop like a bad lasso (the hand was young),

then making the tether.

In a postcard I keep of "Mud Beetle and Blue and White Dish:

Leaf from *Album of Insects and Plants*"—where Ch'i Pai-shih's dish is two ovals,
nested—the white of the dish is the white

of the "leaf" (the page). (The begging bowl.)

The dashing magician in white tie—

here memory, as it can, conflates two or more men
in tuxedoes—ran the length of the long table to retrieve another dish—

revving, in passing, the supports of a few of the fifteen already twirling ones
(by then the first, the one at the head of the table, wobbling terribly . . .
he barely saved it)—and raced to the foot again to eddy up this last. With a
    fanfare,
before briskly lifting each of them down,
palms flourished he looked out at us, proud—astonishing, really—
he kept so many spinning

on their rods.

Something there. Something
white there under the water.

Tugged on its moorings.

I know, only seen as—seeing (white), tugged:
I am That.

JULIANA SPAHR

J ULIANA SPAHR HAS developed one of the most haunting voices in American poetry today. Strongly influenced by Gertrude Stein in her use of repetition, she turns a given bit of language over and over until it opens from the inside out, becoming talismanic. As such, many of her works take on the feeling of chants prefiguring rituals yet to be established. And as is so often the case with ritual, social repair even more than social critique is her core concern. Often directly addressing contemporary political situations, she achieves a paradoxical "clear opacity" in which the language both speaks out and becomes concrete.

Throughout her career, Spahr has been involved in a number of editing projects aimed at developing a strongly responsive poetic community. Beginning with her Leave Books, which she began while working on her PhD at Buffalo, she went on to co-found and co-edit with Jena Osman *Chain*, a formally inventive journal that explores the junctions of visual and verbal art, and to be a founding member of the Subpress Collective. She also co-edited with Claudia Rankine the anthology *American Women Poets in the 21st Century*, focused on the fusion between the lyric tradition and Language poetry. She has published a volume of critical work, *Everybody's Autonomy: Connective Reading and Collective Identity*, in the University of Alabama Series, and numerous essays in journals and on the Web. Spahr's first book of poetry, *Response*, was chosen for the 1995 National Poetry Series, and subsequent collections have been published by Wesleyan University and the University of California Presses. For years a professor at the University of Hawai'i, she currently teaches in the MFA program at Mills College in Oakland, California.

WE ARRIVED AND EVERYTHING WAS INTERCONNECTED:

as twining green maile shrub,
as huehue haole,
our response was to uproot and to bunker.

We arrived and the rain soaked us regularly
as it soaked others and fed rivulets and streams.
It was gentle and warm
but still we built and we bunkered.

This growing and this flowing into all around us confused us.
We didn't know the right and the wrong.
We couldn't tell where we began and where we ended with the land and with
    the others,
where we loved and where we didn't and where we weren't even though we
    longed.

And because we could not figure it out bunkering was a way for us to claim
    what wasn't really ours, what could never really be ours and it gave us a
    power we otherwise would not have had and we believed that this made
    the place ours.
But because we were bunkered, the place was never ours, could never really
    be ours, because we were bunkered from what mattered, growing and
    flowing into, and because we could not begin to understand that this place
    was not ours until we grew and flowed into something other than what
    we were we continued to make things worse for this place of growing and
    flowing into even while some of us came to love it and let it grow in our
    own hearts, flow in our own blood.

WE ARRIVED.

We arrived by air, by 747 and DC10 and L1011.
We arrived over the islands and we saw the green of them out the window.
We arrived and then walked into this green.

Things were different.
The air was moist and things were different.
Plants grew into and on top of and around each other and things were
    different.
The arrival of those before us made things different.

We tried not to notice but as we arrived we became a part of arriving and
   making different.
We grew into it but with complicities and assumptions and languages
and kiawe and koa haole and mongeese.
With these things we kicked out certain other things whether we meant to or
   not.

Asking what this means matters.
And the answer also matters.

NEW WORLD SONNET

How to speaking. Parle ceci. Parle ceci.
How to speaking each to other.
How we spoke cuézale to the furnace.
How we threw the variance vom feuer.
How we took and infected.
How we burned and didn't listen unless we heard it all as us.
In the space. In the language.
In the taking and the burning.
In the cómo usted que habla.
In the como a falar. And the vous parlez des vous que des kommentars.
In the taking and the burning.
In the space. In the language.
Comment ici nous sommes. How we are here. Languages from elsewhere.
   Languages besides. Languages except. Languages less than. Languages less
   of one. Languages of not belonging, of overtaking. Wie hier wir sind. As we
   are here. And having troubles with our loving the other parts of we and hav-
   ing troubles with our liking the other parts of us and credit of troubles with
   our liking the other sections of us and the accreditation of the difficulties
   with ours. Quanto qui siamo. We are here. In the space, in the language, in
   the taking, in the burning. In the space, in the language, in the catch, in the
   burn. In the workstation, in the language, the interlock, the fire. In the job
   station, in the language, the switch of emergency, the fire. In the station of
   the work, in the language, the interruptor of the emergency, the fire. In the
   station of the work, in the language, the switch of the emergency, the fire.
   Como aqui nós estamos. As if we were always here. They are we here and on
   the desire and the hour they are we here taken to traverse completely suf-
   ficiently in the hope or in the desire and in the hour they are we here. Cómo
   aquí estamos.
We are here but how we need listening. How we need listening to the furnace.

DECEMBER 8, 2002

Beloveds, those astronauts on the space station began their trip home a
few days ago and sent ahead of them images of the earth from space.

In space, the earth is a firm circle of atmosphere and the ocean and the land
exist in equilibrium. The forces of nature are in the blue and the white and the
green.

All is quiet.

All the machinery, all the art is in the quiet.

Something in me jumps when I see these images, jumps towards comfort and
my mind settles.

This, I think, is one of the most powerful images in our time of powers.

Perhaps it isn't lovers in our beds that matter, perhaps it is the earth.

Not the specific in our bed at night but the globe in our mind, a globe that we
didn't see really until the 20th century, with all its technologies and variations
on the mirror.

Beloveds, when we first moved to this island in the middle of the Pacific I
took comfort from a postcard of the islands seen from space that I bought in a
store in Waikiki. There was no detail of the buildings of Waikiki in the islands
seen from space. No signs of the brackish Ala Wai that surrounds Waikiki.
Everything looked pristine and sparkled from space. All the machinery, all the
art was in the pristine sparkle of the ocean and its kindness to land. The ocean
was calm.

Beloveds, this poem is an attempt to speak with the calmness of the world seen
from space and to forget the details.

This is an attempt to speak of clouds that appear in endless and beautiful
patterns on the surface of the earth and that we see from beneath, out the
window from our bed as we lie there in the morning enjoying the touch of
each other's bodies.

This is an attempt to speak in praise of the firm touch of yours hands on my
breast at night and its comfort to me.

An attempt to celebrate the moments late at night when yous wake up with kindness.

An attempt to speak away.

And when I say this what I mean is that I am attempting to speak to yous of these things in order to get out of our bed in the morning in the face of all that happened and is yet to happen, the spinning earth, the gathering forces of some sort of destruction that is endless and happens over and over, each detail more horrific, each time more people hurt, each way worse and worse and yet each conflict with its own specific history, many of them histories that we allowed to be formed while we enjoyed the touch of each other in the night.

But the more I look at the pattern of the clouds from our bed in the morning, the more it seems the world is spinning in some way that I can't understand.

Oh this endless 20th century.

Oh endless.

Oh century.

Oh when will it end.

In recent days, I hear rumors that ships are being fueled and then are slipping out of port slowly at night.

I hear rumors from mothers in the street talking to other mothers.

I hear rumors from lovers in line at the grocery talking amongst themselves.

I hear rumors from friends at parties.

I hear rumors of ships refueling and of ships slipping out of port while we sleep in our bed, even as I can't see them in the news.

In the news I learn that Iraq is ready for war but most there are too busy to notice the refueling of ships here in my corner of the world and their beginning of that long journey to their corner of the world.

Even as I can't see the refueling of ships I see ten killed in the Bureij refugee camp by shells from Israeli tanks on Thursday and then one more killed in Gaza on Sunday and then five in east Nepal by a bomb that might have been set by

Maoists and then one hundred and twenty in Monoko-Zohi by various means because of civil war.

Beloveds, how can we understand it at all?

Oh how can the patterns stop.

All I know is that I couldn't get out of bed anymore at all without yous in my life.

And I know that my ties with yous are not unique.

That each of those one hundred and thirty six people dead by politic's human hands over the weekend had numerous people who felt the same way about them.

Chances are that each of those one hundred and thirty six people dead by politic's human hands had lovers like I have yous who slipped yours hands between their thighs and who thought when their lovers did this that this is all that matters in the world yet still someone somewhere tells ships to refuel and then to slip out of port in the night.

Chances are that each of those one hundred and thirty six people dead by politic's human hands had parents and children with ties so deep that those parents and children feel fractured now, one or two days later, immersed in a pain that has an analogy only to the intensity of pleasure.

Chances are that each of those one hundred and thirty six people dead by politic's human hands had pets and plants that need watering. Had food to make and food to eat. Had things to read and notes to write. Had enough or had too little. Had beautiful parts and yet also had scars and rough patches of skin. Had desire and had impotence. Had meannesses, petty and otherwise. Had moments of kindness. Were nurtured for years by someone who was so devoted to them that they sacrificed huge parts of themselves to this nurturing and who today feel this loss of what they nurtured so intensely as to find their world completely meaningless today and will for some time after today.

And yet still someone somewhere tells ships to refuel and then to slip out of port in the night.

And it doesn't even end there.

The Greenland glaciers and Artic sea ice melt at unprecedented levels and still a ship fuels up and slips out of port.

Winona Ryder has thirty prescriptions for downers from twenty different doctors and still a ship fuels up and slips out of port.

Marc Anthony and Dayanara Torres renew their vows in Puerto Rico and still a ship fuels up and slips out of port.

Light and aromatherapy might help treat dementia, a patient sues a surgeon who left in the middle of surgery to pay his bills, cruise passengers continue to have diarrhea and nausea and yet continue to go on cruises, fires burn in Edinburgh, Hussein apologizes for invading Kuwait, United Airlines continues to lose eight million a day, Mars might have been a cold, dry planet when it was first formed, the Cheeky Girls knock Eminem off the charts, and still a ship fuels up and slips out of port.

SUSAN STEWART

S USAN STEWART'S WORK, through all its formal variations, is united by an elegance and clarity of language. She places the problematic tension between nature and culture at the center of her poetic project; titles such as *The Forest* and *Columbarium* set the parameters, and her poems run the gamut, playing timelessness off of history made present through shadows of its poetic forms, such as the georgic, and echoes of its thinkers, from Augustine of Hippo to Merleau-Ponty. Though kept light and active through a delicate attention to sound, her work mounts a rigorous search for a classical balance, while the edge of regret that often filters through is an entirely postmodern recognition of the contemporary relation between humankind and earth.

Stewart's five books of poems, most recently *Red Rover*, are one facet of a larger intellectual endeavor that also includes translations from Italian and ancient Greek, and a range of collaborations in, and meditations upon, literature, art, and music. The author of five works of literary and art criticism, she won both the Christian Gauss Award and the Truman Capote Award for *Poetry and the Fate of the Senses* (2002). Her poetry has won her many honors, including a Lila Wallace Individual Writer's Award, grants from the National Endowment for the Arts and the Pew Charitable Trust, and fellowships from the Guggenheim Foundation and the John D. and Catherine T. MacArthur Foundation. Her book *Columbarium* received the National Book Critics Circle Award in 2003. Susan Stewart is a Chancellor of the Academy of American Poets and a member of the American Academy of Arts and Sciences. The holder of an MA in poetics and a PhD in folklore, she is the Annan Professor of English at Princeton University.

THE FOREST

You should lie down now and remember the forest,
for it is disappearing—
no, the truth is it is gone now
and so what details you can bring back
might have a kind of life.

Not the one you had hoped for, but a life
—you should lie down now and remember the forest—
nonetheless, you might call it "in the forest,"
no the truth is, it is gone now,
starting somewhere near the beginning, that edge,

Or instead the first layer, the place you remember
(not the one you had hoped for, but a life)
as if it were firm, underfoot, for that place is a sea,
nonetheless, you might call it "in the forest,"
which we can never drift above, we were there or we were not,

No surface, skimming. And blank in life, too,
or instead the first layer, the place you remember,
as layers fold in time, black humus there,
as if it were firm, underfoot, for that place is a sea,
like a light left hand descending, always on the same keys.

The flecked birds of the forest sing behind and before
no surface, skimming. And blank in life, too,
sing without a music where there cannot be an order,
as layers fold in time, black humus there,
where wide swatches of light slice between gray trunks,

Where the air has a texture of drying moss,
the flecked birds of the forest sing behind and before:
a musk from the mushrooms and scalloped molds.
They sing without a music where there cannot be an order,
though high in the dry leaves something does fall,

Nothing comes down to us here.
Where the air has a texture of drying moss,
(in that place where I was raised) the forest was tangled,
a musk from the mushrooms and scalloped molds,
tangled with brambles, soft-starred and moving, ferns

And the marred twines of cinquefoil, false strawberry, sumac—
nothing comes down to us here,
stained. A low branch swinging above a brook
in that place where I was raised, the forest was tangled,
and a cave just the width of shoulder blades.

You can understand what I am doing when I think of the entry—
and the marred twines of cinquefoil, false strawberry, sumac—
as a kind of limit. Sometimes I imagine us walking there
(. . . pokeberry, stained. A low branch swinging above a brook),
in a place that is something like a forest,

But perhaps the other kind, where the ground is covered
(you can understand what I am doing when I think of the entry)
by pliant green needles, there below the piney fronds,
a kind of limit. Sometimes I imagine us walking there.
And quickening below lie the sharp brown blades,

The disfiguring blackness, then the bulbed phosphorescence of the roots.
But perhaps the other kind, where the ground is covered,
so strangely alike and yet singular, too, below
the pliant green needles, the piney fronds.
Once we were lost in the forest, *so strangely alike and yet singular*, too,
but the truth is, it is, lost to us now.

AWAKEN

Now in the minute, in the half-life when the rose
    light lights the high leaves, rises,
and then the sun itself appears, when
    the shadow at the back of something like
a thought, implacable, still clouds,
    what, what is it? The vaguely milky half-light,
a tick or jolt—*what was it?*
    Now goes sun over wood, over antennae—
belt on the shoe, dust on the glass: a mote
    (motet, motel?)
              fades, as the lens pulls back
and the mind's screen blurs: news that isn't
    exactly news.
          You tell me your
dream and I'll tell you mine.

                              The wire-
          wheeled crib in the attic, the acorns clustered
in the rusted tin: "We had another child
          and forgot all about it—we'd forgotten
it, left it, in the crib in the attic,
for months or days."
                              Ridiculous—how could
you forget? How could anyone forget?
          The swaddling unwrapped,
          unwrapped, unravelled; the wife of Lot came back,
—no *Lazarus* came back. The prodigal
          son came back, the quarreling squirrels
are what you heard. It wasn't the teeth
          falling out, all the classical worries—
musty, dumped, ineffable. Laughable.
          And yet the moral horror might drag
on and on as it does in the dream of the drifting
          boat, the idyll of the two on the slate-dark
water; something snags as the sleepers
          fall deeper into sleep and the dreamer
who watches is helpless to wake them.

          Are you half as happy as they are, or half
as happy as even that?

The dove sang who whoo
along the hard path
at twilight each star
alone seemed a sign.
Nothing was joined,
nothing was lost.
Others in line
lifted their hands.
Some seemed to pray
some seemed to dance.
The dove sang who whoo
along the hard path.
I looked for you,
but you were gone.

          Now that the world's contracted thus, the cover
thrown off to where—where are we now?

Do you call that a nightmare or a wish?
Saying so doesn't make it so.

I saw in the diminishment of every
living thing the radiance of its end.
I heard in the interval, in the intake
of your breath, the cell's pulse, the quick
and mortal pendulum.

You tell me my
dream and I'll tell you yours.
The fleck and the pool, the bright stain,
obdurate,
        left by the too-long
look at the sun—there in your eyes
I saw what lingers.
I awakened to the world as it was given.

VARIATIONS ON *THE DREAM OF THE ROOD*

In the wood there stood a tree and in the tree there lived a wood
that was a cross without form
      until it stood upon a hill,
    bleeding like a man
        and in the man there lived a god.

In my dream, I thought, wait—
    I can't yet
cease for a while, so midnight
      give me some
        order, some rest.

Inside me stood a dream and in the dream there was a treasure,
a chest drenched with jewels that spilled
    as slow as blood,
        unmeasured, sticky strands
        of pearls and silver
        beads along
        a vein. Along
      a vine,
        dewy strung.

If a tree speaks, it says "bear me down
      shouldering, bear me,
           then stand me up
               up like a tree again."

It says, "I was a cross in the form of a man: I was made
      from a tree, and like a tree.
          And I had arms like a man and
             was like a man,
               and from the man
               a god took form."

Then from his side the soul flew, sudden.
Like a cloud, the soul flew, flown.

Rust sinister, visible
      wounding from nails.
          Endured on a hill, wracked with wires.

Wait, I thought, I can't yet cease for a while
      while a god lies, stretched, severe.
Wait, I said, I can't yet cease for a while
      while clouds fly darkly weeping,
          while clouds fly dark as shadows flowing

I sank down, sorrow-bent
and yielding, as the talkers dismantled the god.

I was a cross from a tree, and, like a tree,
      cut down like a felled man, falling.

Like a body wet with pain, and punctured.

They cut the rock-tomb, sang the corpse cold, hewed me
      and put me in a pit
          then found me
             and covered my wounds
             with silver, draped my wounds
             with silver and gold.

Hear me, adorn me, sing me for healing.

Now I will cease for a while yet,

Joy came back with wonder born from fire

and the fire was born from the wood

     that lived within a tree

         and I dreamed beneath that tree until I woke.

JOHN TAGGART

O VER THE PAST forty years, John Taggart's work has continually reflected his position at the core of American experimental poetry rooted in the Objectivist tradition and the Black Mountain School. His doctoral dissertation "Intending a Solid Object: A Study in Objectivist Poetics" was one of the first in-depth studies of the work of Zukofsky and Oppen. His work often takes serial form, focusing attention on the connections between poetic units as well as on the concrete surface of his non-metaphorical language. "Taggart echoes the world in which he's lived, making particular the mind and heart's persistent need," writes Robert Creeley of his most recent book, *Pastorelles*, set in rural Pennsylvania. "The pastoral tradition is *the* Western Tradition," Taggart stated in a recent interview, and his work, ongoing proof of the importance of continual experimentation, implicitly acknowledges tradition as crucial for delineating the fundamentals and structures of thought.

Born in the Midwest and raised in small towns in Indiana, John Taggart was educated first at a Quaker college and then at the University of Chicago, where he received an MA, and at Syracuse University, where he took a PhD in interdisciplinary studies, blending writing, art, and music. From the mid-1960s to the mid-1970s, he published the influential literary journal *Maps*, which produced special issues on Louis Zukofsky, Charles Olson, David Smith, John Coltrane, Robert Duncan, and others. His own work appeared in the seminal experimental journals of the sixties and seventies, including *Origin*, *Paper Air*, *Sulfur*, and *Temblor*, and has been published in over ten books. The recipient of two NEA Fellowships, Taggart taught at Shippensburg State University, Pennsylvania, from 1969 to 2001. His papers are held in the Mandeville Special Collections Library at the University of California at San Diego.

HENRY DAVID THOREAU/SONNY ROLLINS

1

Two years and two months
alone in the woods
where he had vast range and circuit

his nights black kernels
never profaned by any human neighborhood
Rishyashringa
and no courtesan with a wound to be rubbed and to be kissed

who heard sounds in his nights
and no courtesan who heard the sounds of owls

sounding like

like *that I had never been born*
like *that I had never been born.*

2

Who rejoiced that there are owls
who rejoiced in reading
in reading the classics "the noblest recorded thoughts"

having spent youthful days
costly hours
learning words of an ancient language
an ancient language of perpetual suggestion and provocation

me phunai nikai
three little suggestions

perpetual

singing if it can be called singing
to sing along with the sounds of owls.

3

Cut of the slash
which cuts
which cuts and which connects

mark
of the cut of
time itself

which leaves a blue mark
black and blue mark
which can be read as a kind of bridge

connecting black and blue and
the abstract truth of
time itself.

4

Fled the clubs
nightclubs meccas of smoke clatter
and chatter amid smoke murmur and murmur of assignation

hegira

for two years
alone with the alone

alone with the alone saxophone
in the air
alone in the night air and high above the East River
heimarmene and black water of the river

without a you to do a something to a me
without a song in the air.

5

In the night air
the seven planets in material orbits
so huge and moving at so great a speed must produce sound

harmonia of heimarmene

ringing and roaring sound the sound of a grinding down
"heavenly harmony" in waves and particles

in the air in the ear in the heart
since birth
in the heart there is a melody of heaven's harmony
ringing and roaring

alone with that
without a song with that.

PASTORELLE 9

Large bird on ice of
our pond

great blue heron according to Toot and Linda

large ungainly bird as if
on stilts on ice

yet another thrown being in the world

cold and no longer transparent
frogs gone gold/bronze fish gone even the pond itself the pond
the pond's muddy bottom

faithless
the bird takes off slowly flapping great blue wings.

PASTORELLE 10

Large round bales at random
on the field
which looks shaven looks pool-table smooth

trees in the woods
around the field the sky above seem bigger more absolute
the field an absolute field a form framed by an arching border of trees

because of the large round bales

Stonehenge-like/free-standing/strange

when the bales are now departed in their rickety and red wagons

everything =
the familiar = the invisible
for which one weeps if one weeps in sheer gratitude.

PARMENIDES/FRAGMENTS 3 AND 15A

1

To think = to be

statement needing to become
image

you will come to know what you think although not when you see
what you say
when you see what it is that you are doing

most gradual of images.

2

Word in the Greek in itself unbroken needing nothing
hudatorizon

rooted-in-water.

3

Conodoguinet small
river locally a creek many turnings

boundary of what the map says is mine
boundary to the west to the middle of its turning bed which remains

undredged
muddy

containing stones ripple
slide of water low because of the heat/drought ripple and slide
around stones

no one kind various colors several shapes

pulled out
hauled away to make not quite regular irregular steps.

4

On each side roses
carrying buckets of water two at a time scent of roses

there can be no argument against penetration.

5

Effort to balance some effort to climb more or less level steps
pause before climbing
down

whole stretch of the mountain mass
and line ridge line of north mountain massive and elongated blue wave

what
I do what I think
climbing up and climbing down.

PASTORELLE 12

By itself/nonbiblical
wood lily

from a wild growth of grasses of brambles and of bushes from under
silver maples
to a bed behind the house

carmine and pebbled flowers three to each stem

nodding/turned downward/away

after pictures after a smiling woman
dream of a smiling woman her opulent dress full of clocks

neither silence nor
obedience
not unconditional present tense joy.

WHY TREES WEEP

Because they're listening to Sainte Colombe's "Les Pleurs"

because those they would love don't
love them flee
from them

because their neighbors are beset with illness/disease experience
pain in movement or

can't move can only sit in gardens going to weeds

Niobe lost all her children.

ARTHUR VOGELSANG

RTHUR VOGELSANG IS known for the wildness of his wit as well as the, at times, bitter edge enlivening his poetry. A Vogelsang poem is also profoundly moving, companionable, and quite funny (or, as John Ashbery puts it, "both fun and harrowing"). Part vaudevillian, part shaman, Arthur Vogelsang is a modern chronicler of that vast catalogue of American absurdities that also provoked Mark Twain and Lenny Bruce. He is a master of the dislodged narrative, a quick-shift artist of the first rank. Always stylistically provocative, Vogelsang uses capacious, serpentine lines to reel out the complex syntax of his stories. Voice-driven and maximal, each its own tonal high wire act, Arthur Vogelsang's poems sear the imagination while either touching or ripping out the reader's heart.

Vogelsang was born in Baltimore, and has lived there and in New York City, Iowa City, Wichita, Philadelphia, Paris, Las Vegas, and Los Angeles—places he has been employed variously as a teacher (University of Redlands, University of Southern California, University of Nevada, Wichita State University, the Kansas Arts Commission, University of Iowa) and as an editor (*The American Poetry Review*, 1973–2006). His books of poetry are *A Planet* (Holt, 1983), *Twentieth Century Women* (University of Georgia Press, 1988); *Cities and Towns* (University of Massachusetts Press, 1996), which won the Juniper Prize; and *Left Wing of a Bird* (Sarabande, 2003). The recipient of a California Arts Council Fellowship and three National Endowment for the Arts Fellowships in Poetry, Vogelsang has traveled extensively in Mexico, Florida, and Delaware.

THE FAMILY

There is a trip over horizontal white and vertical blue lightning
Which can go low but can't go high to
Where Judy is sleeping confidently
And the pilot is sweating black water, his forehead some black steam.
Those around him say it is not actually black
But is like black or like you saw black.
They are sailing easily like sailing if you understand
There are no essential propelling moving parts
Only air passing over and turning the blades or sails or fans
In four tubes and they call these jets.
It is simple and safe and they are going fast
As you all have smoothly and the co-pilot is sweating, on his forehead,
Brown mud (very light brown, very thin, mud).
The attendant says it is not mud but reminds her of mud.

Why is the girl, who I know best, sleeping well?
Because they are sailing smoothly. Why are the pilots'
Bodies cooling them with disquieting jarring sweat?
Because they are passing over horizontal white and vertical blue lightning.

I'm tracking (on a good computer) this. Continental shows it
As a cartoon real plane over Indianapolis with dark gray jagged lines around it.
Later it will be over Harrisburg with light grey lines hopping around it.
Our dead daughter and our dead son
Are napping in the next room, through two archways.
How may that be? Why are the pilots
Emitting brown and black steam?
Are they reminded of their wars (each in different wars)
When the man-made light with bad intentions continued upward sometimes
     slightly faster
And sometimes slightly slower than they could go,
And boy could they go then, faster than the noise
Of words in a room person to person (you think it's simultaneous,
The sound of talking, don't you, until you think about it)
And sometimes the noise of no noise at all in the plane or in the room
Like two people sleeping in another room
Without moving for hours or you sleeping in a plane and then you were there
     arrived
And they were here, awake and speaking to me,
Me the living, as if the living were on earth.

THE FAMILY II

Storms to their grown cousins the clouds
Are always an infant at birth flailing violent
Messy but nevertheless a person
Who can scream good and be bloody mucous
But unable to stand to reach the ceiling
Or despite the uncontrollable thrashing force kill
Premeditated any certain individual or go
To a series of meetings as Judy has done
(The meetings she did) and is flying back
Way over vicious bolts (it is unusual to look down on the lightning
So far below, a funny angle) blue and white
And flailing or as if the observation deck in the hospital were in the ceiling
Not the wall and as if with five hours to blow
She was there looking down at yet another vicious safe birth
The little person blasting away at everything
As the billion billion have person after person dropped from women
Screaming on the forest floor or infinite energy undirected on the forest floor
Each little person the same blue fire this way white fire that
So after a while from the observation deck in the hospital
Each birth is a repetitive boring dangerous storm
That is endless or anyway 275,000 years old and on the computer
The real cartoon plane returning to me has been over Ontario yes
That far north from New York and over Manitoba yes that far north
From New York to get away from the little devil babies
Blue and white below and is "too high" though of course not
And the jagged lines were around it in Canada which I stared at to use up time
But now it is over Nevada and sliding downhill to L.A. clear
In the calm high pressure that blesses us and blesses our dead forests the
Deserts and blesses our surf where we came from but the two pilots are
    decaying
In their seats, no cause for alarm, everybody
Dies, you know that already, everybody decays
Unless you choose to be burnt and that won't happen
To this plane it is as if
They are desiccated in their strong, fancy seats
But why? There are no spooks in my (our) house
In the next room (beckoning the pilots), no girl spook resting there
No little boy spook is resting, it is sort of me who are them, though
Yes, we've found two more planets in another system,
Not ours, one with an orbit of two days, not 365, one has an orbit of twenty
    days

It says on the computer which has a news screen too
Before you are here arrived on Continental's screen
On its animated plane the size of Rhode Island
Which you are in forty minutes but it is hot,
Seven hundred degrees, four hundred degrees,
But that doesn't stop us from looking and looking and looking, does it?

KOMODO

It is still easy to get lost on the earth,
though the huge number of roads is connected, and
it is much farmed in rows, many dwellings, many
people, different useful kinds of airplanes,
our own space ships taking photos of fire hydrants
and blades of grass and directing
personal conversations to the right person
if you've got a good battery in your hand and all that.
For years tiny humans (their bones and their stuff)
were hidden or lost. Tinier than possible. They were three foot three
and hunted rats I can't repeat the size
and shape of because you'd think I was pulling
your chain. Also they hunted little elephants and Komodo
dragons. Yes, there were and are Komodo dragons but if you wanted to
     denigrate
them you'd call them lizards—not belching fire, no spikes. The
rats were the size of Lassie. The elephants
were only the size of the biggest football player
but had outrageously thick legs and were slower even than our elephants.
The dragons were the size of horses and, dear
God, fast as automobiles. We know because some archaeologists
got lost, looked in the wrong place, and found
in a cave with perfect humidity bones of everything and everybody
above, and remains of fires. The very small people's brains,
which fit in their heads, were smaller than chimps'.
Yes, they weren't too smart. If you keep fish
now in London or Tokyo or San Francisco
you know their size depends on their pond,
big pond big fish, room aquarium same fish smaller, so,
let's see, the elephants had less to call their own,
so they weren't too big, the rats had a lot more
that they more or less owned than now,
and the dragons, Jesus H. Christ, could go wherever they wanted

and do whatever came to mind. "Came to mind," har! Their brains
were the size of walnuts or our prostate glands
and the brains smelled like ammonia due to their high ammonia content
and of course it was the ammonia more than their size and speed
that made them the real dragons they really were. What I've
told you, everybody who's a scientist believes. Now
I'm going to think on my own a little. The little
people hated the dragons most of all
and herded them with fires backfired into other fires
and laughed at their unique screaming and at the convenient
cooking. It is a shame they couldn't make pictures
of their activities, or themselves. They weren't as smart
as Jackson Pollock, who was pretty dumb and
drank beer all the time. There are eight caves,
a lot of undisturbed, undessicated bones. The news has gotten out of hand.
A lunatic has even suggested they were all quite handsome
and gay, I mean bi-sexual, *that* handsome, and the women were
beautiful, like skinny midget actresses. The government of their country
has closed all the caves, or rather, put yellow police tape
and guards around them and sent packing all the archaeologists
and said no more of any kind of person can
come there. It is in Indonesia. I guess
I really think somebody will find yet smaller people somewhere
and bigger creatures faster even than heavy dragons fast as cars
and this will go on and on, backward, smaller. Yes, these spoke
to each other and had all, exactly all, our same organs. Scientists
(back to the facts now) say the bacteria in the dragons' mouths
was so virulent (and still is) that prey died immediately after minor injuries
or scratches and this was why the teeny people did revenge with fire and the
    teeny
(yes the word is in the *Times* twice) people were in each other's
arms against the damp frequently (frequent holding and frequent
damp) and in their loving arms at night talked over and laughed satisfied
at the tenor-like screaming from the day. Maybe find
some more even smaller in a joke state like New Jersey thereby
giving it some gravitas or where you'd expect,
Idaho, where nothing is and nobody goes,
larger dragons, even smaller elephants, even smaller people, Idaho
where the hateful lunatic, smart as a whip, Ezra Pound, was born
though he grew up in Philadelphia
and maybe it will be there in some pristine deep hole under a bank.

MOTHER'S FIRST AIRPLANE

(I talk to her the whole trip)

The light and its friends the Grimaldis, and its friend
the personal pull shade of your window seat
(how many friends it has! is that because it is faster
than everyone? and anything? yes
it is a lie that it just lies there brightly around us
it is moving.) How fast, son? So's
you can't see it. The Grimaldis our neighbors
are all dead, Marie and her husband
and their daughter Marie the Second
and her grandparents and greatgrandparents.
Naturally from natural causes this was forty years ago and Marie,
little Marie, from swallowing a needle.
Peggy her friend cried and cried. Peggy was twenty-three
like Marie. Marie the First was forty-three.
Peggy is my sister. The light has no brother.
Now you have listened carefully (there's nothing else to do
on a plane, now you know) and know I'm not
shitting you from the tone of my voice, yes,
the light and the ages of people are the closest of friends
the light has many friends, OK, I will repeat it
it is moving it isn't just lying there around us and above
us we are simply in its way when above seems to have no light
but ma, back to the people's ages and the light
if the light did not move all the Grimaldis could be here
some would say would be here whether or not Peggy hoped it. I swear
I never heard a woman cry like that
and never intend to or at least never hope to it was hideous
and I was thirty-six. Marie did not die
from swallowing a needle she swallowed a needle
but she didn't die they got it out perfectly and she died
in a car wreck. Ma, this is the point too,
which I'll explain later, it is much closer to the truth
that if the light did not have everything and everybody
as its friends then the Grimaldis would be here, more true
than it is true that Marie died from a wreck as you say rather
than a needle. Let me put it another way. My ass and my thighs
are sore from riding on this airplane, we
are turning (slowly to you, fast to me, properly as far
as the light is concerned that sees its friends the sun and
the plane moving so well together) turning, OK, I'll call it

slowly and slightly to have at our side the blazing sun so pull down the shade,
I'll take a walk to the back and pretend to pee (yes,
I walk in the aisle for exercise, give it a try) and will come back
and put it another way. I'm sorry
I said you'd be going faster than the plane
if you walked the other way in the aisle
to pee or pretend to pee. Now that I'm back
here's the thing, if the light did not move
and did not have every single thing as its dear friend
what I wanted to do would happen before I did it.
Excuse my language son, but wouldn't that be
a mess, a steady stream of screw-ups and make us all
upset and uncertain all the time?
Yes ma it would, the reading lamp up there would go off before
I touched it, for instance. I could just intend to do it
and it would go off as I was reaching for it
and all the Grimaldis would come back
not at Peggy's wish or mine
but that would be the way it would be
the dead Grimaldis faster than their former best friend the light.
No the light does not hope for a sister.

ANNE WALDMAN

A NNE WALDMAN'S POETRY is deeply rooted in the performative; even when read on the page, it has a vigorous energy that inflects the words with flashing eyes and sweeping gestures. Large spiritual questions lie at its core, yet Waldman refuses abstraction, always keeping those questions rooted in contemporary political realities from global capitalism to U.S. foreign policy. She maintains a prominent international profile, frequently participating in academic exchanges, conferences, and poetry festivals throughout North and South America, Europe, and Asia. As a young woman, Waldman played a crucial role in bridging New York School poetry with the Beat aesthetic. A prominent member of the "second generation" of each, she was raised in an artistic household in Greenwich Village and ran the Poetry Project at St. Marks in the 1960s and 1970s. With the poet Lewis Warsh, she founded *Angel Hair* magazine and books, then left New York to join with Allen Ginsberg in founding the Jack Kerouac School of Disembodied Poetics at the Naropa Institute (now University) in 1974.

A practicing Buddhist, Anne Waldman teaches in the Naropa MFA program and is the Artistic Director of its annual summer session. Her forty-nine books and chapbooks range from the rhizomic epic *Iovis* and the serial poem *Marriage: A Sentence* to a non-fiction collection, *Outrider* (2006). She has collaborated with many musicians and visual artists and has edited several collections of historical and theoretical texts, including *The Beat Book* and, with Lisa Birman, *Civil Disobediences: Poetics and Politics in Action*. Her papers are held by Hatcher Graduate Library at the University of Michigan.

from IOVIS 3: OCULIST WIT: BOOK OF LIGHT

2

this is the image dance, reality exposed for all to see . . .
these are the sainted ones, tinted, resolved, blurred at edges
these are the postures we surmise in light . . .

Across from me is a crossing of leg, across from me, a gray striped sock, long
underwear, red, which is a zipper which is an intruder writing in a slant way,
head turned right gazing, then it goes another way, slanted, as if to say Notice
this, notice this detail before you lose interest, before something interrupts
the ordinary obscure paragraph, and you stop adding on your long lines of
narration, the premium story of a cosmology or origin myth on the relative
differences between genders, the way you receive the sun moon stars into your
habitat, into— your "oculist wit," for that's what it seems to be, help me out
here see a way through a chaotic time, the face of these images, turn blood to
stone, turn stone to fire, making a limb dance toward ozone, carried by a force
you are capable of making a lineage picture of: dream of a dust bowl, dream of
a prophet, dream of a maimed soldier, the dawn of a pre-Raphaelite, dream a
Machiavellian sports announcer, sentence that leaves you cold, all the embers
down, you have no refuge, talk about Paris now, the vision when you stood in
the doorway lintel, and all did not seem strange.

It was the day before the movie shoot, day before the funeral, the day before the
self-immolating attack, when incendiary meant simply "hot", and you could say
it about a lover: "hot" if you were so inclined, day before the discotheque folded,
the day before so many were wounded, and you could make something North
American about it, including all the continents that would keep a Polaris missile
out of their midst, and then it all came back to you, opposite me, leaning over
your instrument of power that would record an inquisitive face,

Not an Agrippa at the control, not a tyrant nor a super errant knight, and you
might ask about threads and stitches and you might inquire about buttons and
harnesses, about exigencies of destroying proof, about all colors matching, about
a reversal of intention before the Mayan long count, before the day we might
go to practice our syllables, and good intention needs to shine on those syllables,
taking them out of the bomb shelter, out of the time warp and onto the street
where you stood waiting for the shutter to snap, shouting "Hold" and then it was
your face that was always needed, face which was always with me and it could
hold anything it wanted to, an unforced perspective, lunar calendar, resistance,
way of thinking, behaving, as spectator to the spectacle, daily life.

& what I saw: *zymosis*

a voix celeste of all the populace
a crumbling of the walls of sight
breathe, intonation,
walls between things, interstices of light
what says the vitreous humor?
back of my eyes, I see
what says the contours of your *mufti?*
the last time I looked I saw
a calendar of a dark age
I see: more rubble
simulacra of a political speech gone mad
see the stratification of desire how might we ever touch again
(cold cold gone cold in the bone)
revive the animal make her sing
bring back a cooing world
utter this warning—solemn, tumultuous
its language at the margin
of imagination——an averted eye
with wide angle lens for sale
"kingdom" with surround-moats for sale
bon mots if you find them selling fast
the joker's keys that could unlock the smallest trunk
celebrity-hood as it swarmed over you & you counted the ways
you could be tortured

1. wily
2. failure in a commercial obligation
3. apology in order over patina & talent
4. sweet defrocking
5. deshabille from a different angle
6. final cut before you could see the sliver of footage
7. quadra-sonic emblems
8. fetishism
9. anonymous sex
10. the blue of the fresco, the sentient being's hand
11. reach out to the Middle East

[this could be a chorus]
[this could be a cloudburst]
[something could sway here, or quake]
gold dust. . . . a dissident serving time

pyrotechnics for sale . . .
incendiary streets . . . painted bright in blood for all to see
(you investigated light to
tantalize the shaman in yourself)
make her dance
protect her tacit nighttime promise
(lower the voice, promise the moon)
lower the boom you might benefit somehow
lift her burqa first, it will be hard
heal mother's miscreant
a lantern would be useful here
o my emigre, my eminence grise
prosper for the tribe
show them all the lights go on at dusk
that they shower you with coins
& you steal the words you like the best

terza rima

        hyperventilation

        syncline

tundra

whim

        whistling swan . . .

clarity will oppose mania
inside the cranium such wonders persist

Inside: I am your scholar—each syllable is my domain
in a delirium of the senses look closely now with an un-blinded eye
scrutinize your algebra, your buoyancy, your war-on-Troy space
I see a world where everything inhabits a container of steel
as one listens & feels the tug of the string she holds
sudden music
dialectical laws of opera materialize
more time! more time!
We moved "light" out of the problem of death
And a character *(how to sound her down?)* was born breathing
And reckoning the end of human time:
Yea tho I am walking
yea tho I walk forever in thy direction which is thy "thyness"
yea tho thy "thyness" be friendly
that it be no shadow, that it be no death

yea that thy "thy" be willing, be aura, be oracular
yea that "thyness" be without gender without godhead
godhead is no way to be walking towards "thy"
thy is no kingdom come
thy is no purple privileged glory
thy is no flag, no rod, no scepter, no staff of brutality
thy is no random particle
thy is a kind site of no dire greenhouse effect
thy is a place with conscientious war tribunals
they is of mercy and follows all the days of tracking war criminals
thy is the hours of constant tracking
thy will keep you awake in any time zone tracking
because thy is observation, is a current affair, is tracking "thy"
thy goes back to any older time you mention
a time the increments of language were simpler, were strange
thy was a module, thy was a repository
thy was a canticle for future discipleship
thy is architecture, thy is the entire book for the things of "thy"
thy is a book of thy "thyness" which is not owned
can you guess the "thy" in all the days of my defiance
yea tho I fear thy terror of "thy" amnesia, thy negligence
yea tho it stalks me in the valley
yea that it beseeches me to lighten up
yea tho it behooves me to abdicate "thy"
I will keep the sleep of ancient times
of Arcady of the holy cities where thy hides
thy could be done, thy could be stationary in any language
and then thy could be moving as I do in pursuit of sanity
that they track the war profiteers
that they track the war criminals
that they track the murderers who slaughter innocents
that they are exposed in the market place
that they are brought to justice, to light

WITHOUT STITCHING CLOSED THE EYE OF THE FALCON

without care without seed pearl without stitching closed the
eye of the falcon without seemly rectitude without the platitude
of o thou muddled media pundit without questionable doubt or
metabolism without a geographic category of speech that will travail
without a hint or glint of "secular" mastery, without ritual framing
without a theatrical sense of illusion and bandying about or on or inside

a thermosphere without it working against you and when it does being
able to go on without it without gavottes without gazelles that you
study in neighboring Persian poetries without spallation and
without a diving bell how will you survive? without rapacious wildcats
without the sense of security you have always expected without your
familiar stage fright without the caves without the bombing of caves
without the mystery of caves without the caves in your memory of that
mystery that lives in caves without caves that long to exist in the
hand print in the cave of that memory without the rivets that hold
the wing together that hold the whole throbbing machine together that
assert the rivet dominion without which you do not have a plan of
fastening together of wings of arms for the automaton that holds
the capital together without its own mind of wheels and cogs and *mudras*
that run the show without all the pixels and efforts of more dominion
without borders to cross without needing to carry things over borders
the invasion of your homeland *(coming? coming soon?)* without it, what
call in the night what call is answered what nuance what tantrum in the night
what martyrdom of dreaming your own birth your own end of history
or end of speculation what call what alarm is sounding deep in the home?

KEITH WALDROP

EITH WALDROP'S WORK blends humor and irreverence with serious metaphysical questioning. Its quick surface—capitalizing on juxtapositions between open statements in a conversational tone and vivid, oblique allusions and glimpses—blends elements drawn from centuries of European and American literature with a distinctly postmodern approach that reflects his detailed knowledge of the avant-garde from the late nineteenth century onward. Mingling history, biography, and philosophical speculation with a poetry that revels in a sheer love of sound, Waldrop's work erodes genre boundaries. He usually does this by allowing the poetic to overflow into other quasi-recognizable modes; but occasionally, as in his "autobiography" *Light While There Is Light*, he approaches from the direction of prose. This is a work that both accurately details his life and demonstrates the breakdown of the sovereign "I" and its reconstruction through language.

Born and raised in Kansas, Waldrop was drafted in 1953 and spent two years in Germany before returning to the States, where he completed a PhD in comparative literature at the University of Michigan. While there, he also became involved in experimental theater and, with his wife Rosmarie, started the magazine *Burning Deck*, which turned into Burning Deck Press a few years later. He joined the faculty at Brown University in 1968 and was a founding member of the Wastepaper Theater, which ran from 1972 to 1992. His first book, *A Windmill Near Calvary*, was nominated for the National Book Award in 1968, and his subsequent eighteen collections have won various awards, including the America Award. A noted translator, Waldrop has published works by some of France's best-known post-'68 experimental poets, and most recently, a new translation of Baudelaire's *Les Fleurs du Mal*. He has received an NEA translation grant and has been made a Chevalier de l'ordre des Arts et des Lettres by the French government. His own work has been translated into French, Danish, and German.

FIRST DRAW THE SEA

(Herr Stimmung's Interludes)

In the outer border of the arch there are angels: angels holding harps, holding lutes, holding other stringed instruments.

And other instruments *perhaps* stringed, vague instruments.

Instruments not always identifiable, the stone being chipped and badly pitted.

=

He is aware that the solar vortex reaches to Saturn's orbit, that Time and the Ocean are brothers.

=

Astra animata.

In their keeping, the harmony of the spheres.

=

Once this corner is turned . . .

=

He shares to some extent that itch which Augustine deplored, not to delight in his body merely, but to use the flesh for exercise. For experiment.

=

Time, to him, is something, not sweet, but sticky. His moments cling.

They cling together.

They stick to his fingers.

If he manages to separate them—these moments—they seek each other out, build themselves into substantial bodies.

They walk the earth.

=

But here is his question, a problem he has set himself to solve:

Why do we search—why this passion, this obsession—for *permanence*, for *certainty*? What strange turn of mind could make us, jumping sights along the way, prefer the *unchangeable*?

=

What do we see in the invisible?

=

He supposes our structure must limit our experience: how could we receive what we have no receptors for?

He would like, nevertheless, to understand various theories (or even any one) that take *things* into account—"things in their thinginess," as the old critic had it.

=

A fog is gathering.

Or, as he describes it, "a cloud on the ground."

=

His words—spoken and unspoken—are hatchings, cross-hatchings, background in progress.

=

Space expands.

I do not mean the universe. I refer merely to the widening prospect as he walks.

=

And time?

No.

Time uncoils.

=

He feels caught between *via dolorosa* and *via negativa*.

And finds meditation, here in the fast lane, unsatisfying.

=

His mourning is disordered, his grief resembles suspense.

Sickness coming, he is sure, not from the unspeakable, but from wrong words, exalted.

=

He wishes he could figure out how memory acts.

Or how an act remembers.

Struck by the intelligence of his hands, he would like to disguise us as animals.

=

Some angels sit.

Some angels stand.

Some dance.

And some are seated, but with their legs in a position suggesting dance.

=

"Wisdom . . ." he thinks.

And halts, appalled at how his thoughts wander.

=

Mortal thoughts they are. Why should they not stray?—slow etymological drift.

=

And a local phantasm, confused and contradictory—must it be rejected out of hand?

Why would we prefer the clarity of unrealizable lines?

For his part, he watches by preference how sun speckles the sidewalk.

=

How houses stand and pages turn.

=

How leaves fall into memory and the memory is forgotten.

=

. . . time's tears in a sea of lead.

=

He hopes for an unfinished epitaph and directs that, before he is buried, his name be removed from his clothing.

=

A great cathedral, newly washed, seen from the Left Bank:

"Ah," he murmurs, admiring. "*Leur Dame*."

=

He searches out apocalypses hidden in the light from street-lamps, lost under sloping roofs, rising sometimes in a vapor from the cellar, suggested by speckles of sun on cement.

He thrives below Saturn and considers himself star-tissue.

Even if God alone—as he has heard it argued—knows the *true* names of the angels; still, we can rename them, as we did with the animals.

=

Reference to cosmic strings brings to mind a blood red carpet and, as if soliloquizing, he walks on.

=

His eye, in this fog, on the fog-eye.

=

He considers that *pass to the opposite* which is 'genesis.'

Not *Genesis*, but some sort of revelation.

=

Scintilla animae.

And *motions of the air, on which the sweetness of the voice depends* . . .

=

Death, a house he never hoped for . . .

=

Somehow, as in so many of his attachments, he loses the thread.

=

Sappho asking, ". . . with what eyes?"

    (The rest of her poem lost.)

=

. . . *this corner turned.*

=

 Unattended ground.

SINGULAR

have spoilt me (you have) bodies of
planets

angels, forced
to postulate *matter*
asked her (I asked) if she would
like to dance, how
crude we are

composed of ether, of
either

is it for such
insults that I have climbed
all these flights

ROSMARIE WALDROP

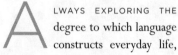

LWAYS EXPLORING THE degree to which language constructs everyday life, Rosmarie Waldrop writes in oblique conversation with a number of philosophers, particularly Wittgenstein. She reads him with a feminist twist entirely her own, one that constantly returns us to the body as the basis of lived experience. The relation of the feminine and the body to language appears throughout her work, and at times, as in her *Key into the Language of America*, she brings themes of immigration and otherness into the mix. The title of her doctoral dissertation and first critical book, *Against Language?*, set the tone for Waldrop's poetics—sometimes she's pushing against language's limitations; at other times, she's leaning against it, shoring herself up. This fruitful ambiguity leaves her poised between traditional meaning making and an evocative, emotionally charged "beyond-sense" that uses the material qualities of language and page to help the reader know what cannot be thought.

Rosmarie Waldrop was born in Germany and came to the United States in 1958. Soon after, she and her husband Keith Waldrop started Burning Deck Press. For the past forty-five years, Burning Deck has been one of the principal publishers of experimental poetry in the country, presenting the work of Barbara Guest, Mei-mei Berssenbrugge, Susan Gevirtz, and many others. Waldrop also publishes "Série d'écriture" and "Dichten =," imprints devoted to French and German contemporary literature. She is one of the most important translators of contemporary German and French poetry into English; her translations include work by Edmond Jabès, Jacques Roubaud, Emmanuel Hocquard, Paul Celan, Elke Erb, and Friederike Mayröcker, and she has been made a Chevalier de l'ordre des Arts et des Lettres by the French government. Waldrop's most recent critical works are *Lavish Absence*, on translation and Edmond Jabès, and *Dissonance (if you are interested)*, essays on poetics. She has published two novels in addition to her sixteen collections and numerous chapbooks of poetry, and has been awarded an NEA Fellowship, the Landon Award for Translation, the Columbia University Translation Award, and a Lila Wallace–Reader's Digest Award, among others. She lives in Providence, Rhode Island.

EVENING SUN

for Sophie Hawkes

1

On a balcony onto the Seekonk stands. And full of thoughts of winter. My friend. And drunk with red wine I. Think of the power. Of a single word. Like for example "fact." When I know what matters. Is between.

•

But how with gnarled hands hold the many and how? The sun and shadow of Rhode Island? Let alone the earth?

•

Down swoops the hawk. From the sky over Providence. The sky over my head. Down to the leaves inward curled on the ground. But not like buds. Yellow. A cat is buried here and the leaves. Swirl up in the wind.

•

In the hour of the hawk. What is meant by: I think? Or even: I sit under clouds in which. Rain gathers weight. I sit in my mother's shawl which is. Threadbare. In my head I sit. By the river Euphrates. Strange like water the skies of the dead.

•

And high from the branches of the maple. Like a prelude to snow. White feathers.

2

But music. Quickens the house down into its shadows. So trembles air in the sun and the shape of the tree blurs as if through a flame seen. Swarms of monarch butterflies stir and brush your cheeks. In celebration. In memory.

•

Almost visible the words of the song. Leave the singer's mouth and rise up into the sun. Which goes crazy instead of down.

•

Floods, storms, fires. But a tank won't be stopped by a word. Not even if you shout it from the middle of the road, with hands thrown forward and fingers spread out.

•

Nor by music. Though its power is great. Like the heat of noon it slants between body and soul. Difficult, then. Unaccustomed as we are to beauty. To know which is effect and which cause.

•

Not merely as a sailor is present in a ship am I. In my body. Intermingled.

3

My father thought he had the gift to read the stars. To know if the light in a person's eyes. Had gone out. To hypnotize. I stayed awake. Weak in the knees am I. Not a spiritual woman. And pulled toward the earth.

•

He said, you have to look from afar: what children we are, so gravely at play. In worn out light, in afterglow. Yet fire present is in words.

•

Which is why we try to read. The stone, the wood and grass, the cloud and lightning and air. And the ancients and poets. And the frogs croak in the swamps.

•

And to stand. Sky around your shoulders high on a mountain. Or balcony. And know you must cast. Like so many shadows. Your words onto the distance. Or paper. But will they span?

•

And the next morning you go to the bakery and ask for a loaf of rye. This too is work and without it the dream crumbles inside its glass case. And we must travel the ocean just to see it.

4

With great force our bodies are pulled out of our mothers. And ever since, we walk like almost orphans. With a scar on the brain.

•

And remember childhood among strings and puppets. Crutches. Knees under the chin tucked. And toy warriors with lance and shield and red badge to ensure courage.

•

Which we need to live in three dimensions. Of dry air. Or wet. Among gauges for measurement made of wire and string. That my father had looked at before.

•

And tapped with his finger to make sure. They were steady, not broken. And hitched his pants against gravity and tried to discern. The tether between particle and wave.

•

Tea has dribbled on his book. The letters under the drops enlarge till a wavy gray absorbs the excess. If however too deep you plunge, he thinks. Into thought. You can't rest till you get to the bottom.

5

Let us take our time, Sophie, fitting bones to the earth. Though they are turning visible inside the flesh, and our blood. No longer overflows and spills.

•

Much work still to be done. And the smell of ripe peaches. And Long-Jing tea. And lungs full of words. And being an opaque body that intercepts the rays of the sun.

SONG

fire tied
under your breast
all angles an apple
could fall

distances traveled
a fish to the West
the leaves blue
as the sun

it is your turn
to think

MEDITATION ON UNDERSTANDING

Even if you were to express everything that is "within you," if the flesh opened.

rain curtains
the eye

Or if it could talk, the bold insect on the page I'm reading, a moving violation pushing its smallness to the brink as exemplary economy. Pulled, as if it were one of the letters, into vain sequence by my eyes.

the surface of
a lake

Is it that I can't foresee the way your thought grows into anger? a body? How nudity is yet another garment? Blurred invasion. Can't stand in your shoes, under your wear, over your soul. Thirsty on awakening. Beside the point. The lake overflows without bringing childhood memories up into the light.

ricochets

The rings on the surface announce events already dissolving, the pebble's fluid migrations among contingent waves.

like
lovers

No deep image. A fault line through the lake. I've never dreamed of hunting though I sleep in a cave. The rain goes on falling. Rust in the bones. The riddle need not have a solution, need not be a riddle. Anyone can dream.

SONG

the king with
all his medals
rides horseback toward
the Sacred

Heart adrift
on the same wall

this is
his real life

meaning can take
but two dimensions

STEPS IN INTEGRATION

Anxiety arises, she says. To signals of the clock. To cut down the forest for the trees. To to. Compulsive ties found embedded.

White, hard piece of chalk. So that the letters resemble hunger. Subtract underwater from fear of parting.

In early childhood, atoms cannot be seen. Not mechanically interlocked. Not in collision. On billboards. Then impulse seems to attach itself, and time so short.

In a run-down neighborhood, the jazz players. The water moves around the trout. No color separation.

Is the ego capable of splitting the object? The atom? Hairs? The clock in winter, extreme context. The forest cut down.

Faced with unpleasant stimuli the organism reacts by fragmentation, considered as a weapon. Letters written in a rage. And space between limbs.

The atomists found the liquid state hard to explain, but the trout stirs under water. A raw world, she says. Out of raw world into commercial zone. And time so short.

The sound of many atoms. The color of drums. The solace of phantasy.

Condition of flight: First plant your right foot and then your left. On noun? Or adjective? Folded in, the flush of omnipotence.

MARJORIE WELISH

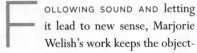

OLLOWING SOUND AND letting it lead to new sense, Marjorie Welish's work keeps the object-nature of language to the fore. Presenting the word as an art material on a par with paint or marble, Welish moves in and out of abstraction, often over a foundation of coherent argument, and often in conversation with the visual arts. Her work is not ekphrastic in the traditional sense of addressing or explicating another work; instead, she creates verbal constructs that write through questions of art criticism and theory. Her poetry's patterns of thought, its mental syntax, draw freely on the devices and forms of the literary and visual avant-gardes, which results in a verbal surface full of surprising shifts, active white space, and wide-ranging cultural allusion.

Born and raised in New York, where she still lives, Welish graduated with a degree in art history from Columbia University. Since then, she has maintained three simultaneous careers—as a poet, a painter, and an art critic. She writes regularly for magazines such as *Art in America*, *Bomb*, *Art Monthly*, *Partisan Review*, and *Textual Practice*. Her criticism has been gathered in *Signifying Art: Essays on Art After 1960*. A book-length study of her work, *Of the Diagram: The Work of Marjorie Welish*, was published by the Slought Foundation in 2003. Her many poetry books include *The Annotated "Here" and Selected Poems*, which was a finalist for the Lenore Marshall Poetry Prize. Her many grants include ones from the Fund for Poetry, the Djerassi Foundation, the New York Foundation for the Arts, and the Trust for Mutual Understanding. She has held the Judith E. Wilson Visiting Poetry Fellowship at Cambridge University and has received a Fulbright Senior Specialist Fellowship for work at the University of Frankfurt.

from ART & LANGUAGE WRITES AN EPITAPH

2

                    Zero
                                        (for two voices)
Indexing initiatives, when
                    Not whenever, NOW!
Modernities, start your engines!
                    The year is 1907.
                                        (create acute annals)
Modernity
                                        (circle of)
Modernity: where ore when?
                    More noise! For some persons, pessimism.
As for modernism
                    Zip open!
When did modernity begin?
                    With laughter we shall bury you!
                                        (Thank you, Stefano.)

Whenever modernity is, there shall be
                    " 'A
                    of a life
                    —and a time' "
                    is Z's ideogram.
When was modernity's beginning?
                    A valve, circa 870
When did modernity begin?
                    19A, Africa
                                        (the very contretemps)
Which modernity?
                    And here's the orchestra to play it for you!

When did modernity make its mark?
                    Mark my voids!
                                        (to mark)
When was modernity?
                    Sleepers, awake!
Modernity ruptured:

                    Death, in sentences.
                    Sentenced To Death
                                        (populist or popular, which?)

                         Wall, you are mine!
Now arriving on platform zero . . .

                                        (from the Arabic)

When did the modern era begin?
                         Ahh!
Is contemporary art modern?
                         Publics, take notice!
When did modernity begin?
                         I don't know.

                                        (ground? groundless?)

                         Death

                                        (Nietzschean)

Has modernity begun?
In a thought experiment, try cosmopolitan

                                        (laughter)

"LOOK, LOOK!"

        "Look, the birds have freed the Stop signs."
        —ROBERT RAUSCHENBERG

    Eyeing Wilson's lecture on Eva Hesse is as an expense
rather than a liaison. . . ,

    where the life-force of Kyrie Eleison lay in pursuit.
While words may point to hallucinatory greenery . . .

    . . . only to learn she had happily reassimilated the attire of ruffled feathers
native to France, for ruffled feathers as

    endgame amuses them, ruffled
feathers happily ever after.

    The ideology of self-possession, "in ellipsis rather than a full stop,"
intervenes artistically at this level.

    "It's impossible?" A little too administrative
for me. Your opinion,

    together with the two annual newsletters.
N.Y. Birdcalls for Övyind Falström, circa 1965.

Ugh! Aargh! Oh. Oh, Anna, you could address us.
Who were to pass? Conferences of hosannas, and your help as well.

Helllp! We would appreciate your help in opening our columns, Palladio.
Thus, it seemed necessary . . .

Writing of zones in non-contradiction, or protocols columnar and in confusion,
you could address us.

Ruffled feathers exciting, agitating protocols,
oh, confusion!

FOR FOUR VIOLINS

Many were fascinated with birth in erratic modes of construal. Meaning?
If keen on jazz, why, I asked, did he borrow [the work of]
    Buxtehude. His name was Ben Paterson.
Ben, Fluxus.
From the start we witnessed birth and death shadow forth a heterodox
    enrollment to replenish the situation.

Measureless, sayable without toil, were Robert Gorham Davis's reappearing
    myths.
His students found places near their neighbors of last week.
By habit, the student preferred the company of one she met by accident once.
Inclusive of retrograde thematics, the manifestation of Davis.

Gather from time, and fourth generation variants, Buxtehude.
A natural situation sensibly represented in suitably receptive persons.
A natural vigilance sensibly represented.
Gather, from time and fourth generation variants, a phase
    elaborated with claim to plausibility.

In 1967, I heard a new release Ben wanted me to hear.
"What do you think?" he said. "Boring," I said. "Keep listening," he said.
"Now, what do you think?"
Steve Reich's new release, *Violin Phase,* interested Ben. He wanted me to hear it.

By habit we sat together.
A few notes rejuvenated when the new young god plays,
    when Paul Zukofsky's vigilant playing wore on.
Technique that elucidates process confers respect upon psycho-acoustic blur.
Common crystallizing devices such as the force of habit.

A minim of disenfranchisement.
"Boring," I said. "Keep listening," he said.
"What do you think?" he said. "Oceanic," I said.
A minim of anomie.

FALSE ISLE

Resilience had expressed some isles
and disappeared, as it were, into the false
commitment of a provident file

cabinet or an edifice of aisles
postulated faultlessly
in the auditorium. These isles

of annihilated numbers are ill
with vapors. Subsumed doors, false,
hypothetical, and filial, adorn the *Isle*

of the Dead by Arnold Böcklin. And why
this esoterica of all else?
this henceforth rusted tranquility? An isle

carpeted in aims and methods, declaring aisles
in sawdust, as though to propose false
mantles. Illegitimate lights and filial

incisions stray across the faun,
threatening the theater of important idleness
that foreshortened literature of our isle
sufficient to lips of a vase, finally.

THE GLOVE

"Always in face, never in fact."
"Always in house, never at home."
"Always leaves a glove longer."
"A horse walks into a bar . . ." where are we now?

". . . a thousand lights in a dish."
". . . comes and goes and leaves a white glove
    at the window."
"How do you make a road broad?"
"A horse walks into a bar."

Once a blue glove folded like this
    like this bronze.
Once a fire unabridged if underweight
    scraped paint away.
Once a face set axes upon which
    hung paradoxes.

"A horse walks into a bar."
"Where once the id, now the ego."
"I, too, once knew Arcadia."
"A horse walks into a bar."
"Once upon a time," alleged.

TEXTILE 5

As if,
    then.
        Such is not always the case

because
        allegations and tougher
                        units

of corresponding bias
            and a vivacious clipping service
                        flash,

or for the reason that

        literature conjectures across texts

              and carcass

with reading.

      For what reason?

For the reason that

      a further allegation can provide

           qualms

as

  intertext,

      three decades of

sand

    as if shadow.

        Shadow

as if sand

     meddled with windshield.

          A further comfort

insofar as

     the forward edge of reading

          made material conjecture.

As if

    conjecture is international: a vivacious clipping service

          and a species of

pavilion.

     For what reading?

        "Pavilion, your rooms are coming down!"

SUSAN WHEELER

S USAN WHEELER'S WORK makes the
most of the contradictions inherent
in contemporary America. Her dic-
tion swings from the archaic to the cybernetic, and her images come as readily
from classical paintings as they do from the street outside her city apartment.
These paradoxical surfaces are rooted in the much deeper dichotomy between
faith and finance that, while an abiding interest, emerges overtly in her fourth
and most recent book, *Ledger*. "One tragedy of consumerist culture," she states in
a recent *Bomb* interview, "is the absolute draining of the spirit . . . so much yearn-
ing is displaced yearning for God." But Wheeler complicates her critique of con-
temporary society by celebrating it as well; full of exclamations and quotations,
she captures the immediate sounds of urban life and arranges them into lyrics.

Wheeler has also explored her interests in race, class, and economy in a
novel, *Record Palace*, set in Chicago's jazz world. A resident of New York, she has
been active in the literary world there for the past twenty years, chairing panels,
interviewing poets, and publishing reviews. Her first book, *Bag o' Diamonds*, was
accepted for the University of Georgia Series and subsequently won the Norma
Faber First Book Award; her second collection, *Smokes*, won the Four Way Books
Award; and *Ledger* won the Iowa Poetry Prize. In addition, she has received fel-
lowships from the Guggenheim Foundation and the New York Foundation for
the Arts, and has been included in seven volumes of *Best American Poetry*. She has
taught at NYU, The New School, Rutgers, and Columbia, and currently teaches
at Princeton.

BEAVIS' DAY OFF

He'd been doing a lot of cull-twanging,
he thought, walking back and forth on the deck
of his battleship *whoa! correction*: loft.

Small fires burned on the outskirts of Soho;
Fanelli's lit up under a stickered sky:
cirrus pitched to the top of its firmament.

How long could he crimp the diesel in the dark?
The bedlam was breathing its own air now;
the parrot shivering in the freezer glared at the hen.

Please it's time said Meg. And each infernal
truism struck a package deal for tin.

What hast thou, O nut job, with paradise?
The sparks O they crested the floor then they floated
and she lay down on fine braids and she cried.

WHITE EXILES

Pittsburgh
"No, it's *fop*. Not sap, fop." "Yeah?—
what century you be blazing in?"
He wanked it twice, for effect.
The bugeyes flared and rolled.

Westport
It was that beverage service!
It even provided the wrong
condiments
and a truckload of calories.

Rochester
Uwanga, uwangalayma
uwanga. The red locust,
from the palm of her hand,
spun out over checkerboard turf.

Wilton
There might be a festoon with which to salve—
perhaps ministrations and some unfolding things—
that will expiate the wrecks you wrought.
What sanguine heads the tufts adorn.

Sudbury
Unguent. A nail flies softly on a cheek,
the candle sputters and then carries on.
He steered the International Travelall
through the wooded, winding roads.

Bennington
Mrs. Ainsworth clicks across the
gallery floor as the Buick pulls up
and three smelly kids run into the minimart
for all-beef sticks.

Woodstock
She was wearing the shiny gold baseball
jacket with the word *Trésor* like
handwriting across the back and leopard
spots across the lapels.

Chicago
The clutch had stuck on the Outer Drive. "Oh,
Perseph—oh dear, you do me so like shaking."
The left turn light had shorted twice. "Your
lap is where I'm pricking. Doll."

New York
So? Whine and be *pissy.* The abrupt
bud in the Hawaiian grove, the cheap chiseler
in the monkey suit, the filaments beneath the sill:
what made me, what I will.

Framingham
Doug shoveled some sand and let it fall.
The disaster that accompanied you
to this moment made it
harder and harder to speak uh, normally.

The rapacious bags at the supermarket
were all packed tight as a drum.
Late in the evening, the stoplight at Warner
swooped in the tumbling rain.

Squish it! the children were yelling
in the garage in the light of the bulb,
And the breath that had left you came back upon you
from your perch in the far sycamore.

LOSS LIEDER

It's an icebox
missing freon,
elevator
that's kaput.
It's a danger
in the stashbox,
fast upon us
citigrade.
Lay your head
on radiators,
drive the needle
through the vein;
I'll be here when
you're no longer,
opal midnight
my refrain.
I'll sing it when
you're mentioned
if the cost is
not too great,
and if I haven't
met you coming
toward us
in the haze.

EACH'S COT AN ALTAR THEN

. . . from the service of self

alone . . .

grasses in low wind high sun

(streamers of starlings)

Joseph hauling the leg with his hands, corn stubble to stalk, horizon no
house—

Low animal flash in the riot of leg–

all such good works as thou hast prepared for us to walk in

This one request I make if it mean foot or glove
Repair, deplete the debt as I am out of love

carrion   calumny

and come into the field of blade poplars glinting,
leg pulled like a cart on the mule of the man
grasshopper of cropduster sprawled in the sun
desperate pastor all yield   green pan

Limb lost? Likely.
Undone? Likely.

Let us grant it is not amiss

who bears the Count Chocula shipment up
who razors the retractable in the joint
who sings the bass of Anthony
who cries for mercy in the placid field,

far now to go.

to reel the streets at noon—
so great weight in his lightness—

So. Bike at door.
On it. Avenue
of the Americas   (against traffic)
a stream.
          The
spareribs hot against
his knees.

                              fiduciary re
                              no sib
                              ability re-
                              spond dis
                              Eisenhower, Eisenhower

                                                                      sty

pend   sur

          plus one is
                    x, solve for.   solve

vent

          A kind of Mamie-dress, that's right, with the bodice—
          no—you'd need darts here first. But that kind
          of print—

                              kind of

a clear light above Joseph and his leg and the dry dry stalks and the clatter he
makes

                    seek a proper return for our labor

TOWARD AUTUMN

                    matted to a dank thing
                    twist of Cape Cod kindling

the shredder   the sprinkler   Symbionese Army—

fall, and a wren has a glossy page clamped into its beak.
The wren balks, the wren pops the clamp and clamps again,
the woman and the machine gun in the sedum browning,
bit wind the leaves loosening, the fairy rose swaying,
a whipping of water at the baby oak.

                    The leaf, its nematode.
                    Cat wary of water, and—

the glossy page, does it predate the summer's dry season?
A reason must I have to return and find one? The green

                    hose snaked by the rose of Sharon,
                    spiraea bobbing fronds in the breeze.

DARA WIER

D ARA WIER'S POEMS have always brought with
them a haunting Southern inflection and
a relaxed colloquial diction that reveals its
wisdoms quietly, purposefully, and at times with a sardonic nonchalance. Yet in
her most recent collections, beginning most explicitly with *Hat on a Pond*, Wier
has determinedly redrawn and enlarged the boundaries of her poetic ambitions.
There is an exuberance and abandon to this recent work that is enthralling, hyp-
notic, and just plain nervy. Both the stylistically innovative *Reverse Rapture* (a
startling book-length meditation that is also a formal rethinking of the line's
internal measure), which was named the 2007 American Poetry Archives Book
of the Year, and *Remnants of Hannah*, with its surreal wit, show a maturity and a
rare sense of urgency.

Dara Wier was born and raised in Louisiana, and attended Bowling Green
State University. She is the author of ten collections of poetry, including the
early, well-regarded collections *Blood, Hook & Eye* and *The 8-Step Grapevine*, as well
as *The Book of Knowledge*; *Blue for the Plough*; *Our Master Plan*; and *Voyages in English*.
She has received grants and awards from the John Simon Guggenheim Memorial
Foundation, the National Endowment for the Arts, and the Massachusetts
Cultural Center, as well as the Jerome J. Shestack Prize from *American Poetry
Review*. Dara Wier teaches in the MFA Program for Poets and Writers at the
University of Massachusetts in Amherst. She is co-director of the Juniper
Initiative for Literary Arts and Action.

DOUBLE SONNET

the table is crazy

If you have arrived
Please write "arrived"
In the sand on this table
You are more beautiful than
Never still moving away see-through water
Sometimes I catch a glimpse of you
By accident in exit exiting in dissolving
Unparticulars
You are more beautiful than
melting hailstones on the back of a run-a-way horse
Absurd
I have finished
It has been described to me
As a real physical feeling

the last and most prolific stage of the forever uncertain

I knew how to do it from childhood, I knew how to do it
From werewolves and bats and dead horses,
Never a day without buzzards somewhere revolving,
Singing in circles they seemed to be scarcely pretending
Not to know they were going, so persistent, so
Casual to never have touched one,
I think of a friend who's being a mother, protecting,
Protecting,
You can feed me
Into one of the frantic
Living machines
I'll come out salty, shredded, astonished
A real physical feeling
Has been described to me

ATTITUDE OF RAGS

It felt like a story sorry it'd lost all its sentences,
Like a sentence looking for its syntax.
All of the words had homeless, unemployed, orphan
Written all over their faces.

It had that parboiled, simmering, half-baked look
Of curiosity about its mouth, like a month of Sundays
Has in the mind of a non-believer, a true back-slider.
One got the impression reluctance was waxing.
One wanted to say passion was taking a beating.
One wanted to say one's prey to one's feelings.
The feathers of their feelings were all scattered.
It was the kind of day were one to see a flock of
Creepy baby angel heads attached at their necks to
Pitch-black aerodynamically preposterous little wings
Clustering at the sum of things, one would rub one's
Eyes, be too faint to respond, much less explain.
It looked the way a fence looks just after the last
Stampede. A big old blood-colored barn collapsed in
Its tracks. Out of hiding came all the hidden cameras.
It looked like streets look after a parade's disbanded.
It was the kind of day in which emotions roaming from
Town to town, free to be themselves, enjoyed their
Rich fantasy lives. This was the kind of day that day
Was. We were rags in the hands of a narcoleptic duster.

INDEPENDENCE DAY

We'd incorporated a laundry lending motion
Detector into the third figure without success.
Everyone commenced dispersing themselves back
To their homes all dejected.
Many fires were set, much ice was cut, a few
Links fell away, a key attached to a braided
Horsehair bracelet got left behind, many more
Samples went into a sample case, midnight unbraided.
Everyone spent the next three days practicing
Free will. They insisted on it. They lived by it.
Was there any other way? That's one thing we wanted
To know. And if there were where would we find it?
Oh, maybe just over there, over the edge of that
Precipice. If no one volunteers we can draw straws.
Everyone spent the next several hours in deep reasoning.
Or at least made it look as if that were what we were
Doing. Then we drew straws to elect a new leader.
Something we suspected not all that pretty was happening
In the cellar. That would have to be saved for later.

We called for a consensus and sure enough we found it.
It looked as if it were perfect. But was it a solution?
Everyone spent the next several days in denial.
Or at least that's what our leader said we were in.
Then we drew straws to elect a new leader.
And sure enough once again it was our old leader who
Drew the shortest straw. And we were back to square one.
But we refused to call it that, we called it progress.
You idiots, our leader said, what have you done with the
Consensus? This caused us everyone to become exceedingly
Sheepish. We who'd been so thoroughly entrusted had
Allowed ourselves to be mightily distracted.
Everyone spent the next several months hanging crepe.
That's what our leader said we should do for the rest
Of our lives. So we drew straws to elect a new leader.
No, we set the straw on fire, it started in the cellar,
Old milk cartons, filters, dead animals, it was a
Ghoul's soup down there, and we made up glorious anthems
To praise the courage of our leader.

THOSE GENERALS' EYES

When I was always the same, someone says,
I was always me. Of course you are, you were,
Someone blurs back, someone shares, as someone
Says, something terrifyingly weird about them-
Selves, something along the lines of if it were up
To me I'd kill us all to spare the pain, not that
Exactly, something worse, something I won't say,
Someone says when I saw them holding hands, says
I wanted to be them then and not be me holding
A different hand, says see, see I looked at who
I was, I saw someone I'd never want to be, some
Of us didn't know what to say, we were speechless,
Our ransacked brains were wild inside their orders,
A full-blooded moon was foaming in our faces.

FAUX SELF-PORTRAIT OF YOU

You are a very uneven person.
You, on the other hand, the one with not quite
five fingers, are a very uneven person.
Look me in the eye I say with conviction and say
you are a person of complete unevenness.
I look away to look for the surface of something
whose unevenness is its main attraction.
Very uneven person, I address you haphazardly,
you are a patchy, jerky lurcher.
You are nonuniform. You are subsubstantial,
I say to you of the fluctuating essence of uneven-
ness. No, I say, I am not a triangle, I do not
fit in the corner. I am an uneven piece of furn-
iture. There is a sirocco in you today.
You are a difficult table. Anything that rolls
rolls off of you almost immediately.
You're not good for a broken string of beads,
Is this not so I say uneven person that you are.
I look down to watch the beads roll where the floor
leans. An odd lullaby passes through my hair.

IT WASN'T EXACTLY LIKE BEING LEFT STANDING AT THE ALTAR

I had on my superfine handy translation glasses
So I could see what you mean.
It was worth selling my soul for
The convenience.
To memorize comes about as easily to me as a mouse
Comes to a cat. But some things I remember.
It was a memorable evening.
So I closed my eyes and spun the globe but it
Was one of those perpetual motion globes, filled
With indecision, with minds of its own.
Remember when I told you about the memory competitions?
Remember how I made my fortune?
Once I wrote a novel & it was made into a movie &
The movie won an Oscar & licensing & franchises
Were gravy.
You remember the story?

At first I wouldn't take any money.
A sinister but loveable band of pranksters with too
Much time on their hands plot to steal everything
From out of all the time capsules there are in the world.
Nothing's too insignificant or unambitious.
They succeed. They go undetected. It's a perfect
Crime. The movie's just a lot of dialog with them
Sitting around in a condemned movie house arguing
About what to do next.
Beats me. You're the one who left me with all that
Time to kill. No dubbing, no subtitles, that's
All I remember about the contract.
What am I telling you this for, you were my agent.
No Rush to Explain

An avalanche of missing concepts one is
Tempted (to call them beautifully truant)
To say it's a mudslide in which therefore
More (than can meet the mind in an instant)
Can be in it than snow and ice only
Snow & ice (surely cascading in real time)
Are (forces of fierce ardent attention)
Far more brokenly open in swift understanding
Appealing (yes, wonder inducing, compulsive)
To ignore which of which thousands of firs
Fell (up in flames remained still another option)
Instead of compelling rocks tangled in roots
Feeling (as if two opposing tidal waves were approaching)
Openly suddenly broken into by ice temptations
Sensational (unapproachably vast conflagrations)
To watch most of an iceberg crash away from its
Glacier (most solemn unending ending procession)
And later the rest of it cleave amidst
Calving (most rare sure opening beginning)
An odd concept to have to be having to have
At this juncture (stepping sideways into the crosshairs)
Just where a choice might stand to be the better
Part of valor (sewn into satin hems on blankets)
I am at wide odds with my maker

EYE CAGES

I was idling in the blue lassitudes,
My louvers half-opened, my shutters
Shut not. My head was a sieve and my heart
Was a sifter. I surveiled surveillance.
I babysat the babysitter. I molted more
Times than money can buy. It was a crime
Among criminals. It was a walk in the
Park in the park. I stumbled upon red.
I said things to myself I could do without.
I diagnosed the diagnosis. And yes, it was
Hopeless. I crossed in the crosswalks &
Switched back into a cattleguard. I was
A good cattleguard, children were afraid
Of me. Next I was a foot bridge. Then
I was a roundhouse. And after that I was
A birdcage. For what seemed a lifetime I
Was a page someone dog-eared in a book about
Noonday devils. I enthused enthusiasms.
I donated donations. Finally I got to be
A thread a friend was pulling from a sleeve.
A blue thread, an indigo bunting. Later
I was not walking but I was the texture of
Walking on a wet sidewalk at five in the
Morning. Streetlamps dimmed as I passed
Under them. I felt a lump in my throat
For every one of them. Soon enough I could
See the edges of a city crumbling in a ditch-
Bank. I could see the blue moon rowing back
To where it had come from. I homed in on the
Drops of water that fell from its oars.

ELIZABETH WILLIS

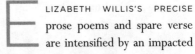

E LIZABETH WILLIS'S PRECISE prose poems and spare verse are intensified by an impacted lyricism that invites the reader into the intimate process of constructing new meanings from familiar materials. The clarity of her syntax leads us to expect the orderly logic of a syllogism, but a freewheeling slippage immediately kicks in, with each new sentence opening up another world—or opening up new ways of interpreting the world we thought we already knew. Though she plays continually with juxtaposition, allusion, and metonymy, there is nonetheless a coherent subject behind each poem, as there is behind each of her books. Taken all together, they display Willis's broad range of interests and influences: from early theories of the earth to the lyricism of William Blake, from film noir to questions of biological, cultural, and political sustainability. Informed by her long-term interest in visual culture, Willis's poems repeatedly present us with alternative ways of seeing.

Raised both in the United States and abroad, Willis studied at the University of Wisconsin and received her doctorate from SUNY Buffalo. She is the author of four collections: *Second Law*, *The Human Abstract* (selected for the National Poetry Series), *Turneresque*, and *Meteoric Flowers*. She has also received awards from the Academy of American Poets, the California Arts Council, and the Howard Foundation. Recently she edited a collection of essays entitled *Radical Vernacular: Lorine Niedecker and the Poetics of Place*. She teaches at Wesleyan University.

THE TREE OF PERSONAL EFFORT

after Charles Rennie Mackintosh

The lost highway of ornament fades into origin. Shipwrecks return like magnets to their builders. In the tree of personal effort, a balloon is lodged or branches are basketed. What did we think we dared to sail away from, an unread book, an aspirin? My body knew I was anchored to earth with flesh. Build a bigger bellows if you want to rise above your life. So sighs the pilot's cloud of word. To imply or intone the whole possibility of human sun. The rose rose unknit with spring. A dragonfly in your hand for luck.

THREE APPLES, TWO CHESTNUTS, BOWL, AND SILVER GOBLET; OR, THE SILVER GOBLET

after Chardin

As in the darkly open science of the foreground, sheepishly at rest as upon air; the rest we stand in. We stand in for the chestnuts, a type of their magnetism, reflecting on the room; or upon the average darkness, aristocratic brown, with hunted things; we come to rest among them. The painted room, locked in a type of kindness. We reflect upon this lovely habit of this hare with whom we are, in the habit of this picture, getting caught. To hide the virtues of a boundless leaping, we regard reflection in the chestnut. As if the painter drew himself as Death into the still life; as of a sculptural stillness, commas in the dark. A figure of ourselves reflected or a type of picture resting; sheepishly as air, locked in a form of capture.

ARTHUR IN EGYPT

Where do you go after a season in Denver? Walking through Africa in shoes of sand. My name was a green flash on the glassy horizon. My pen leaked until there was nothing else to say. When my feet were gone I rowed ashore, beached on the word, *pure*. What happens once can never come again, even in a dream. So I moved on, or it passed through.

CONSTABLE'S DAY OFF

Loving the human bird—
the bright converse
of yellow-flowered grasses—

why aren't we lying
in miles of weedy clover?
The bright boat, tumbling through it
the blue of it—Or,
taking the kid out of the picture
(what you loved to see)
a girl who talks to birds—Don't go
Let's delay or—like Shakespeare—"fly"
all disappointment
in the green and untidy
molecular air

A FISHER KING

Falling in the alley
or shadow of debt

beauty yields
beyond all earning

A glitter train
against the sun

inventing a Bobby
Fischer to live through it

Dear comet
dear rook

who couldn't see
the stardom on your body

empires of loneliness
on board

Hand against
the flyaway clock

a lasting silver lid
or gulf you fancied youngly
for a day

Like Turner with his legs
upon the Orly grass

thinking treed hills
in tweedy blue

his mothered shadow
a lavender turbine

an ancient wisteria
lugging up groundwater

What you take
onto the surface

above the brow
is fierce emergence

O hero of the leafy mind

you're out of reach
in parabolic lamplight

its burning eye
whatever you wanted

THE SIMILITUDE OF THIS GREAT FLOWER

These vines are trim, I take them down. I have my mother's features in my heart, the darkest gem, tripping in the tar, an affinity for Iceland. The world is clanking: noun, noun, noun. Sand in the shoe doesn't make you an oyster. This river runs constantly. "The similitude of this great flower," its violent fame. Forfeit your interests while moonlight chucks the sun. Is the dog behind glass, glassed in? Heaven's voice has hell behind it. I'm looking at the evil flower, a fly in the keyhole trying to read the wall. It says we haven't died despite the cold, it sells the green room's sweat and laughter. It's misty in the dream. It says you promised to go on.

ON THE RESEMBLANCE OF SOME FLOWERS TO INSECTS

A smoky vessel drifts east like a slippery elixir. By simple rotation night collapses with its head in the dirt, though from the heights it appears more like cubist swagger. Suddenly curtains. What lives in a room takes on the spirit of the room. This is true even of television. Imagine deciding the gulley a life will follow as if choosing breakfast over diligent labor. I don't remember my first brush with pollen, yet I've watched words flower sideways across your mouth. In a month we'll be dizzily older. Moths will leave singed paper on the stoop. Is this my design? An ant crosses my shadow so many times looking for its crumb, I think it's me who's needlessly swaying. Its path is busy eloquence while I'm merely armed, like a chair leaving the scent of large things on the breeze.

VERSES OMITTED BY MISTAKE

Were I invited
to draft that flower

an unfixed wilder thing
would fix upon my palm

Those wolves are numbered
to a government rifle

If Lucy rules
the castle of indolence

I joy to dream
a more fortunate planet

OIL AND WATER

One person's idyll is another's confinement. Midnight everywhere is praying through the noise, a token of the obvious. Hours blurt out buds like synonyms of battle. Depending on your subject, a cup may be a sword, dropped on the tile like a capital "is." To put away, to be instant, like "the sands of Iwo Jima," an eager policy toward the nearest sea. Someone dreamed a fire would quench it, something drew a finger through the fire.

ANCIENT SUBTERRANEAN FIRES

When I crossed the road, I burned with the heat of its traffic. Time as movement, a government of rushes. All those itching satellites, blind among the dreaming guns. A bee in its lace is the author of something. Easy work is out there, just beyond the mines. A cab into heroic legend, the first of its kind. To look back on gasoline as hoof and leaf. A moving eye, scrolling through the weeds. Just another carnivore frozen at the spring. As dirty as heaven, a skeleton key.

NOCTURNE

I'm thinking of the heat in the reins
A gear in love with itself,
two parts that fit
I'm thinking about your face:
there's nothing to invent
Driven to distraction
or just walking there,
the edge of my mind
against the edge of yours
An astrolabe isn't thinking
of a concrete lane
or unconquerable interior
Abiding by its class and
country church, a kitsch picture
is not "sincerity"
though I am native to it
A nation has this sound
of being born   The human
is not its ill-begotten ad
A hemisphere is not your hair
in its Parisian rooms
An astrolabe is not
a metaphor for love
though love contain the mortal roots
of congress, like a peasant
inside the name you give its ruins

THE OLDEST GARDEN IN THE WORLD

Something drives out
from the fate I was hungry for
A body that fulfills its face
carries into day
what fades behind it
In *Natural History*
Sophocles loved
Asphodel, but Asphodel
loved William Carlos
Williams as hyacinth
loved France, and honey
loves a toothache
Is that a crime
or just a form of currency
like big tobacco, moving on
with shady radar
over our greenery?

BOHEMIAN RHAPSODY

after anonymous Virgin and Child *(1345–50), Zbraslav*

A boy in the hand, and a bird
in his hand

like a "magic city"
He wrestles with his mother

A foot in translucent water
ready to go

Let the old man sleep
falling into his book

Let the foot reach shore
The painting grasps its afterimage

The bird is dead
before the paint is dry

This structure won't hold
the stone accoutrements of wealth

So the child is crushed beneath them
and rising up is felt as a descent

The letters come
directly to the point

like a Guide for the Perplexed
The boy so insect-like, so young

The letter behind
its piece of green silk

An appointment floating toward you
with nothing to declare

C. D. WRIGHT

O F THE CHOICES revealed to me," notes C. D. Wright, "crime and art were the only ones with any sex appeal." In her dozen collections of poetry, Wright has infused everything from the romantic lyric to the book-length-long poem with a vibrant urgency. Her language experiments less with syntax and fragmentation than with dialect, slang, and the foreign. Her recent work has been increasingly formally inventive, eroding the boundaries of poetry and overflowing into other media. She has done a number of collaborations with the photographer Deborah Luster, which have resulted in exhibits at the Corcoran, S.F. MoMA, and other museums and galleries, and in the books *One Big Self*, which won the Lange-Taylor Prize from the Center for Documentary Studies at Duke, and *Just Whistle: A Valentine*. Born and raised in the Ozarks, Wright's work is often rooted in place; during a Wallace Foundation Fellowship, she created a "walk-in book of Arkansas," a multimedia touring literary event, and she has resurrected the genre of the literary map, creating ones for Arkansas and Rhode Island.

C. D. Wright was named the State Poet of Rhode Island for 1995–99. She has received fellowships and awards from the NEA, the Guggenheim Foundation, the Lannan Foundation, and the Whiting Foundation, and in addition to her poetry, has written a book of critical meditations, *Cooling Time: An American Poetry Vigil*. In 2004, she was named a MacArthur Fellow, and in 2005 she received the Robert Creeley Award and was elected to the American Academy of Arts and Sciences. She teaches at Brown University, where she is the Israel J. Kapstein Professor of English.

ANIMISM

> *We have degenerated into people.*
> —DUO DUO

We are back from the ark, almost.
Is it always this dark?
Who was here first?
Since it is so lush why does everything have that chemistry-set smell?
Is there still time for a crisis?

It rained. Or did it? There is water yet standing.
When in the late afternoon, everything gets hungry.
If my head should fall off, please don't put it in a sack.
Does one start with the face. Save the jam for the end?

The sign said grave-digging two bodies a day,
sixty cents an hour.
How does one decide what to leave for the others?
If the cheese were all that is left
How would that be ascribable to me?
When the light doesn't cover itself up
then will you see the incision of my words?
We are back from the dark, almost.

What is a savannah anyway?
Dogs everywhere are close kin. Like Amish.
Jesus, the Cistercian biology teacher told them, had 23 chromosomes
And was the spitting image of his mother.

Carcass of love, carrion of the wedding feast.
Go ahead, pick my bones
I dreamed I was biting his arm.
I dreamed he was taking me to Nebraska on foot
for our honeymoon. And this was the best I'd felt in a long time.
Those who question the primacy of the phallus
Are surely in for it.

It stopped raining. But made no discernible difference.
The thirst was and will be with us forever.
And after the dogs, the others would come.
First two, then more; in pairs, then more.

And the hewed stones formed a pair as well. Blackened. Fallen.
Perhaps from a monument. A marker for a significant boundary.
Toppled. Here in the savannah.
Because it is beautiful you should not walk alone.
Because it is beautiful you should not go without shoes.
But take a long look. For the rest of nature is nearly morte.
When I think of dying. I think of the ultimate release from fear.
When I think of dying, I get so scared my body refuses to lie down.
There is always time for a crisis.

    Even here, another Fourth, everyone is prey to the heat
and the drums. Cars supplant the beasts.
    Where was he. He said he would be back before the clouds
broke. And the headlights began streaming down County Road.
    Or he would stay until the final minutes before the finale and
the cars became belligerent and began to degenerate into people.
    He knew the ark would not wait.
    He knew they were booked to the rafters.
    He knew we could lose our cheap seats in the reaches
Where the Juilliard students stand up reading the scores.
And therefore, we have to wait for the hyenas to get hungry
enough to kill for their supper. Then we will come
with our napkins tucked under our chins
and our cutlery gleaming. Things seem more eternal
elsewhere. Where one eats until one is eaten.
    Never eat to be eating.
    There was a sheen on the road soon after we entered
the city limits. The air, splendid, freshly wetted.
    Have you ever attempted to count the storage tanks when you
passed them on the way back. Have you ever reeled
under the magnitude of petroleum's ruin.

The beast involuntarily turns its rack of ribs up for the pack.
He has pulled into the breakdown lane, burning oil.
If these rags are edible, we will live.

I am the last one in the house to go to bed.
Listen. The insects resume where the fireworks left off.
Or, if not, the insects collect at the light
with their silent scores.

Isn't the engine turning over. Almost.

There must be a re-set button for this machine.

Let's be realistic. We are never coming back.

LIKE PEACHES

change   speak   sway
keep lingering smell
protected by a succulent seal   a burr
yield one's earthly wand   one's earthly sac   into this vessel
trace   blaze   clear
the foliage at the wrought gate
the serrated tongue   rescinded   along with the dream
of urinating in three streams
sunscalded

Forever Lynne   riddles the water tower   of a dying town
ripen   cling   drop
what would it be like to fell   this mess of twigs   to graft
the shaking body   to lyric   the seasoned body   to stem
to shake   the lyric body   to season
the stemmed   to trail   the fallen . . .
slather   shudder   lower
drupe

things that are not written in this book
don't go boring your nose in the fork of a tree not even present
arise   refreshed   wormed
pulpy   opaque   ecstatic
lingering innocence
of perfect nexus   shave the epicarp   collect the juices
we orchard

WHY LEAVE YOU SO SOON GONE

Ah well   Be well   Be iron   On rock

sharpen yourself   Remember   heat goes out the top

Follow thought   migration of stars   Detach

from the surrounding sound   Be resistant

to disease and evil   Take the path worn by the walker

the dreamline   Take the dreamline   inalienable map

of rivers and lovers   in subtle and effortless tones   Say yes

when the month begins   Take ginger   Chew garlic

If you won't wear the watch cap   We miss   Remember

your hood   Don't forget the subjunctive   the usual nostrums

Never a glove   *So* like your father   Listen to me

You're going to need this   way up there   Don't forget

The tip jar   You're going to need   When you're moving

at the speed of loneliness   and your papers pile up in drifts

Call back later   your words   breaking up in this ear

Tell the truth   the trees tell   as their boughs bend

to the forces   leaves spray in all directions   their limbs rend

as they come crashing   across invisible fencing

the privet   the shingles   the insulated glass   the horsehair

plaster crumbles in my head   their leaves shattering the light

Sharpen yourself   on rock   Say yes   Don't forget

BIENVENU EN LOUISIANE

The septuagenarian murderer knits nonstop

One way to wear out the clock

In Tickfaw miracles occur

This weekend: the thirteenth annual Cajun joke contest

They will/will not be sending the former governor to Big Gola

I pinch a cigarette and stare at Rachel's wrist scars

By their color they are recent

That the eye not be drawn in

I suggest all courage is artificial

Her sister did not fail

Noses amuse us and hers not less so

   short smart butch

Utterly unsure of herself

Whichever you see as sadder

A jukebox or a coffin

A woman's hand will close your eyes

On the surface she is receptive

I wear the lenses of my time

Some run to type, but I am not qualified

Hectored by questions that have to do with the Forms of Harm,
   the Nature of the Beast, Mercy, etc.

Last seen yesterday morning in a one-piece swimsuit

The popular sixteen-year-old is 5'7", 127 lbs

The K-9 unit given her long white prom gloves, her pillowcase

Do you wish to save these changes
      yes   no   nevermind

The stinging caterpillars of Tickfaw pour onto the bark
      in the form of a cross

A random book skimmed from the women's shelf

In which an undine-like maiden
      is espyed feeding white daisies to a bear

Something on anarcho-syndicalism wasn't really expected

      poetry   time   space   death

Church marquee: AFTER GOOD FRIDAY COMES EASTER
      GOD ALWAYS WINS

Drive-in marquee: Lenten Special
      POBOYS   FRIES   DRINK

The men pretty much all have ripped chests

Knitting wasn't really expected

Sign on the weight machine: PUSH TO FAILURE

Whoever becomes a DRUNKARD must be taken to the Whipping Post

Dino's out, he'd like his pictures
Dino blowing smoke out the holes of his beautiful nose

She is so sweet you wouldn't believe she had did
      all the things they say she did

      That one, she's got a gaggle of tricks up her you know what

Drawn on a wall in solitary by a young one
      MOM   LOVE   GOD
      Before he had a face on him

CHARLES WRIGHT

C HARLES WRIGHT IS a poet of spiritual pilgrimage. The reflections of a luxuriant memory (of his childhood/adolescence in Tennessee and his young adulthood in Italy) meld with Wright's meditative reckonings about a desired salvation and his pursuit of the sublime. The ghosts of St. Augustine, St. John of the Cross, and Buddha echo within these poems. Initially using the models of Pound and Montale, Wright has developed over the course of his career a distinctive, supple, and sculptural poetic line capable of stylistic fluidity and linguistic surprises. Influenced by a variety of artists—painters as various as Cézanne, Mark Rothko, Milton Avery, and Cy Twombly, as well as by Chinese poetry and the writings of John Cage—Charles Wright remains a protean and restlessly inventive poet, capable of sliding from an echo of the Episcopal liturgy to a demotic drawl to a jazz-inflected slang in the space of a single line.

The author of nineteen collections of poetry, most recently the book-length poem *Littlefoot*, Wright's many awards and prizes include the National Book Award in Poetry; the National Book Critics Circle Award; the Lenore Marshall Prize; the Los Angeles Times Book Prize; and the Pulitzer Prize. *Scar Tissue* (2007) was the international winner for the Griffin Poetry Prize. He has also published two books of criticism: *Halflife* and *Quarter Notes*. His translation of Eugenio Montale's *The Storm and Other Poems* was awarded the PEN Translation Prize. Wright's other honors include the American Academy of Arts and Letters Award of Merit Medal; the Ruth Lilly Poetry Prize; and the Rebekah Johnson Bobbitt National Prize for Literature from the Library of Congress. In 1999, he was elected a Chancellor of the Academy of American Poets. He is Souder Family Professor of English at the University of Virginia in Charlottesville.

BODY AND SOUL II

(for Coleman Hawkins)

The structure of landscape is infinitesimal,
Like the structure of music,
                              seamless, invisible.
Even the rain has larger sutures.
What holds the landscape together, and what holds music together,
Is faith, it appears—faith of the eye, faith of the ear.
Nothing like that in language,
However, clouds chugging from west to east like blossoms
Blown by the wind.
                    April, and anything's possible.

Here is the story of Hsuan Tsang.
A Buddhist monk, he went from Xian to southern India
and back—on horseback, on camel-back, on elephant-back, and on foot.
Ten thousand miles it took him, from 629 to 645,
Mountains and deserts,
In search of the Truth,
                         the heart of the heart of Reality,
The Law that would help him escape it,
And all its attendant and inescapable suffering.
                                            And he found it.

These days, I look at things, not through them,
And sit down low, as far away from the sky as I can get.
The reef of the weeping cherry flourishes coral,
The neighbor's back porch lightbulbs glow like anemones.

Squid-eyed Venus floats forth overhead.
This is the half hour, half-light, half-dark,
                              when everything starts to shine out,
And aphorisms skulk in the trees,
Their wings folded, their heads bowed.

Every true poem is a spark,
                    and aspires to the condition of the original fire
Arising out of the emptiness.
It is the same emptiness it wants to reignite.
It is that same engendering it wants to be re-engendered by.
Shooting stars.

April's identical,
                        celestial, wordless, burning down.
Its light is the light we commune by.
Its destination's our own, its hope is the hope we live with.

Wang Wei, on the other hand,
Before he was 30 years old bought his famous estate on the Wang River
Just east of the east end of the Southern Mountains,
                                        and lived there,
Off and on, for the rest of his life.
He never traveled the landscape, but stayed inside it,
A part of nature himself, he thought.
And who would say no
To someone so bound up in solitude,
                        in failure, he thought, and suffering.

Afternoon sky the color of Cream of Wheat, a small
Dollop of butter hazily at the western edge.
Getting too old and lazy to write poems,
                                I watch the snowfall
From the apple trees.
Landscape, as Wang Wei says, softens the sharp edges of isolation.
Don't just do something, sit there.
And so I have, so I have,
                        the seasons curling around me like smoke,
Gone to the end of the earth and back without a sound.

THE SECRET OF POETRY

The second Chinese said, all that you need to find poetry
Is to look for it with a lantern.
Tonight, one night after full, the full moon feminine
Is all you would need,
The lunar essence, the blind structure of matter,
                                        perfection of pain,
Discharging unwilled and processional across the landscape.

Snow, and snow and ice, and snow again,
Came yesterday, before the moonlight.
                                It's hard to find,
Despite what the Chinese said.
It's hard to find despite what the moonlight jukes and joins.

Now that the snow and ice have stopped, and the light's come back,
It hurts, and it's difficult to see.

The north wind in the bard limbs of the oak trees bears down on us.
The song of the north wind fills our ears with no meaning.

'54 CHEVY

Sam's Gap, the Tennessee side,
Kiss-your-ass curve and white house on the poor field's aneurysm,
A handful of Alzheimered apple trees across the highway,
South Mountain back to the right,

Delicate short grasses, bird flocks in the trees, pasture
and cupped orchard
                          green against the unendable blue
Of North Carolina sky just over the hill.
                                    And the heart,
That legless bird, circling and circling, hoping for anywhere to land.

A moment that should have lasted forever and forever
Long over—
            it came and went before I knew it existed.
I think I know what it means,
But every time I start to explain it, I forget the words.

SINGING LESSON

This is the executioner's hour,
                          deep noon, hard light,
Everything edge and horizon-honed,
Windless and hushed, as though a weight were about to fall,
And shadows begin to slide from beneath things, released
In their cheap suits and eager to spread.

Out in the meadow, nothing breathes,
                          the deer seem to stop
Mid-jump at the fence, the swallows hanging like little hawks in the air.
The landscape loosens a bit, and softens
                          Like miniature exhalations,
Wind stirs in the weeds, a dog barks, the shadows stretch and seep out.

Therefore, when the Great Mouth with its two tongues of water and ash
Shall say, Suffer the darkness,
Suffer the darkness to come unto you,
                                    suffer its singsong,
And you will aide,
Listen to what the words spell, listen and sing the song.

WAKING UP AFTER THE STORM

It's midnight. The cloud-glacier breaks up,
Thunder-step echoes off to the east,
                                    and flashes like hoof sparks.
Someone on horseback leaving my dream.

Senseless to wonder who it might be, and what he took.
Senseless to rummage around in the light-blind stars.
                                                Already
The full moon is one eye too many.

HAWKSBANE

There are things that cannot be written about, journeys
That cannot be taken they are so sacred and long.

There is no nature in eternity, no wind shift, no weeds.

Whatever our vision, whatever our implement,
We looked in the wrong places, we looked for the wrong things.

We are not what is new, we are not what we have found.

from LITTLEFOOT

32

Backyard, my old station, the dusk invisible in the trees,
But there in its stylish tint,
Everything etched and precise before the acid bath
—Hemlocks and hedgerows—

Of just about half an hour from now,
Night in its soak and dissolve.
Pipistrello, and gun of motorcycles downhill,
A flirt and a gritty punctuation to the day's demise
And one-starred exhalation,
                              V of geese going south,
My mind in their backwash, going north.

The old gospel song from 1950
                              by Lester Flatt and Earl Scruggs,
"Reunion in Heaven," has a fugitive last verse
I must have heard once
Although it wasn't included when they recorded it.
So I'll list it here,
              that it won't be disremembered.

Just in case.
I am longing to sit by the banks of the river
There's rest for the ones by the evergreen trees
I am longing to look in the face of my Savior
And my loved ones who have gone, they are waiting for me

When what you write about is what you see,
                              what do you write about when it's dark?

Paradise, Pound said, was real to Dante because he saw it.
Nothing invented.
One loves a story like that, whether it's true or not.
Whenever I open my eyes at night, outside,
                              flames edge at the edge
Of everything, like the sides of a nineteenth-century negative.
If time is a black dog, and it is,
Why do I always see its breath,
                              its orange, rectangular breath
In the dark?
It's what I see, you might say, it's got to be what my eyes see.

So many joys in such a brief stay.
Life is a long walk on a short pier.

∎

If poetry is pentimento,
                    as most of its bones seem to show,
Remember the dead deer on Montana 92,
Lincoln County, last Monday scrunched in the left-hand ditch.
Raven meat-squawks for two days.
On Thursday, south wind through the rib cage,
Ever-so-slightly a breathing,
                    skull-skink unmoved on the macadam.
Its song was somewhat, somewhat erased.

∎

I'm early, no one in the boat on the dark river.
It drifts across by itself
Below me.
            Offended, I turn back up the damp steps.

∎

The dragonflies remain a great mystery to me.
Early October.
                At least a dozen of them are swarming
Like swallows over the dying grass
And browned leaves of the backyard,
Each tending to recompose a previous flight path
With minor variations.
So beautiful,
            translucent wings against the translucent sky,
The late afternoon like litmus just under our fingertips.

∎

The berries shine like little stigmata in the dogwood trees,
A thousand reminders of the tree's mythology
As the rain keeps polishing them,
                    as though it could rub it clean.

Such red, and Easter so far away.

JOHN YAU

M

UCH OF JOHN YAU'S quick, sharp poetry has a wry humor that underscores its urban pace and its oblique approach to sentiment. And while it reveals a number of influences, they're ones that are rarely seen together: there are echoes of Surrealism in his vividly inventive, careening imagery, something of the New York School in his immediacy and casual tone, the intimations of contemporary painting in his subject matter, his use of patterning, and his open-ended inconclusiveness—and all juxtapose a strong narrative impulse. His incorporation of popular culture in the form of borrowed characters such as Boris Karloff and Peter Lorre (both of whom played Asian characters in their movies) points to his subtle but consistent concern with identity. Yau's take is neither confessional nor theoretical, but offhand, letting issues of name and renaming rise up amid other quotidian concerns. A recent book, *Ing Grish*, looks directly at the effects of a multilingual background on self-definition, while his latest collection, *Paradiso Diaspora*, treats issues of identity and community more broadly.

Yau has published over thirty books of poetry, fiction, and criticism. A prolific writer on the visual arts, he has written book-length works on Jasper Johns, Andy Warhol, and Ed Moses, and countless articles and catalogue essays. He is also the founder and editor of Black Square Editions/Brooklyn Rail Books, a small press that focuses on contemporary international poetry. His own poetry has earned him a National Poetry Series selection, the Lavan Award from the Academy of American Poets, and fellowships from the National Endowment for the Arts, the New York Foundation for the Arts, and the Guggenheim Foundation. Known also for his vivid short stories, Yau is the editor of the fiction anthology *Fetish*. He lives in Manhattan, and is an Associate Professor in the Visual Arts Department at Mason Gross School of the Arts, Rutgers University.

THE LATE TALE

then several (like five) venture there
(site: transparent teal blue plane)
maybe meet several (like nine) more
then several (more like ten)
gather flesh outside
(nerve directions: encase)
erect spines near several others
then several (imagine eleven)
see several others being erect (maybe noble)
then five (maybe seven) chatter
opposite downtrodden eight (maybe less)
then maybe less help maybe more
duel several others (maybe even more)
then the then dwindles beside the the
leaving even less gathered
none erect
then the superbly sculpted supine figures
(imagine neat pile)
are raised
open-mouthed because haunted
then the several open-mouthed
but haunted figures venture
near quiet abodes
(they penetrate cement castles, insect domiciles)
then several armed (some men)
dangle celery before children
dressed like donkeys (possible sacrifice)
then the donkeys (maybe they are children)
shed their purple capes
before fleeing their haunted parents
then more meet less even then the less faces more
then the darkness divides itself
releasing molten red cascades
fiery tongues descend
demanding more donkeys
then the donkeys aren't children anymore
because different celestial effects
infect their heads
then the dreamers
(imagine one maybe three)
tell their tale near the fire

then the tale (maybe more)
explodes above the telling
then the donkeys
(are they haunted children)
slide like stale bubbled cream
inside the children
their red smiles
then the disguised children descend
demanding larger purple capes
then several more stories are recited beside the fire
then these stories
unable to extinguish the stories preceding them
(note: noises [notes]
begin breaking
ice-clogged lake,
teal green plane)
because each tries extinguishing the others
their frozen syllables dissolve
more tales
(are they holes
are they moles)
emerged
then several marriages break
leaving the children wandering
then the wandering comets
(imagine children) return
their blue stones
exciting the cimmerian darkness
then several figures
(some are comets
others are children)
converge inside the wooden abode
(termite-eaten table
rotted cellar-beams
master's teak lined bedroom)
where the dreamer
leaves the dream
others seek
believing therein lies the answer
forgetting they have the lake
the ice
the comet
the red stone

then the answer becomes the little haunted question
(imagine comet)
suspended above the lacustrine drinker
(green marble statue)
then once more the then
begins breaking factories
little sweatshops crammed together
under the fiery planets
the children swear opposite the donkeys
the donkeys are secretly infidels
disguised hermits
large drudge machines
they (donkeys perhaps children) become heroes
when they reduce their drivel quotient
then the children hidden inside the donkeys
begin exhausting their parents
several disinherit their progeny
others take downhearted hikes
then the ice age begins once more
(maybe twice)
then the children are cooled inside the frozen lake machine
the parents become delirious
(huge venomous parties)
the donkeys are freed
everyone rejoices
then the donkeys make their mistake
they dance beside the fire
then several (maybe more) meet several others
(some venture where
they once gathered erect)
then the celestial delivery systems begin their bombardment
then the here (imagine infinite more) empties itself
before the darkness becomes the emblazoned shield
whose foretelling occurred
(inside the faded flame once called time)
when the tale began loosening the blackened tiles
lodged inside the infinitely broken sea

UNPROMISING POEM

I am writing to you from the bedroom of my ex-wife, where I have been
stenciling diagrams on sheets and ceiling, intricate star charts of the paths
modern soldier ants take to reach the lips waiting at the end of their long
journey. There are no red messages in the balloons floating overhead, no tasty
tidbits left from the first meeting. I have been told that the soft meat gets
softer in the harsh helixes of the second sun.

I am writing to you from the bedroom of my ex-wife, the room in which
flocks of birds have returned to the shelves of their one-syllable caves. Dust
settles on the eyelids of those who yet to emerge from the shadows. Blue
sparks etch the edges where the sky falls away, and black clouds fill the
chalkboards with sleeping children.

I am writing to you from the bedroom my ex-wife keeps in her bedroom, the
Library of Unusual Exceptions, Book of Gaudy Exemptions, Ledger of Lost
Opportunities, wavelengths of archaeological soot drifting through the screen.

I am writing to you from the sleeping car temporarily disabled in the bedroom
of my ex-wife. Dear Corraded Clouds, Dear Correspondence Principle, Dear
Axle, Enzyme, and Ash, Dear Example of Excellence, are you Frigg or Freya?
Hoop Snake or Hoosegow?

O turtle in a kirtle, why must you chortle so?

Dear Hangman of Harbin, why did I wake in the bedroom of my ex-wife?

Dear ex-wife, I have learned to accept the small pleasures that come with
being called the Hangman of Harbin.

EGYPTIAN SONNETS (7)

Do you copy each hour of the double horizon?
Its gold torso, azure head, and emerald light?
Bandaged sun bleeding into rivers
Proud to have bequeathed its demonic power.
Are you oar and heir? Do you recline among lions?
Red heaven accompanies this worm-eaten boat
Through plumes of sulphurous battle smoke.
It sings: O brief insect dying with the dying day
Do our hearts dilate? Can we ever announce our joy?

The two regions of the sky have met and departed
I grow among flowers dwelling in dust is my name
I rise from a couch of snow atop a rotting mountain
I make my nest in the rafters of a metallic sky
I stand naked and alone in a public fountain

EGYPTIAN SONNETS (11)

Night, dispassionate scholar of our fears
Opens its portfolio, and unwraps
Our bracelets of tears again
How ghostly this train
Quiet as a forest
Hung about in smoke
And a poet
In a sudden fit
Falls weeping
A monstrous serenity
Rainbow salts, smooth lipped
The sculpture frozen in oratory
Lunar horns spreading
From its silver forehead

ROBERT DESNOS WRITES

What strange sound glided the length of the bannister down to where the transparent apple was dreaming?

I don't know the answer to that question or the one before, or the ones before that. A key chain without keys is all that I feel beneath my pillow. Now how will I ever find my way back to the Saskatchewan night car?

I nudge him again, but he has already fallen asleep at the table. And, as if his head has been removed by one-armed bandits and placed in a copper basket lined with potted plants, he has started speaking into the waterlogged tape recorder:
If your horoscope mentions scissors, scorpions, or scrapbooks, you should post an ad for a woman who can prove to you her name is Robert Desnos. She will look like me and she will sound like me, but the poetry she writes will be neither hers nor mine.

Please copy what I have said, including the part that begins, "please copy . . ."

Shortly after the last clock in town tolls midnight, black carriages begin lining up outside The New Archive Luncheonette. A swarm of iridescent gnats hovers above the main shed of the obsolete gondola repair depot. In an adjacent frame, two policemen discuss ways to improve their uniforms, how their epaulets might be emphasized to greater effect. On a quaint suburban street near the fireworks factory, a team of champion wrestlers practice hauling the corpse of a pink walrus into an illegally parked armored car.

This is how we meet, beneath a billboard of a burning city, above a car named after a beach, in a room ablaze with citron stripes. You are painting, and the room is filled with a warm liquid called "light." Don't bash the squash, you scribble in the air with your brush. The sky is a black horse pawing the ocean, I scribble back with my fingers. Both of you are brazen with gibberish, the smoke scribbles in its entrails.

The fortune teller looks up from her deck of cards. Why don't you see yourself as a mathematical object, a creeping blue buttercup, one inkling plum among many? I do, which is why I want to report how I found the world, the poet whispers to the philosopher who has accompanied him to this infernal basement.

Where did you say you were taking me?

But you are smoke, and I and my many unembraced selves cannot carry you anywhere, because you go wherever you want. O smoke, want is never the issue on which your laws are written.

Yes, the smoke heard itself answering, though it was sure it wasn't doing the speaking.

Yes, I am poetry and its residue settling onto the wig of a man who appears to have fallen asleep, all alone beneath his tiny wooden star.

DEAN YOUNG

DEAN YOUNG HAS revolutionized the use of humor in American poetry. Often ironic, often painful, often sad, his poems also often make you laugh out loud, which increases their irony, pain, and sadness. Influenced by the New York School and by French Surrealism, Young's work has a quick step and a constant shiftiness in which Pop culture poses side by side the timeless and the mythological. His more radical use of juxtaposition gives the surface of his work a certain edginess in which the many voices that inhabit it are never entirely at ease. Instead, they, like the reader, must be ready to shift direction, to follow a tumultuous flow that is often logical, but even more often a little odder than that. And underneath it all is a fascination with natural history revealed through his attention to daily wonders such as flies' wings and the mating habits of orchids.

Dean Young was born and raised in Pennsylvania and educated at Indiana University. He has held a Stegner Fellowship as well as fellowships from the Fine Arts Work Center in Provincetown, the National Endowment for the Arts, and the Guggeneheim Foundation. His *Strike Anywhere* won the Colorado Prize in 1995, and his most recent book, *Elegy on a Toy Piano*, was a finalist for the 2006 Pulitzer Prize. Young is also a visual artist; his minute, energetic abstracts are on the jackets of several of his books and have been exhibited in group and solo shows. He has taught in the Warren Wilson low-residency MFA program and at the Iowa Writers' Workshop, and currently teaches at the University of Texas at Austin.

WITH HIDDEN NOISE

I am a teapot and this is my song.
I am award winning and this is my song.
What genius decided we needed a fire engine now?
Maybe I'm a postindustrial bunny and this . . .
Look, big ears, this is MY song
and no one needs your rabbity bull around here.
I am an exchequer and this is my retinue.
No one knows precisely what I do.
Where to put the excess of speaking voice?
But Professor, there's too much
nitrogen up there for any known life-form
to survive! I am the breasts of a starlet
and this is my lab coat. Did you say
lifeboat? Watch out for the nails
coming out the other side. I am
a liminal state and this is my program.
Misbegotten pang, open your oh.
Did you say sleeping voice?
We can no more invent ourselves
than the ticks of a clock can invent the clock.
Are you sure this is the way to go?
I am Walt Whitman but so?
Everybody's Walt Whitman.
Clouds of unlimited portent.
Insert anecdote here.
The idea is to get the heart-rate up
and sustain it. What happened?
shouts the hero rushing into the study room.
Mung magph naagh, replies the heroine
still in her gag. Insert flap A
into slot A. X-rays inconclusive.
Want to hear me count to 1,000 by 17s?
Beep hexagonal, my puppeteer.
I hate your dog.
I am a 2-CD set of the world's greatest arias
No wonder no one gets nothing done.
Clearly we need a new filing system.
After a while it all sounds the same.
Saaaaaaammmmme.
Enter Fortinbras.
I am your waiter and this is your orchard

This can't be what I ordered.
Next question.
Now try it on your own at home.

YAWN

No one owns a yawn. Sometimes
it seems to be passed along
so you may think wrongly it is mine,
here, I give it to you. The same is true
of leading a person up to a waterfall
then unblindfolding her. You do not own
the waterfall to give and now neither does she.
To see a snake yawn explains
how he can swallow such larger-than-him prey
like a magician making his head disappear.
Due to the mandibular bone
constricting the external auditory meatus
thereby tautening the tympanic membrane
as a result of increased pressure,
yawning may inhibit hearing.
What huh?
It is 11:30 in the evening, night really,
under us like the passage of underground
conveyances: yawns.
None of them are green with red rings,
none of them are blue with green wings.
To look at an audience and see yawns:
horrible, even if you're singing lullabies.
In college I thought Theodore Dreiser
was trying to kill me but a yawner
is never fatal, there is no record
of a person turning from the tiresome novel
to the rain-tapped window,
yawning and living no more.
At least as attributable to the yawn.

BATHED IN DUST AND ASHES

Maybe Heraclitus was right, maybe
everything is fire. The lovers,
exhausted, unknot like slick ribbons,
the sirens fade to silver ash. Knock
at the door, no one there, voices

coming through the floor, spring
all morning, winter by afternoon,
dense rhymes of foliate argument,
laughter from passing cars. Fire
swallowed and regurgitated from which

all life comes, bees returning
to their hives to dance, hawks feeding
their gaping chicks, variables
in alternate currents you almost
lived, if you had married him,

if you had stayed, a future begun
as marks on a nearly transparent page.
So the shadows vanish and return
carrying their young in their jaws,
and the man who still thinks he's a man

and not a column of smoke, sits
in his idling care, and the woman
who still thinks she's a woman and not
climbing a staircase in flames,
bites her lip before she speaks.

SPECK

What I have in common with people of the future:
they don't exist either.
What I have in common with people of the past:
mother forgets me, I'm late for work.
Oh exquisite hammer, you liar.
The monkey do be loop da loop
in orthopedic shoes. Down monkey, down!

I dial a wrong number, still no answer.
It's hard to keep the conversation alive
but on one can find the do not resuscitate order.
I be very lonely overcome leaf.
I doth not keep my chattel safe.
Great battlements appeared in snowstorms
but we were too tired to reach them,
too tired our quadrupeds.
The emperor will be gravely grieved
and take it out on the sea.

The people of the future send out a scout.
The people of the past seep.
I had been mean to a wife long distance.
I scoured the marsh for bioluminescence.
I applied to install solar panels.
Are children too grass?

I walked towards the bridge
that represented soaring aspirations
as well as not having your body recovered for days.
The people of the future might hate you less
but the people of the past won't know what to think.
By then your important parts will be lint.
But hey, take it easy,
little bird of fire.

HOMAGE TO RICHARD TUTTLE

What a relief
no presiding intelligence
no vanishing point no quiz.
A piece of wire worthless
so what does that make its shadow?
Stuff had been picked up along the way.
Most of the lightbulbs didn't work.
I always feel more people should be laughing
but that's my problem: delight.
You could imagine every bit of it discarded
requiem somewhere else
except for the catalogue a measly 30 bucks.
It's not the same.

No penitentiary kickplates
so breath moves shreds.
It's okay to feel excited about trying to draw a line.
Or glue.
You mean we can have as much as we can use?
Some of it bound to be ugly.
Then whammo.
Well, not ugly
preparatory
waiting.
The job was the wrong tool.
Making some people angry
but try to love them anyway
they're looking for a different church.
Cardboard: an essay on mortality, futility, protection, fate.
Which.
Totalizing toddler?
Which end of the brush is the brush end?
The policeman arrests a leaf
then releases it under its own recognizance.
Paper boat.
Confidence with a cricket.
It's not easy to install a window in the soul.
Maybe your hiding places were too good.
Crayon, wood, cardboard, wire, glue.

MAN IN RED

You didn't even know
you were accruing an immense debt,
a debt that would ensure your everlasting

so when you died suddenly—
how many times did you forget
plankton was your step brother?
how many machines did you avoid
being fed into?

so when you die suddenly at last
figuring out solitude was not ice,
that wretchedness was part of the rainbow,

each of the sixty billion mourners,
their carefully made-up faces ruined
by harsh backlighting,
their wings vestigial,
their hearts' voltage snarling,

pause for five seconds
in their channel surf

to watch a single pigeon feather
pretend to be a snowflake
and be shunned by the other snowflakes

but what do snowflakes know
in their unrepentant geometries
about being the step brother of plankton,
the half sister of an ice skate
at the bottom of a lake,
spending a life's savings
on a guitar Johnny Cash played once?

They vanish with nothing in their stomachs,
none of their teeth are porcelain
glued to crumbling roots.

Even an insect sometimes gets to perish
in the glass skull of a lightsource.

Even a blade of grass
can be tracked into an elevator.

Even the letter O can be beaten
against a page
until its center fills
with dark debris
and it ceases crying out.

DONALD REVELL: "My Trip," "My Mojave," and "Picnic" from *My Mojave*. Copyright © 2003 by Donald Revell. Reprinted with the permission of Alice James Books. "Zion," "Conquest," and "Landscape with Tityrus in Vermont" from *Pennyweight Windows*. Copyright © 2005 by Donald Revell. Reprinted with the permission of Alice James Books.

ELIZABETH ROBINSON: "The Little Matchgirl" from *Apprehend* (Fence Books, 2003). Copyright © 2003 by Elizabeth Robinson. Reprinted by permission of Fence Books. "The Snow Window" from *Pure Descent*. Copyright © 2002 by Elizabeth Robinson. Reprinted with the permission of Green Integer Books. "Allege or Elegy" and excerpt from *Hovenweep*. Copyright © by Elizabeth Robinson. Reprinted by permission of the author.

MARTHA RONK: "In a landscape of having to repeat," "You couldn't read a book about it," "In the house," and "Vertigo" (all eleven sections) from *In a landscape of having to repeat* (Omnidawn, 2004). Copyright © 2004 by Martha Ronk. Reprinted by permission of the author and Omnidawn.

MARY RUEFLE: Reprinted from *Tristimania*: "Penciled," "The World as I Left It," "Go Verbatim," "Where Letters Go," "Concerning Essential Existence," and "Minor Ninth Chord" by permission of Carnegie Mellon University Press. Copyright © 2004 by Mary Ruefle. "Naked Ladies" and "Impresario" from *Apparition Hill* (CavanKerry Press, 2001). Copyright © 2001 by Mary Ruefle. Reprinted by permission of CavanKerry Press.

REGINALD SHEPHERD: "A Parking Lot Just Outside the Ruins of Babylon" and "Direction of Fall." Copyright © Reginald Shepherd. Reprinted by permission of the author. "Turandot," "You Also, Nightingale," and "The Tendency of Dropped Objects to Fall" from *Fata Morgana* by Reginald Shepherd. Copyright © 2007. Reprinted by permission of the University of Pittsburgh Press.

ELENI SIKELIANOS: "Thus, Speak the Chromograph" and "Essay: At Night the Autoportrait" from *Earliest Worlds*. Copyright © 2001 by Eleni Sikelianos. Reprinted with the permission of Coffee House Press. "A lady just asked" from *The California Poem*. Copyright © 2004 by Eleni Sikelianos. Reprinted with the permission of Coffee House Press. "World Is Weird." Copyright © 2008 by Eleni Sikelianos. Reprinted by permission of the author.

ROD SMITH: "Ted's Head" from *Music or Honesty* (Roof Books, 2003). Copyright © 2003 by Rod Smith. Reprinted by permission of the author. "the egret says," "egret lights," and the first twelve sections ending at "& it is real" from *The Good House* (Spectacular Books, 2001). Copyright © 2001 by Rod Smith. Reprinted by permission of Spectacular Books. "The Strength" reprinted from *Deed*. Copyright © 2007 by Rod Smith. Reprinted by permission of the University of Iowa Press.

CAROL SNOW: "Le Déjeuner." Copyright © 2008 by Carol Snow. Reprinted by permission of the author. "Gallery" from *The Seventy Propositions: Poems* (University of California Press, 2004). Copyright © 2004 by The Regents of the University of California. Reprinted by permission of the University of California Press. "Bowl" from *For* (University of California Press, 2000). Copyright © 2000 by The Regents of the University of California. Reprinted by permission of the University of California. "Vantage" from *The Seventy Propositions* (University of California Press, 2004). Copyright © 2004 by the Regents of the University of California.

INDEX